Learn QGIS
Fourth Edition

Your step-by-step guide to the fundamental of QGIS 3.4

Andrew Cutts
Anita Graser

Packt>

BIRMINGHAM - MUMBAI

Learn QGIS
Fourth Edition

Copyright © 2018 Packt Publishing

All rights reserved. No part of this book may be reproduced, stored in a retrieval system, or transmitted in any form or by any means, without the prior written permission of the publisher, except in the case of brief quotations embedded in critical articles or reviews.

Every effort has been made in the preparation of this book to ensure the accuracy of the information presented. However, the information contained in this book is sold without warranty, either express or implied. Neither the authors, nor Packt Publishing or its dealers and distributors, will be held liable for any damages caused or alleged to have been caused directly or indirectly by this book.

Packt Publishing has endeavored to provide trademark information about all of the companies and products mentioned in this book by the appropriate use of capitals. However, Packt Publishing cannot guarantee the accuracy of this information.

Commissioning Editor: Richa Tripathi
Acquisition Editor: Prachi Bisht
Content Development Editor: Anugraha Arunagiri
Technical Editor: Aniket Iswalkar
Copy Editor: Safis Editing
Project Coordinator: Ulhas Kambali
Proofreader: Safis Editing
Indexer: David Punnoose Muthukaden
Graphics: Tania Dutta
Production Coordinator: Shraddha Falebhai

First published: September 2013
Second Edition: December 2014
Third Edition: March 2016
Fourth Edition: November 2018

Production reference: 1221118

Published by Packt Publishing Ltd.
Livery Place
35 Livery Street
Birmingham
B3 2PB, UK.

ISBN 978-1-78899-742-3

www.packtpub.com

For Catherine and Elodie

– Andrew Cutts

Mapt

mapt.io

Mapt is an online digital library that gives you full access to over 5,000 books and videos, as well as industry leading tools to help you plan your personal development and advance your career. For more information, please visit our website.

Why subscribe?

- Spend less time learning and more time coding with practical eBooks and Videos from over 4,000 industry professionals

- Improve your learning with Skill Plans built especially for you

- Get a free eBook or video every month

- Mapt is fully searchable

- Copy and paste, print, and bookmark content

Packt.com

Did you know that Packt offers eBook versions of every book published, with PDF and ePub files available? You can upgrade to the eBook version at www.packt.com and as a print book customer, you are entitled to a discount on the eBook copy. Get in touch with us at customercare@packtpub.com for more details.

At www.packt.com, you can also read a collection of free technical articles, sign up for a range of free newsletters, and receive exclusive discounts and offers on Packt books and eBooks.

Contributors

About the authors

Andrew Cutts is a Geospatial freelancer based in West Sussex, UK. He has almost 20 years industry experience across several sectors. He holds a degree in geography and a masters, in GIS (awarded in 2002). Andrew consults for clients worldwide and gives training in Geospatial technology. The themes covered include Python, GIS, and Earth Observation. Andrew writes extensively on the topic of Geospatial technology on his blog (www.acgeospatial.co.uk) and is the co-host of the #scenefromabove podcast. You can follow him on Twitter at `@map_andrew`.

Anita Graser is a spatial data scientist, open source GIS advocate, and author, with a background in geographic information science. She is currently working with the Center for Mobility Systems at the Austrian Institute of Technology in Vienna and teaching QGIS classes at UNIGIS Salzburg. She serves on the QGIS project steering committee and has published several books about QGIS. She also develops tools, including the Time Manager plugin for QGIS. You can follow her on Twitter at `@underdarkGIS`.

Packt is searching for authors like you

If you're interested in becoming an author for Packt, please visit `authors.packtpub.com` and apply today. We have worked with thousands of developers and tech professionals, just like you, to help them share their insight with the global tech community. You can make a general application, apply for a specific hot topic that we are recruiting an author for, or submit your own idea.

Table of Contents

Preface	1
Chapter 1: Where Do I Start?	5
Installing QGIS 3.4	5
Installing QGIS on Windows	6
Installing QGIS using the OSGeo4W installer	7
Latest QGIS release	7
Advanced installer (to specify version)	9
Installing on Ubuntu	10
Running QGIS for the first time	11
Plugins	13
What is new in QGIS 3	15
Introducing the QGIS user interface	15
Menu bar	17
Toolbars	17
Information bar	21
Layers and browser panels	22
Map	24
Finding help and reporting issues	26
Summary	26
Chapter 2: Data Creation and Editing	27
Data formats	28
GeoPackage	28
Loading data	28
Getting data into QGIS	29
Interacting with data	32
Navigation	32
Data attributes toolbar	33
Inspecting the data	34
Measuring data	35
Selecting data	36
Vector data	40
Editing attribute data	40
Building your own vector data	47
Projections	49
Creating data	51
Create a ShapeFile	51
Editing tools	53
Snapping	56
Mistakes and correcting with editing	57

Table of Contents

      Populating attribute data   62
   Data joins   63
   Using temporary scratch layers   68
   Checking for topological errors and fixing them   69
      Finding errors with the Topology Checker   69
      Fixing invalid geometry errors   72
Raster data   73
Other data   77
   Creating a GeoPackage   77
      Exporting to a different format   81
   Spatial Databases   81
Summary   82

Chapter 3: Visualizing Data   83
   Styling data   84
      Interactive styling   84
   Styling raster layers   85
      Layer styling – Terrain   86
      Layer styling – satellite image   89
         Raster Toolbar   91
      Styling data – landcover map   92
   Saving styles   95
   Styling vector layers   96
      Creating point styles – an example of an airport style   97
      Simple marker   101
         SVG   102
         Default symbols   103
      Creating line styles – an example of a river   105
      Creating polygon styles – an example of a landmass style   109
   Summary   114

Chapter 4: Creating Great Maps   115
   Communicating with data   116
   Labeling   116
      Interactively editing labels   119
      Displaying more information using labels   121
      Line labels   124
      Polygon labels   127
   Creating a map   129
   Loading data   131
      Adding layout items   133
         Add a title (or any text)   135
      Further map creation options   138
         Adding Grids   139
         Adding an overview map   140
         Adding an attribute table   141

Map outputs	143
Saving maps to share	143
Creating an Atlas	144
Presenting Maps online	145
Exporting a web map	145
QGIS2Web – an excellent way to export your data in openlayers or leaflet	146
Exporting a 3D web map	147
Summary	151
Chapter 5: Spatial Analysis	**153**
Processing toolbox	**154**
Analyzing raster data	**154**
Clipping rasters	154
Analyzing elevation/terrain data	156
Terrain projections – slope maps	160
Using the raster calculator	161
Combining raster and vector data	**166**
Converting between rasters and vectors	166
Raster to vector	166
Vector to raster	169
Accessing raster and vector layer statistics	171
Computing zonal statistics	174
Creating a heatmap from points	177
Advanced vector and raster analysis with processing	**179**
Finding nearest neighbors	179
Converting between points, lines, and polygons	181
Building workflows with processing tools	183
Identifying features in the proximity of other features	184
Sampling a raster at point locations	186
Mapping density with hexagonal grids	188
Calculating area shares within a region	192
Batch processing multiple datasets	198
Automated geoprocessing with the graphical modeler	199
Create a model that automates the creation of hexagonal heatmaps	201
Documenting and sharing models	205
Summary	**206**
Chapter 6: Extending QGIS with Python	**207**
Adding functionality using actions	**207**
Configuring your first Python action	208
Opening files using actions	211
Opening a web browser using actions	214
Getting to know the Python console	**214**
Loading and exploring datasets – vector data	215
Loading and exploring datasets – raster data	217
Styling layers	218
Filtering data	220

Table of Contents

Creating a memory layer	221
Exporting map images	222
Creating custom geoprocessing scripts using Python	**224**
Writing your first processing script	224
Building a basic buffer script	226
Running the script	229
Extending the script	230
Developing your first plugin	**232**
Creating the plugin template with Plugin Builder	233
Accessing qgis.core from the command line external to Python	237
Setting up the pb_tool	238
Assigning a logo to the plugin	241
Customizing the plugin GUI	242
Implementing plugin functionality	244
Adding a message box when OK is clicked	246
3D view	**246**
Summary	**251**
Other Books You May Enjoy	**253**
Index	**257**

Preface

QGIS is a user-friendly, open source Geographic Information System (GIS) that runs on Linux, Unix, macOS, and Windows. The popularity of open source GIS, and QGIS in particular, has been growing rapidly over the last few years.

This book will take you, as a new user, on a journey from the first time you fire up QGIS, all the way through to being on the cusp of developing your own processing pathway. We will travel together through familiarization with the user interface, loading some data, editing it, and then creating data. QGIS often surprises new users with its mapping capabilities. We will unlock these doors by looking at styling and creating your first map. And that is not all! Learning about spatial analysis and the powerful tools in QGIS will form the final part of this introductory book, before we end our journey by looking at the Python processing options.

Who this book is for

This book is for users, developers, and consultants who know the basic functions and processes of GIS and want to learn how to use QGIS to analyze geospatial data and create rich mapping applications.

What this book covers

`Chapter 1`, *Where Do I Start?*, covers the installation of QGIS 3.4, major changes since QGIS 2.x, UI, and getting help.

`Chapter 2`, *Data Creation and Editing*, covers data formats, loading data, interacting with it, and vector and raster data.

`Chapter 3`, *Visualizing Data*, explains how to interactively style vector and raster GIS data.

`Chapter 4`, *Creating Great Maps*, covers the labeling of data, creating maps, and map outputs.

Preface

Chapter 5, *Spatial Analysis*, explains the *Processing Toolbox*, spatial analysis of vector and raster data, batch processing, and modeling.

Chapter 6, *Extending QGIS with Python*, *covers* actions, the Python console, plugins, and 3D applications.

To get the most out of this book

We will cover installation in Chapter 1, *Where Do I Start*. This book steps through the basic tasks of QGIS 3.4 through to the advanced topics, such as Python programming. To get the most from this book, it is recommended to follow the chapters in sequence.

Download the example code files

You can download the example code files for this book from your account at www.packt.com. If you purchased this book elsewhere, you can visit www.packt.com/support and register to have the files emailed directly to you.

You can download the code files by following these steps:

1. Log in or register at www.packt.com.
2. Select the **SUPPORT** tab.
3. Click on **Code Downloads & Errata**.
4. Enter the name of the book in the **Search** box and follow the onscreen instructions.

Once the file is downloaded, please make sure that you unzip or extract the folder using the latest version of:

- WinRAR/7-Zip for Windows
- Zipeg/iZip/UnRarX for Mac
- 7-Zip/PeaZip for Linux

The code bundle for the book is also hosted on GitHub at https://github.com/PacktPublishing/Learn-QGIS-Fourth-Edition. In case there's an update to the code, it will be updated on the existing GitHub repository.

We also have other code bundles from our rich catalog of books and videos available at https://github.com/PacktPublishing/. Check them out!

Download the color images

We also provide a PDF file that has color images of the screenshots/diagrams used in this book. You can download it here: `https://www.packtpub.com/sites/default/files/downloads/9781788997423_ColorImages.pdf`.

Conventions used

There are a number of text conventions used throughout this book.

`CodeInText`: Indicates code words in text, database table names, folder names, filenames, file extensions, pathnames, dummy URLs, user input, and Twitter handles. Here is an example: "But what about the remaining 13 rows? They will now have no entry for the `small_area` field."

A block of code is set as follows:

```
my_features = v_layer.getFeatures()
for feature in my_features:
    print (feature.attributes())
```

When we wish to draw your attention to a particular part of a code block, the relevant lines or items are set in bold:

```
my_features = v_layer.getFeatures()
for feature in my_features:
    print (feature.attributes())
```

Any command-line input or output is written as follows:

```
[1, 18, 78.0, 'NOATAK', 'Other']
[2, 18, 264.0, 'AMBLER', 'Other']
[3, 26, 585.0, 'BETTLES', 'Other']
```

Bold: Indicates a new term, an important word, or words that you see on screen. For example, words in menus or dialog boxes appear in the text like this. Here is an example: "This can be done by going to **Layer Properties** | **Style** | **Save Style** | **QGIS Layer Style File**, or, alternatively, you can use any other style you like."

Preface

> Warnings or important notes appear like this.

> Tips and tricks appear like this.

Get in touch

Feedback from our readers is always welcome.

General feedback: If you have questions about any aspect of this book, mention the book title in the subject of your message and email us at `customercare@packtpub.com`.

Errata: Although we have taken every care to ensure the accuracy of our content, mistakes do happen. If you have found a mistake in this book, we would be grateful if you would report this to us. Please visit `www.packt.com/submit-errata`, selecting your book, clicking on the Errata Submission Form link, and entering the details.

Piracy: If you come across any illegal copies of our works in any form on the internet, we would be grateful if you would provide us with the location address or website name. Please contact us at `copyright@packt.com` with a link to the material.

If you are interested in becoming an author: If there is a topic that you have expertise in, and you are interested in either writing or contributing to a book, please visit `authors.packtpub.com`.

Reviews

Please leave a review. Once you have read and used this book, why not leave a review on the site that you purchased it from? Potential readers can then see and use your unbiased opinion to make purchase decisions, we at Packt can understand what you think about our products, and our authors can see your feedback on their book. Thank you!

For more information about Packt, please visit `packt.com`.

Where Do I Start?

Welcome to QGIS. There has never been a better time to start using QGIS, you have made a great choice! You may have already started using QGIS 3.4, you may have experience with older versions, or you may be familiar with other GIS software. No matter where you are on your learning journey, the first time you install any software can be a little daunting.

This chapter is all about getting a feel for the software, building your confidence, and developing the urge to explore. By the end of this chapter, you will grasped some of the basic ideas and concepts. You will be in the perfect position to begin working with data, designing and styling it, and working toward creating a map.

In this chapter, we will cover the following topics:

- Installing QGIS
- What has changed since QGIS 2.x?
- Toolbars and GUI
- Getting help
- Setting up
- Community of users

Installing QGIS 3.4

QGIS runs on all operating systems; it is even possible to install it on a Raspberry Pi. The QGIS project provides ready-to-use packages as well as instructions to build from source code at `http://download.qgis.org`. Here, we will cover how to install QGIS on two systems: Windows and Ubuntu.

> Full installation instructions for every supported operating system are available at `http://www.qgis.org/en/site/forusers/alldownloads.html`.

Where Do I Start?

Like many other open source projects, QGIS offers you a choice between different releases. For the tutorials in this book, we will use the QGIS 3.4 **long term release** (**LTR**) version. We recommend installing this version in order to follow this book with ease. As you build familiarity and confidence, you may wish to work with different versions. The core QGIS functionality generally remains the same. Newer versions will include the **latest release** (**LR**), which is normally updated every four months, or the **developer version** (**DEV**) for which you can get nightly builds, if needed. While exciting, the DEV version should not be relied on for anything other than testing or inspecting new features.

> You can find more information about the releases as well as the schedule for future releases at http://www.qgis.org/en/site/getinvolved/development/roadmap.html#release-schedule.
> For an overview of the changes between releases, check out the visual change logs at http://www.qgis.org/en/site/forusers/visualchangelogs.html.

Installing QGIS on Windows

On Windows, we have two different options for installing QGIS. These are the OSGeo4W and the standalone installer.

The OSGeo4W installer is a small, flexible installation tool that makes it possible to download and install QGIS and many more OSGeo tools with all their dependencies. The main advantage of this installer over the standalone installer is that it makes updating QGIS and its dependencies very easy. I recommend that you use OSGeo4W where practical. You can download the 32-bit and/or the 64-bit OSGeo4W installers from http://osgeo4w.osgeo.org. You can download directly from http://download.osgeo.org/osgeo4w/osgeo4w-setup-x86.exe for the 32-bit version. If you have a 64-bit version of Windows, you can also download from http://download.osgeo.org/osgeo4w/osgeo4w-setup-x86_64.exe. Download the version that matches your operating system and keep it. In the future, whenever you want to change or update your system, just run it again.

If you prefer, you can use the standalone installer. This is one file to download (approximately 400 MB in size). It contains a QGIS release, the **Geographic Resources Analysis Support System** (**GRASS**) GIS, and the **System for Automated Geoscientific Analyses** (**SAGA**) GIS in one package. For a beginning, this is the easiest installation option.

Installing QGIS using the OSGeo4W installer

In this section, we will focus on installing QGIS using the OSGeo4W installer. This is a convenient way to install QGIS and a host of other open source GIS tools.

> **TIP**: QGIS 3.4 will, in February 2019, become the first LTR of QGIS 3 replacing 2.18.

Latest QGIS release

Start by double-clicking on **OSGeo4W** executable. This will lead you to the following screenshot:

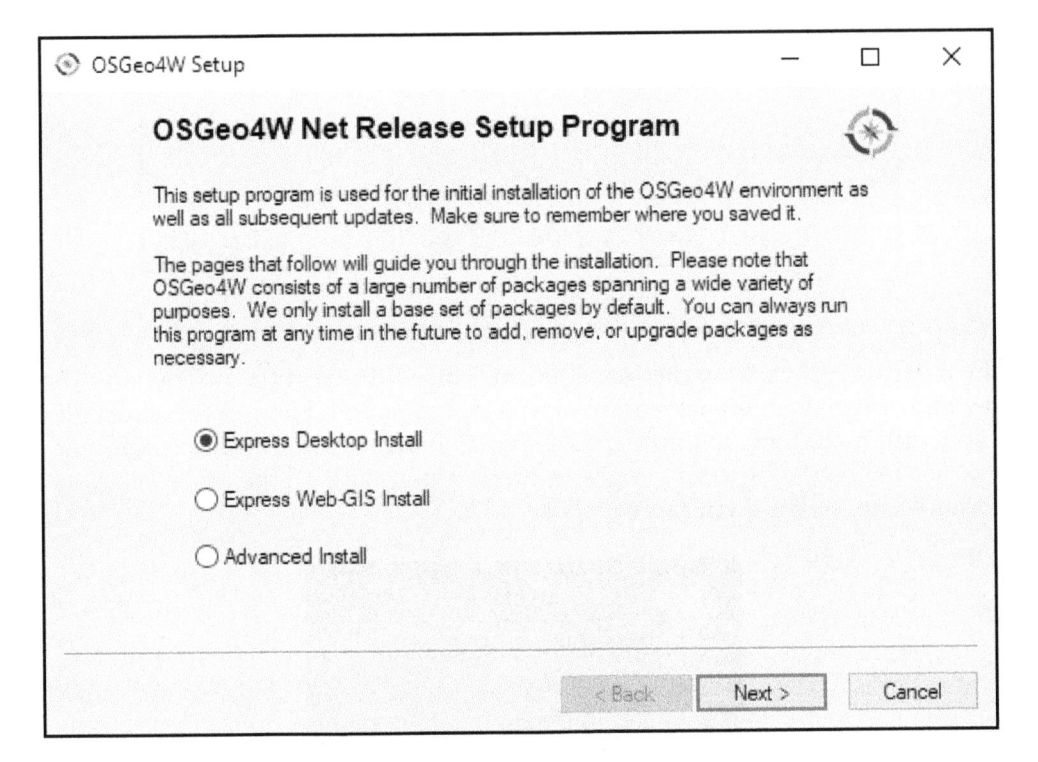

OSGeo4W setup screen

Where Do I Start?

Select the **Express Desktop Install** radio button. **This may not install QGIS 3.4.** If you wish to specify a version, please see the next section on *Advanced Installers*. The **Advanced Install** radio button is useful if you want to customize your installation, or choose your installation version or perhaps by install the development version of QGIS:

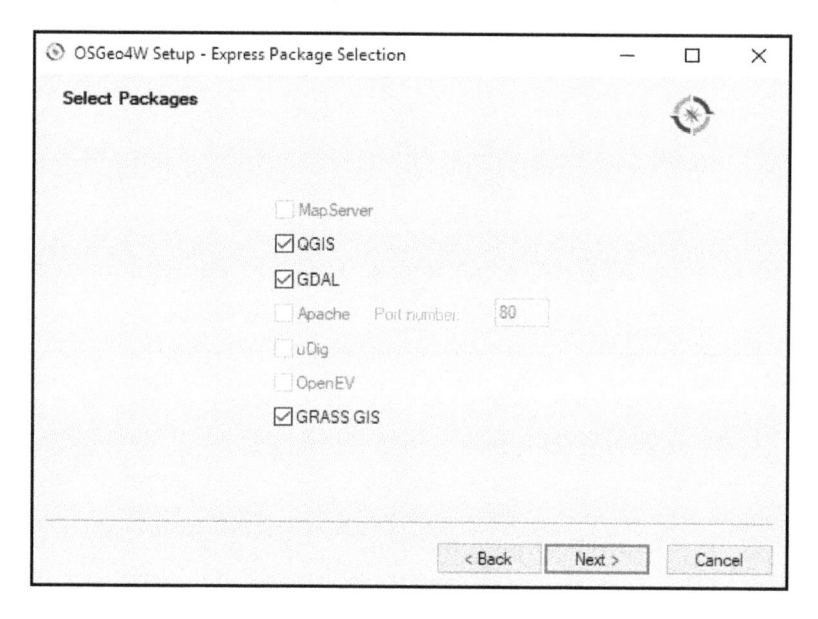

Setting the express package selection

Accept the defaults and click on the **Next** button. This will set off the download process. Progress will be displayed as each component is downloaded. Having these installed will provide you with more tools to perform Geospatial analysis. After a short period of time, you should see OSGeo4W in your programs menu along with all the other installed software, similar to the following screenshot:

How QGIS appears in Windows

If QGIS is appearing in your programs menu, then it is now installed on your machine.

> **TIP**
> It is possible to have multiple versions of QGIS installed on Windows. This may mean that you could have QGIS 2 and QGIS 3 running on the same machine. Please remember QGIS 3 projects will not open in QGIS 2. You may need to have two versions installed if you are reliant on a plugin that is no longer supported or has as yet to be ported to QGIS 3.

Advanced installer (to specify version)

Select the radio button next to **Advanced Install**, as shown in the following screenshot:

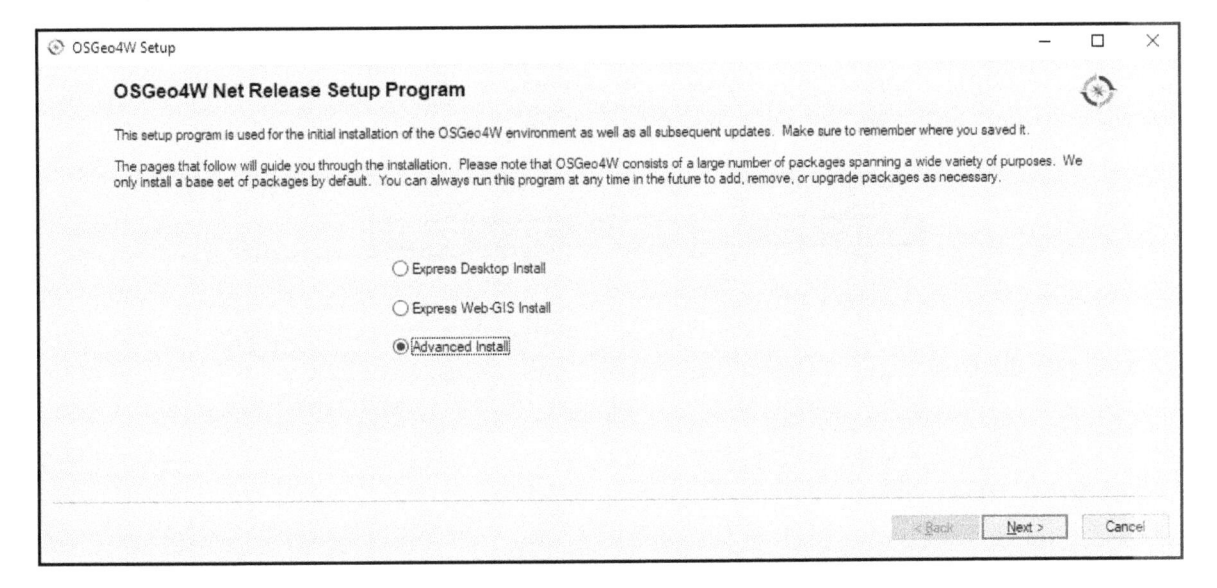

Advanced installer

Where Do I Start?

Step through the installation wizard. When you get to the Select Packages, choose the version you require. In the following screenshot I have selected the **3.4.0-1** release:

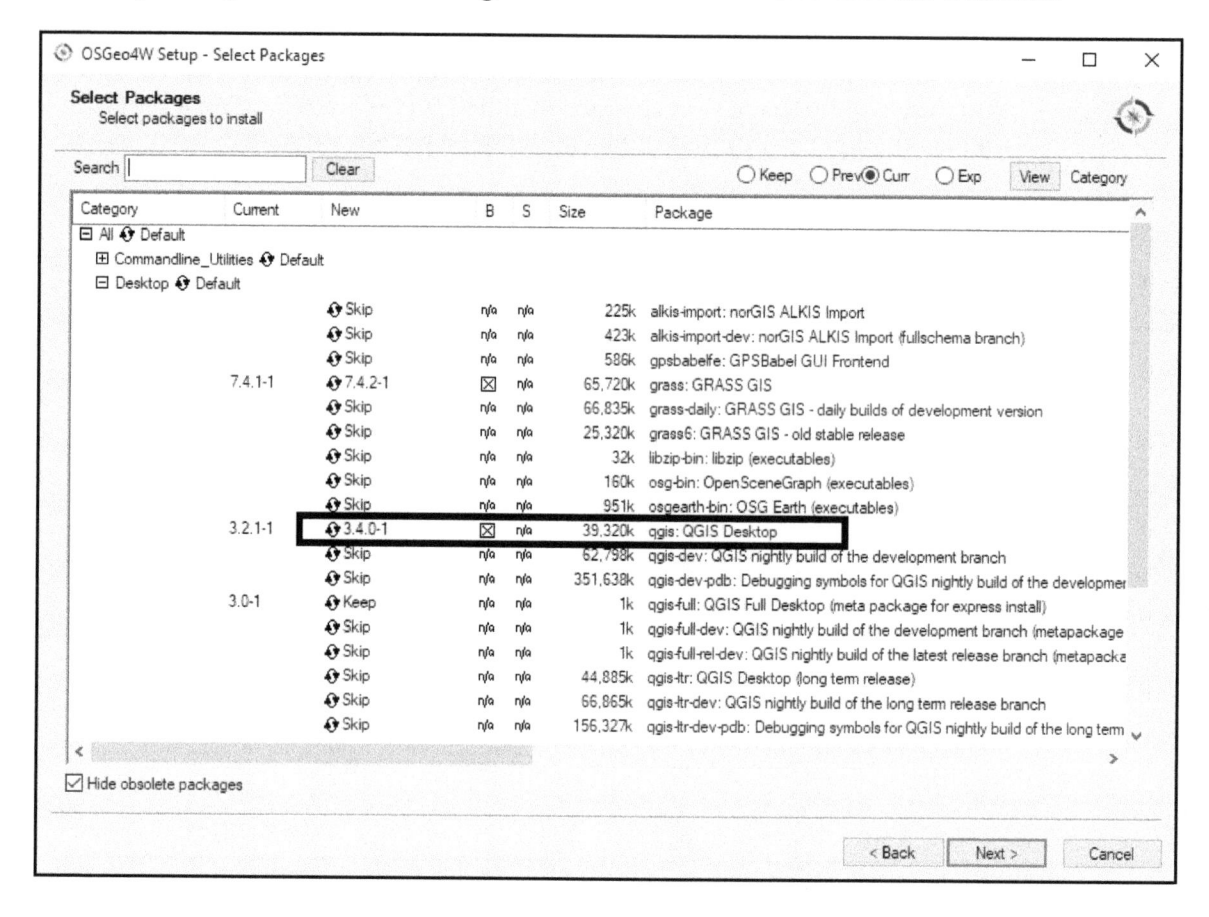

Installing QGIS 3.4 via advanced install

You can select other packages if required. Once you have chosen the software, click on the **Next** button. Step through the wizard by accepting the defaults and the installation will begin.

Installing on Ubuntu

On Ubuntu, the QGIS project provides packages for the LTR, LR, and DEV versions. For this book, we recommend installing the LTR version of 3.4 if available (release date: February 2019).

To avoid conflicts that may occur due to incompatible packages, make sure that you only add one of the following package source options. The specific lines that you have to add to the source list depend on your Ubuntu version. The following version is latest release for Debian stretch:

```
deb      https://qgis.org/debian stretch main
deb-src  https://qgis.org/debian stretch main
```

After choosing the repository, we will add the `qgis.org` repository's public key to our apt keyring. This will avoid the warnings that you might otherwise get when installing from a non-default repository. Run the following command in the terminal:

```
wget -O - https://qgis.org/downloads/qgis-2017.gpg.key | gpg --import
gpg --fingerprint CAEB3DC3BDF7FB45
gpg --export --armor CAEB3DC3BDF7FB45 | sudo apt-key add -
```

> You might need to make adjustments based on your system. For an updated list of supported Ubuntu versions, check out `http://www.qgis.org/en/site/forusers/alldownloads.html#debian-ubuntu`. By the time this book goes to print, the key information might have changed. Refer to `http://www.qgis.org/en/site/forusers/alldownloads.html#debian-ubuntu` for the latest updates.

Finally, to install QGIS, run the following commands. The first will fetch any updates to packages on your system, and the second will install QGIS, the python library, and the grass plugins:

```
sudo apt-get update
sudo apt-get install qgis python-qgis qgis-plugin-grass
```

Running QGIS for the first time

In recent years, QGIS has become the most popular open source desktop GIS software. Some people are using it just to view and query data, while others are using it for much deeper analyses. Maybe you are an ecologist or a town planner needing to use GIS as part of your job. Maybe you have a background in proprietary GIS software and want to migrate some of your common workflows to open source. Or maybe you are a student that needs to use GIS for a project. Whatever your driving reason is for opening this book, welcome to an amazing community that is passionate about open source and GIS.

Where Do I Start?

The following screenshot shows how QGIS 3.4 will look when it is first opened. In this case, there are no recent projects here and the interface is uncustomized:

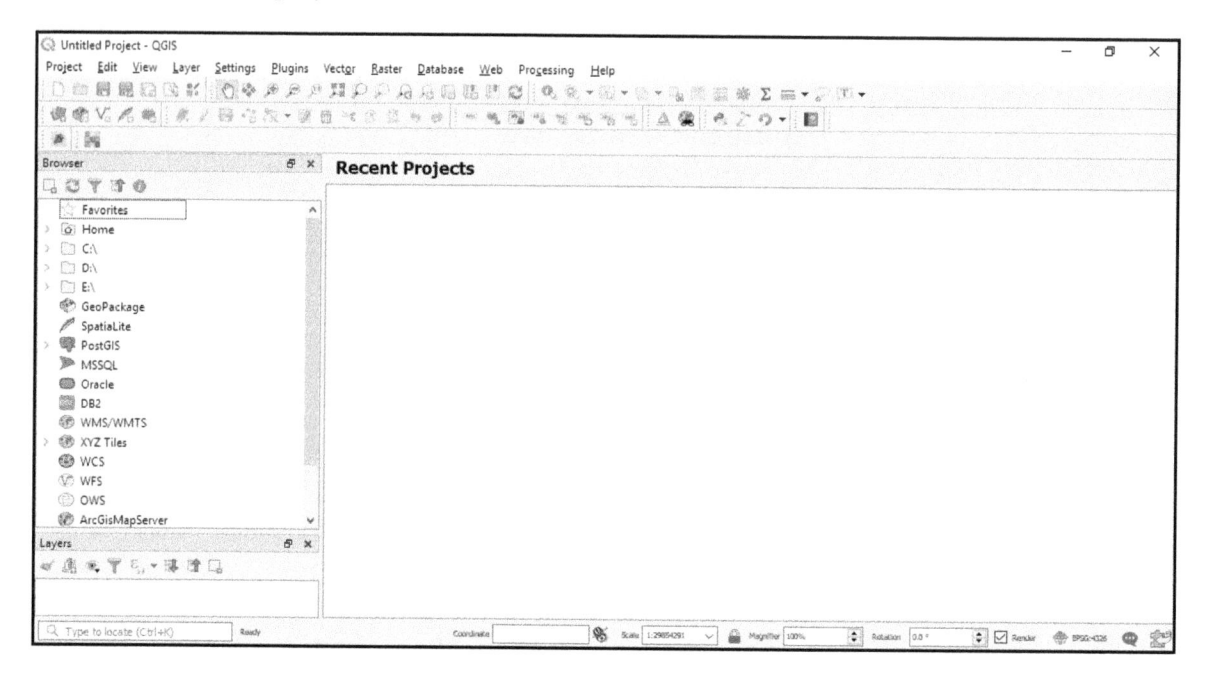

How QGIS appears once opened for the first time

On the first run, not all toolbars are enabled. You can enable all the default toolbars (meaning the ones not associated with any additional plugins) via **Toolbars** in the **View** menu. Set up the QGIS environment according to your personal preferences via the **Toolbars** option shown in the following screenshot:

[12]

Chapter 1

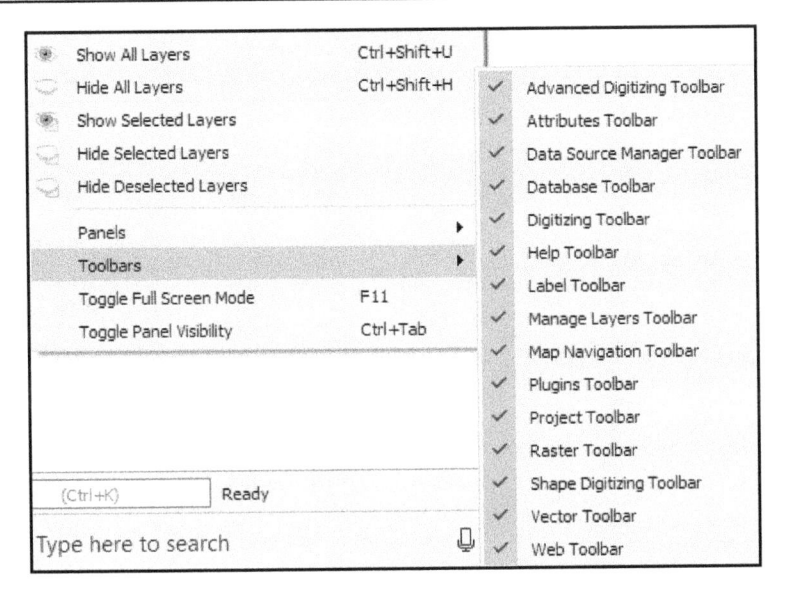

Setting the toolbars

> **TIP:** Leave the default settings enabled for this book. We will guide you through the toolbars and panels in detail in later sections.

Plugins

Plugins are a unique feature of QGIS. In Chapter 6, *Extending QGIS with Python*, we will cover how to build your own. Plugins are available to be installed as you need them to enable further analysis. If what you want to do is not available within your current QGIS setup, search in the plugins as someone may have developed a tool to help you reach your solution. To access the Plugins, navigate to **Plugins** in the menu and then select **Manage and Install Plugins**:

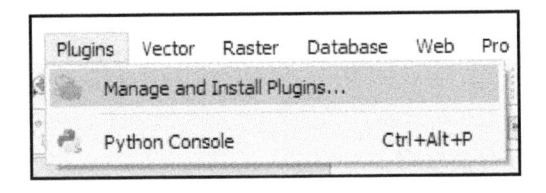

Opening the Plugins menu

[13]

Where Do I Start?

By clicking on the preceding option, the following window will be displayed:

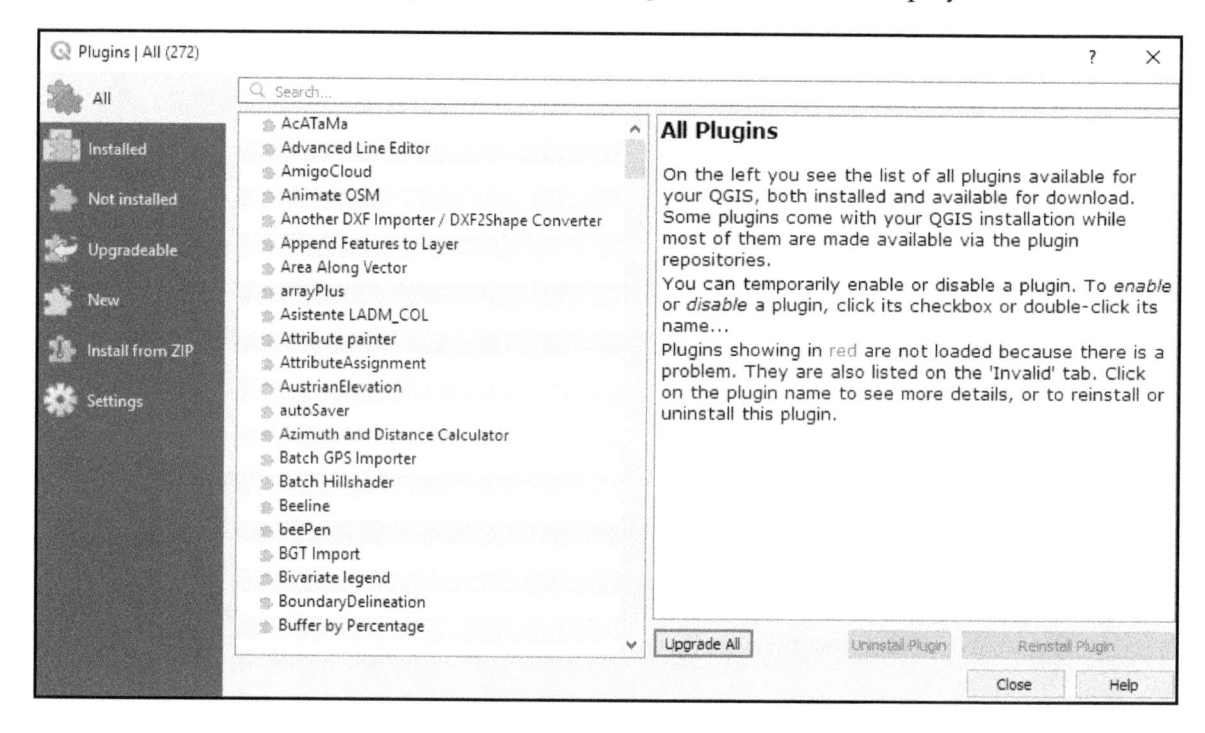

List of plugins currently installed

The **Plugins** window will display the number of plugins installed in parentheses. In the preceding example, 272 are shown. You can search for plugins in the search box, install or upgrade individual plugins, or **Upgrade All**. Plugins are activated by ticking the check boxes beside their names. In QGIS 3.4, an icon will appear in the bottom-right corner of the information bar if there are any updates available for the your installed plugins.

> **TIP**
> For a list of all the available Plugins, including the latest and most popular, navigate to `https://plugins.qgis.org/`. This is an ever-growing list!

[14]

What is new in QGIS 3

QGIS 3 has been ported to support Python 3, so if you are familiar with previous versions of QGIS, some of the older plugins may not be compatible. These will either have been updated or will be in the process of being updated, some are also obsolete (because their functionality is now part of QGIS core) or abandoned by the original developer. In terms of the GUI, not a great deal has changed. If you have previous experience, it should be mostly familiar to you.

Some of the major changes that have taken place for QGIS 3 include processing in the background. This enables you to continue working while processing continues, rather than waiting for QGIS to complete tasks. The processing toolbox has been updated, meaning that many of the tools now execute faster than in QGIS 2.x. There has also been a significant update in the way maps are authored and data is styled. We will be covering this in detail in Chapter 3, *Visualizing Data*. There is a really useful search feature in the bottom-left corner of the QGIS information bar, allowing you to search for tools, layers, and features. Finally, QGIS now supports GeoPackage and is using it as its default GIS format.

We will cover all of these new features in this book using examples to bring QGIS to life.

> For a comprehensive list of all the major updates, please see the change log at http://changelog.qgis.org/en/qgis/version/3.0.0/. To see the latest changes between version, check out https://qgis.org/en/site/forusers/visualchangelogs.html.

Introducing the QGIS user interface

Now that we have set up QGIS, let's get accustomed to the interface. The following screenshot shows a breakdown of QGIS. The main part of the screen is dominated by the map display, which can be adjusted as needed.

Where Do I Start?

- **Map Navigation**: This toolbar contains the pan and zoom tools, as well as bookmarks (customized zoom) and map refresh:

Map Navigation

- **Attributes**: These tools are used to identify, select, open attribute tables, and measure:

Attribute toolbar

- **Label**: These tools are used to add, configure, and modify labels
- **Plugins**: This currently only contains the Python Console tool, but will be filled in by additional Python plugins
- **Database**: Currently, this toolbar only contains DB Manager
- **Raster**: This toolbar includes histogram stretch, and brightness and contrast control
- **Vector**: This currently only contains the Coordinate Capture tool, but it will be filled in by additional Python plugins
- **Web**: This is currently empty, but it will also be filled in by additional Python plugins
- **Help**: This toolbar points to the option for downloading the user manual

All these toolbars are shown in the following screenshot:

Many of the common tools grouped together

[18]

On the left screen border, we place the Manage Layers toolbar. This toolbar contains the tools for adding layers from the vector or raster files, databases, web services, and text files. It also contains the tools for creating new layers:

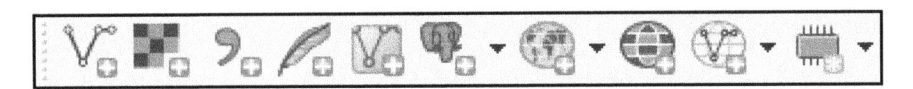

Manage layers toolbar

- **Digitizing**: The tools in this toolbar enable basic feature-creation and editing.
- **Shape Digitizing**: Useful for quickly building different shapes when editing.
- **Advanced Digitizing**: This toolbar contains the Undo/Redo option, advanced editing tools, the geometry-simplification tool, and so on. When activated, the right part of the screenshot is accessible:

All the editing tools

- The data source manager toolbar contains buttons to quickly create new geopackage files and shapefiles, as well as calling the data source manager and creating temporary scratch layers:

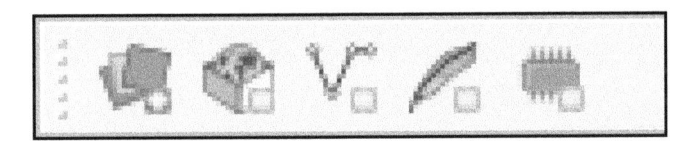

Data source manager toolbar

Toolbars can be accessed by right-clicking on a menu or toolbar, which will open a context menu with all the available toolbars and panels. All the tools on the toolbars can also be accessed via the menu. If you deactivate the Manage Layers Toolbar, for example, you will still be able to add layers using the Layer menu.

Where Do I Start?

As you might have guessed by now, QGIS is highly customizable. You can increase your productivity by assigning shortcuts to the tools you use regularly. You can do this by going to **Settings | Configure Shortcuts**. Similarly, if you realize that you never use a certain toolbar button or menu entry, you can hide it by going to **Settings | Interface Customization**:

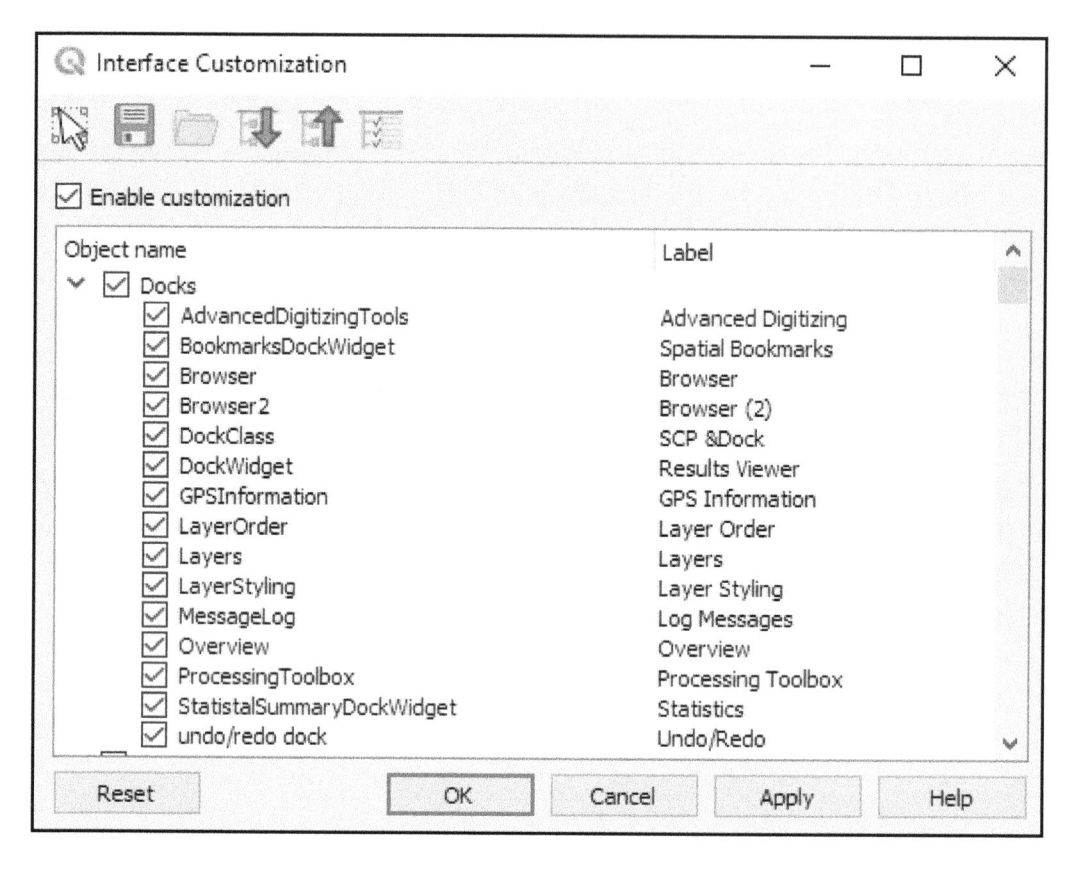

Customization of the user interface

Chapter 1

Information bar

The information bar is useful for finding out about the projection and navigation of the map. The information bar also contains icons about any log messages (potential errors) and any plugins with updates pending. It is shown in the following screenshot, and is located at the bottom of the QGIS window:

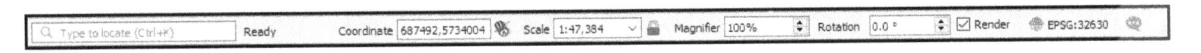

Information bar

The search function is one of the new features in QGIS 3 and this helps to find processing tools or layers. You can use the shortcut keys shown in the following screenshot:

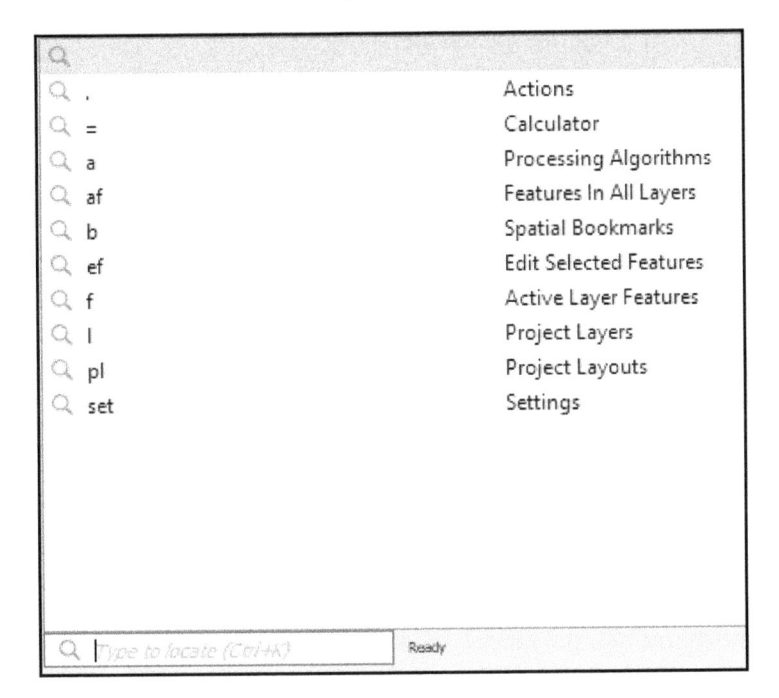

.	Actions
=	Calculator
a	Processing Algorithms
af	Features In All Layers
b	Spatial Bookmarks
ef	Edit Selected Features
f	Active Layer Features
l	Project Layers
pl	Project Layouts
set	Settings

Using the shortcut keys

[21]

Where Do I Start?

Alternatively, you can search directly for what you are looking for. For example, you can simply search for a `buffer` in the information bar search and the results will be similar to the following screenshot:

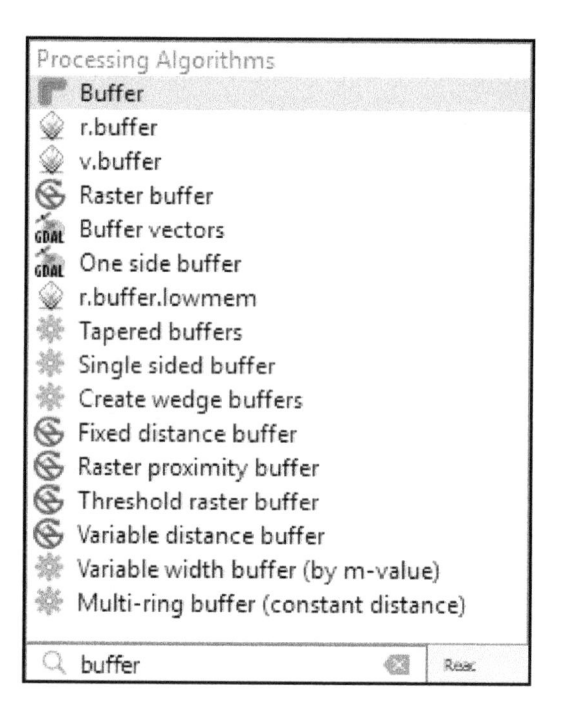

Processing Algorithms
- Buffer
- r.buffer
- v.buffer
- Raster buffer
- Buffer vectors
- One side buffer
- r.buffer.lowmem
- Tapered buffers
- Single sided buffer
- Create wedge buffers
- Fixed distance buffer
- Raster proximity buffer
- Threshold raster buffer
- Variable distance buffer
- Variable width buffer (by m-value)
- Multi-ring buffer (constant distance)

buffer

Searching for buffer tools

Layers and browser panels

Browser and Layers panels describe where data is stored and how that data is displayed. Now is a great time to download some sample data. Head over to https://qgis.org/downloads/data/ and download `training_manual_execise_data.zip`. Extract it in a folder of your choice and then navigate to that folder in the Browser window.

[22]

Chapter 1

I have located the `basic_map.tif` and `forest_stands_2012.shp` files and dragged them both into the **Layers** window. We will look at styling layers in `Chapter 3`, *Visualizing Data*, and then cover how to create a map in `Chapter 4`, *Creating Great Maps*. Lets take a look at **Browser** and **Layers** Panels in the following screenshot:

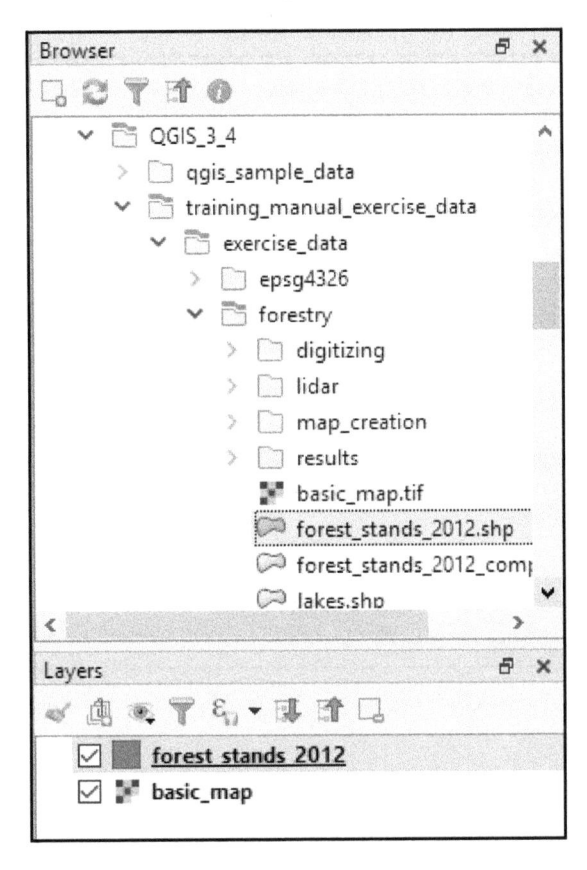

Browser and Layers Panels

Where Do I Start?

Map

Now that we have added some data to the **Layers** window, the data will appear in the map. The following screenshot shows two layers that I have added to the map: one vector (**forest_stands_2012**) and one raster (**basic_map**):

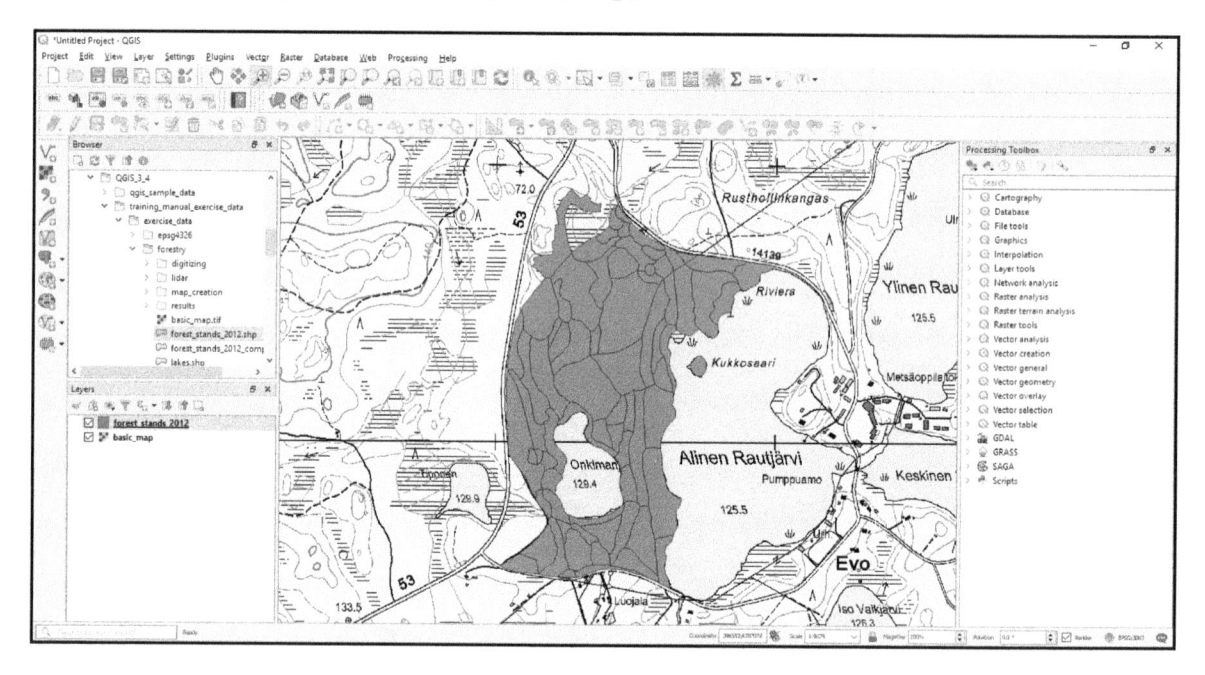

QGIS with some data added

The data has appeared! Notice that the projection in the information bar has changed; QGIS 3 supports on-the-fly projections. Finally, we have to save the project. The new default format is .qgz. Select **Project | Save**, and the window shown in the following screenshot will appear:

[24]

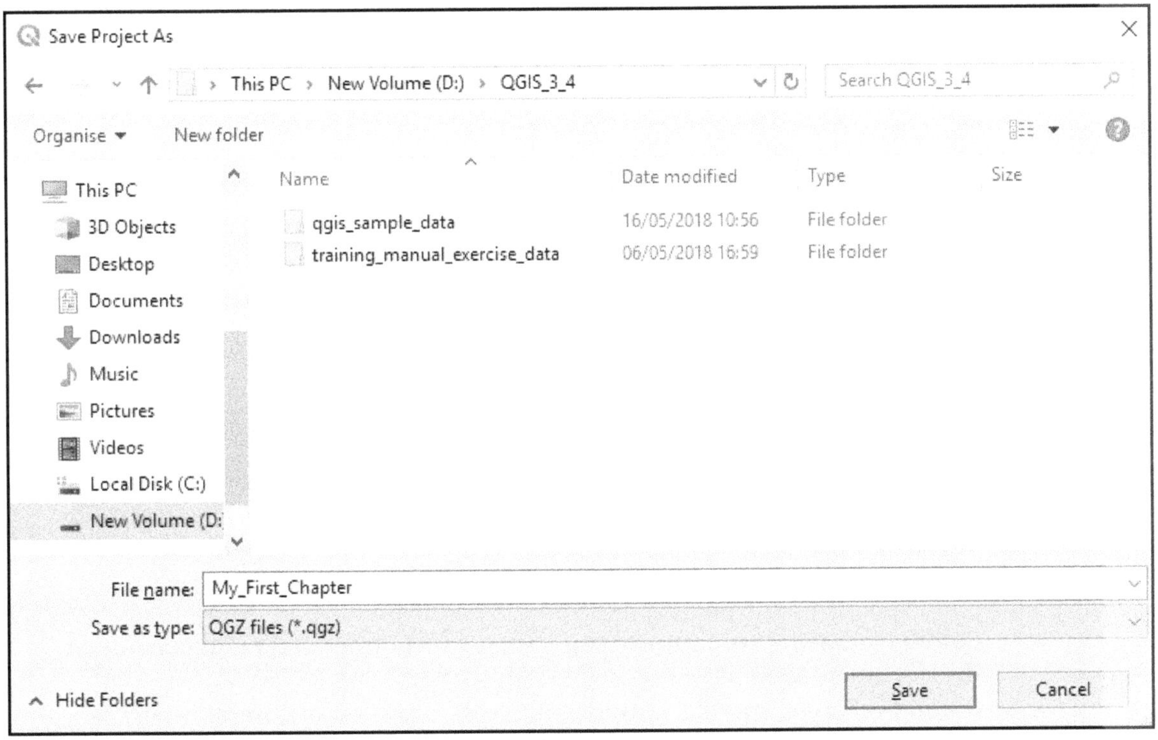

Saving a QGIS project

If you now click **Project** | **New**, you should see your saved project in the **Browser** window:

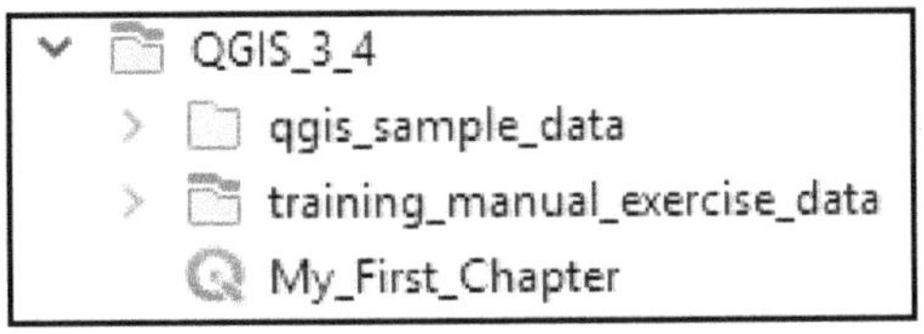

How the project appears in the Browser window

To load the project again, double-click on the project name.

TIP

You can sometimes open QGIS 2.x projects in QGIS 3, but you cannot open QGIS 3 projects in QGIS 2.x, so be careful.

Finding help and reporting issues

The QGIS community offers a variety of different community-based support options. These include the following:

- **GIS StackExchange**: One of the most popular support channels is http://gis.stackexchange.com/. This is a general-purpose GIS question-and-answer site. If you use the tag qgis, you will see all QGIS-related questions and answers at http://gis.stackexchange.com/questions/tagged/qgis.
- **Mailing lists**: The most important mailing list for user questions is qgis-user. For a full list of available mailing lists and links to sign up to, visit http://www.qgis.org/en/site/getinvolved/mailinglists.html#qgis-mailinglists. To comfortably search for existing mailing list threads, you can use Nabble (http://osgeo-org.1560.x6.nabble.com/Quantum-GIS-User-f4125267.html).
- **Chat**: A lot of developer communication runs through IRC. There is a #qgis channel on www.freenode.net. You can visit it using, for example, the web interface at http://webchat.freenode.net/?channels=#qgis.

> Before contacting community support, it's recommended to take a look at the documentation at http://docs.qgis.org.
>
> If you prefer commercial support, you can find a list of companies that provide support and custom development at http://www.qgis.org/en/site/forusers/commercial_support.html#qgis-commercial-support.
>
> If you find a bug, please report it because the QGIS developers can only fix the bugs that they are aware of. For details on how to report bugs, visit http://www.qgis.org/en/site/getinvolved/development/bugreporting.html.

Summary

In this chapter, we installed QGIS 3.4 and took a first look at the interface. We highlighted some of the exciting new features in the QGIS 3.4 release and looked at how they will impact us. We also explored the panels, toolbars, and menus that make up the QGIS user interface. At the end of the chapter, we interacted with the browser and the layers panel by dragging our data in and looking at how to save a project. Finally, we covered where to find help and report issues. In the next chapter, we will use QGIS to work with data.

Data Creation and Editing

At the core of any GIS is data. Without it, we cannot create maps or perform spatial analysis. In this chapter, we will load, edit, and create data. We will look at the large range of formats and types and how QGIS 3.4 helps us to work with them.

If you are familiar with GIS, then you will already know that we often work with vector data, namely points, lines, polygons, and raster data, as **pixels**. Vector and raster data are the core data types that we use in a GIS. However, text files, databases, and web services can also be integrated into GIS. We can use a location associated with a file (such as a coordinate), or we can perform joins to extend or spatially enable our existing data.

In this chapter, we will explore all of the data options in QGIS. The topics covered in this chapter are as follows:

- Data formats
- Loading data
- Interacting with data
- Vector data
- Attributes
- Editing and creating data
- Data joins
- Raster data
- Other data in spatial databases

Data Creation and Editing

Data formats

QGIS supports many GIS data formats. It makes use of the OGR library for vector data and the GDAL library for raster data.

> **TIP**: To see the latest list of OGR vector formats, check out http://www.gdal.org/ogr_formats.html, and to see a list of GDAL raster formats, visit http://www.gdal.org/formats_list.html. If you can't find your format on the list, it is probably not supported in QGIS at this time.

Shapefiles are the most common form of vector data today, and QGIS supports this format. Similarly, GeoTIFF are probably the most common form of raster data, and QGIS also supports these. In this book, we will work with and use these formats, as well as the new GeoPackage format.

GeoPackage

QGIS 3 has chosen GeoPackage as its default format. This is an open format, unlike the Shapefile, which is proprietary. GeoPackage also supports rasters. It is built on a SpatiaLite database, has no file size limitations, and works as one file. The format was developed by the Open Geospatial Consortium and is increasingly being adopted by organizations around the world. A GeoPackage has a .gpkg extension, which unlike the Shapefile has several extensions.

Loading data

We are going to start by loading data into QGIS 3.4. You may have some of your own data that you wish to use, but all of the techniques are applicable to any GIS data you have. We will use the QGIS sample data for these examples. Over the following chapters, we will use the sample dataset to eventually build maps.

> **TIP**: Download the QGIS sample data from https://qgis.org/downloads/data/ and look for the qgis_sample_data.zip file. Download and extract this data to a folder on your computer.

Getting data into QGIS

Loading data into QGIS can be done in several ways. The three most common ways are as follows:

- You can drag data directly from a folder straight into the map.
- You can drag data from the browser panel (shown in Chapter 1, *Where Do I Start?*) onto the map.
- You can click **Layer** | **Add Layer** and choose what type of layer to add.

In the following screenshot, we are choosing to load a Vector Layer, which can also be done using the *Ctrl + Shift + V* shortcut:

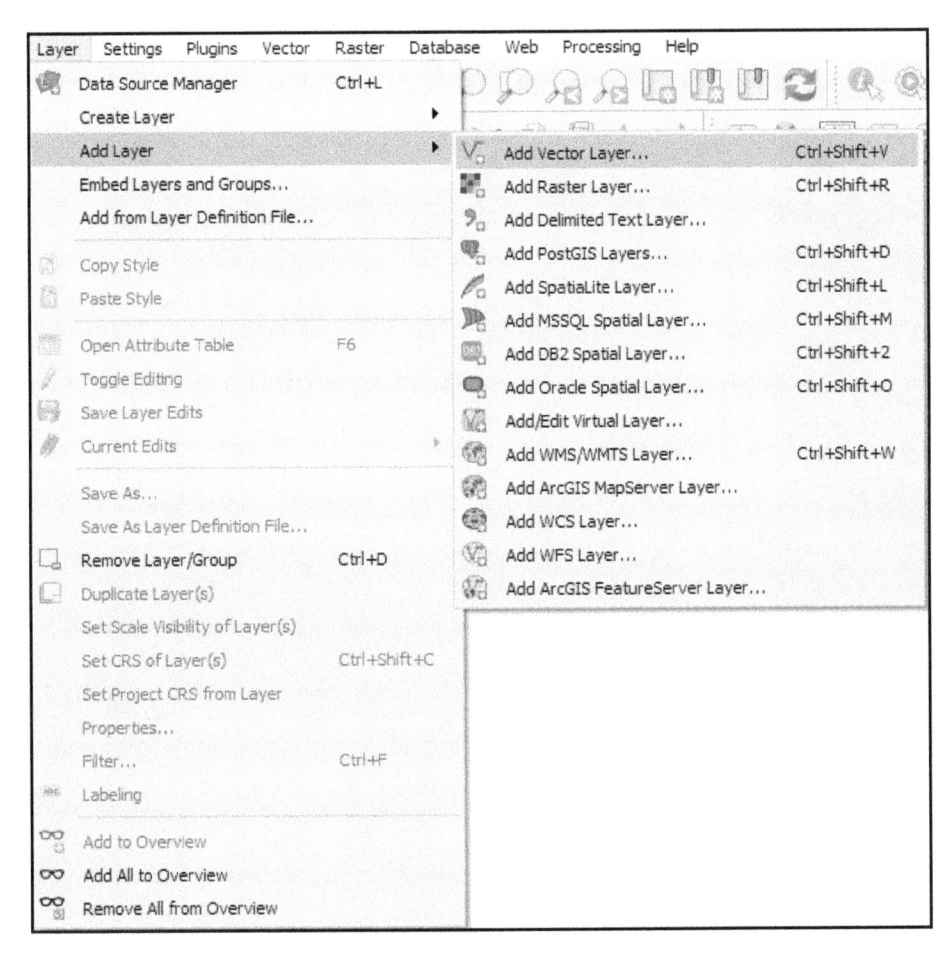

Adding a vector layer

Data Creation and Editing

By choosing this method, the **Data Source Manager** window will appear, with **Vector** highlighted, as follows:

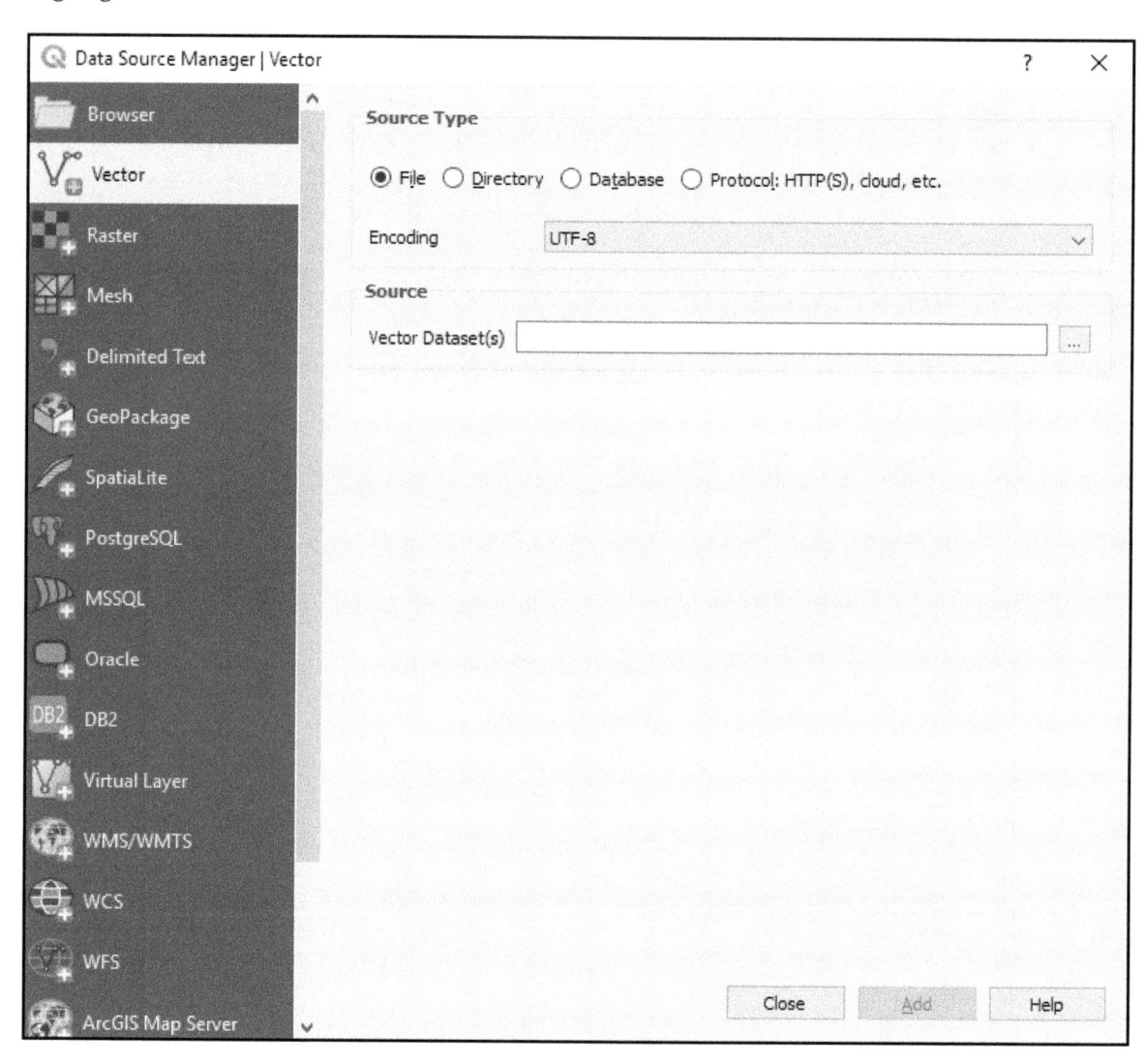

The QGIS Data Source Manager

Click on the ellipsis for **Vector Dataset(s)** and navigate to the layer you wish to load. In the following example, the `alaska` Shapefile is selected. You can load more than one layer at the same time by holding down the *Ctrl* button and clicking on multiple files:

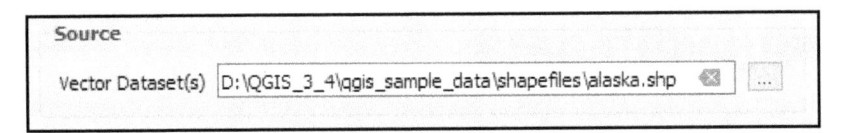

Loading data in the data source manager

If you then click the **Add** button at the bottom of the **Data Source Manager** window, the data will be added to your **Map** window as well as the **Layers** window. The **Data Source Manager** window will remain open, and you can also load other layers. Close the window and your Shapefile will appear in the map, as follows:

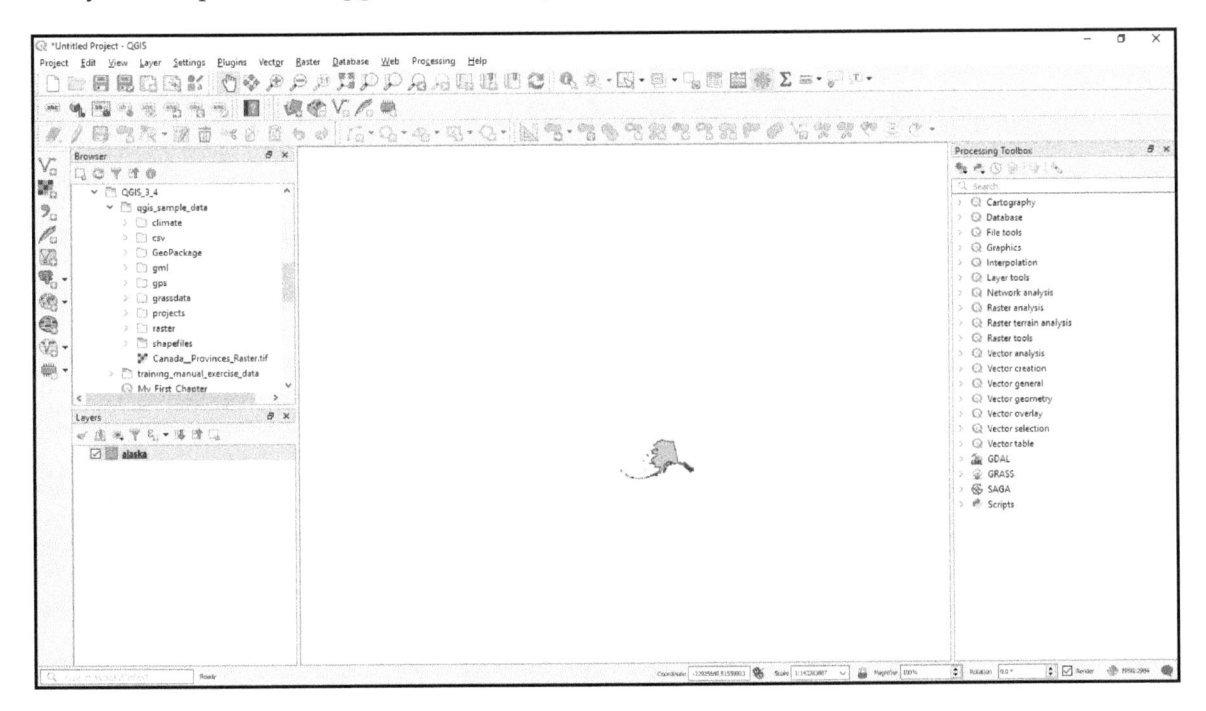

Data loaded into the map panel in QGIS

Data Creation and Editing

In the next section, we will look at how to interact with the data to zoom in and inspect its attributes.

Interacting with data

When you loaded the Alaska layer, you probably noticed that the data appeared as a relatively small object. In this section, we will cover some of the basic interactions we can perform with data. Let's start with zooming in.

Navigation

Later, we will show you how to zoom in on a layer to look at it in more detail. But first, let's remind ourselves of the project and navigation toolbar:

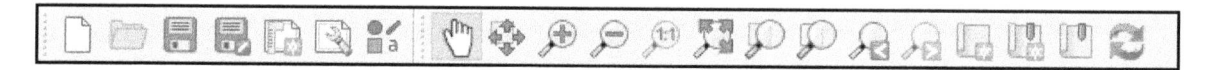

Project and Navigation toolbar

These tools are the workhorse of the GIS. They allow us to move around, inspect, measure, and select data. All are critical in any GIS, and if you have used mapping software before, you should be familiar with them.

Start by clicking on the zoom-in icon (a magnifying glass icon with a + in it). When this option is selected, it will be highlighted in a different shade, just like any other interactive button in QGIS. This is demonstrated in the following screenshot:

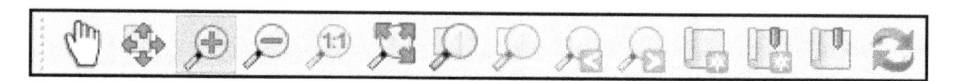

Clicking on the zoom tool in the navigation toolbar

[32]

Left-click and draw around the Alaska shape. The map window will quickly refresh around the shape you have drawn. You can then click on the white hand to pan around the map to adjust to your preference. You can also use the scroll button on your mouse to zoom in and out of the map. Some of these navigational tools are grayed out; this is because a setting or event has not happened yet to enable them.

The bookmark tool is shown in the following screenshot and highlighted in the red box:

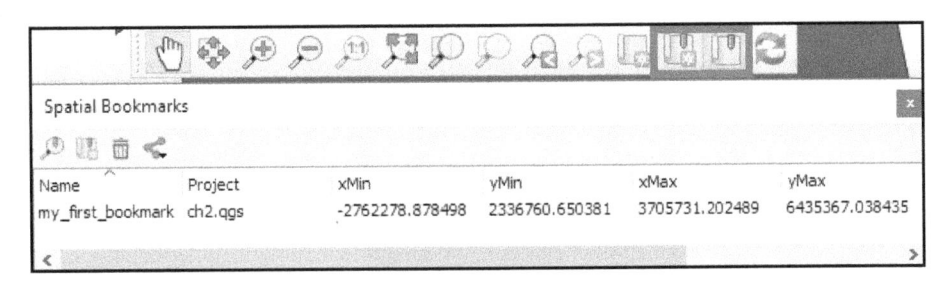

Spatial bookmarks

Spatial Bookmarks allow you to save your current map extent. This means that you can return to this bookmarked view later, or in another project. In the preceding example, I have created a bookmark called `my_first_bookmark`.

Data attributes toolbar

Here is the attributes toolbar:

Attributes toolbar

This contains tools to inspect, measure, and select data, among other tools. In order to be able to use these tools, we need to have a layer selected in the layers window. Left-click once on the Alaska layer and this toolbar will have all of its options available.

Data Creation and Editing

Inspecting the data

Click on the blue **i** button in the attributes toolbar and then click on the layer in the map. This will display the feature attributes in a new panel, which will dock by default. Like all panels, you can move them around and resize as needed. Your QGIS project should look similar to the following diagram:

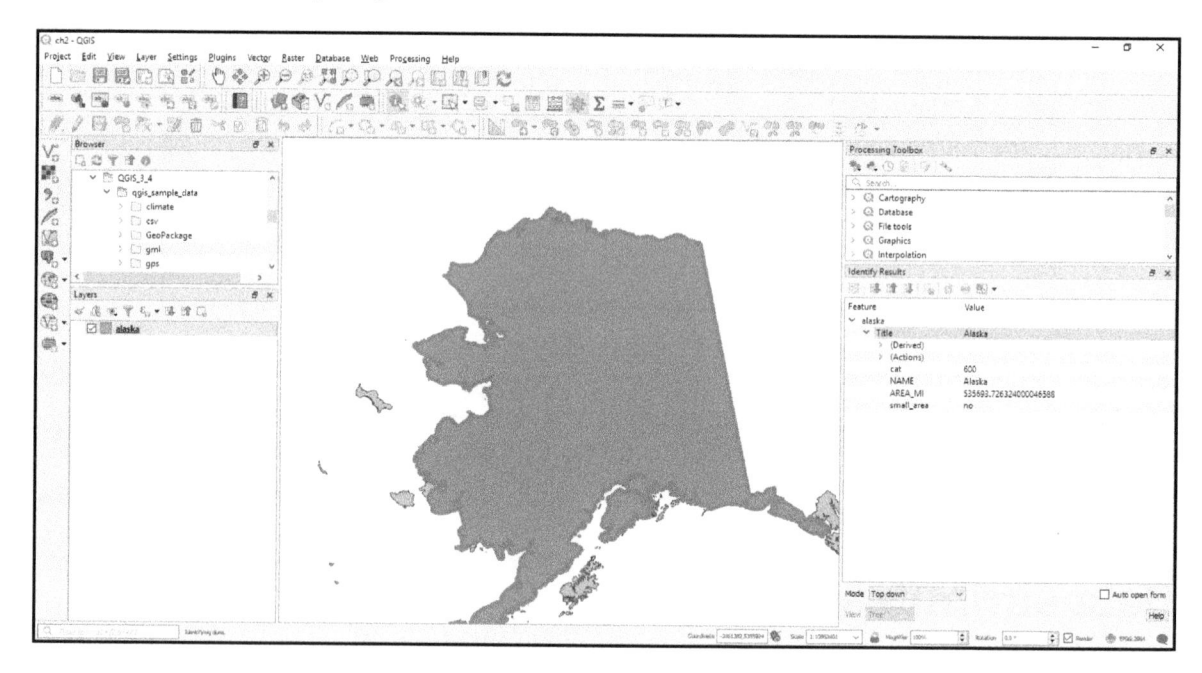

Inspecting data in QGIS

The new panel is called **identify results**. In this case, attributes include a **Category**, a **Name**, and an **Area value**. Later in this chapter, we will look at creating and editing data, as well as adding attributes.

[34]

Measuring data

The measure tool does not require a layer to be selected in the layer panel in order for it to work. This means that it is independent of a layer(s). The measure tool can measure length, area, or angle, and you can use the drop-down button next to the tool to select the required option. In this example, let's measure length. Select the measure line option and then left-click on the map to begin the measurement. After doing this, left-click again to measure the segment. Continue to left-click to measure segments of the line or right-click on the end point to finish measuring.

The following diagram shows a series of left clicks on the Alaska layer:

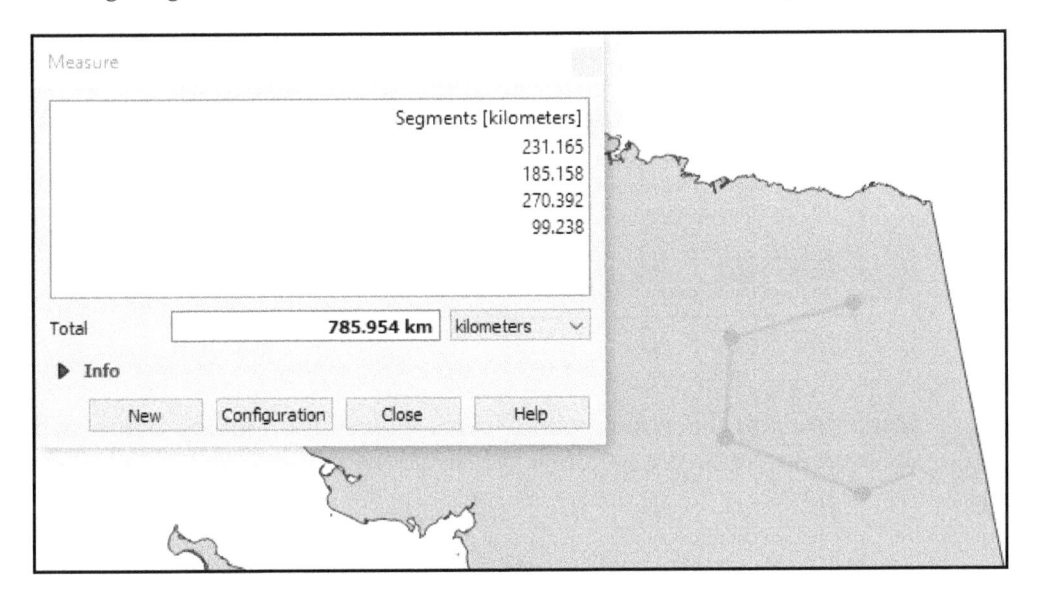

Measuring distance in QGIS

Use the drop-down boxes to adjust the units of measurement you require. The default is set to **meters**; we have changed ours to **kilometers** to obtain a more usable distance unit.

Data Creation and Editing

If you expand the arrow next to **Info** in the **Measure** toolbox, you will get more information about how the measure tool is calculating the distance/area. An example is shown in the following screenshot:

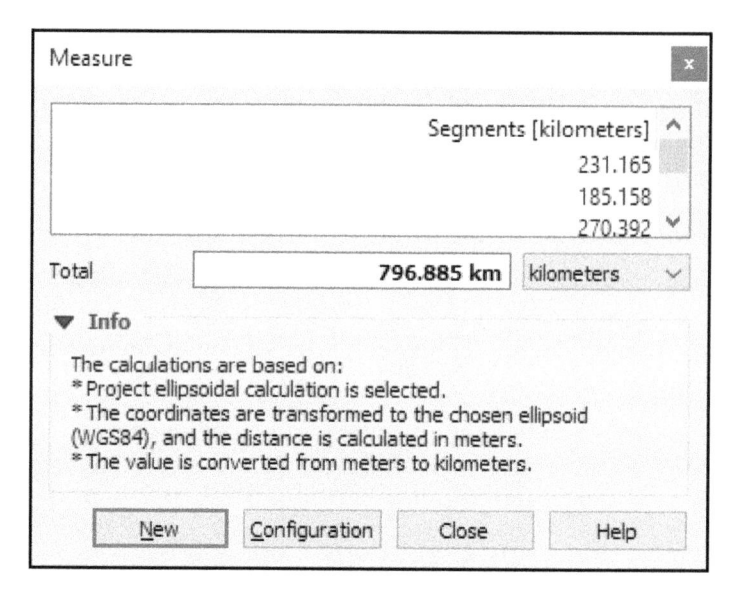

The measure tool info box

> **TIP**: Make sure you check that you are in the expected projection before using the measure tools. We will look at Projections in the *Vector data* section of this chapter.

Selecting data

Selecting data is very useful in GIS. We can create a new layer from a selection, or we could add new data specific to that selection. QGIS allows multiple ways of selecting data, and we will cover some of these here. Later, in `Chapter 6`, *Extending QGIS with Python*, we will look at spatial selections. The data attributes toolbar allows selecting by area (this means drawing on the map by hand) and selecting by value (this means passing a query to select the data). The selection tools are highlighted in the following screenshot:

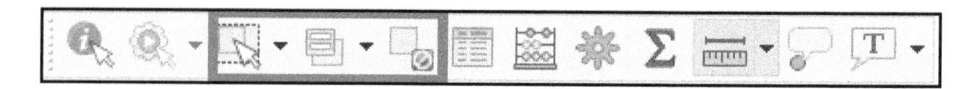

The select data tools

[36]

Chapter 2

Working from left to right, the tools are Select by Area, Select by Attribute, and Clear Selection. Click on the Select by Location button and click on the largest area associated with the Alaska layer. It will change to yellow to highlight the selected layer. The following screenshot shows the other Select by Area options in the drop-down list:

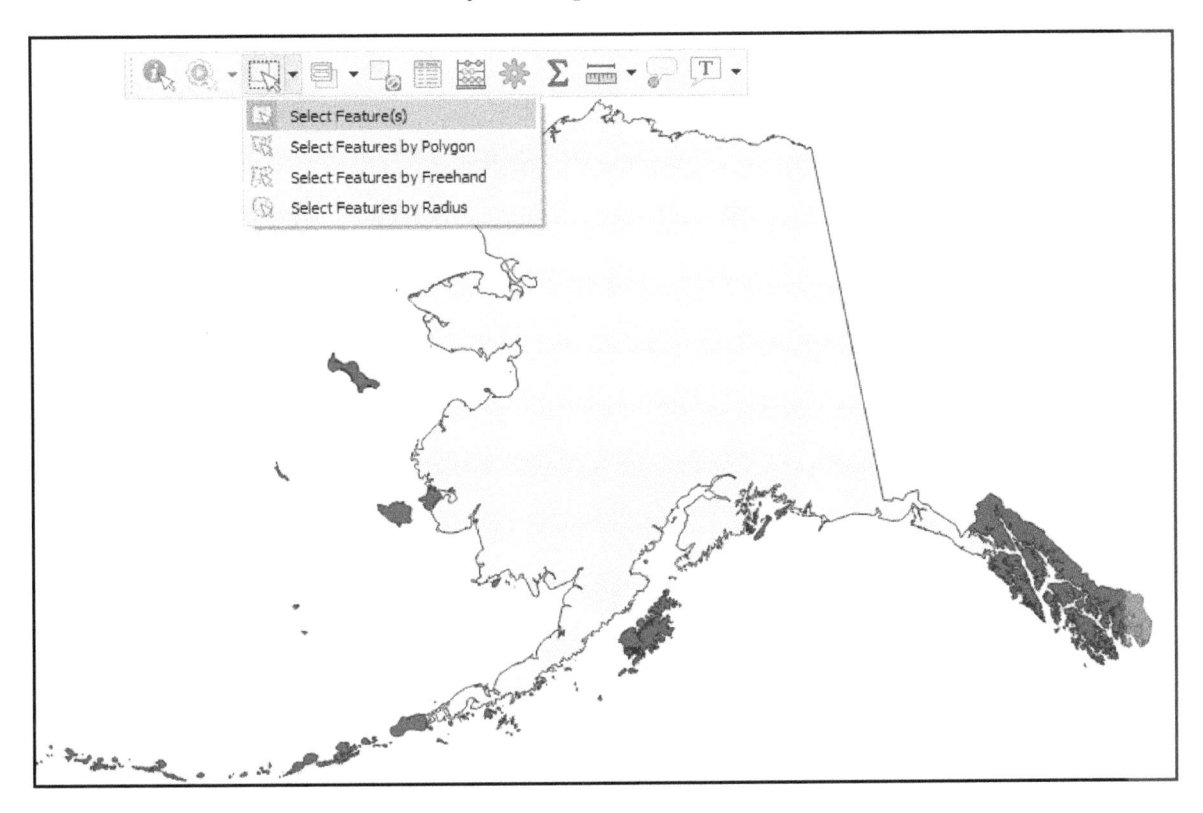

Feature selected in QGIS

Click on **Clear Selection** to remove any selections from the layer.

[37]

Data Creation and Editing

The **Select by Value** button is the second button on the toolbar described previously. Click on this button to open a new window:

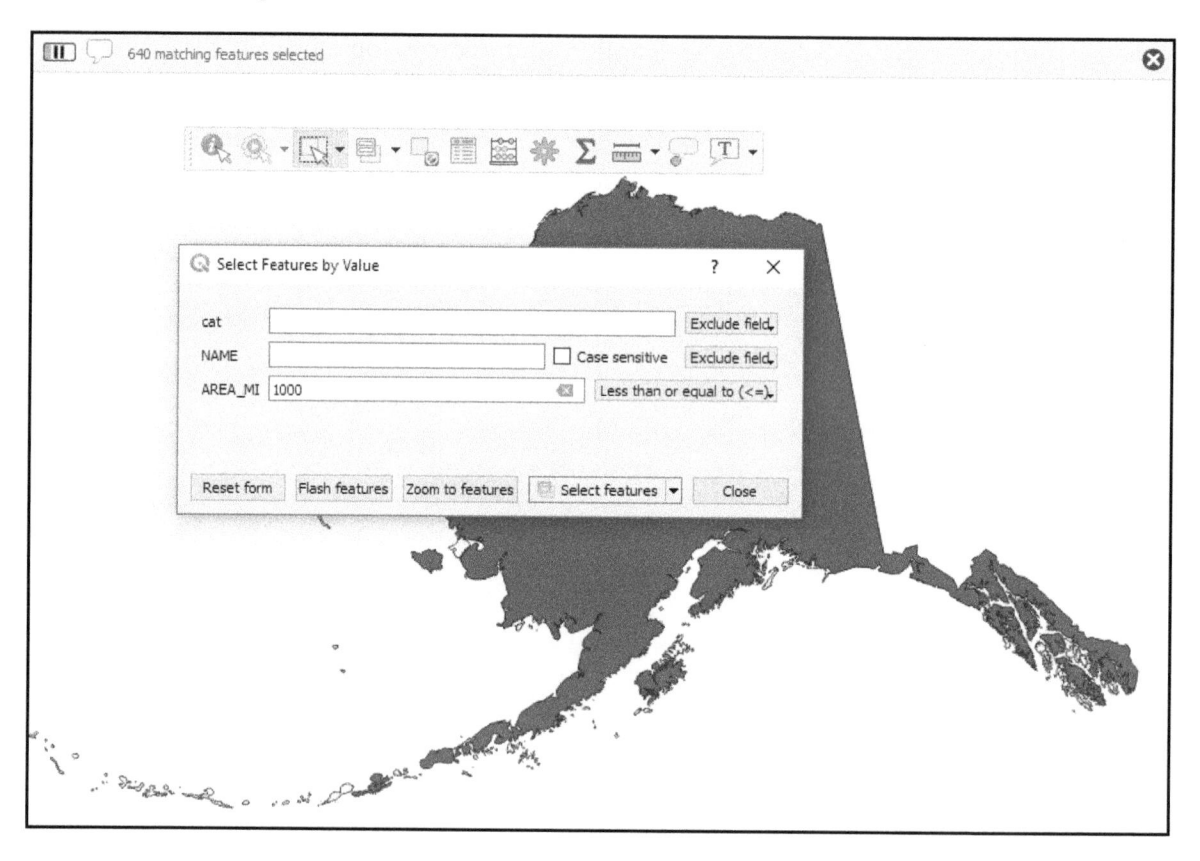

Map showing the selected features by value option

In the **Select Features by Value** window, we have clicked on the **Exclude field** button associated with **AREA_MI** and selected **Less than or equal to (<=)**. As a parameter, we have typed 1000 into the box. We then clicked **Select features** and QGIS selected the features that match this expression. At the top of the screen, a notification tells us how many features have been selected. In this case, it is 640.

If we click on close and then press *F6* or click on the button immediately to the right of the **Clear Selection** button, the attribute table will appear with the selected rows highlighted. This attribute table for the **Alaska** layer is shown as follows:

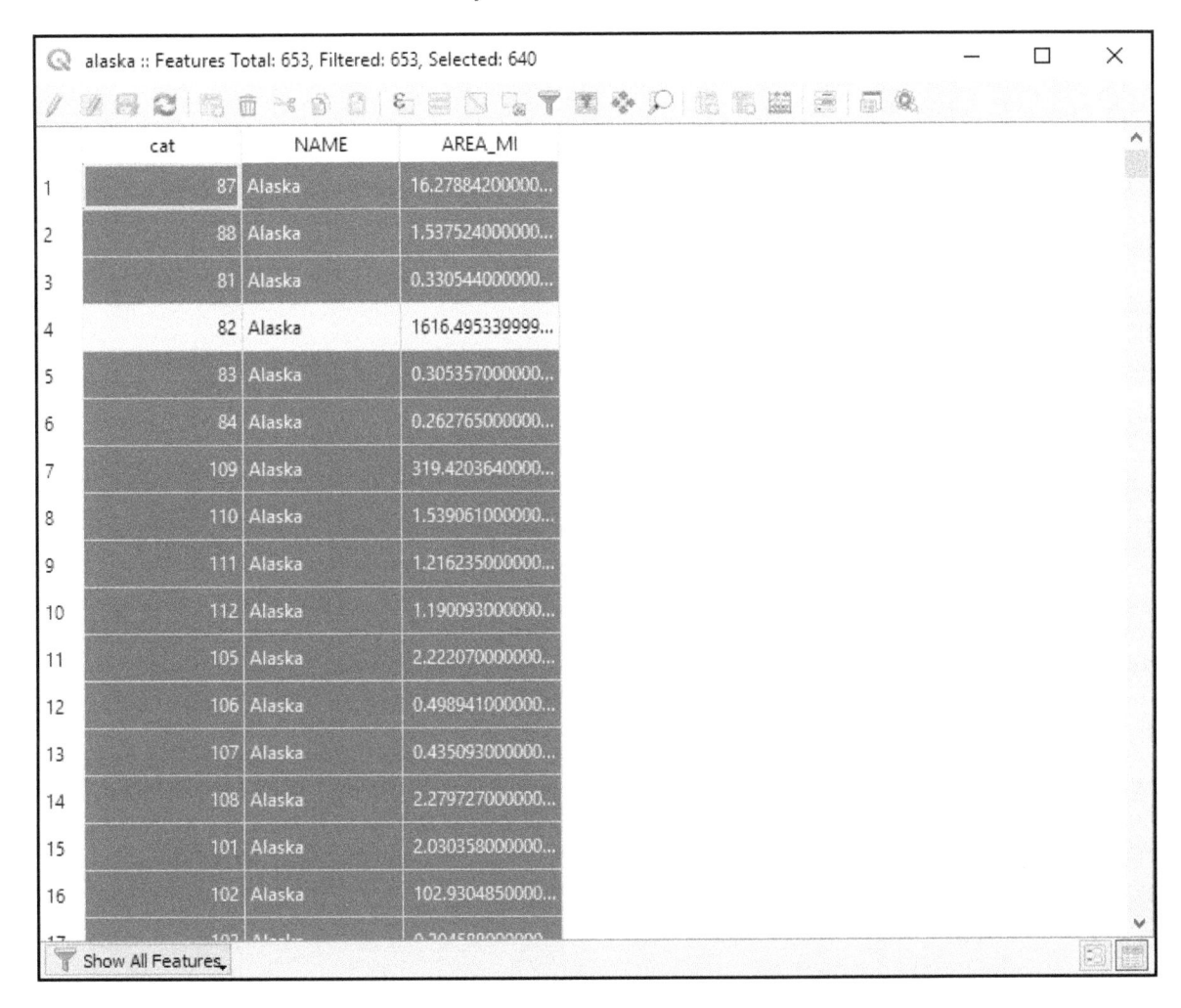

	cat	NAME	AREA_MI
1	87	Alaska	16.27884200000...
2	88	Alaska	1.537524000000...
3	81	Alaska	0.330544000000...
4	82	Alaska	1616.495339999...
5	83	Alaska	0.305357000000...
6	84	Alaska	0.262765000000...
7	109	Alaska	319.4203640000...
8	110	Alaska	1.539061000000...
9	111	Alaska	1.216235000000...
10	112	Alaska	1.190093000000...
11	105	Alaska	2.222070000000...
12	106	Alaska	0.498941000000...
13	107	Alaska	0.435093000000...
14	108	Alaska	2.279727000000...
15	101	Alaska	2.030358000000...
16	102	Alaska	102.9304850000...

Attribute table with features selected

When you are finished inspecting this table, close it down by clicking the close button, on Windows this is an X symbol in the top-right corner. Keep this selection handy, as we will use it in the next section.

Data Creation and Editing

There is one more very useful tool worth mentioning, and that is the **Field Calculator** tool. This button looks like an abacus and is next to the **Attribute Table** button. We will use this tool next to begin creating our own data.

Vector data

Now that we have become more familiar with inspecting, selecting, and interacting with data within QGIS, it's time to create data. In this section, we are going to edit attribute data, create vector data, and join data.

Editing attribute data

With the **AREA_MI** <= 1000 selection, let's add a field and populate it with a marker based on this selection.

Click on the **Field Calculator** button in the attributes toolbar to open up the field calculator.

This window contains considerable information; there is a great deal of power within the field calculator. In our case, we want to create a new field called small_area and assign yes if it is =< 1000, or no if it is >1000. As with many of the tools in GIS, there are several ways of doing this. The method we will use is designed to help you to build confidence first. In chapter 6, *Extending QGIS with Python*, we will look at more complex queries and show how this particular query could be addressed in one step.

As shown in the following screenshot, the first check box is ticked. This tells QGIS to only apply the calculation to the selected data. The second check box tells QGIS to create a new field. We could update an existing one if we wanted, but at this point we want to build a new field and populate it. Set the field name to small_area and the type to **Text**.

Chapter 2

Accept the defaults for field length and in the expression window type `yes` (including the single quotations). Your **Field Calculator** should now look like this:

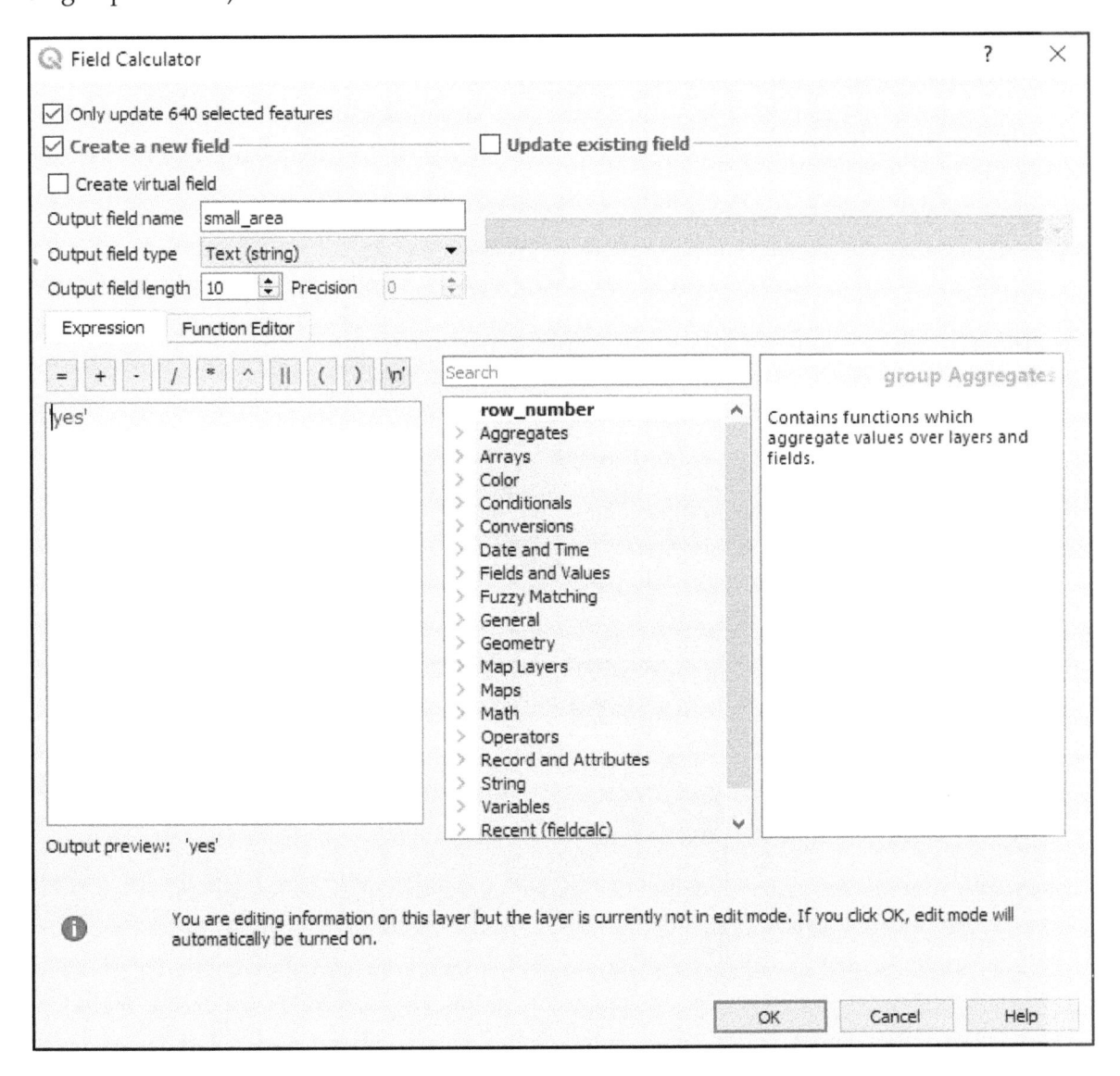

Field Calculator

Data Creation and Editing

By clicking on **OK**, you will have started an edit session and populated a field with `yes` based on your **Selection by Value** selection. Your screen will look similar to this:

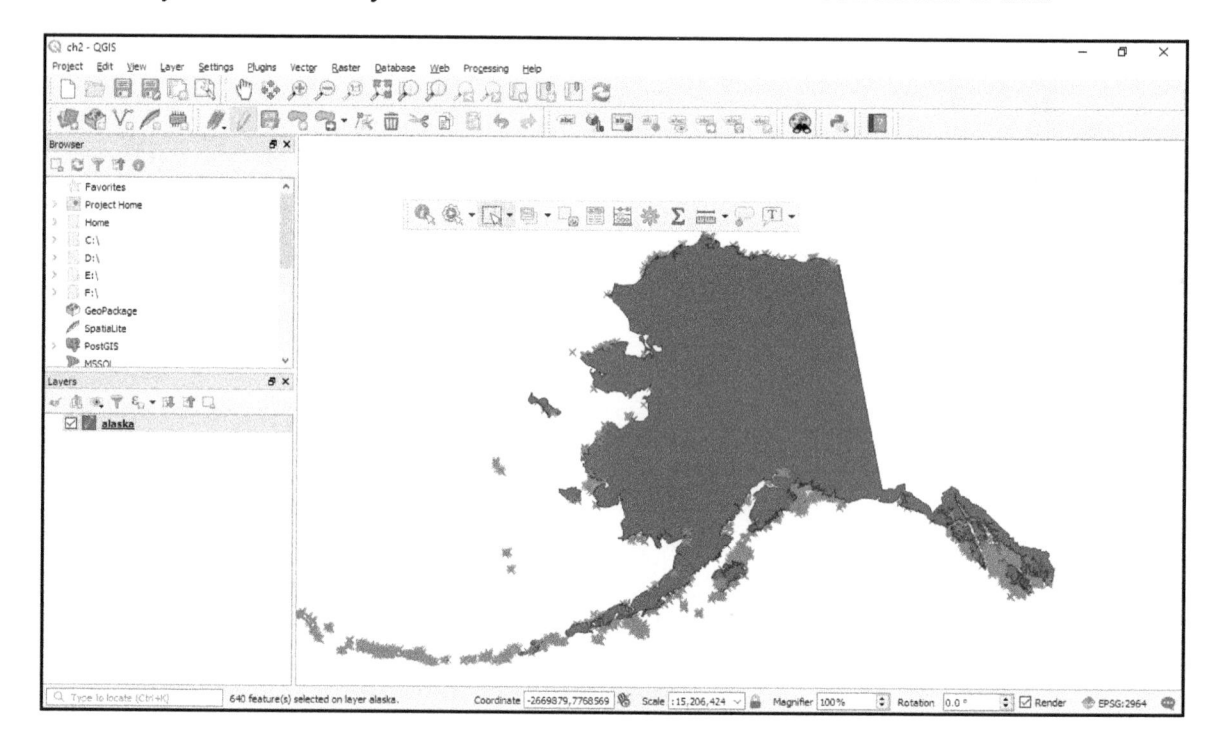

An edit session in QGIS

In the **Layers** window, there is a pencil icon on the toolbar. This tells us that this layer is currently open in an edit session. Let's take a look at the attribute table; press *F6* or click on the **Attribute Table** button in the attribute toolbar. It should look like this:

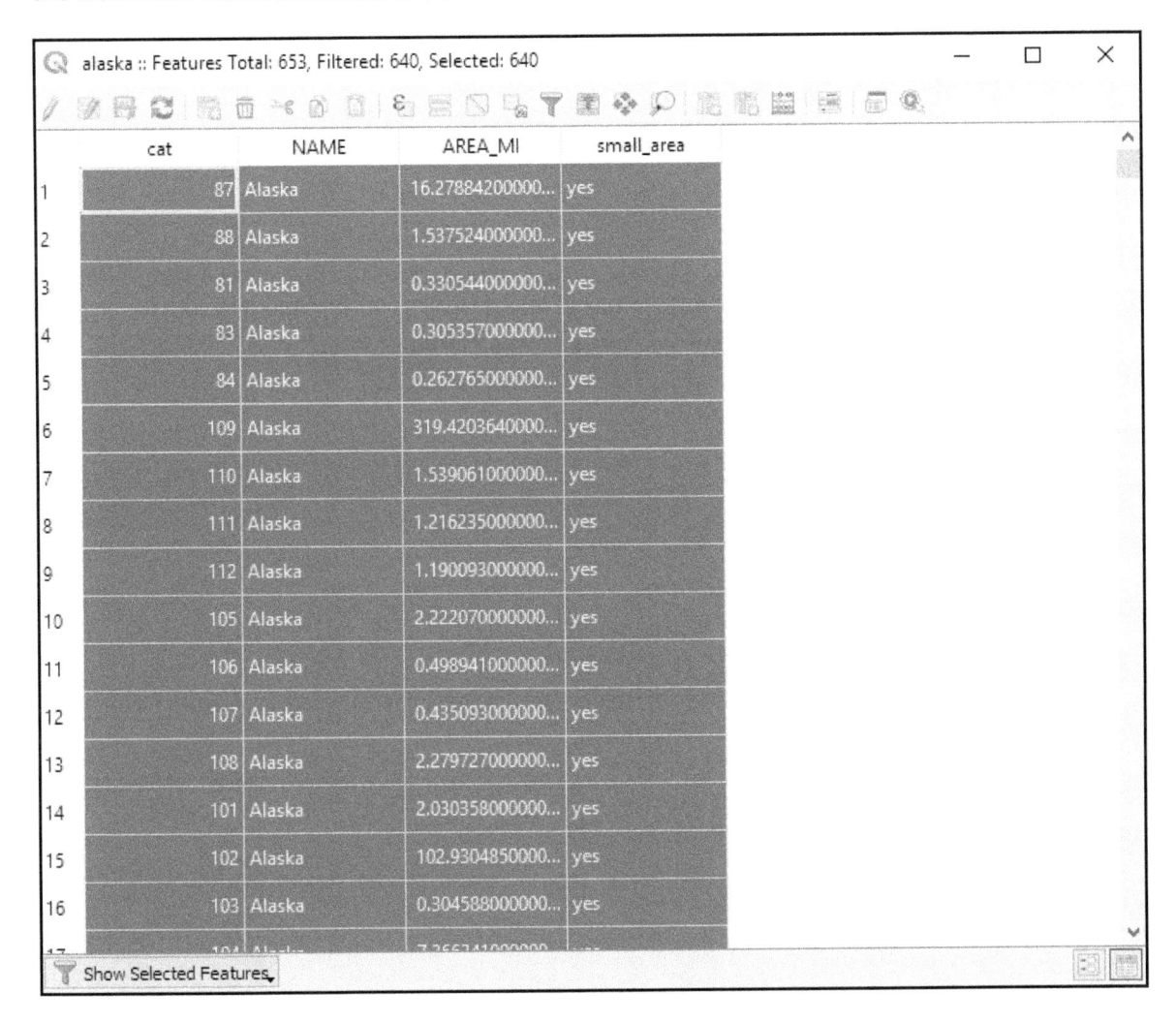

	cat	NAME	AREA_MI	small_area
1	87	Alaska	16.27884200000...	yes
2	88	Alaska	1.537524000000...	yes
3	81	Alaska	0.330544000000...	yes
4	83	Alaska	0.305357000000...	yes
5	84	Alaska	0.262765000000...	yes
6	109	Alaska	319.4203640000...	yes
7	110	Alaska	1.539061000000...	yes
8	111	Alaska	1.216235000000...	yes
9	112	Alaska	1.190093000000...	yes
10	105	Alaska	2.222070000000...	yes
11	106	Alaska	0.498941000000...	yes
12	107	Alaska	0.435093000000...	yes
13	108	Alaska	2.279727000000...	yes
14	101	Alaska	2.030358000000...	yes
15	102	Alaska	102.9304850000...	yes
16	103	Alaska	0.304588000000...	yes

alaska :: Features Total: 653, Filtered: 640, Selected: 640

The attribute table with the selected features and the new field with the values populated

[43]

Data Creation and Editing

Congratulations! You have now created some data! Six-hundred and forty rows of data have now been updated with `yes` in the `small_area` field. But what about the remaining thirteen rows? They will now have no entry for the `small_area` field. Let's change that. Click on the **Invert selection (Ctrl +R)** button in the attribute table. It looks like this:

Inverting a selection

This will invert your selection. Once clicked, it may appear that you have lost everything. However, click on the button at the bottom left of the attribute table and click **Show Selected Features**. It will look like this:

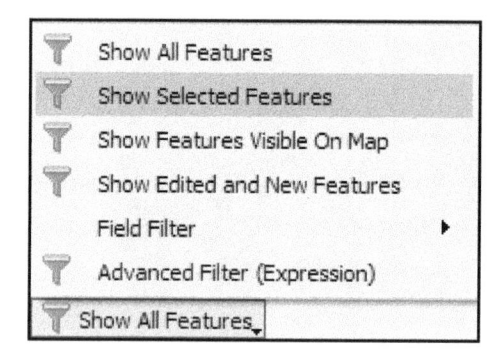

Show all features option

Now we have effectively selected all features with an **AREA_MA** > 1000. You can see that the `small_area` values associated with this area are set to `NULL`:

[44]

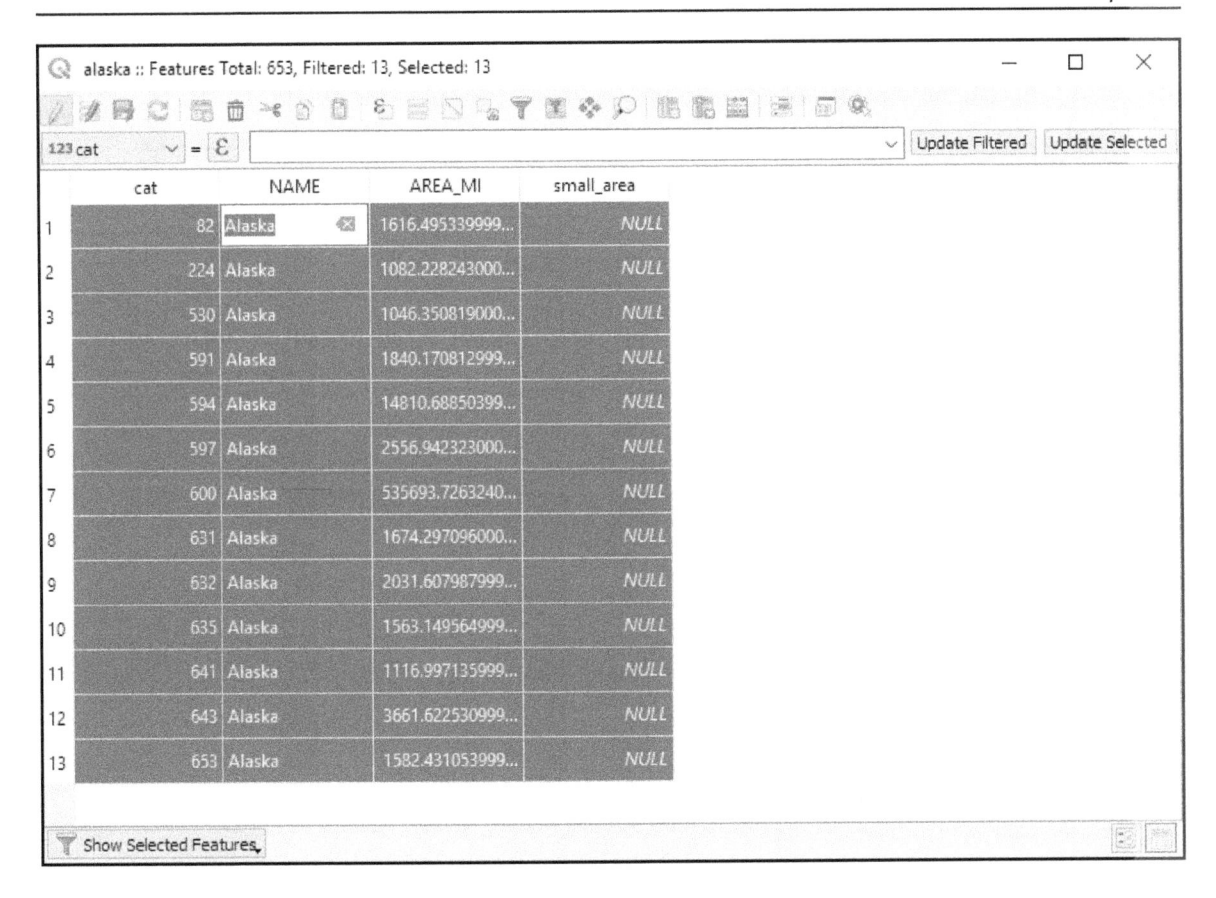

Attribute table after inverted selection

You may have already noticed that the attribute toolbar is not only in the main display of QGIS, but it is also in the attribute table. In this toolbar, select the **Field Calculator**. This time we are going to set the selected rows to no. Remember, this time we are not creating a new field, but updating one.

Data Creation and Editing

Your field calculator should look similar to the following screenshot. We have highlighted the important difference compared to when you are creating a new field:

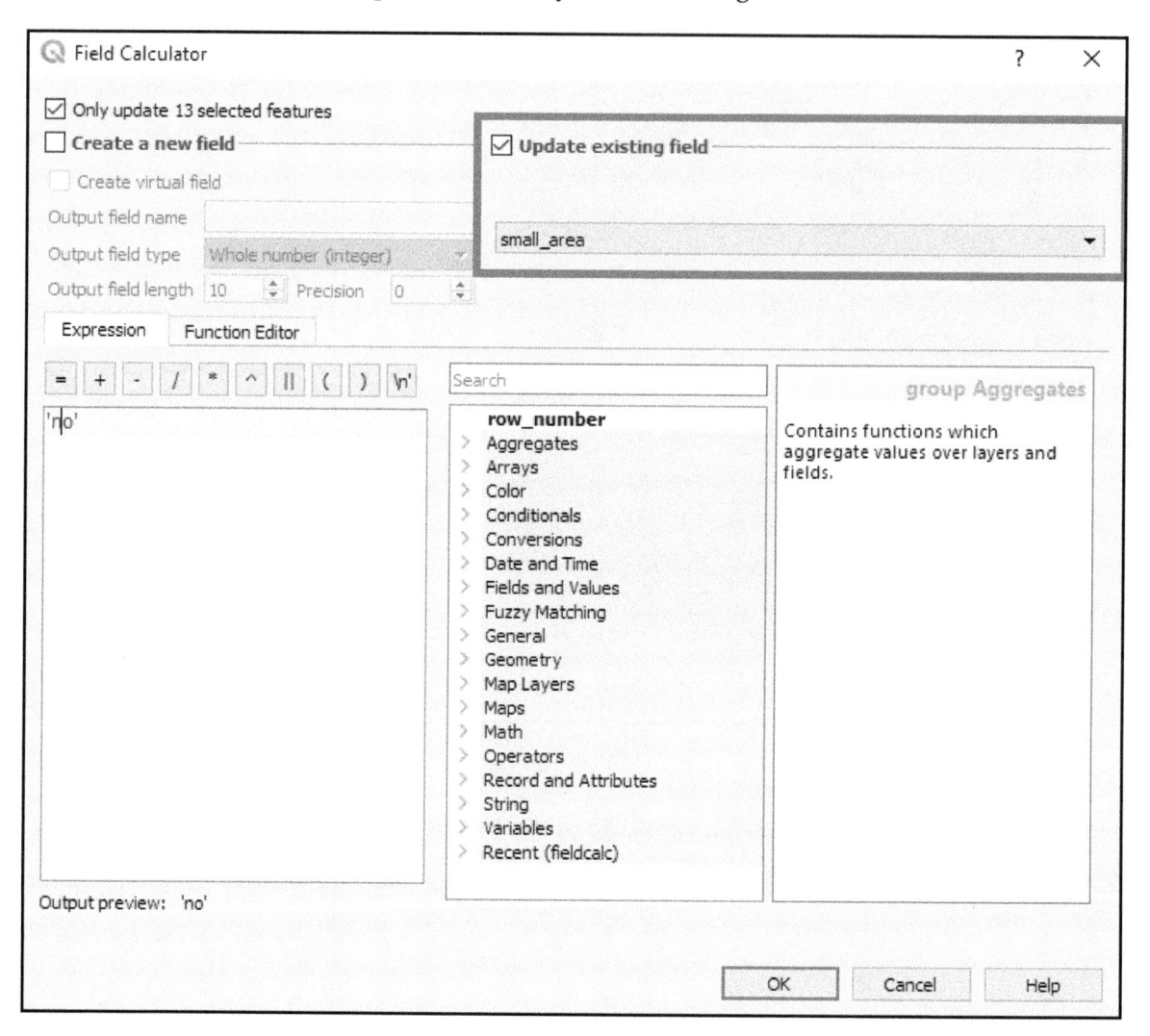

Field calculator shows how to update an existing field, with selected features set to No

Chapter 2

Click **OK** and then **Clear Selection**. Stop the editing session by clicking on the single pencil and then select `yes` to save the edits:

Editor toolbar

We have just edited attribute data in QGIS.

Building your own vector data

Start a new project in QGIS by either clicking **Project** | **New**, pressing *Crtl + N*, or clicking on the new project icon on the project toolbar. You will get a prompt if you wish to save the project; if you are following through this chapter, there is no need to save the project.

In a new project, scroll in the **Browser** window to the **XYZ Tiles** and expand the dropdown. In here, you will find **OpenStreetMap**:

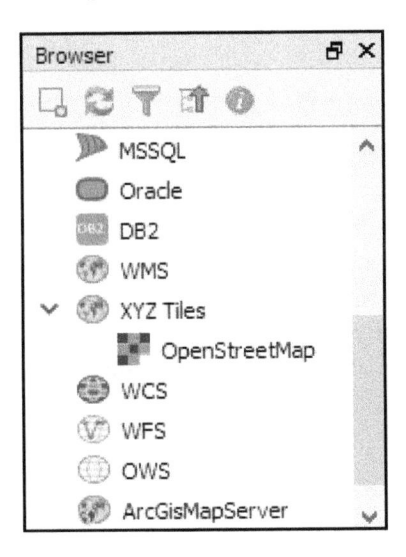

Browser window

[47]

Data Creation and Editing

Drag **OpenStreetMap** into the **Layers** window. The **OpenStreetMap** data will appear in the map view. Have a look in the bottom-right corner of the screen at the projection. This has changed to **EPSG 3857** (Web Mercator) as this is the native projection of the **OpenStreetMap** data you have just loaded. Your screen should look similar to this:

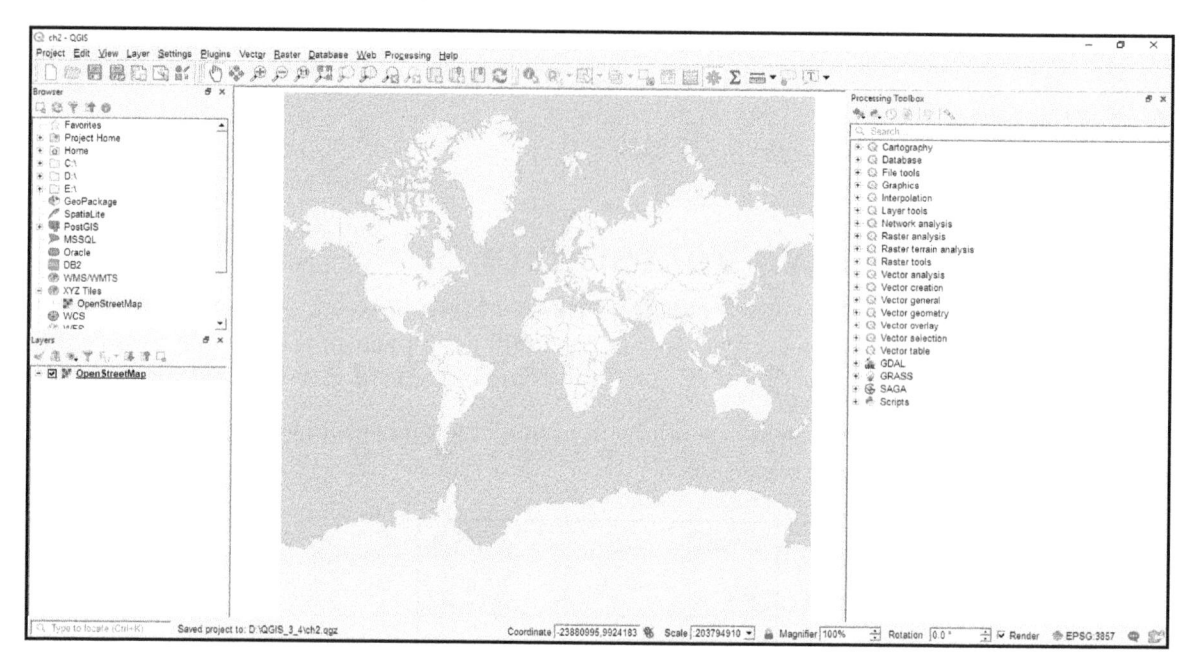

QGIS with OpenStreetMap layer loaded

Find the `Alaska.shp` that we used previously and load that into QGIS as well. Use the map navigation tools to zoom and pan to the data. The following diagram shows the data loaded together. The projection in the bottom-left corner has not changed, even though the projection of the **alaska** layer is different to the **OpenStreetMap Tile**. This is because QGIS 3.4 re-projects on the fly:

[48]

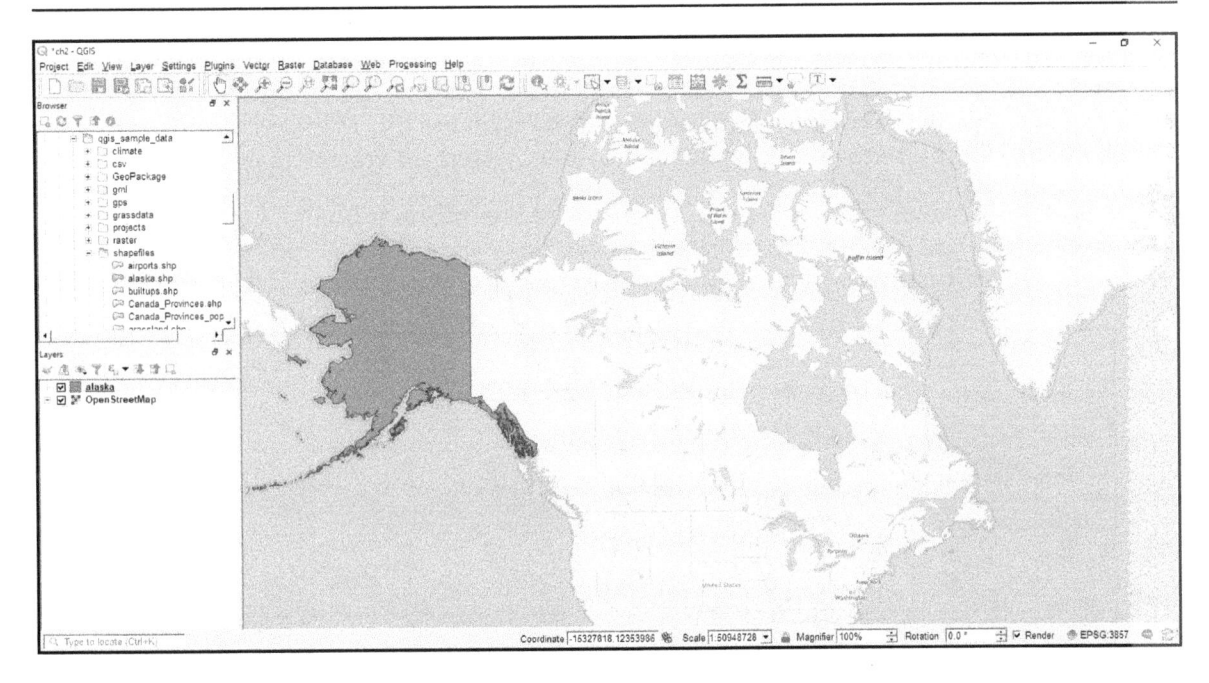

Alaska Shapefile loaded and re-projected on the fly into QGIS

> **TIP**
> You can right-click on any layer in the **Layers** window and look for the **Source** tab; it will contain information about the layer's projection.

Projections

The default projection for QGIS (on load the first time) has the EPSG code 4326 (WGS 84). Unless changed, the default settings in QGIS allow the projection of the map to be set by the projection of the first layer loaded into the map, assuming that the data has a projection associated to it. If you are interested in learning more about this, a good starting point is the QGIS entry on Geographic Coordinate Systems:
```
https://docs.qgis.org/testing/en/docs/gentle_gis_introduction/coordinate_refere
nce_systems.html
```

Suffice it to say that getting the projection correct in your GIS is fundamental to any analysis, mapping, or derivation of knowledge from your data. The world is not flat, and projecting your data is the process of taking the part of the Earth's surface you are working on and mathematically shrinking and distorting it so it fits on a plane. You can move from one projection system to another by transforming your data.

Data Creation and Editing

Let's use the Alaska layer as an example. The projection of the layer is **EPSG 2964**, and on load of this data, your QGIS project will be set to this projection. If you add data in another projection, QGIS will make re-projections of your data on the fly. This is very powerful and useful, but be careful that you know what projection system *all* your data is in.

To find out and change your map projection, look at the information bar. On the bottom-right corner, you will see that the projection is currently set to **EPSG 3857**, as we have loaded the **OpenStreetMap** data. Click on this to bring up the projection properties dialog:

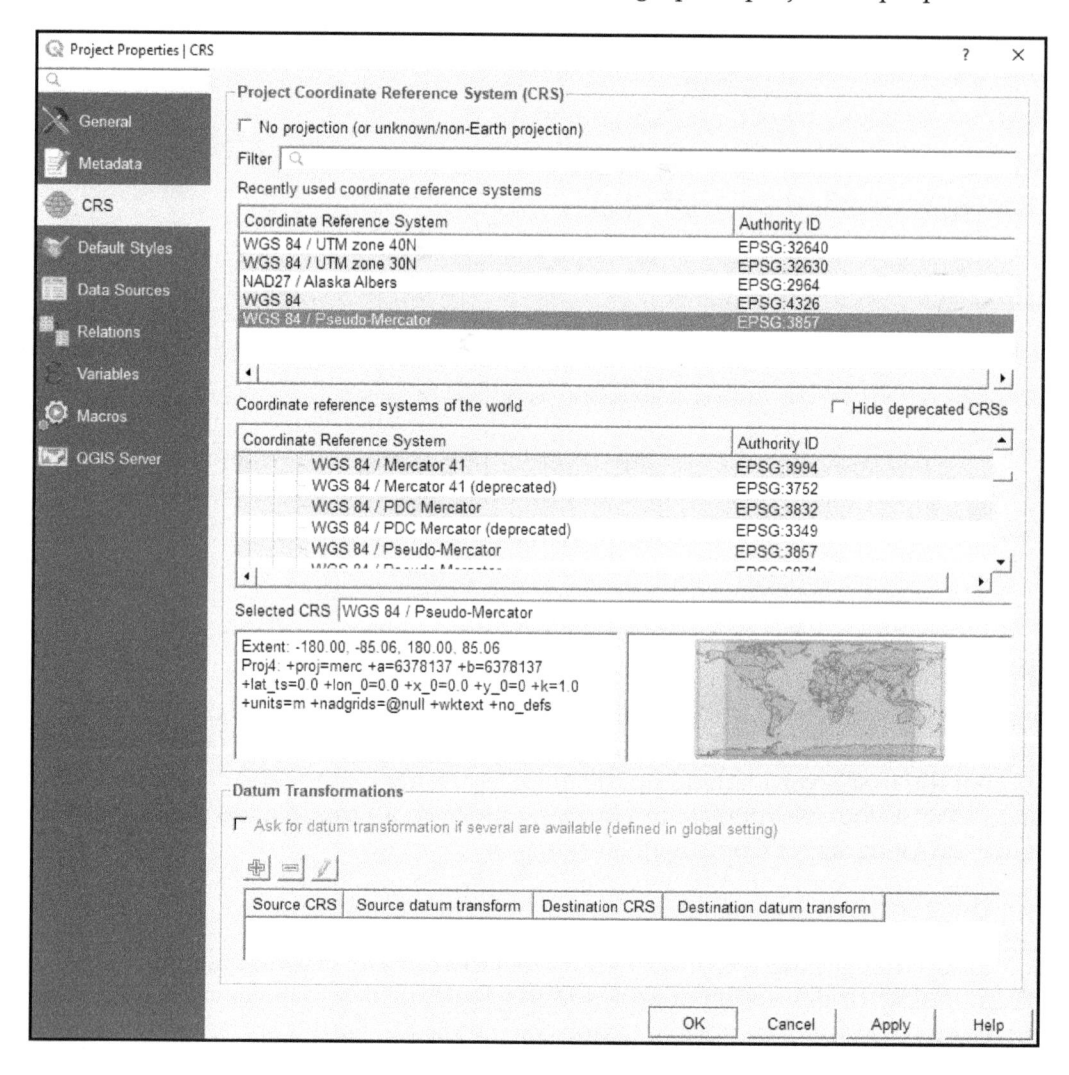

Projection properties

In the next section, we will create some data in this using this projection. Click on **OK** to close the coordinate properties dialog box.

Creating data

We will now create some data. During this exercise, we will be using digitizing tools to map two provinces in Canada. We will create a field in the attribute table and assign values in this table.

Create a ShapeFile

To create a Shapefile in QGIS 3.4, click on **Layer | Create Layer | New Shapefile Layer**:

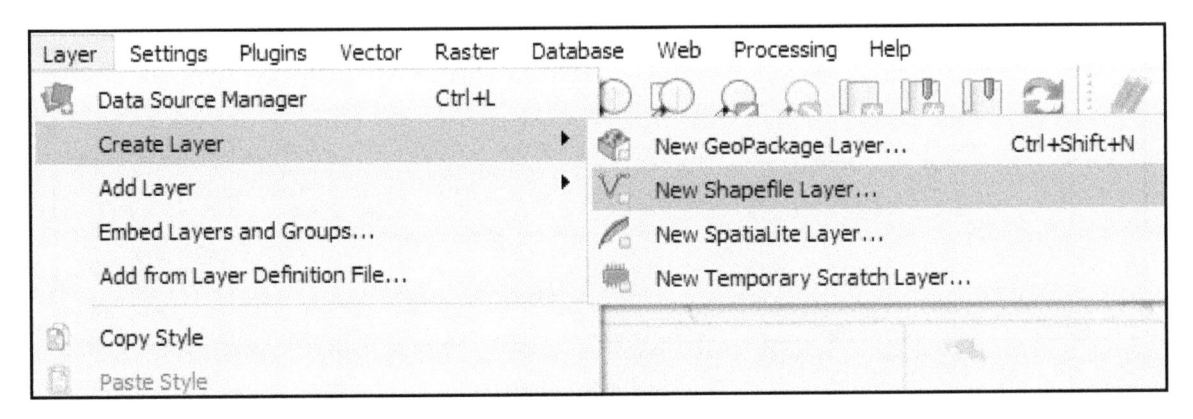

Creating a New Shapefile Layer

Again, we are going to be creating a new **Polygon** layer. We are assigning the name `Canada_Provinces.shp` in the `Shapefiles` folder or `qgis_sample_data` (where `Alaska.shp` is stored). The **Geometry** type is set to **Polygon,** and we have accepted the default project (as defined by the projection in the map window). We are not assigning any additional fields in the table at this point, but this is one way that you could define fields.

Data Creation and Editing

The dialog box should look similar to this:

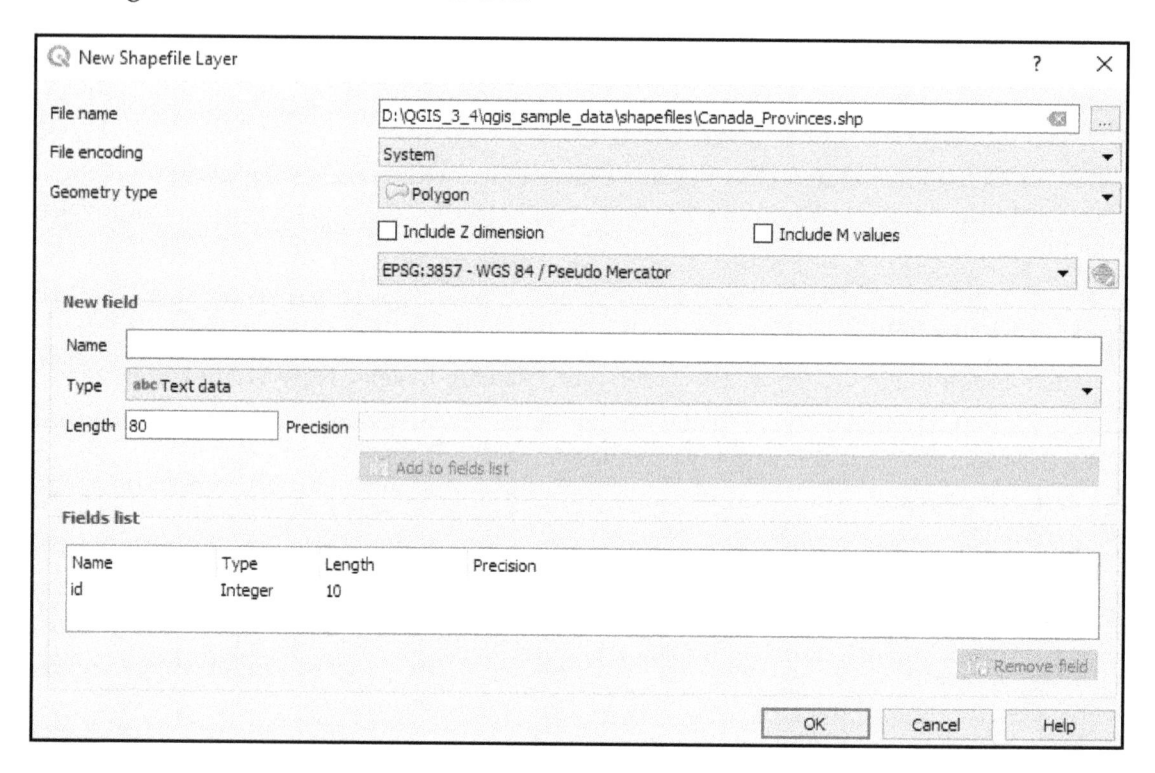

New Shapefile Layer	
File name	D:\QGIS_3_4\qgis_sample_data\shapefiles\Canada_Provinces.shp
File encoding	System
Geometry type	Polygon
	☐ Include Z dimension ☐ Include M values
	EPSG:3857 - WGS 84 / Pseudo Mercator

New field

Name	
Type	abc Text data
Length	80 Precision

Add to fields list

Fields list

Name	Type	Length	Precision
id	Integer	10	

Remove field

OK   Cancel   Help

Creating a New Shapefile Layer dialog box

Click on **OK** and the newly created Shapefile will be added to the map, the **Layers** window, and the **Browser** window. The layer also becomes the active selected layer in the **Layers** window, as shown in the following diagram:

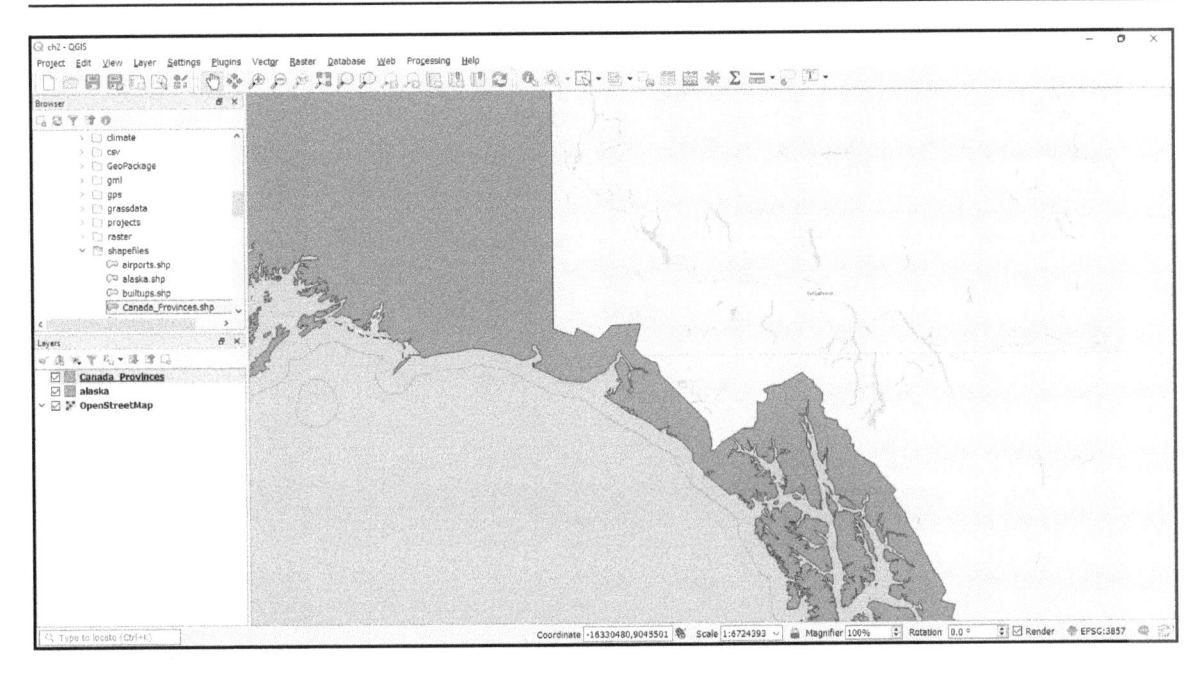

The Canada provinces ShapeFile added to the layers panel

If, like me, you didn't define any fields when you created this Shapefile, when you open the attribute table (right click | **open** attribute table, or click on the attribute table icon in the attribute toolbar), you will just have an **ID** field and an empty table. To change this, we will need to begin an editing session.

Editing tools

The editor toolbars we saw earlier in Chapter 1, *Where Do I Start?* If they are not displaying, select **View** | **Toolbars** | **Digitizing** for the Digitizing toolbar. Repeat for the advanced digitizing and shape digitizing toolbars. The following editing example also applies to any vector format, including the GeoPackage format. For this example, we will work with the Shapefile we previously created.

Data Creation and Editing

Make sure your newly created Shapefile is the selected layer in the **Layers** windows, then click on the pencil, and you will start your editing session. Before we start drawing, let's add a couple of fields that we can assign data to. Open the attribute table and click on the **Add Field** button (highlighted in the following screenshot), create a new **Text** field called Name, and select **OK**:

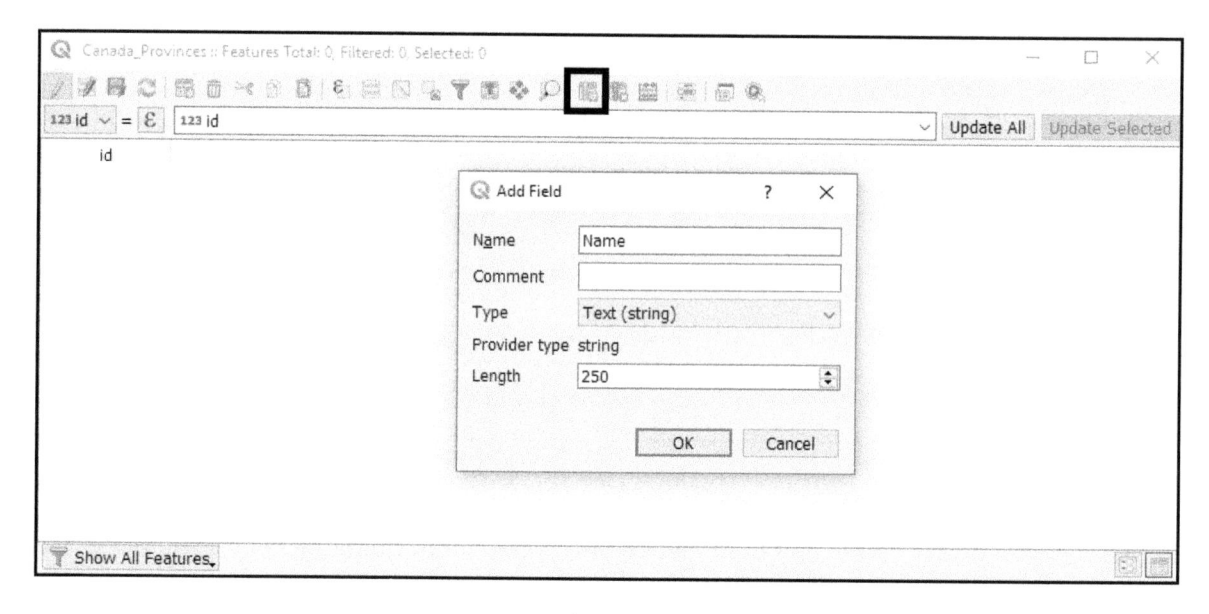

Adding a field

Add another field called Area, then set the **Length** to 10 and the **Precision** to 2:

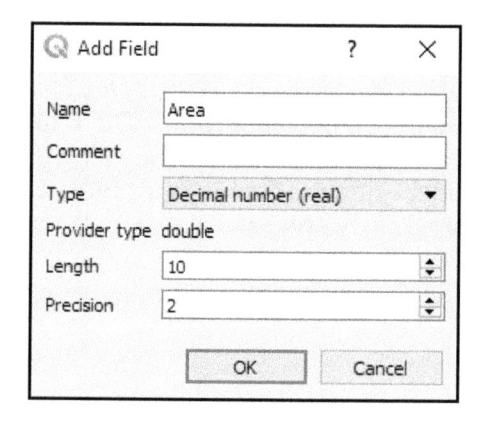

Defining the new field

[54]

Click on **OK,** and you should now have three attribute fields, **id**, **Name**, **Area**, which we will populate. Close the attribute table. We will now digitize a Canadian province. In the Digitizing toolbar, click the Add Polygon Feature button, shown here as a green polygon with a yellow star underneath:

The editing toolbar with the add polygon feature button selected

As your cursor hovers over the map, it will look like a target with crosshairs. To begin digitizing, left-click with the mouse. When you have finished, right-click to complete the shape. The shape you are drawing, in our case the approximate province of **Saskatchewan**, will be shown in a faint red:

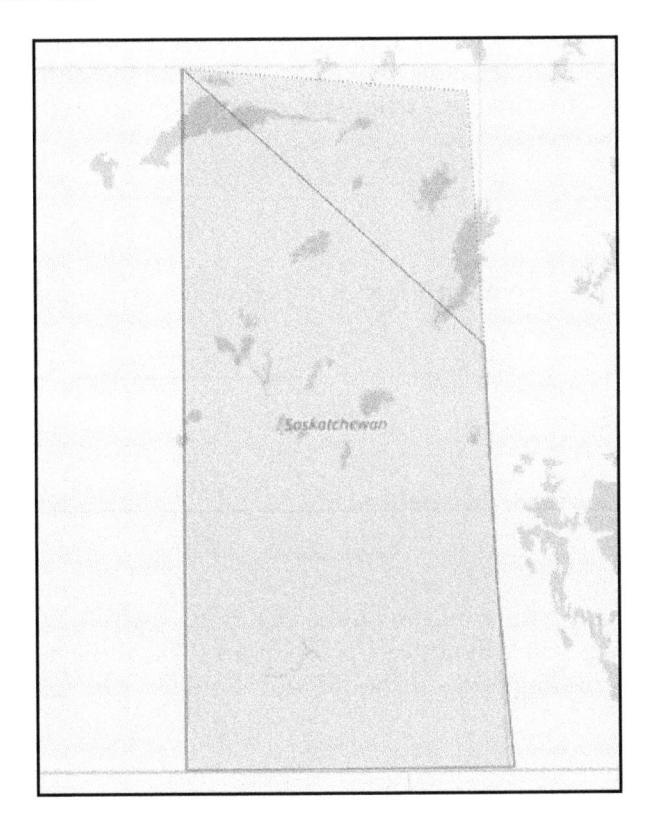

Drawing a new feature

Data Creation and Editing

After we have right-clicked and completed the polygon, the feature-attribute form appears. We are going to populate the **id** and the **Name** field:

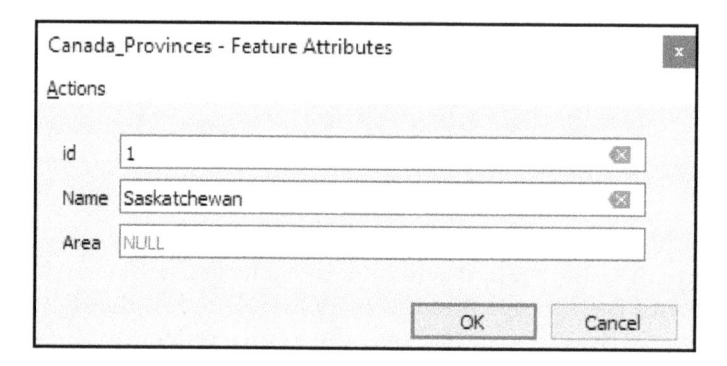

Creating new attributes

Click on **OK** to complete the entry, and then click on **Save** in the digitizing toolbar. Let's create another province. This time, we will use snapping tools to make sure we don't leave any gaps between the two polygons.

Snapping

Enable the snapping toolbar from the **View** menu and click on the magnet icon in the toolbar:

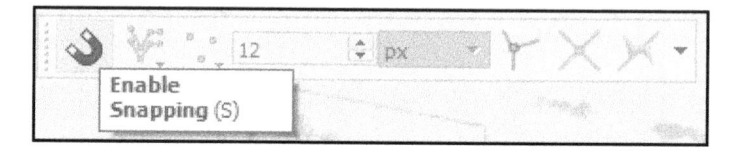

Enable snapping tool

Click on the Add Polygon Feature button on the digitizing toolbar, and as you move your mouse to begin digitizing, you will notice a pink square. This indicates that when you left-click, it will snap to the existing node. It should look similar to the following screenshot:

Chapter 2

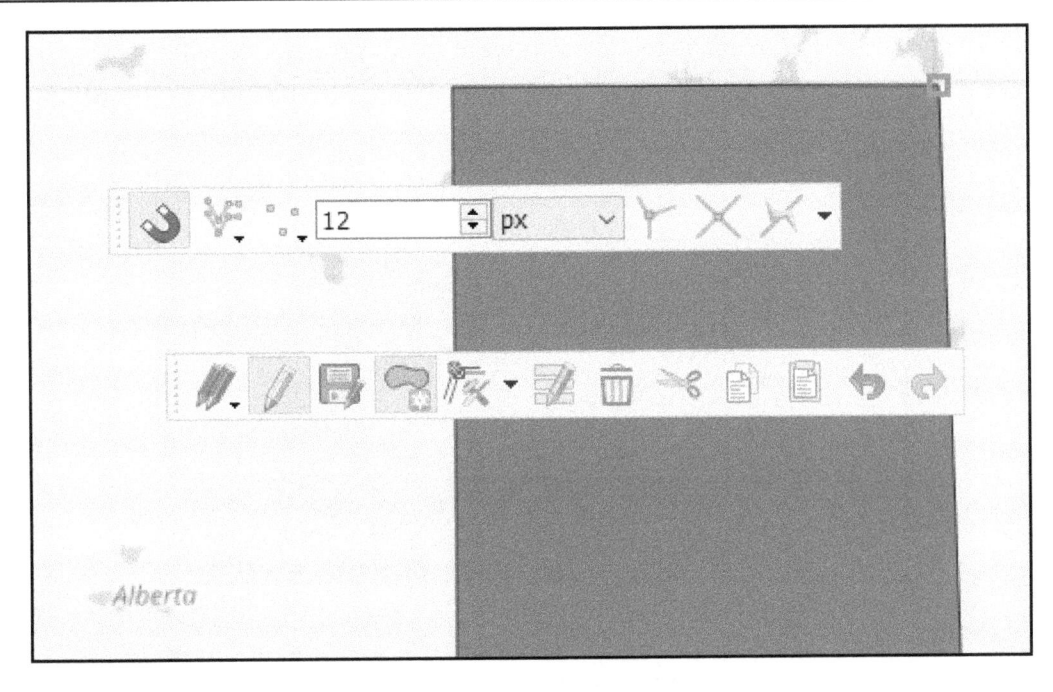

Snapping node highlighted

Continue editing as you would normally and assign the **ID** as 2 and the **Name** as `Manitoba` (assuming you are digitizing the province of Manitoba). Go ahead and capture Alberta using the same method and assign the **ID** to 3.

Mistakes and correcting with editing

When editing and creating geometries, mistakes often occur. Mistakes such as a misplaced click or a missed snapped point are common errors that you could introduce. A simple way to correct any poorly placed nodes is to use the vertex tool when editing has been toggled on. Click on the Vertex Tool and select the **Vertex Tool (Current Layer)** option:

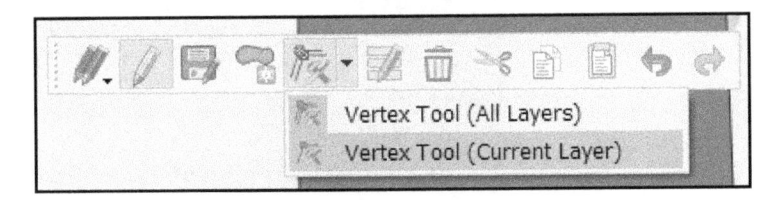

The editing toolbar with the vertex tool selected

[57]

Data Creation and Editing

As you move your mouse over the feature you want to edit, the nodes will show up as red dots. Left-click once on the red dot to select the node and then reposition it as required:

Editing a segment

You can add a node by double-clicking on the segment you wish to add to the node, and then dragging this to the desired location. A dashed red line will appear on the screen as you move your mouse. This is shown in the following diagram:

New node added to the feature

> **TIP**
> Alternatively, when the mouse cursor hovers over a line segment, the editing tools also display a potential new node candidate at the center of the line. This candidate node can be clicked and moved to a new location. This should be less error-prone than adding new nodes by double-clicking.

Finally, you can edit the coordinates of each node individually if necessary. Left-click on the feature and select **Vertex editor** from the pop-up menu. This will open another panel below the layers browser, which lists the coordinates; navigate to the point you wish to edit and make the adjustments in the corresponding table. This is shown here:

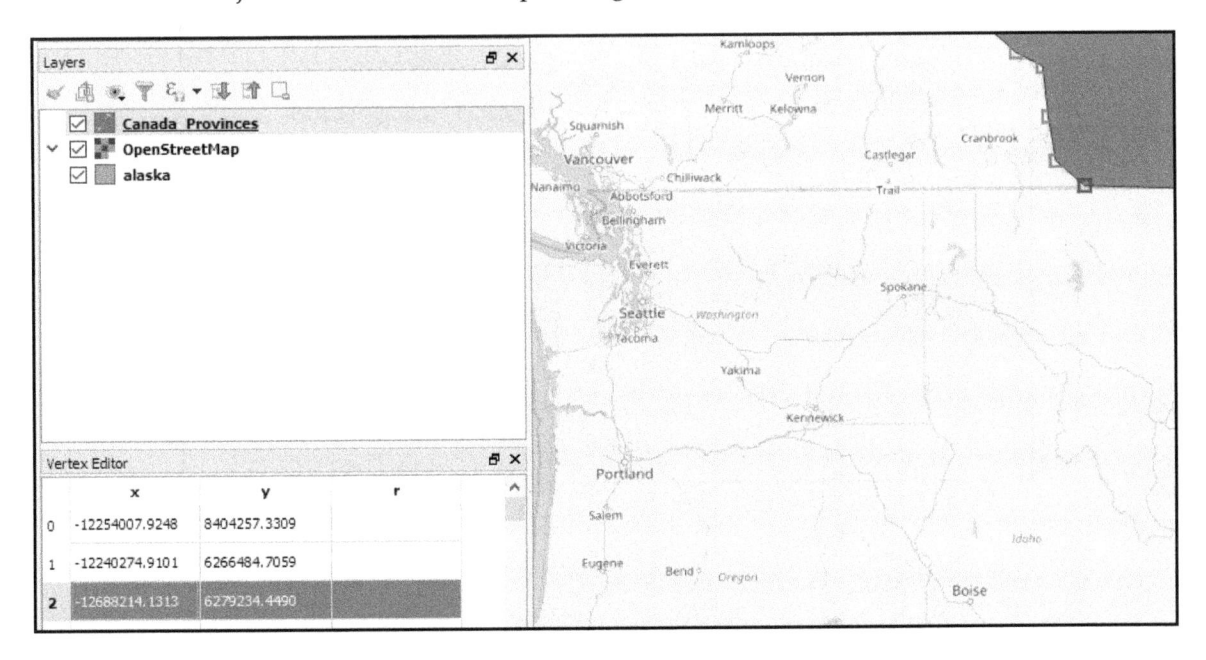

Vertex editor panel opened

Data Creation and Editing

This is the most time-consuming way of editing nodes, and is not recommended. Use the snapping tool alongside the **Vertex** tool for best results.

Finally for this section, if you wish, you can use the **Check Validity** tool via the **Vector | Geometry Tools** menu:

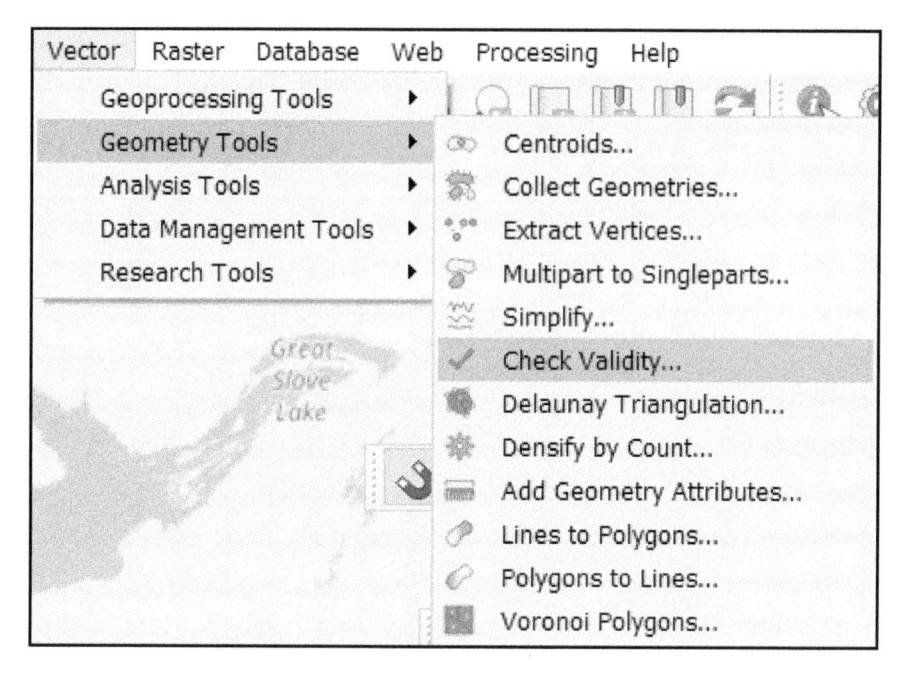

Checking the validity of the geometry

Chapter 2

This will bring up an interface that reports any errors topologically:

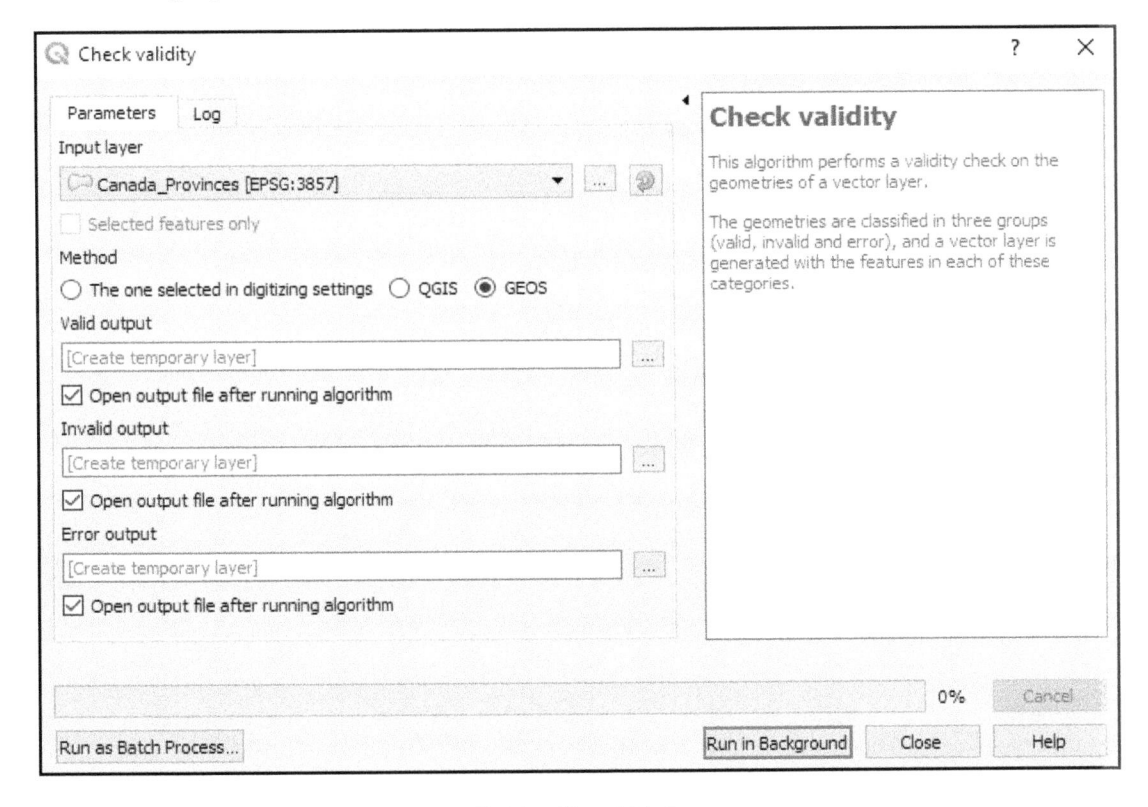

Check the validity tool dialog box

Running the **Check validity** tool (shown in the preceding screenshot) will create temporary files that will be displayed as new layers in QGIS (shown in the following screenshot). These can guide your corrections:

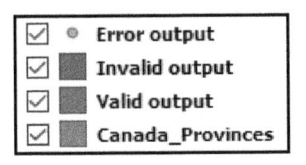

Output in the layer panel

There are further tools to help clean up editing errors that we will explore in Chapter 6, *Extending QGIS with Python*.

[61]

Data Creation and Editing

Populating attribute data

Finally, let's populate the **Area** field. Open the attribute table and click on the **Field Calculator**. We will update the **Area** field and use the **$area** from the **Geometry** section. In the following screenshot, we have searched for an area and doubled-clicked **$area** to move it to the **Expression** window:

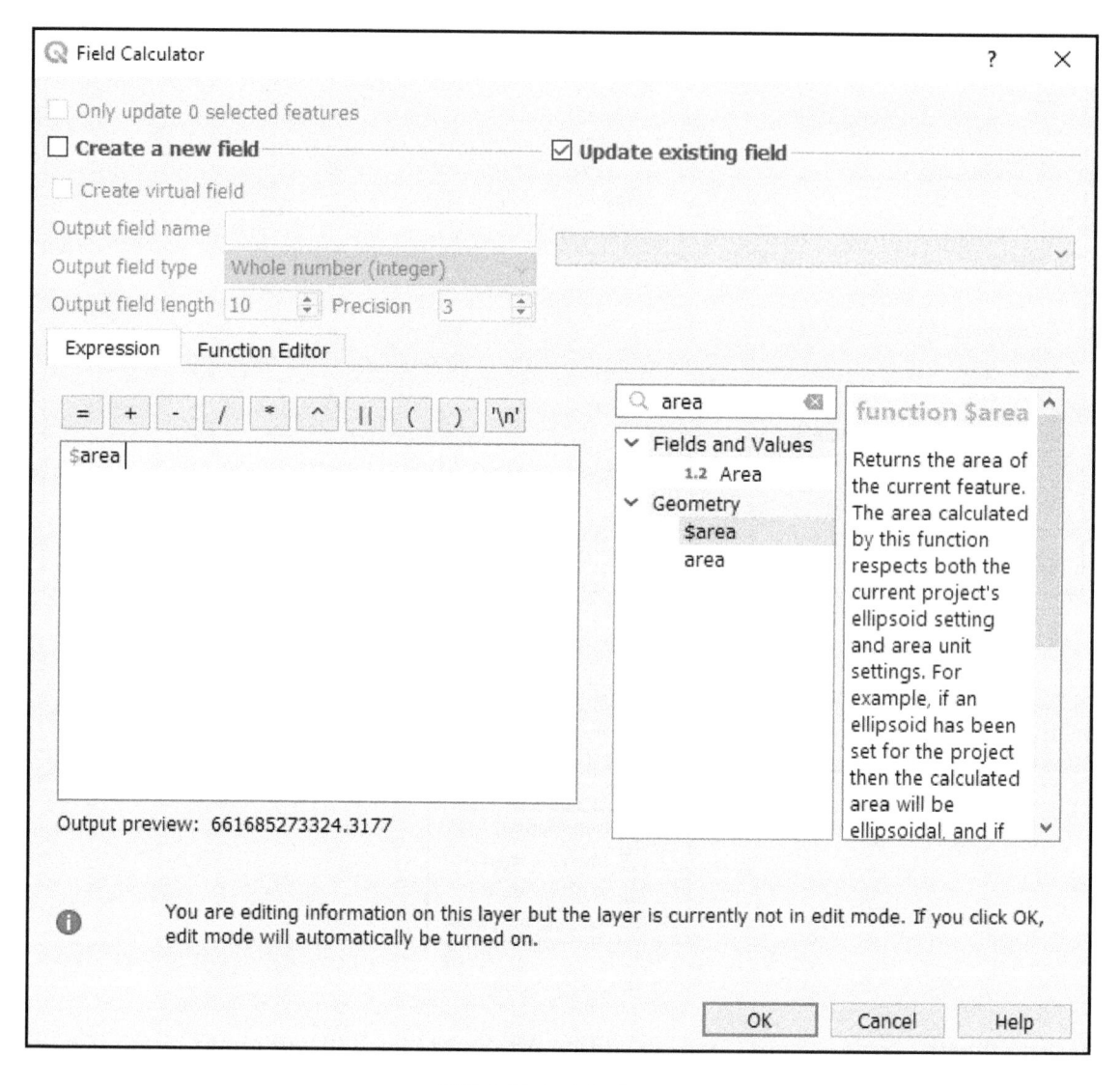

Field calculator to calculate the area

[62]

When done, click on **OK** and look at the attribute table. It will not be exactly the same as mine, as you have manually digitized these areas. You should have values populated, and this will look similar to the following screenshot:

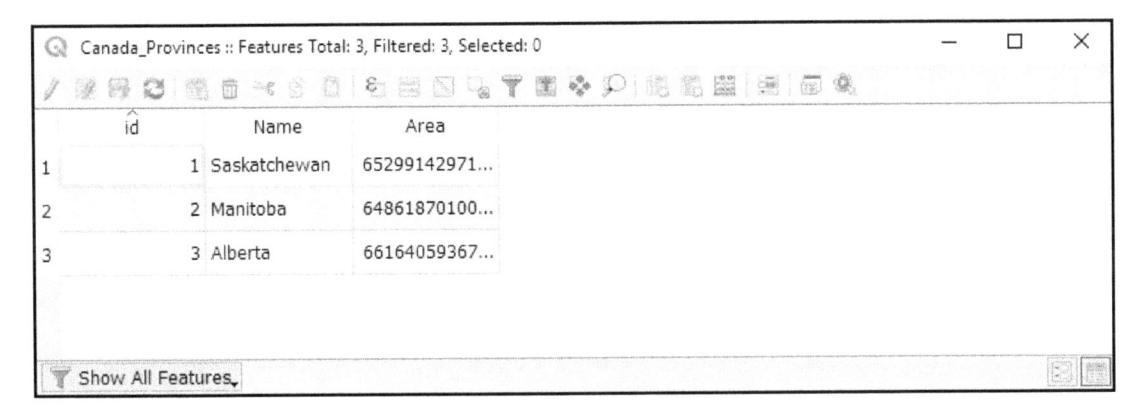

	id	Name	Area
1	1	Saskatchewan	65299142971...
2	2	Manitoba	64861870100...
3	3	Alberta	66164059367...

Attribute table with updated area values

We will discuss how to use these and other attributes to symbolize our data in `Chapter 4`, *Creating Great Maps*. We will then explore how to use these symbolized layers to create maps in `Chapter 5`, *Spatial Analysis*.

Data joins

Data joins serve an important function in any database. It often means that we can join data with a common identifier, extending the original data. In this section, we will create a simple table and join it to the `Canada_Provinces` Shapefile that we have just created.

Data Creation and Editing

Using the data on the corresponding Wikipedia pages for each of the three provinces that we have captured, I have created the following `.csv` file:

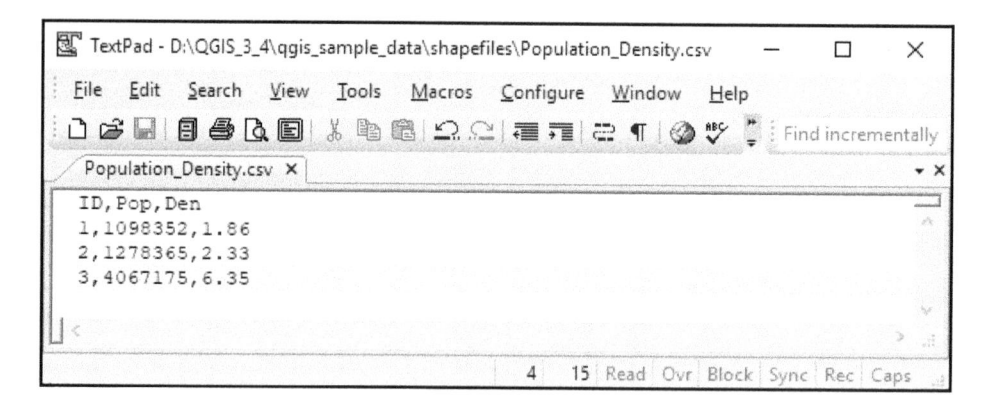

Create a simple .csv file to join to our Canadian provinces data

Here, I have kept the **ID** the same as the one we created in our Shapefile. I have saved this `.csv` file in the same place as my `Canada_Provinces.shp`. Create this layer in a text editor of your choice. Then add this text layer by clicking **Layer** | **Add Layer** | **Add Delimited Text Layer**:

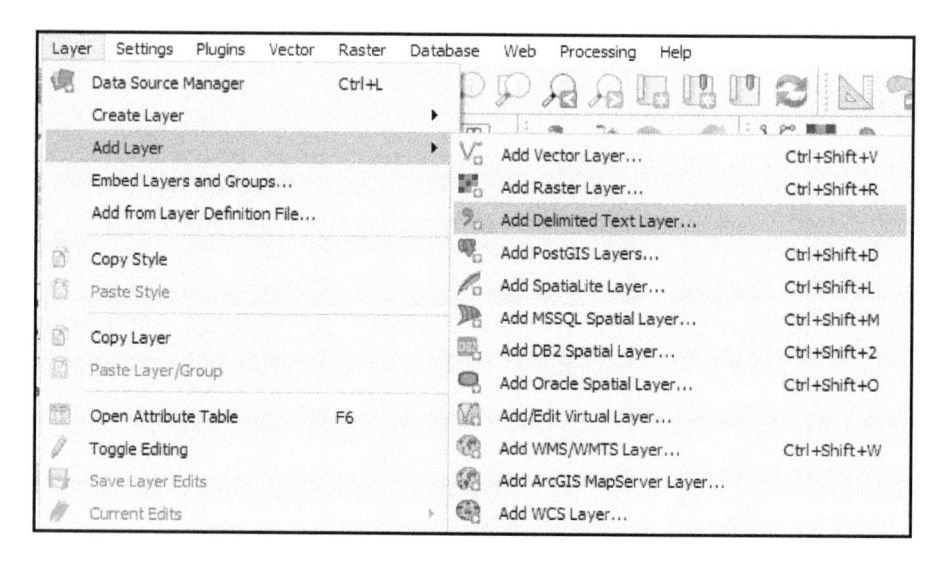

Add Delimited Text Layer

[64]

Chapter 2

In the resulting dialog box, make sure in the **Geometry** definition you select **No Geometry (attribute only table)**:

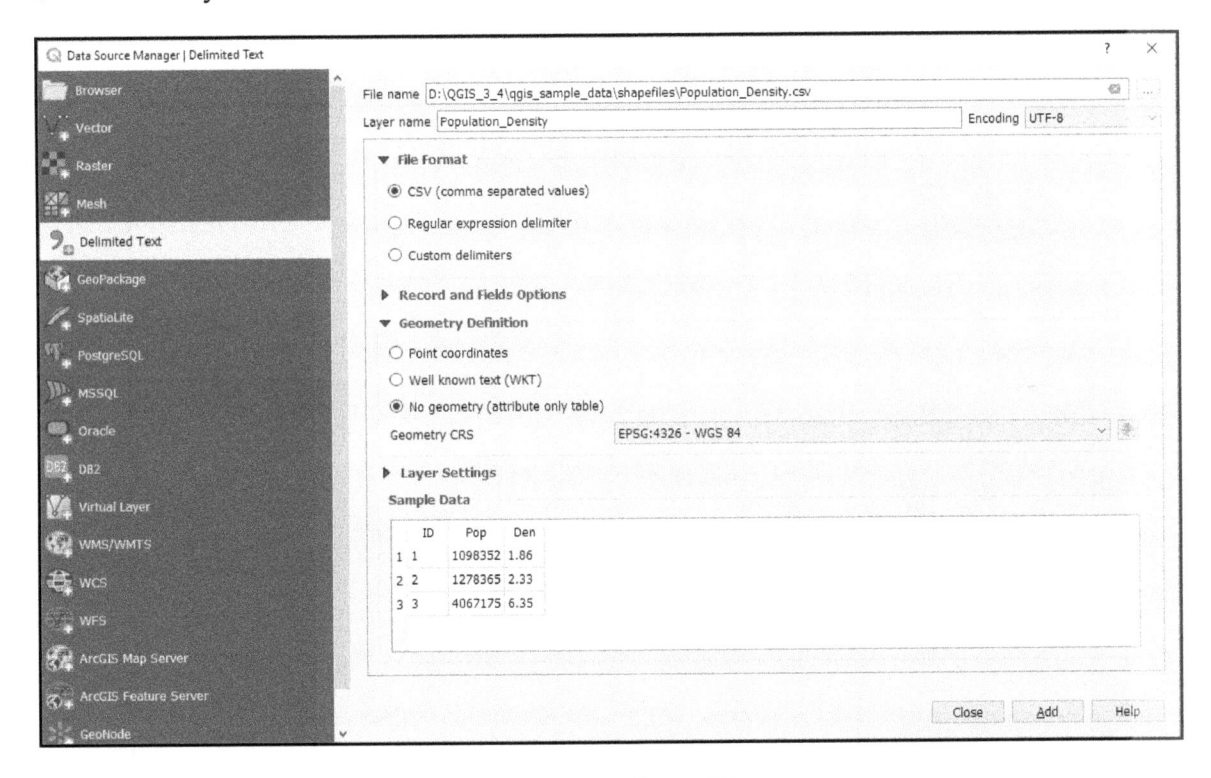

Data source manager to add non-spatial data

Click **Add**, and the csv will be added to the layers panel. If you open the attribute table, your screen should look similar to the following screenshot:

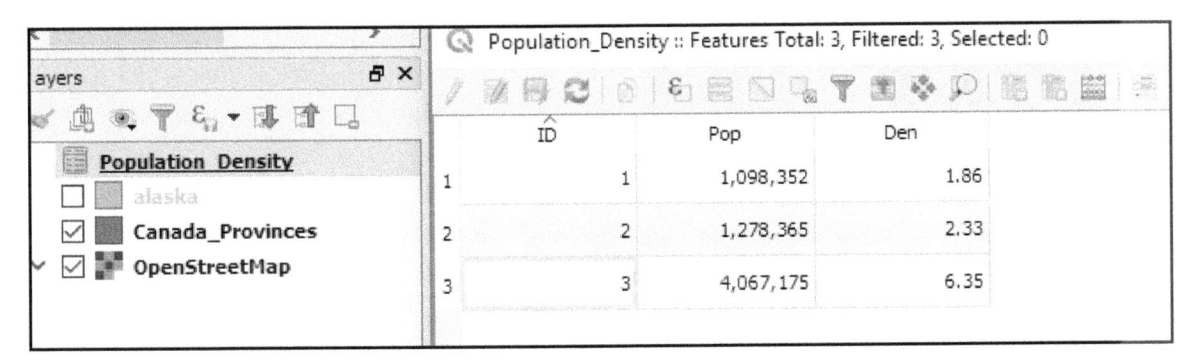

The newly added csv file in the layers panel

Data Creation and Editing

To join this data to our **Canada_Provinces** layer, close the **Population_Density** table, right-click on the **Canada_Provinces** layer, and select **Properties** | **Joins**. You will have the **Layer Properties** dialog box open (which we will explore extensively in `Chapter 4`, *Creating Great Maps*), which should look similar to the following screenshot:

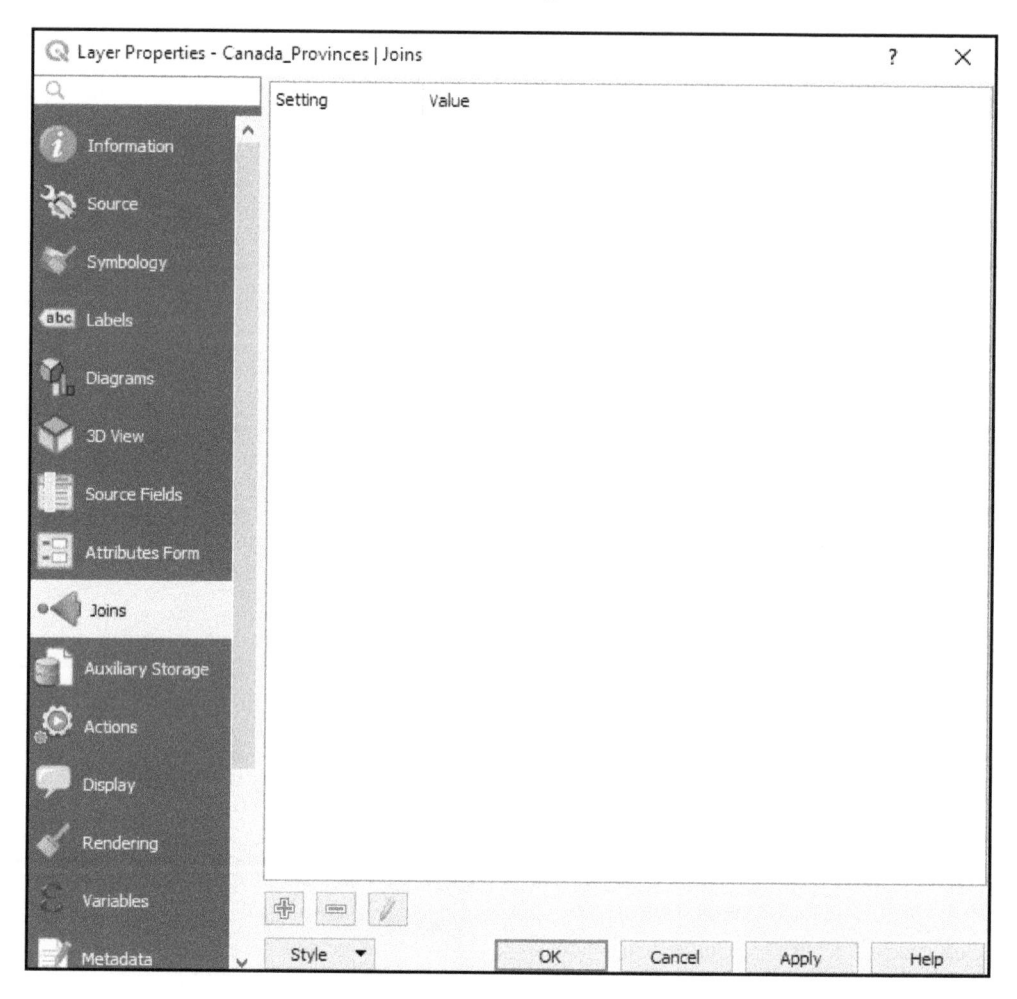

Layer properties Joins option

Chapter 2

Click on the green + button in the bottom left and set up the join layer as the **Population_Density** layer, the **Join field** as **ID**, and the **Target field** as **ID**, and then click **OK**. The join dialog box is shown here:

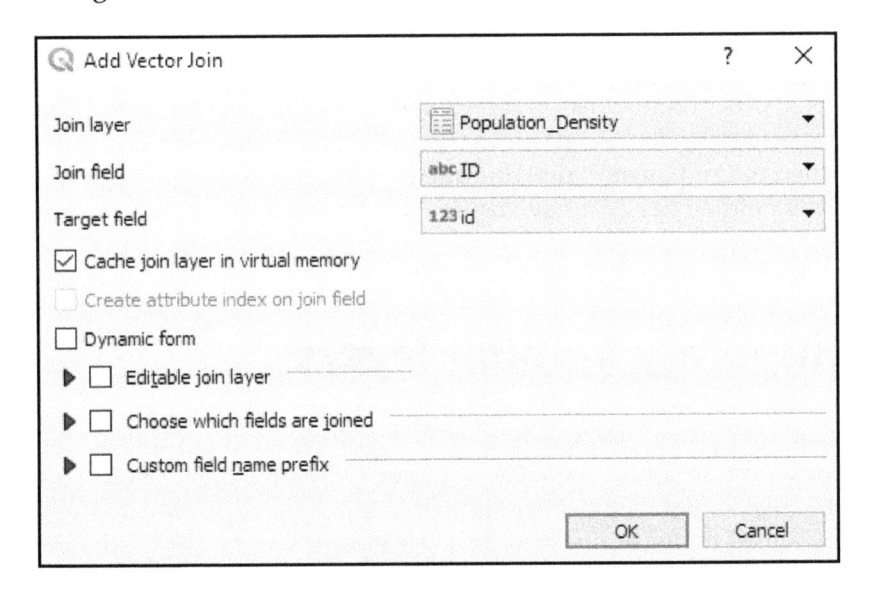

Add Vector Join dialog box

Close the **Layer Properties** dialog box and reopen the attribute table for the **Canada_Provinces** layer. The population data will now be joined:

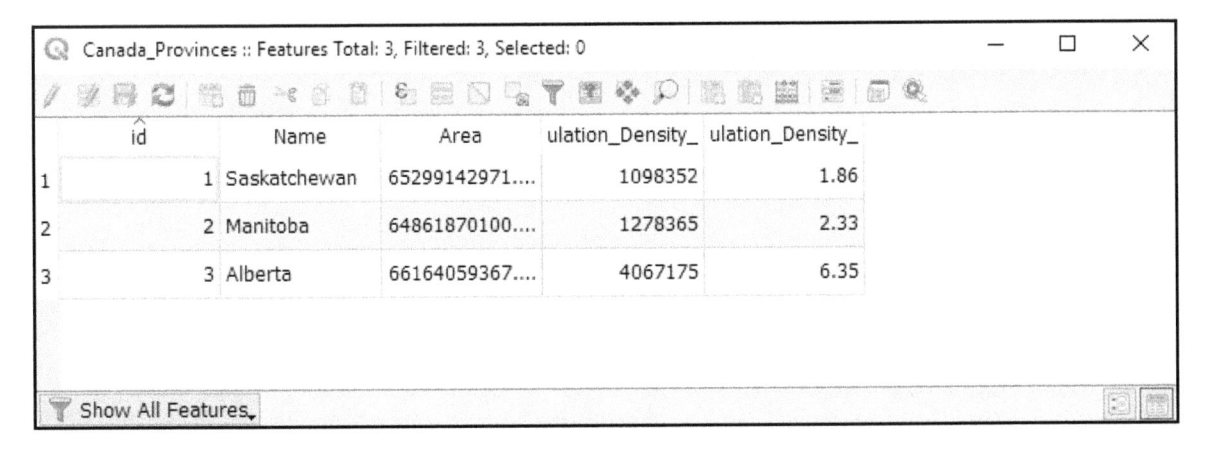

id	Name	Area	ulation_Density_	ulation_Density_
1	Saskatchewan	65299142971....	1098352	1.86
2	Manitoba	64861870100....	1278365	2.33
3	Alberta	66164059367....	4067175	6.35

The attribute table with the joined data

[67]

Data Creation and Editing

> **TIP**: When joining data, care is needed to ensure that there is a common join. This process of data wrangling is often the slowest part. However, the reward is an expanded dataset that we can then use to symbolize and build maps.

Finally, if you want to make this join permanent, you need to save the **Canada_Provinces** layer as a new Shapefile. Right click on the **Canada_Provinces** layer, select **Save As**, set the new name as `Canada_Provinces_population.shp`, and click **OK**. The newly created layer will be added to the **Layers Panel** and the map. When you right-click to inspect the attribute table, the field names will have been abbreviated to fit in with the field name restrictions of the Shapefile format.

Using temporary scratch layers

When you just want to quickly draw some features on the map, temporary scratch layers are a great way of doing that. The benefit is that you don't need to think about file formats and locations for your temporary data. Go to **Layer** | **Create Layer** | **New Temporary Scratch Layer** to create a new temporary scratch layer. As you can see in the following screenshot, all we need to do to configure this temporary layer is pick a **Geometry type**, a **Layer name**, and a CRS. Once the layer is created, we can add features and attributes as we would with any other vector layer:

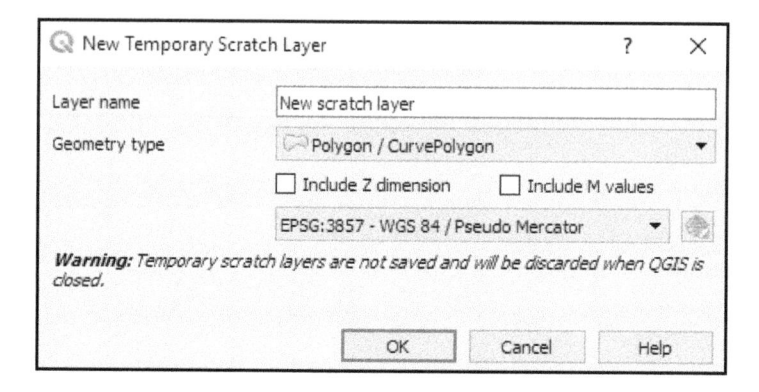

Creating a New Temporary Scratch Layer

As the name suggests, temporary scratch layers are temporary. This means that they will vanish when you close the project, so use them with care. A temporary layer will appear with a circular icon on the right next to it in the Layer Panel. This will remind you which layers will be lost when you close the project. This is shown here:

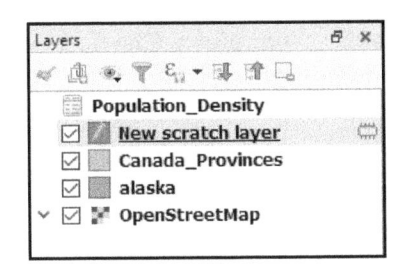

> You can convert a scratch layer to a permanent layer by right-clicking and saving it as a new layer, just as we did with the joins. Alternatively, you could install the memory-saver plugin, which will save all the temporary layers with the project.

Checking for topological errors and fixing them

Sometimes the data that we receive from different sources or data that results from a chain of spatial processing steps can have problems. Topological errors can be particularly annoying since they can lead to a multitude of different problems when using the data for analysis and further spatial processing. Therefore, it is important to have tools that can check data for topological errors and that know ways to fix discovered errors. Care must always be taken when changing topological errors on batch, so make sure any corrections work on a few geometries before scaling across all your data.

Finding errors with the Topology Checker

In QGIS, we can use the Topology Checker plugin; it is installed by default and is accessible through the **Vector** menu **Topology Checker** entry (if you cannot find the menu entry, you might have to enable the plugin in **Plugin Manager**). This shown in the following screenshot:

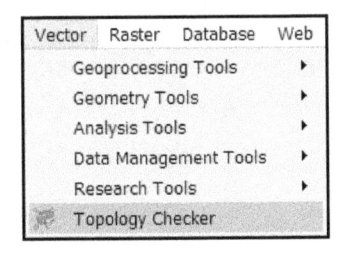

Topology Checker in the Vector menu

Data Creation and Editing

When the plugin is activated, it adds a **Topology Checker** panel to the QGIS window. This panel can be used to configure and run different topology checks and will list the detected errors.

To see the **Topology Checker** in action, create a temporary scratch layer with polygon geometries and digitize some small polygons that overlap. As you can see from the following screenshot, we have made the fill transparent. Right-click on the layer, select **Properites** | **Symbology**, and then set the Fill Color to transparent (`Chapter 3`, *Visualizing Data*, will help if you are unsure about how to do this). This overlap is highlighted in the following screenshot:

Overlapping topology

In the topological checker, create a new rule by clicking on the configure button which (looks like a wrench tool button). Set a rule to say that the **New scratch layer must not overlap** each other. This is shown in the following screenshot:

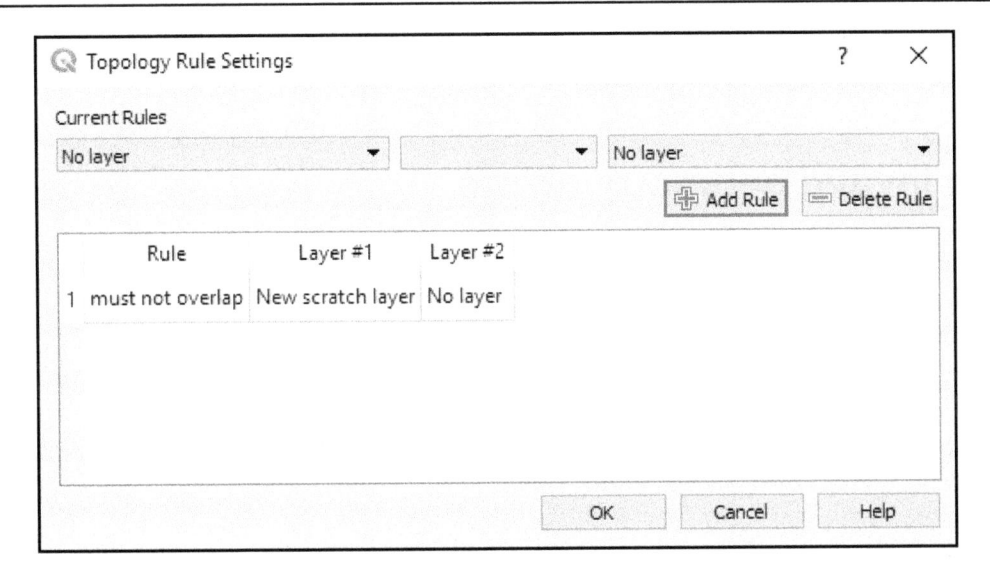

Chapter 2

Setting the Topology rules

Click on **OK**. In the **Topology Checker** panel, click on the yellow check mark to validate the rule. The overlap we have created will return one error highlighted in red. This is shown in the following screenshot:

Highlighted error based on the rule set

[71]

Data Creation and Editing

Now that we have highlighted an error, we need to fix it. In the next section, we will use the v.clean tool to do this.

Fixing invalid geometry errors

To get rid of these overlapping polygons, we can use the **v.clean** tool. Search for **v.clean** in the **Processing Toolbox | Cleaning tool** option and set to **rmarea** (meaning remove area), which is also available through the **Processing Toolbox**. In the example shown in this screenshot, the **Threshold (comma separated for each tool) [optional]** value of `10000` tells the tool to remove all polygons with an area less than 10,000 square meters by merging them with the neighboring polygon with the longest common boundary:

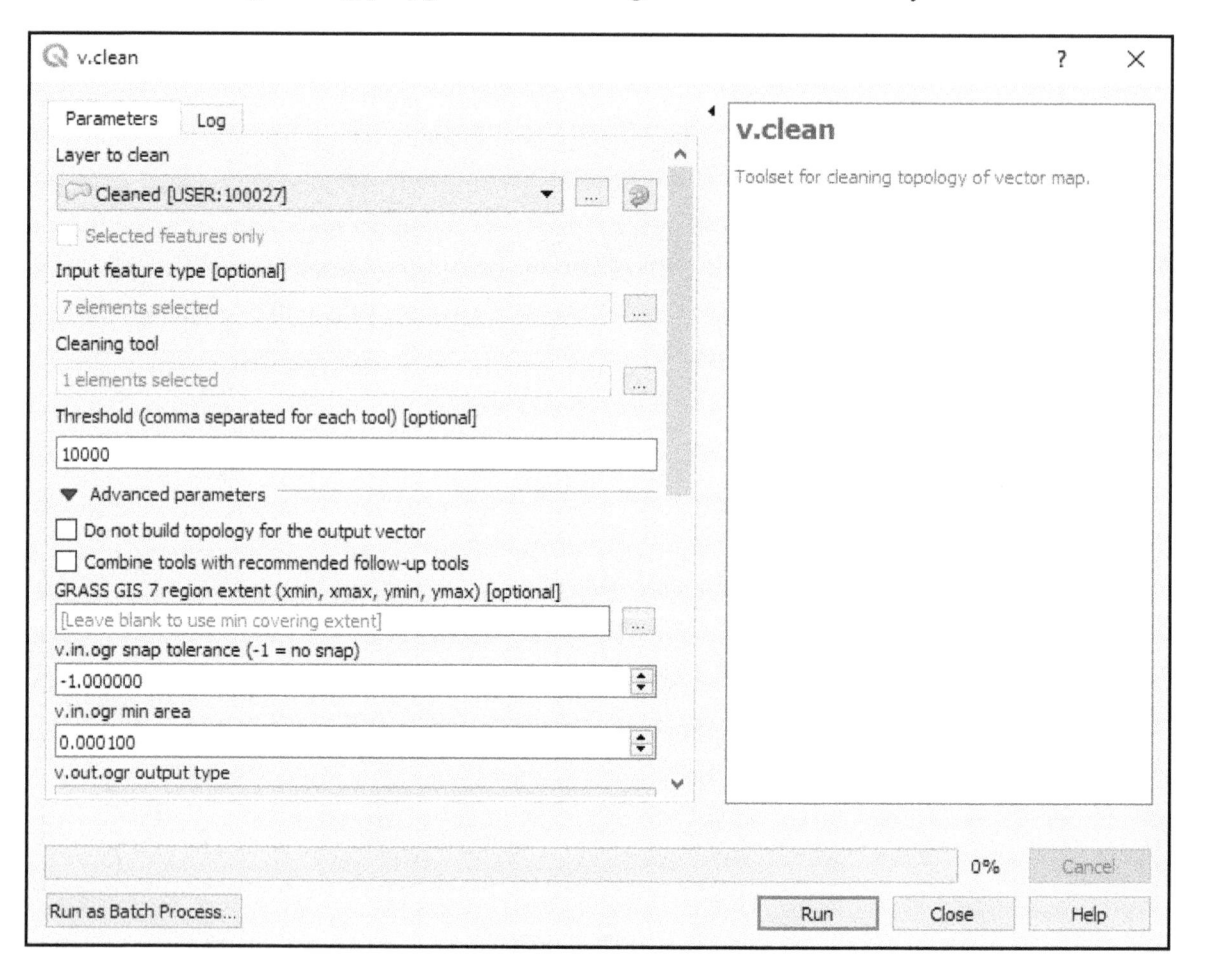

Fixing the errors with v.clean

Check the size of your overlap area and adjust this value accordingly. Click on **Run** when you are ready to run the **v.clean**. The resulting layer is called **Cleaned**. My new data looks like the following screenshot:

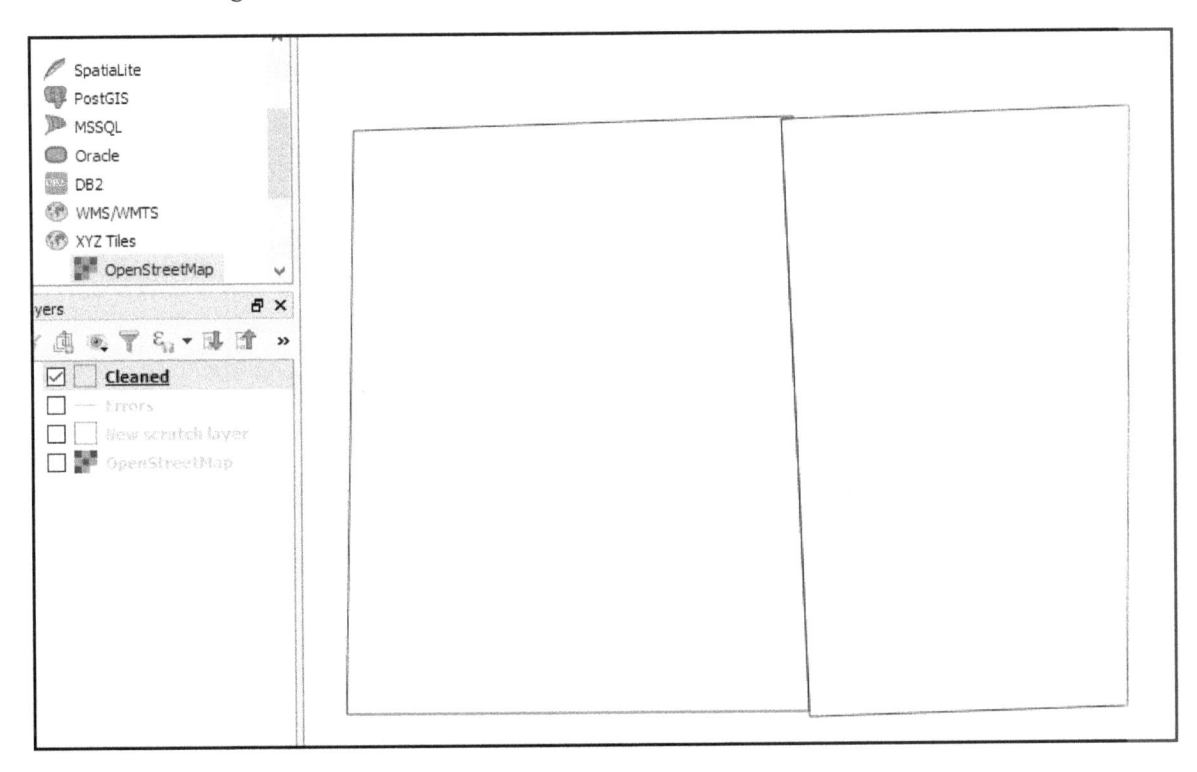

The resulting cleaned layer

Raster data

Raster data is not created like vector data. Quite often, raster data is created from other raster data, such as creating a slope raster from a topographic raster. Raster data can also be created from vector data, which can be done by gridding a series of coordinates/points. QGIS has the ability to perform all of these functions. We will further explore raster visualization in Chapter 4, *Creating Great Maps*, and processing rasters in Chapter 6, *Extending QGIS with Python*.

[73]

Data Creation and Editing

In this section, we will convert our `Canada_Provinces.shp` to a raster. In the menu, click **Raster | Conversion | Rasterize (vector to raster),** as shown in the following screenshot:

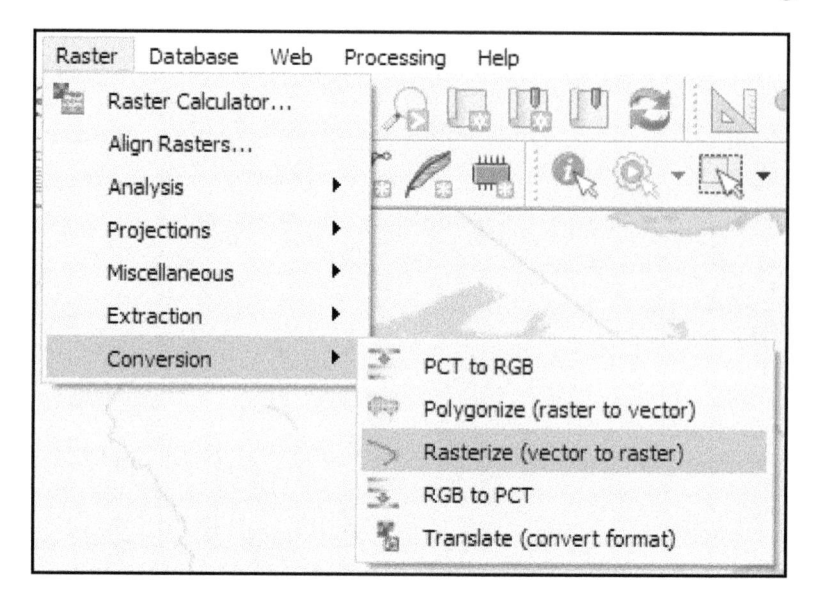

Vector to raster

In the following dialog box, enter these parameters:

- **Input Layer**: `Canada_Provinces`.
- **Burn-in value**: **id**.
- **Output raster size units**: **Pixels**.
- **Width**: 10 (this will create a raster with a width of 10 pixels).
- **Height**: 10 (this will create a raster with a height of 10 pixels).
- **Output extent**: Select the **Use layer/canvas** and then click on `Canada_Provinces` to auto-populate.
- **Rasterized**: Save the `Canada_Provinces_Raster.tif` filename.

Chapter 2

Your screen should look similar to this:

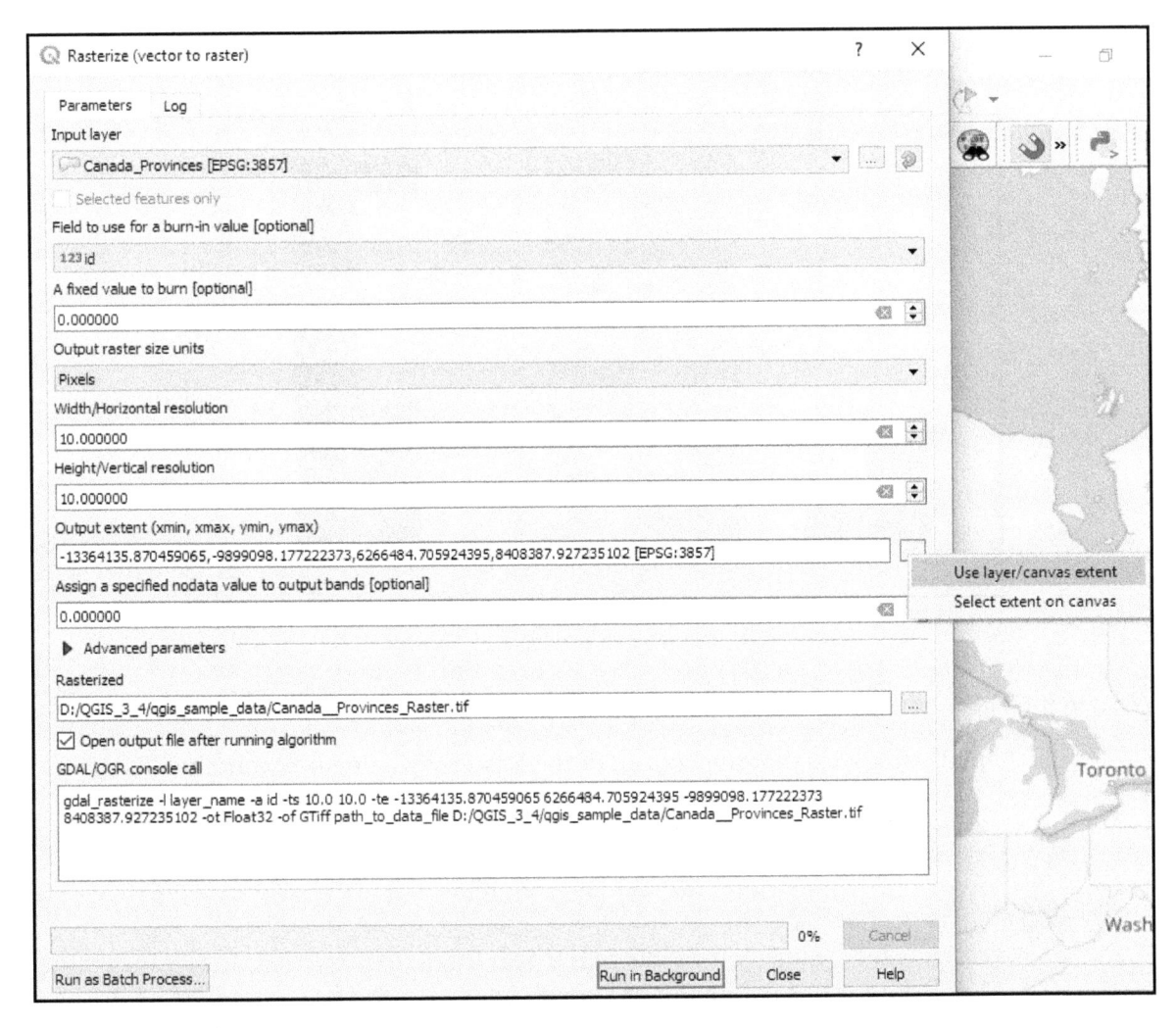

Rasterize the vector layer dialog box

Data Creation and Editing

Now select **Run in Background** (a new feature of QGIS 3). Once this has been done, the dialog box will remain open. You can close this down if no errors are reported.

The result will be shown in the map, and this should be similar to the following screenshot:

Raster result

We will look at shading and displaying Raster datasets in Chapter 3, *Visualizing Data*.

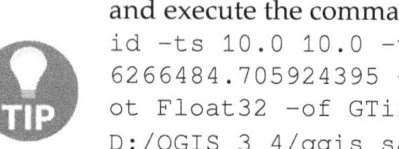

> **TIP**
> Did you notice that the bottom of the Rasterize dialog box contained a GDAL command? You could copy and paste this into the OSGeo4W shell and execute the command there: `gdal_rasterize -l layer_name -a id -ts 10.0 10.0 -te -13364135.870459065 6266484.705924395 -9899098.177222373 8408387.927235102 -ot Float32 -of GTiff path_to_data_file D:/QGIS_3_4/qgis_sample_data/Canada__Provinces_Raster.tif`. Look out for this command in later chapters. As you grow familiar with QGIS, you will begin to notice the `gdal` commands that are running in the background.

Other data

Finally, we will take a look at databases and the process of creating data in the new GeoPackage format.

Creating a GeoPackage

At the start of this chapter, we looked at data formats and the GeoPackage format. Remember that, in QGIS 3, the GeoPackage format is the default format. So, let's finish this chapter by creating data in the GeoPackage format:

Create a new GeoPackage layer by clicking **Layer** | **Create Layer** | **New GeoPackage Layer**...:

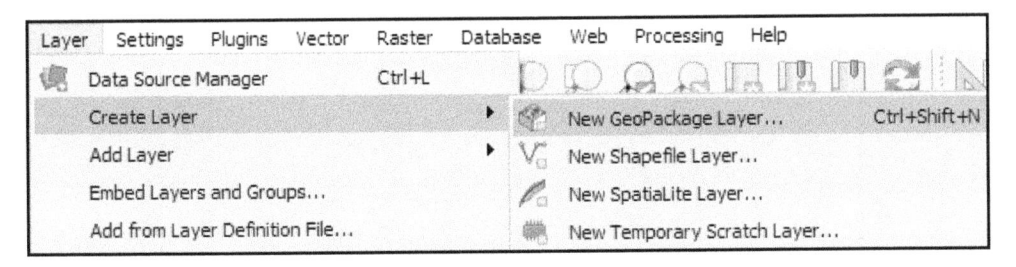

Create a New GeoPackage Layer

Now fill in the resulting dialog box. Let's create a GeoPackage called `My_first_GeoPackage`, set the **Geometry type** as a **Point**, and add the **ID** and **Name** fields.

Data Creation and Editing

It should look similar to the following screenshot:

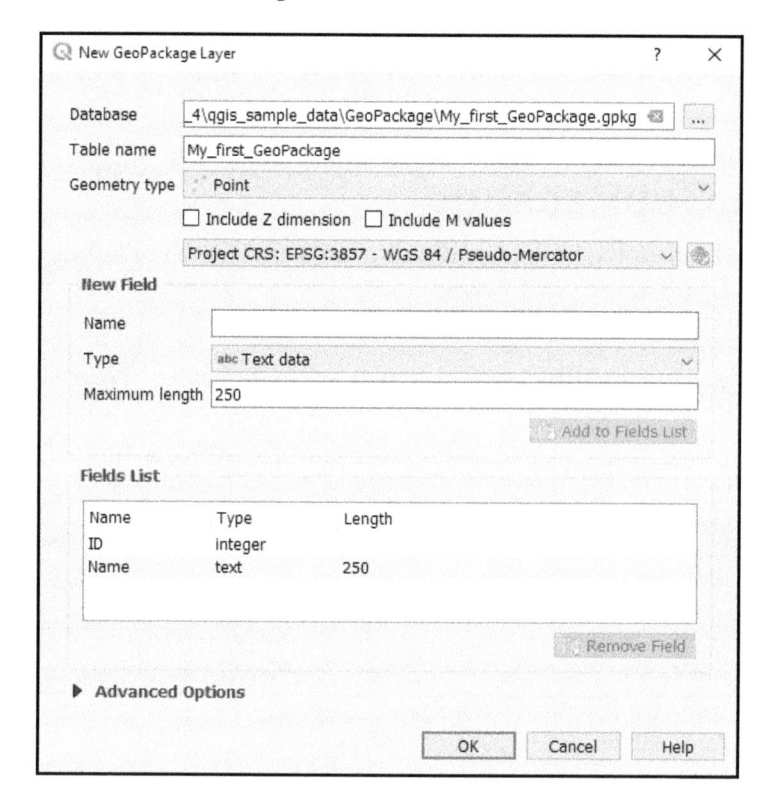

New GeoPackage Layer dialog box

Use what you have already learned in this chapter to select this layer, toggle editing on, and then capture a point. Fill in the associated attributes, which are similar to what we can see in the following screenshot:

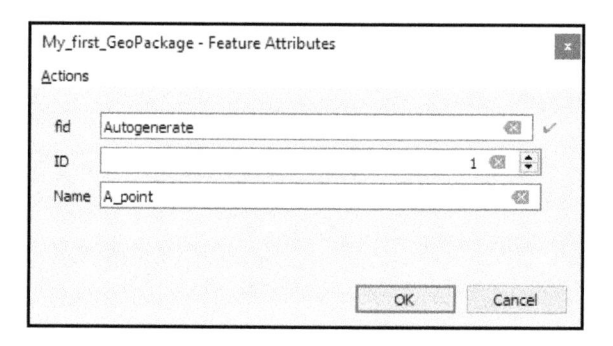

Adding feature attributes

Chapter 2

Click **OK** to confirm this, and you have officially created your first point layer in a GeoPackage. You can add another layer with a different geometry type within the same GeoPackage. This is a change from working with a Shapefile. You can create a new GeoPackage layer by clicking **Layer** | **Create Layer** | **New GeoPackage Layer**, but this time, point it at the existing GeoPackage. Create a new **Table name**, select **Geometry type** as **Polygon**, and add fields:

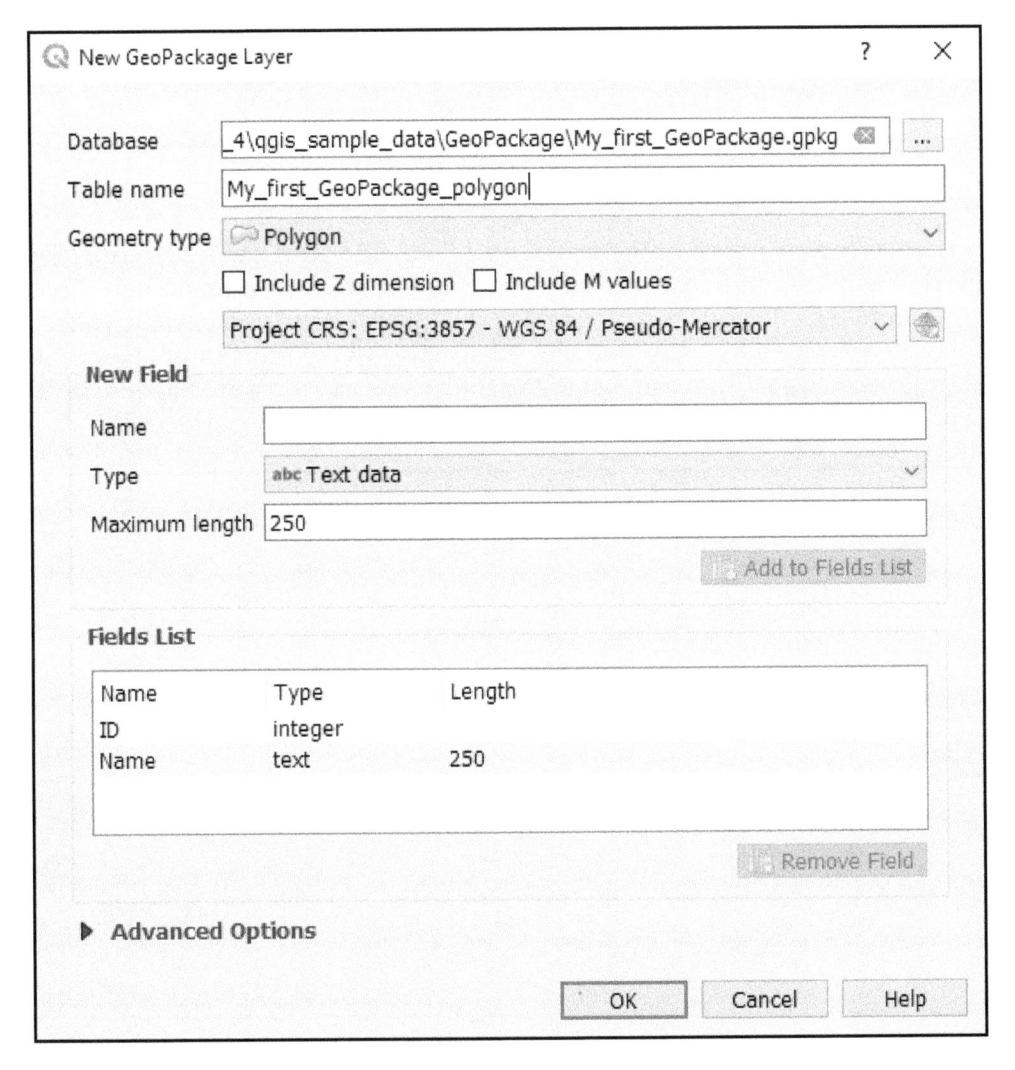

Adding a new layer to the GeoPackage

Data Creation and Editing

You will get an overwrite message, as shown in the following screenshot. Here, click on **Add new layer**:

Add new layer dialog box

Edit your new layer as we have previously with a Shapefile. This can be repeated for different layers with different feature types. After saving all of your associated files and projects, close down QGIS and then navigate to the folder where you created your GeoPackage. Here, you will see just one file, irrespective of the number of layers you have added to the GeoPackage. Compare that to the folder you saved your Shapefile in. The following screenshot shows one file for many layers with different geometries:

The GeoPackage in the folder directory in Windows

Exporting to a different format

Reopen QGIS and load in a layer from your GeoPackage. Right-click on the layer in the **Layers** Panel and select **Export | Save Features As.** In the resulting dialog box, you can choose the format you wish to export to. This process is the same for any Vector or Raster layer.

If you wish to export a Shapefile into a GeoPackage, you could, in the **Browser** Panel, click and drag the Shapefile into your GeoPackage. This is a super simple layer to import data into a GeoPackage:

Importing into GeoPackage

Your original Shapefile will still exist. You have just imported a copy.

Spatial Databases

Let's conclude this chapter by briefly mentioning Spatial Databases. DB Manager is a great way of handling connections with Spatial Databases, including PostGIS, Oracle Spatial, SpatiaLite, and GeoPackage. To open the **DB Manager**, click **Database | DB Manager**:

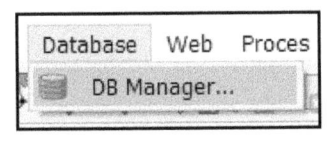

Opening the DB Manager

You will be presented with the ability to connect to all of the databases listed above. To connect, right-click on the database. A GeoPackage is a database container, which means it supports direct use. In the DB Manager, let's connect to our newly created GeoPackage layer. Right-click on GeoPackage and select **New Connection**. Navigate to the location in which you stored it, and then click **OK**.

Data Creation and Editing

You should see the connection displayed in the following screenshot:

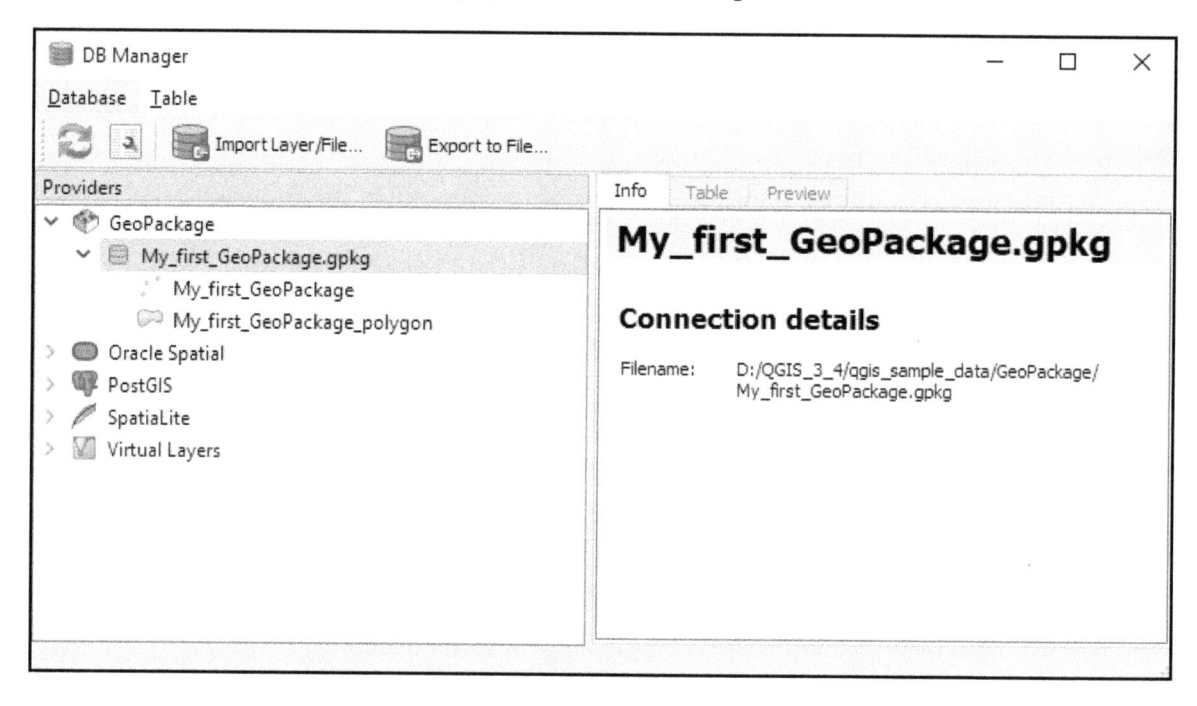

The DB Manager

You can drag and drop these layers into QGIS. You can then upload new data, export existing data, and run SQL on the data. The DB manager performs the same function for all the GIS database types previously listed. If you have access to a database, such as PostGIS, then the DB manager is a very convenient place in QGIS to interact with the data.

Summary

In this chapter, you learned the basics of using data in a GIS. QGIS 3.4 supports all the formats in OGR and GDAL. The default format for QGIS 3.4 is the GeoPackage. We also looked at creating and editing Vector data, as well as attribute tables and geometries. Furthermore, we joined data and used snapping tools to preserve topology. Don't ignore Raster data though; we will use it many times throughout this book. In this chapter, we briefly reviewed its creation and hinted at the powerful GDAL tools built into QGIS. Finally, we looked at spatial databases in QGIS 3.4 and connected to them in DB Manager.

In the next chapter, we will look at styling and visualizing this data.

3
Visualizing Data

In this chapter, we will look at visualizing GIS data. We will build on the knowledge gained in Chapter 2, *Data Creation and Editing,* in which we learned how to load, create, and edit GIS data. QGIS automatically styles data when added to the map. This is useful for a quick inspection, but to convey more meaning, we need to style our data so that the information presented becomes more intuitive. That is what this chapter is all about.

The topics covered in this chapter are as follows:

- Styling data
- Interactive styling
- Styling Rasters
    - Styling Terrain data
    - Styling Satellite imagery
    - Raster toolbar
    - Styling landcover maps
- Saving styles
- Styling Vectors
    - Points
    - Simple markers and SVG
    - Lines
    - Polygons

Styling data

We are going to style both Raster and Vector data. QGIS 3 has significantly updated and improved its ability to visualize GIS data. In this chapter, we will show how styling in QGIS can be used to convey more meaning to data.

> **TIP**: We will again use the QGIS sample data from `https://qgis.org/downloads/data/` – look for the `qgis_sample_data.zip` file. Download and extract the data to your computer if you have not already done so.

Interactive styling

A major visualization improvement in QGIS 3 is the ability to style GIS data interactively. There are now two main ways to style your data. You can either left-click on a layer and select properties, or you can click on **View | Panels | Layer Styling Panel**, as shown in the following screenshot:

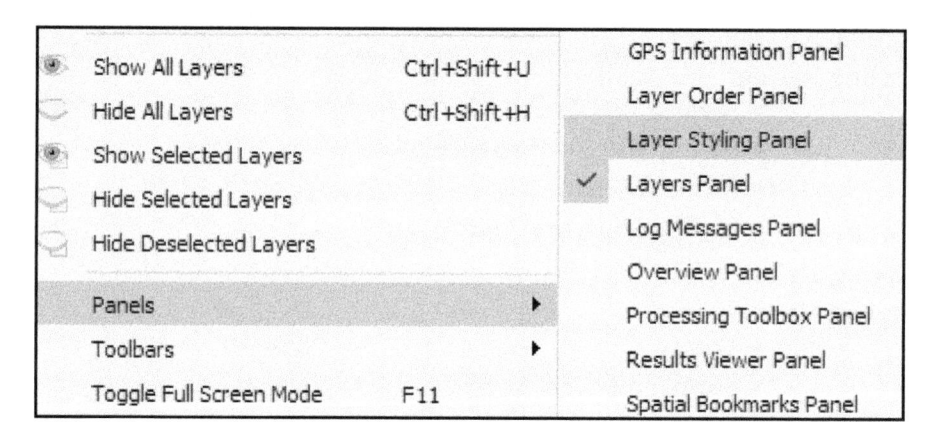

Selecting the Layer Styling Panel

The Layer Styling Panel provides fast feedback, but does take up a lot of screen space. In the **Layer Styling Panel**, check the box next to the **Live Update** option to see changes in real time. In this chapter, we will be predominantly working with the **Layer Styling Panel**, but you will achieve the same results by accessing the layer properties dialog box if you prefer.

Styling raster layers

From the QGIS Sample dataset, load the `SR_50M_alaska_nad.tif` and `landcover.img` files from the `Raster` folder. Turn on the **Layer Styling Panel** if it is not already on, and then load the `RGB_LandsatARD.tif` file from this book's download page.

> **TIP**: Download the extra material for this book from `www.packt.com`.

Your screen should look similar to the following. The three raster layers loaded into the QGIS layers panel are shown here:

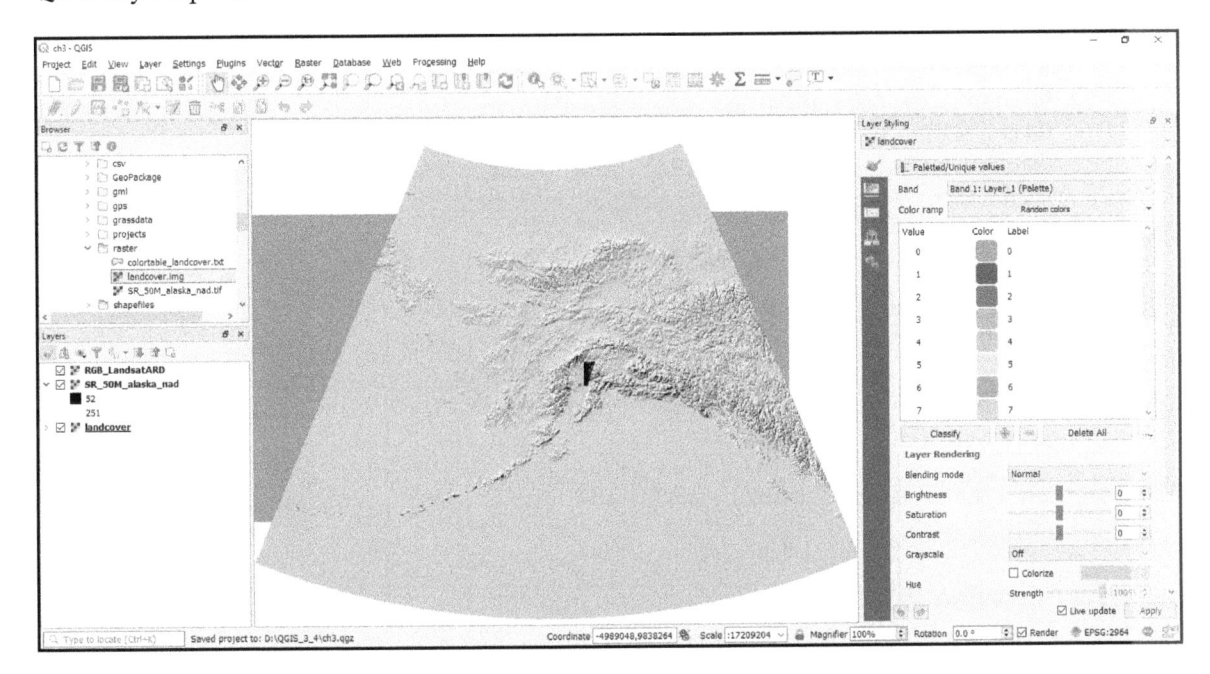

QGIS with the raster datasets loaded

[85]

Visualizing Data

In the map window, we now have three of the most common types of Raster datasets: a Satellite image (this is Landsat 8 Analysis-Ready Data), a Terrain dataset (Hillshade data that covers the whole of Alaska), and a `landcover` dataset that has been loaded as a paletted image by default.

In QGIS 3.4, there are five methods for styling your raster. These methods consist of the following:

- **Multi-band color**: This style is used if the raster has several bands. This is usually the case with satellite images with multiple bands.
- **Paletted**: This style is used if a single-band raster comes with an indexed palette.
- **Single-band gray**: If a raster has neither multiple bands nor an indexed palette (as is the case with elevation models), they will be rendered using this style.
- **Single-band pseudo-color**: Instead of being limited to gray, this style allows us to render a raster band using a color map of our choice.
- **Hillshade**: This is useful for any DEM-derived rasters, such as Hillshade. It gives us the ability to alter the angle at which these datasets are displayed. Think of this option as an on the fly Hillshade for Raster. We will look at how Hillshade Rasters are created in `Chapter 5`, *Spatial Analysis*.

Layer styling – Terrain

The **Layer Properties** dialog box or the **Layers** panel contains similar styling options in the dialog box. We are now going to look at the styling options for terrain data, Satellite RGB data, and landcover/paletted data.

Click on the **Layer Styling** tab button, as shown in the following screenshot:

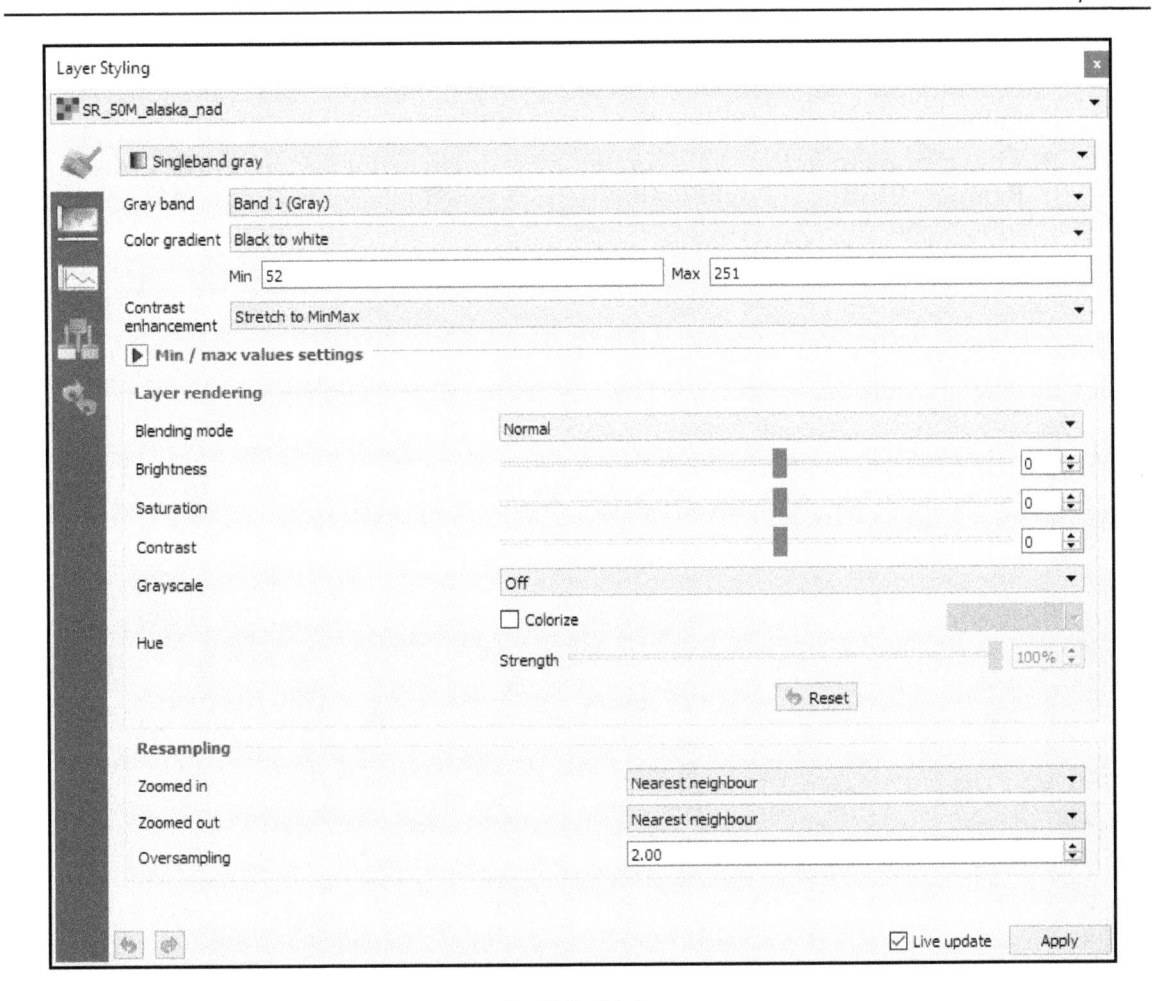

Layer Styling dialog box

There are several useful parameters in here that display the data in the best way. These parameters include:

- **The renderer**: This is set to **Singleband gray** for this image. Change this to **Single-band pseudo-color**. If you are working in the **Layer Styling** panel as I am, you will see the impact of this change immediately.
- **The Min/Max values settings**: This is how we stretch our image. Zoom to the extent of the RGB_LandsatARD layer, change the statistics to the current canvas, and click on the **Mean +/- standard deviation** radio button to alter the way the data is displayed. This is known as **stretching**.

Visualizing Data

- **The Interpolation drop-down box**: This allows the color ramp to be blended using Linear Interpolation or Discrete in order to use the values as shown in the following color ramp. Leave this setting as Linear.
- **The color ramp option**: Click on the drop-down menu and select **All Color Ramps | Viridis**. This color ramp is more suited to terrain display. This setting is shown here:

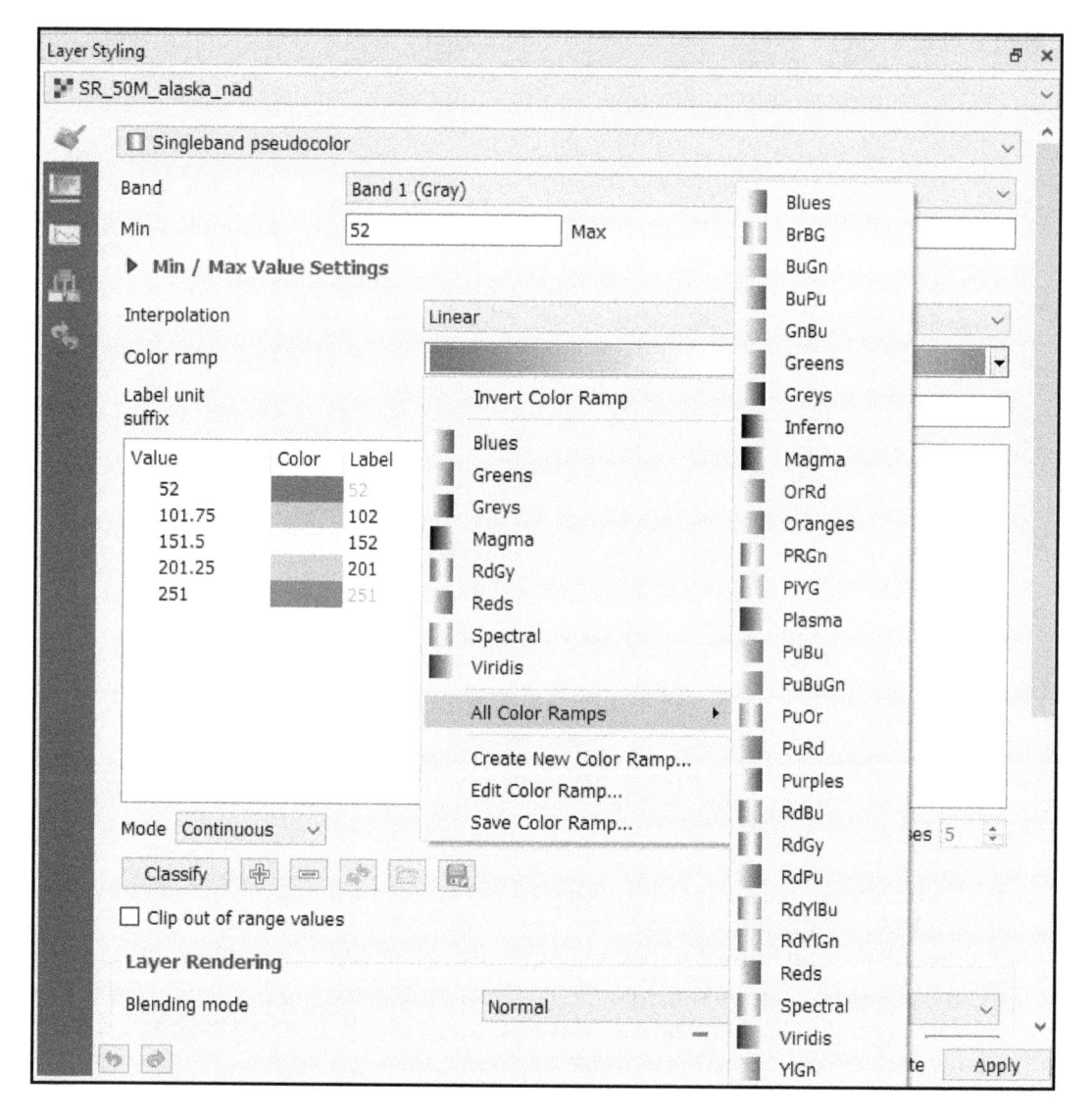

Color ramps in QGIS

- **The mode option**: This enables you to change the way the data is split up into classes. By default the setting is **Continuous**, though you can change to Equal Interval or Quantile. With these settings, you can adjust the number of classes you wish to display.

Under the color settings, we can find a section with more advanced options that control the Raster **Resampling**, **Brightness**, **Contrast**, **Saturation**, and **Hue** options that you probably know from image-processing software. By default, resampling is set to the **Nearest-neighbor** option. To get smoother results, we can change to the Bilinear or Cubic method. For this example, we will set resampling as **Cubic**.

There is one final layer **Rendering** option: **blending**. Leave this setting as normal for this layer. As we build up our map, this setting helps us to integrate this data visually. Turn off the **Layer Styling** panel and zoom to the extent of the **SR_50M_alaska_nad** layer. Your terrain data should look similar to the following screenshot:

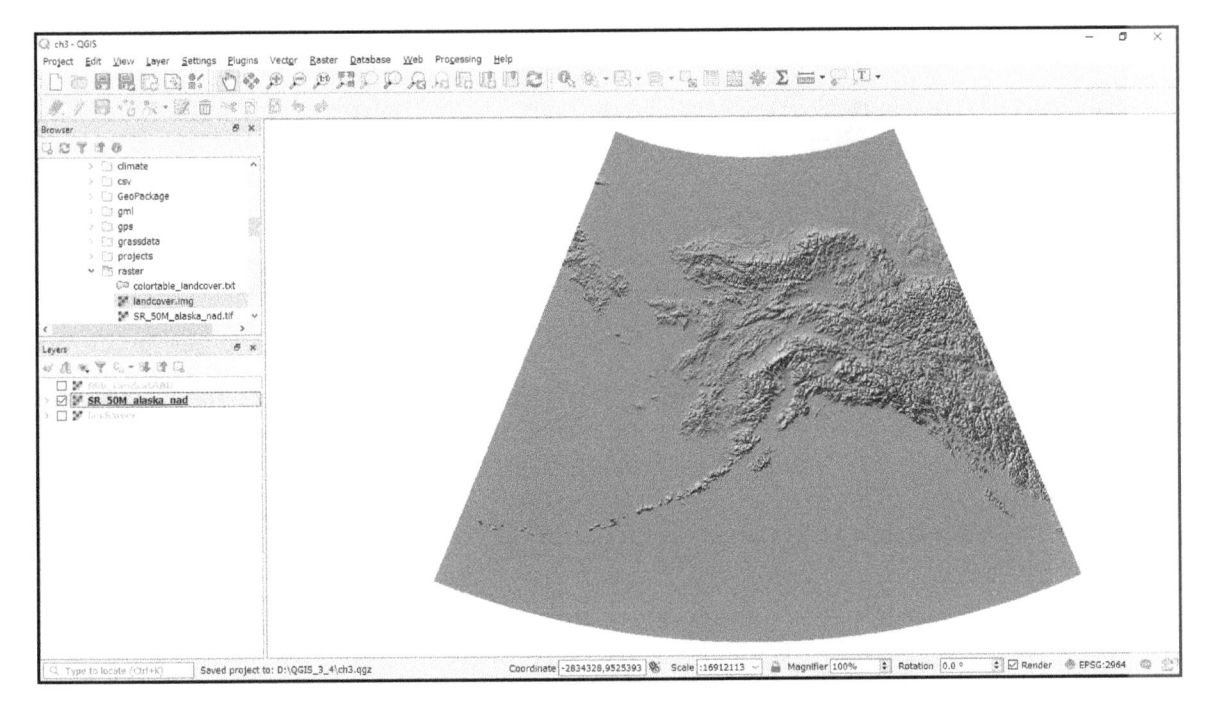

Terrain rendered in QGIS

Visualizing Data

Layer styling – satellite image

Turn on the **RGB_LandsatARD** layer and zoom in to it. If you haven't stretched or altered the layer, it should appear similar to the following screenshot:

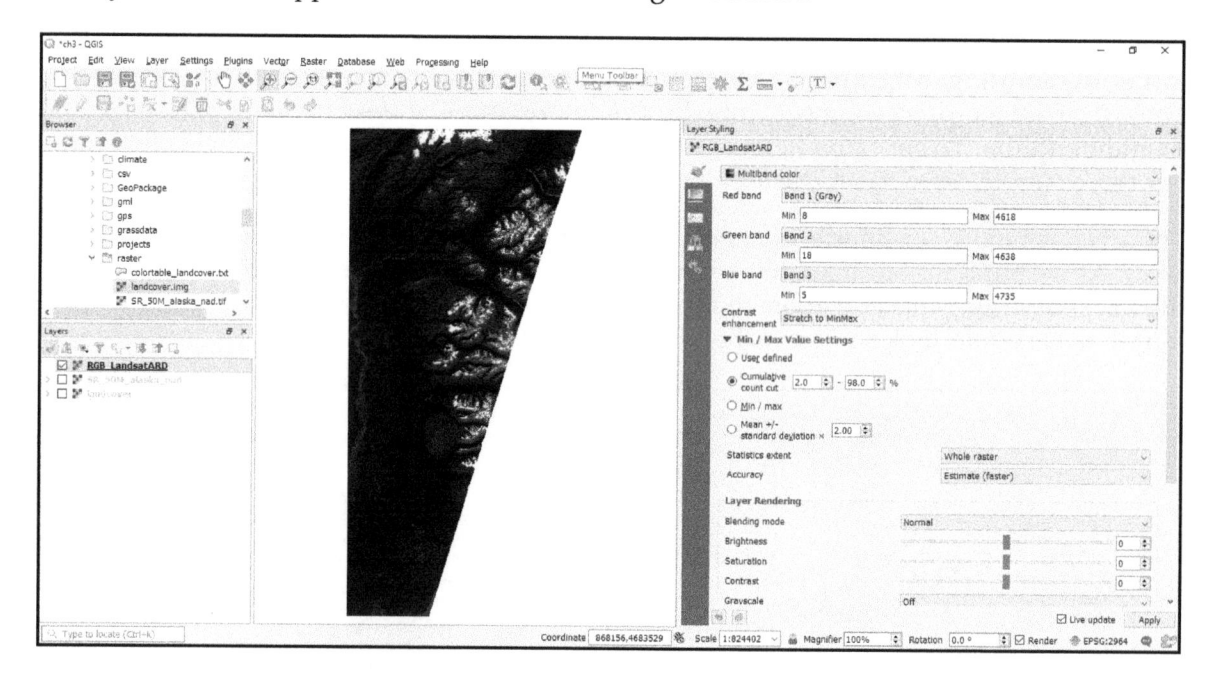

Landsat ARD in QGIS

This data is Landsat **Analysis Ready Data** (**ARD**), which was downloaded from the **US Geological Survey** (**USGS**) in May 2018. All Landsat data is open source and is increasingly becoming part of many GIS workflows. The ARD data means that we do not have to perform any atmospheric correction to the data; it is already converted to surface reflectance and therefore is in a usable format.

The first thing to do with this layer is to change the order of the bands from RGB 123 to RGB 321. To do this, set the **Red band** to Band 3, the **Green band** to Band 2, and the **Blue band** to Band 1. Set the **Contrast enhancement** to **Stretch** and clip to **MinMax**. Zoom into the data and set the **Statitistic** extent to **Current canvas**. Leave all other parameters as default. The Landsat data should appear similar to the following screenshot:

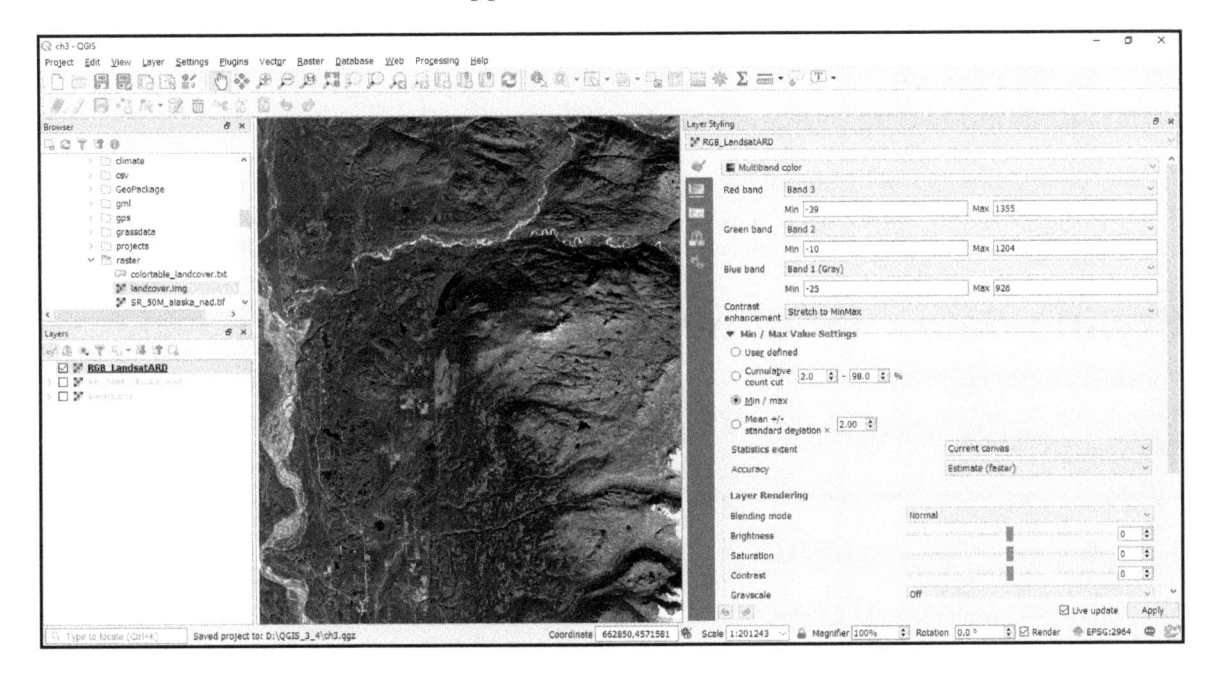

Stretching satellite data using the Layer Styling panel

Raster Toolbar

The Raster Toolbar (**View** | **Toolbars** | **Raster Toolbar**) is a very useful way of quickly stretching and displaying Raster data. It is especially useful for RGB satellite images. The toolbar looks like this:

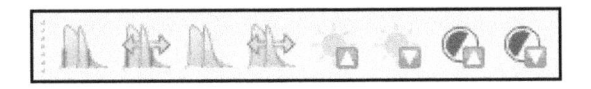

Raster toolbar

Visualizing Data

The first four buttons (displaying the histogram graphs) are useful for stretching the data, while the final four buttons adjust the contrast and brightness. Furthermore, the histogram buttons can alter the data depending on your current view extent.

- The first of these buttons is a local cumulative cut stretch set to the extents of your current map extent
- The second is a local cumulative cut stretch set to the extents of your data
- The third is the local histogram stretch
- The fourth is the histogram stretch to the extents of your data

This toolbar is one of the hidden gems of QGIS. Once you have defined the bands to be displayed, this is often the simplest way of creating a nicely balanced image.

Styling data – landcover map

To conclude this section on styling raster data, let's take a look at the landcover map. By default, when data is added to the layer panel, the landcover map will look similar to the following screenshot:

Displaying landcover data in QGIS

In the same way as for layer styling within the terrain section, we have the ability to make several changes to the `landcover` layer. We are not going to alter the color ramp here. `Landcover` raster datasets are often based on or generated from classifications of Satellite data. If your `landcover` class has an appropriate color, then this will help the end user to understand the data that is being presented to them.

It is also often useful to add a meaningful label to a dataset such as this. If you double-click on the **0** label and set it to **Other** as well as setting the next label to **Class 1**, you will see the **Layers** panel update at the same time:

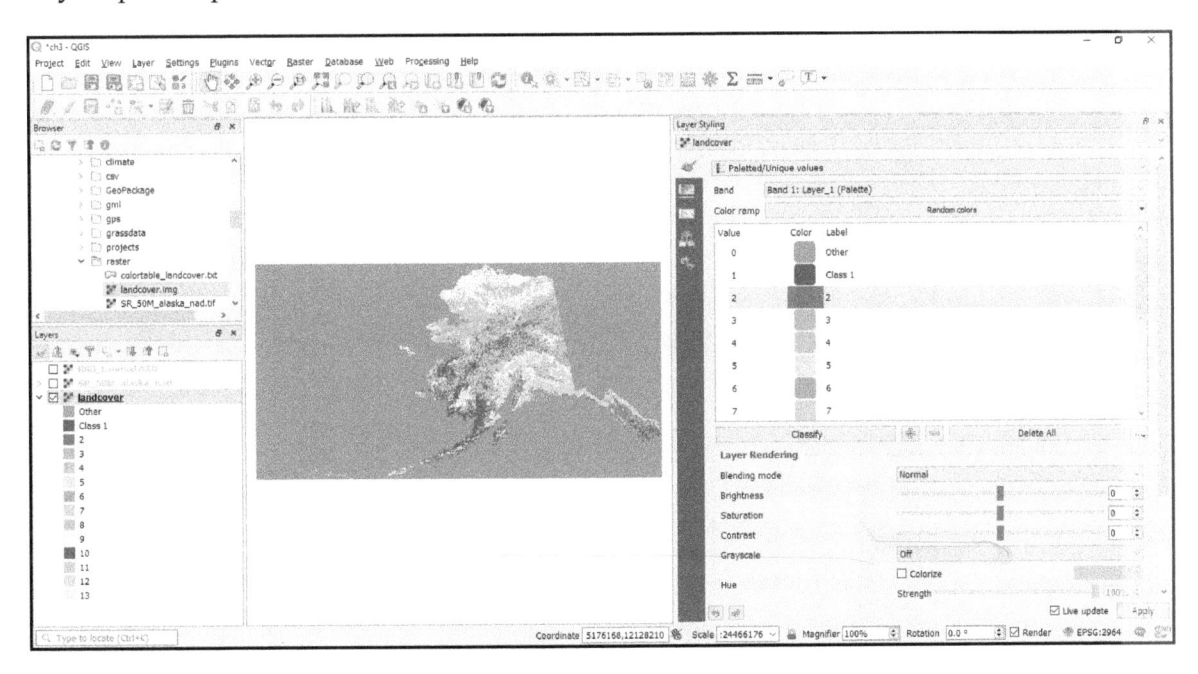

Changing the landcover dataset in QGIS

Visualizing Data

Continue to label all of the other labels in this way. After you have labelled them, double-click on the blue color which corresponds with Value 0 . Alter the **Opacity %** to 0%, as shown in the following screenshot:

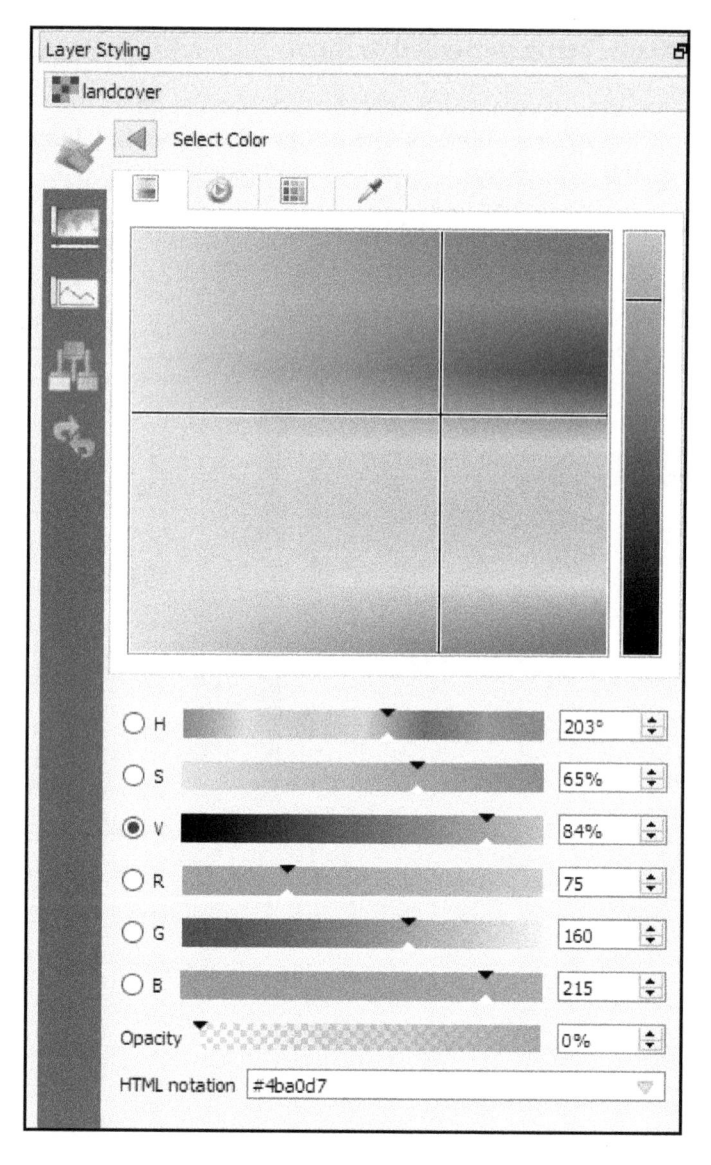

The color picker

This will make the blue color transparent. Finally, let's look at the blending options in the Layer-rendering section on the layer-styling tab. First, turn on the **SR_50m_alaska** layer. Next, set the **Blending** mode to **Lighten** and see the impact on the display. In this example, I want to combine the **SR_50m_alaska** layer with the landcover layer in an attempt to show more details and highlight the geomorphology of Alaska. To do this, I will set the **Blending** mode to **Multiply** and leave the other settings at their default options. As I zoom into the data, I can see the impact of the Hillshade combined with the landcover classification. It should look similar to the following screenshot:

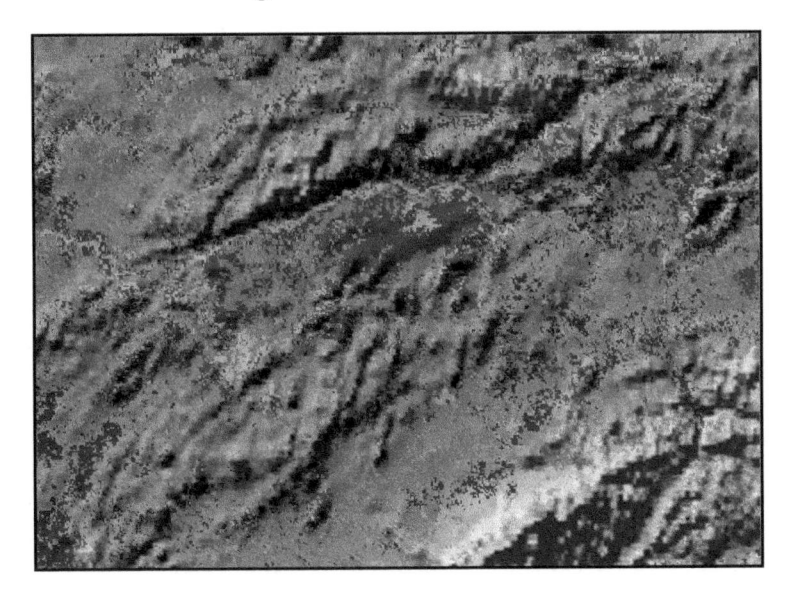

Combining the raster datasets

Saving styles

Before we move on to styling vector layers, it is worth noting that whenever you style your data, you can save the style. This means that you can reuse it again on other layers and in other projects.

Visualizing Data

To do this, right-click on the **Layer** in the **Layers** panel and select **Properties**, then click on the **Style** button in the bottom left of the **Layer Properties** dialog box and select **Save Style...**, as shown in the following screenshot :

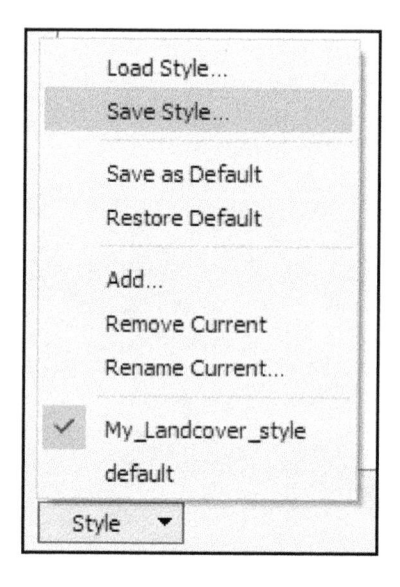

Saving the style

A `.qml` file will be saved to your disk. Follow the same process to generate qml styles for all the layers and then save your map. Alternatively, you can right-click on the **Layer** in the **Layers** panel and select **Export | Save as QGIS Layer Style File**.

> **TIP**: Saving to Styled Layer Description (`.sld`) files can be done with the SLD4Raster plugin. This useful plugin will allow you to upload your styling directly to Geoserver as well. An SLD file is an OGC format. For more information, see http://www.opengeospatial.org/standards/sld.

Styling vector layers

As we saw when we loaded vector layers, QGIS renders them using a default style and a random color. In the following exercises, we will style point, line, and polygon layers. You will also get accustomed to the most common vector-styling options.

Regardless of the layer's geometry type, we always find a drop-down list with the available style options in the top-left corner of the Style dialog. The following style options are available for vector layers:

- **Single Symbol**: This is the simplest option. When we use a Single Symbol style, all points are displayed with the same symbol.
- **Categorized**: This is the style of choice if a layer contains points of different categories. For example, a layer that contains the locations of different animal sightings.
- **Graduated**: This style is great if we want to visualize numerical values, for example, temperature measurements.
- **Rule-based**: This is the most advanced option. Rule-based styles are very flexible because they allow us to write multiple rules for one layer.
- **Point displacement**: This option is only available for point layers. These styles are useful if you need to visualize point layers with multiple points at the same coordinates. For example, students living at the same address.
- **Point Cluster**: As with Point displacement, this option is only available for point layers. By default, the Point Cluster shows a numerical label if the points overlap with the count of the points.
- **Inverted polygons**: This option is available for *polygon layers only*. By using this option, the defined symbology will be applied to the area outside the polygon borders instead of filling the area inside the polygon.
- **Heatmap**: This option is available for point layers only. It enables us to create a dynamic heatmap style.
- **2.5D**: This option is available for polygon layers only. It enables us to create extruded polygons in 2.5 dimensions.

Creating point styles – an example of an airport style

From the sample data, load `airport.shp`. For context purposes, you can keep the Raster layers we just used if you like, or you can start a new project. I am going to keep them in as layers.

Visualizing Data

Open the **Layer Styling** panel. As was the case in the *Raster Styling* section, any changes you make will be seen in the map as you make them. In order to see the points on our hillshade map from before, set the symbol size to 4 and the color to red. In styling options for the Hillshade layer (SR_50M_alaska_nad), I have set the symbology to **Singleband grey**. If you are following along, the QGIS should look similar to the following screenshot:

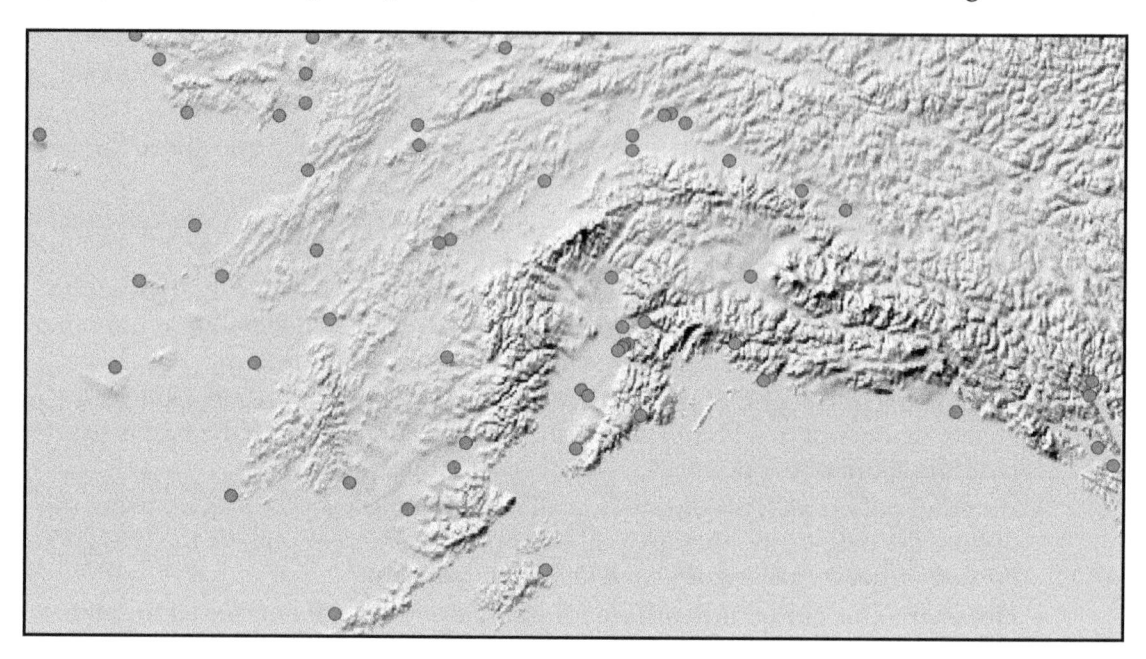

Airports plotted as dots on the Hillshade raster

We will return to the single symbol styling in the following subsection. First, let's take a look at all the options for styling a point layer. Change the **renderer** to **Categorized** and select the the fk_region column as the category. As with the landcover raster, if you change the labels, the data in the table of contents will also change.

Chapter 3

This is an important point to remember when it comes to making maps in `Chapter 4`, *Creating Great Maps*, as the Legend will contain this information. QGIS should look similar to the following screenshot:

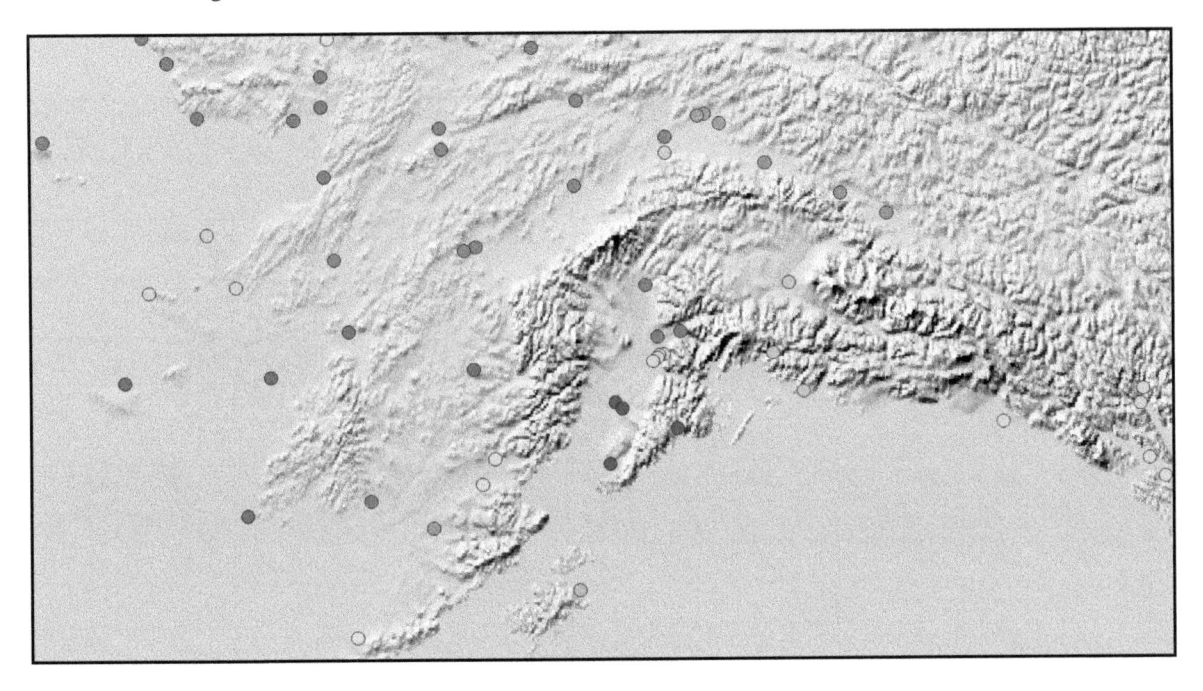

Airports plotted as colored dots on the Hillshade raster

This is useful if your data has categories you wish to highlight. This is also a fast way to spatially inspect your data and a good aid for the quality control of a project. This is especially important when digitizing and manually entering data into fields.

Visualizing Data

Reset the symbology of the layer by setting the styling back to single symbol. Then click on Point Cluster (Point Density will do a similar thing but will move the clustered points around a point; when making maps, choose the option that best fits your data). Clicking on Point Cluster will, depending on your zoom level, display the number of points at the same geographical location. This should look similar to the following screenshot:

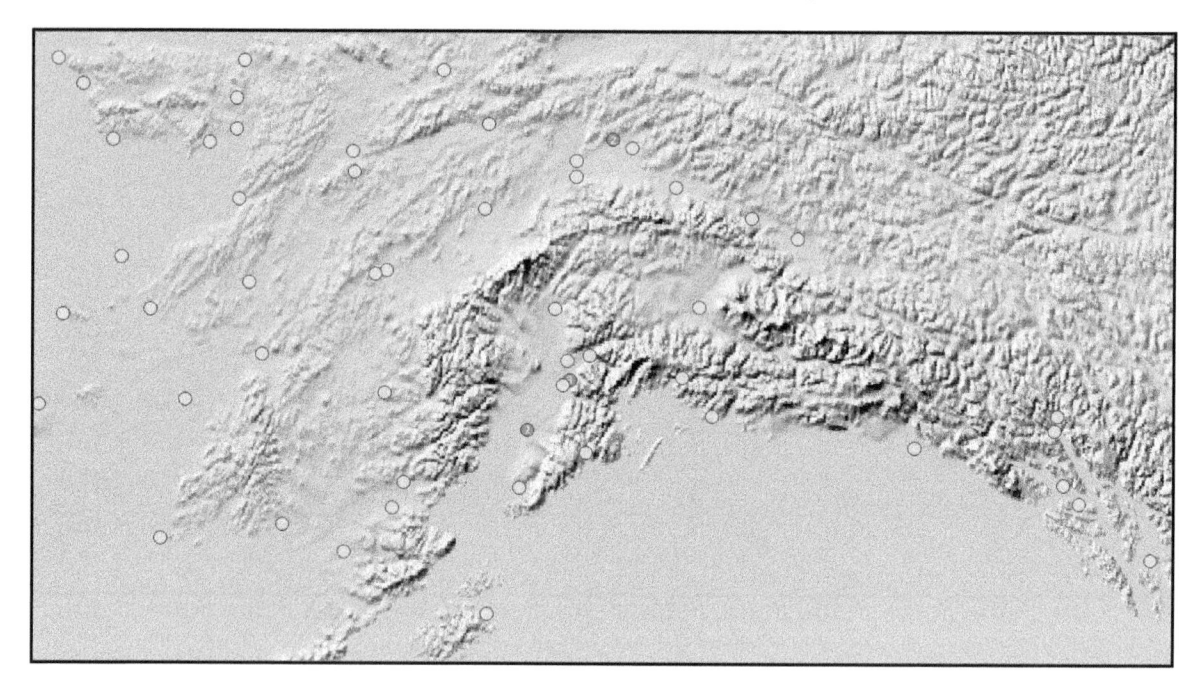

Point clustering

> **TIP**: Be attentive to the scale you are working on. This is *airport location* data, and it is very unlikely that airports will share the same x,y coordinates. However, as you zoom out and the scale changes, clustering occurs. Be sure that you do not misinterpret your data.

Set the point styling to heatmap and change the color ramp to **Spectral**. This option will build a heatmap raster on the fly to show areas of clustering (hot areas) in your data. It should look like the following screenshot:

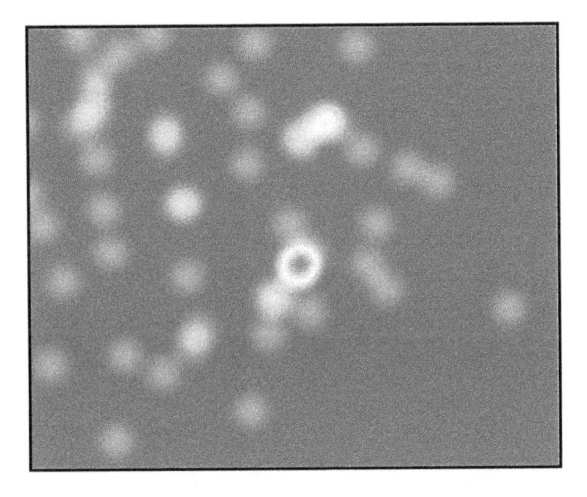

On-the-fly heatmap

We will return to heatmaps in `Chapter 5`, *Spatial Analysis* where **Kernel Density Estimation** (**KDE**) has been added in the default Processing Toolbox.

Simple marker

The simple marker tool deserves its own section. In this section, we will use the **Layer Properties** dialog box. Right-click on the layer in the **Layers** panel and select **Properties**. The options available for simple markers include Colors, Size, Rotation, and Form. However, sometimes a symbol that you want is not available. If this is the case, you can either create your own SVG files or import an existing one.

> **TIP**
>
> Download the SVG Mapbox symbol set from `https://www.mapbox.com/maki-icons/`.

[101]

Visualizing Data

SVG

In the **Layer Properties** dialog box, select **SVG**. Set the height to 4 and the width to 4. At the bottom of the dialog box, point to the `airport-11.svg` file downloaded from Mapbox, as shown in the following screenshot:

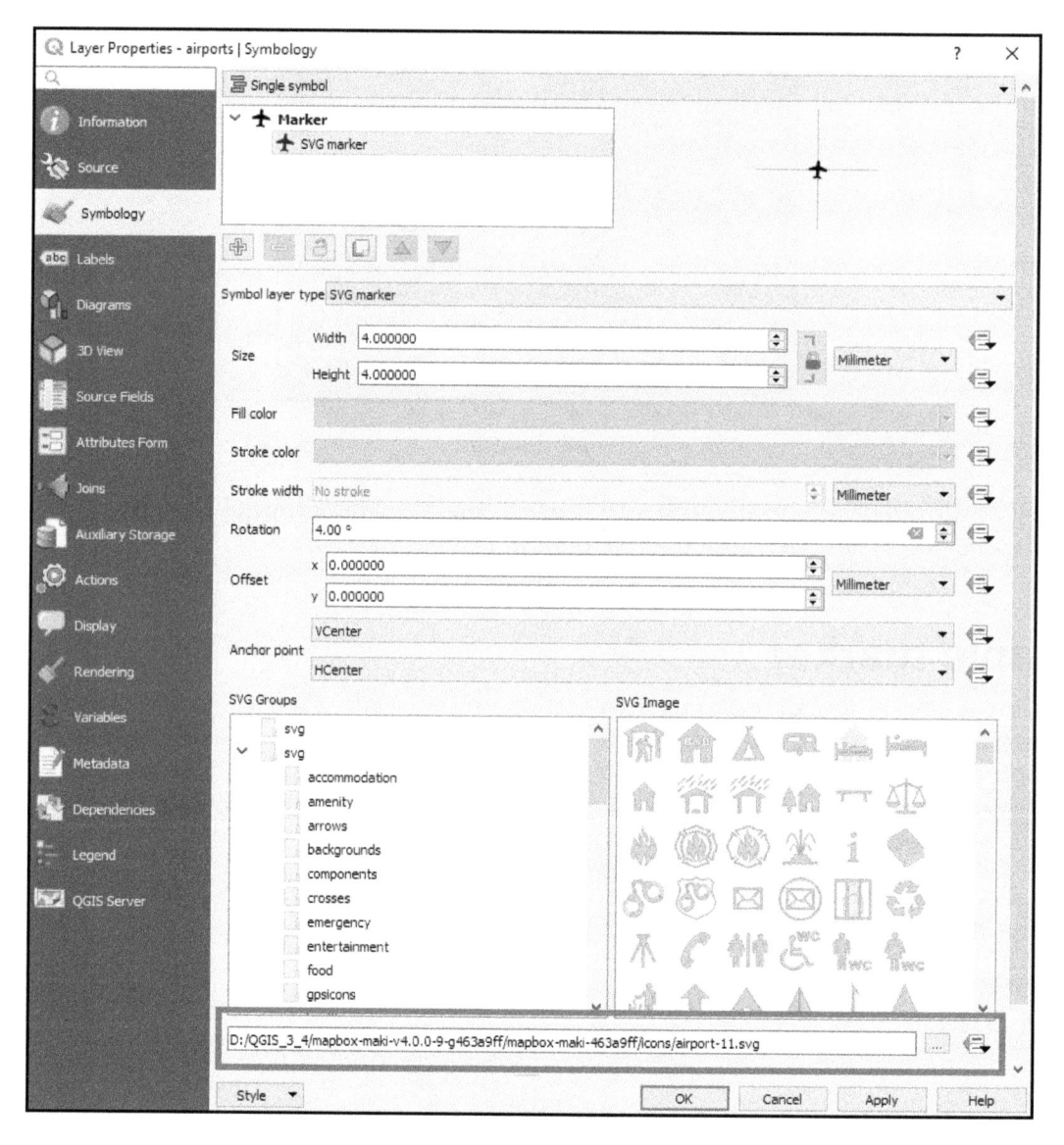

Layer property settings

When you select **OK**, small black airplane symbols should appear and replace the points on your map. There are a variety of SVG files available online if the symbol you need is not available as standard.

> **TIP**: SVG marker: Each QGIS installation comes with a collection of default SVG symbols. Add your own folders that contain SVG images by going to **Settings | Options | System | SVG Paths**.

Default symbols

In QGIS 3, there is an airplane symbol in the default library. Look for topo airport in the symbols window in the **Layer Properties** dialog box. Select the bottom SVG marker and set the **Stroke color** to black. When you have done this, your screen should look similar to the following:

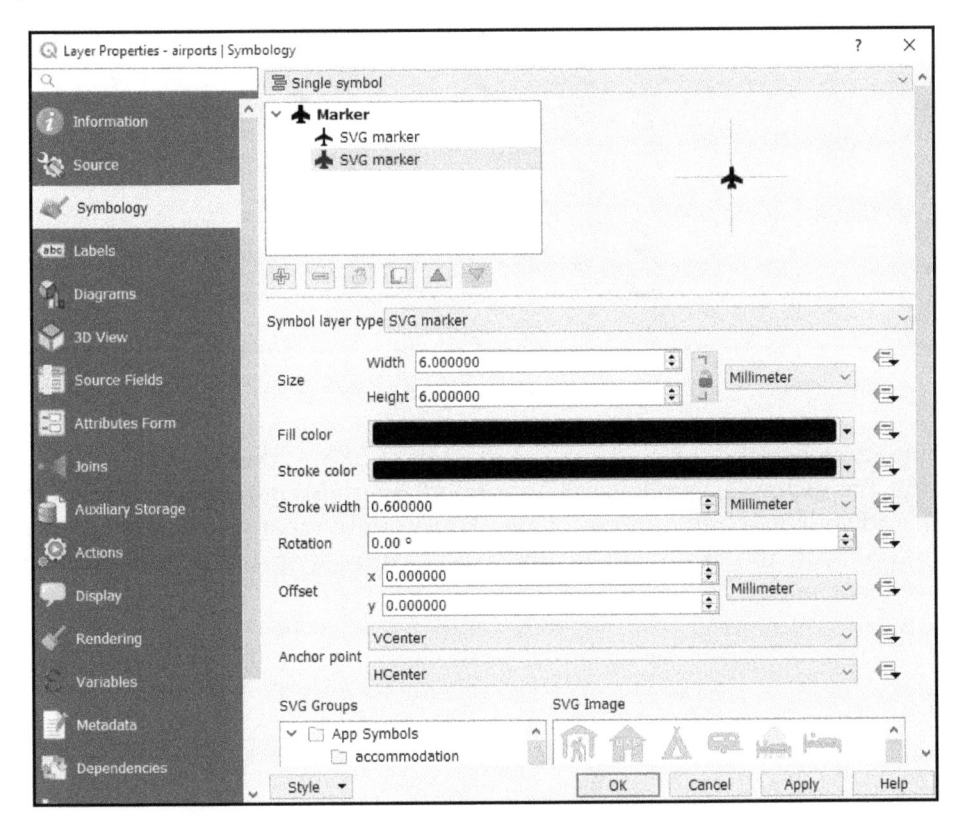

Marker symbols

Visualizing Data

By clicking on the **OK** button, this will apply a black airplane with a white outline symbol to your map, which is slightly clearer than before. Finally, we can take this symbol and, like before, display it according to the `fk_region` category. Now choose **Categorized** from the style drop-down box, select **Random colors** in the color ramp, and click the **Classify** button in the bottom-left of the screen. Click on the **OK** button and your map will consequently look similar to the following screenshot:

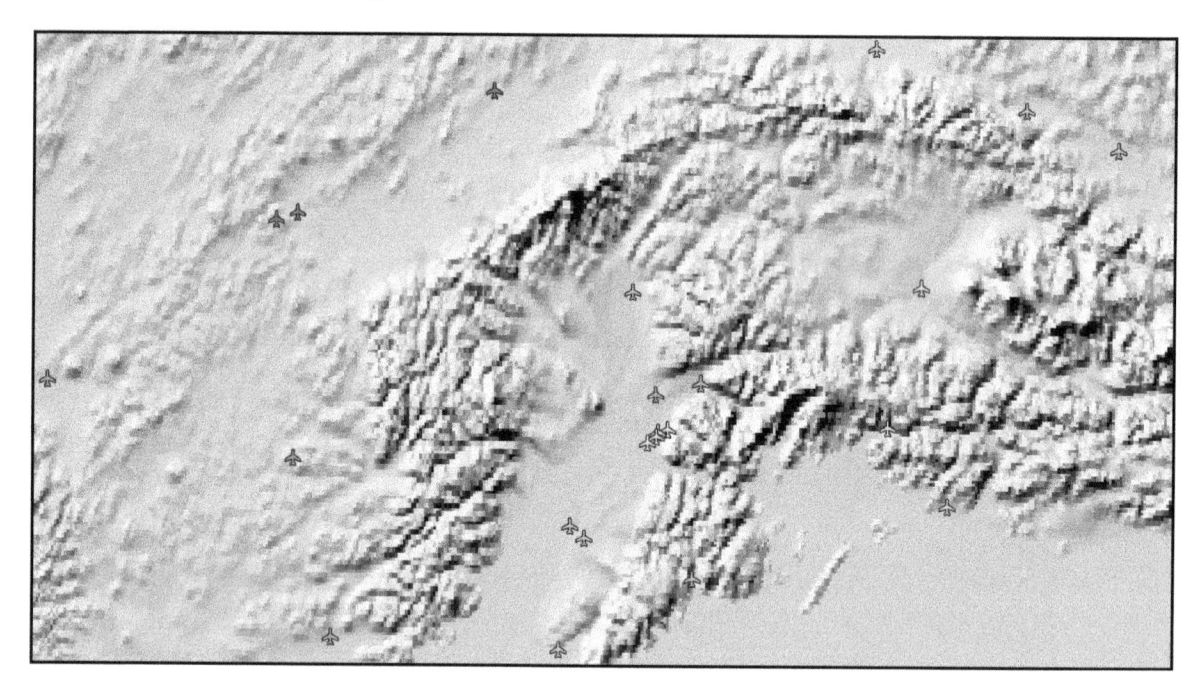

Colored marker symbols on Hillshade raster

We have only scratched the surface with the display of points; there are many combinations. For example, symbols can be rotated, overlaid on each other, and offset from the location and style in many different ways. Think about what you wish to convey and how best to convey it, and QGIS will be able to accommodate many variations of the examples we have shown.

Creating line styles – an example of a river

Load `majrivers.shp` into QGIS. We will use this data to create a line style that consists of two colors: a fill color and an outline color. To do this, open the **Layer Styling** panel and select a single symbol. Beneath this symbology, click on the green plus icon to add a new **Simple line**. You should now have two lines showing, which look similar to the following screenshot:

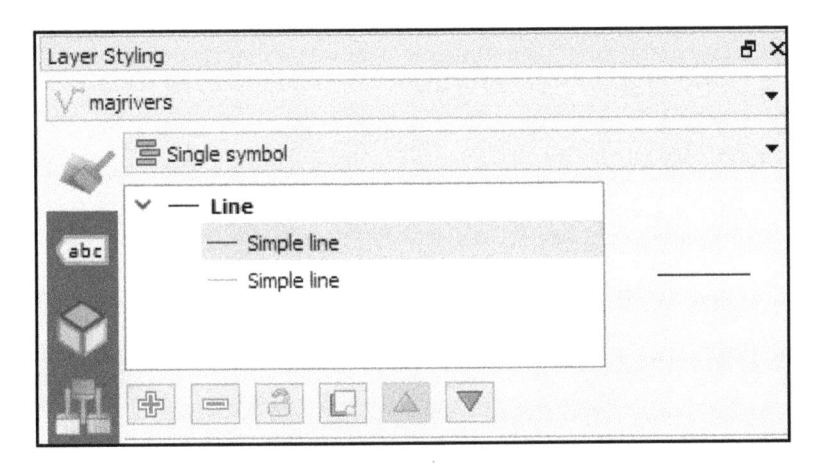

Layer styling on lines

The lower line will be our outline color, and the upper one will be the fill color. Select the upper simple line and change the color to blue and the width to 0.5 millimeters. Next, select the lower simple line and change its color to gray and the width to 0.8 millimeters, which is slightly wider than the other line. Check the preview and select **Apply** to test how the style looks when applied to the river layer.

Visualizing Data

You will notice that the style doesn't look perfect yet. This is because each line feature is drawn separately, one after the other, and this leads to a rather disconnected appearance. To change this, select the Line entry in the symbol layers list and click on the **Symbol Levels** dialog of the **Advanced** section (the button in the bottom-right corner of the style dialog), as shown in the following screenshot:

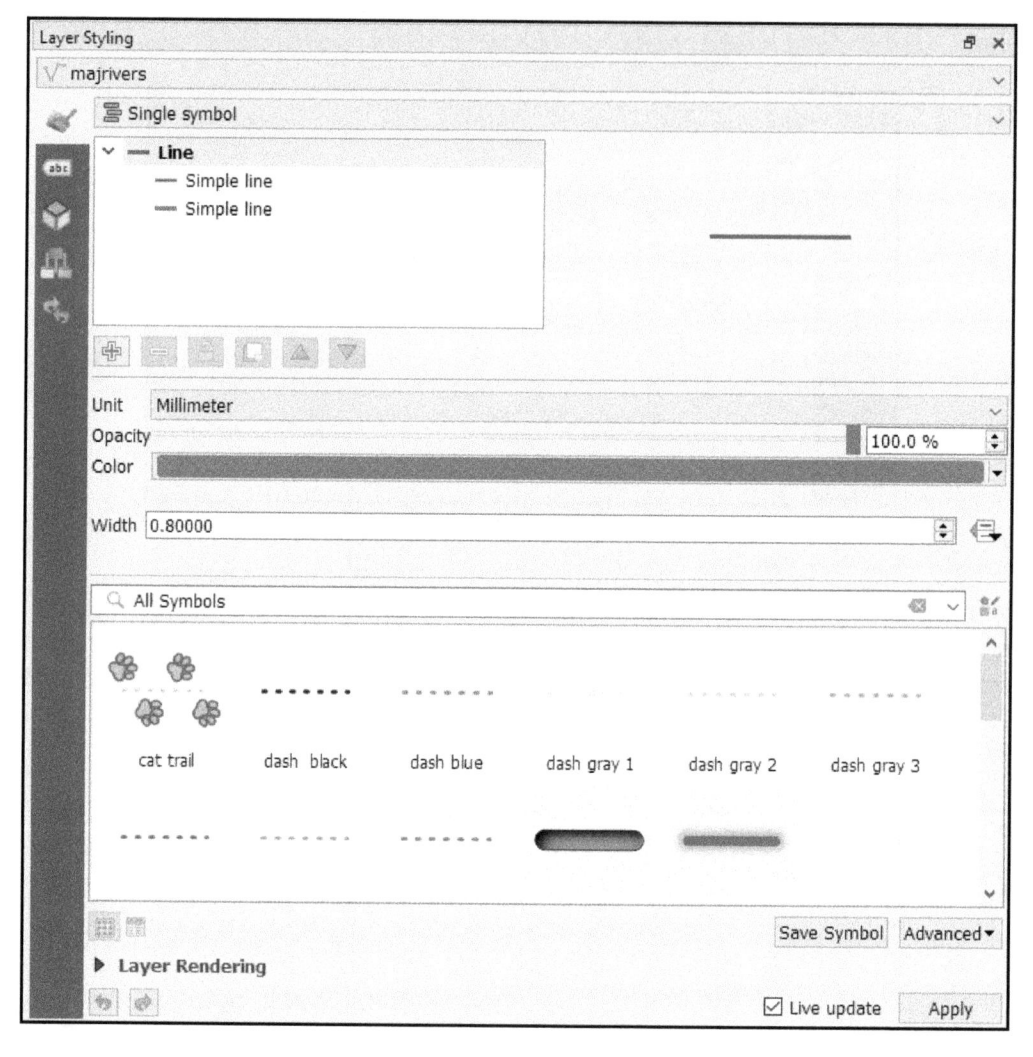

Adjusting the layer styling for a line dataset

[106]

This will bring up a new window. Now select Enable symbol levels and your river layer should change. Your map should now look similar to the following screenshot:

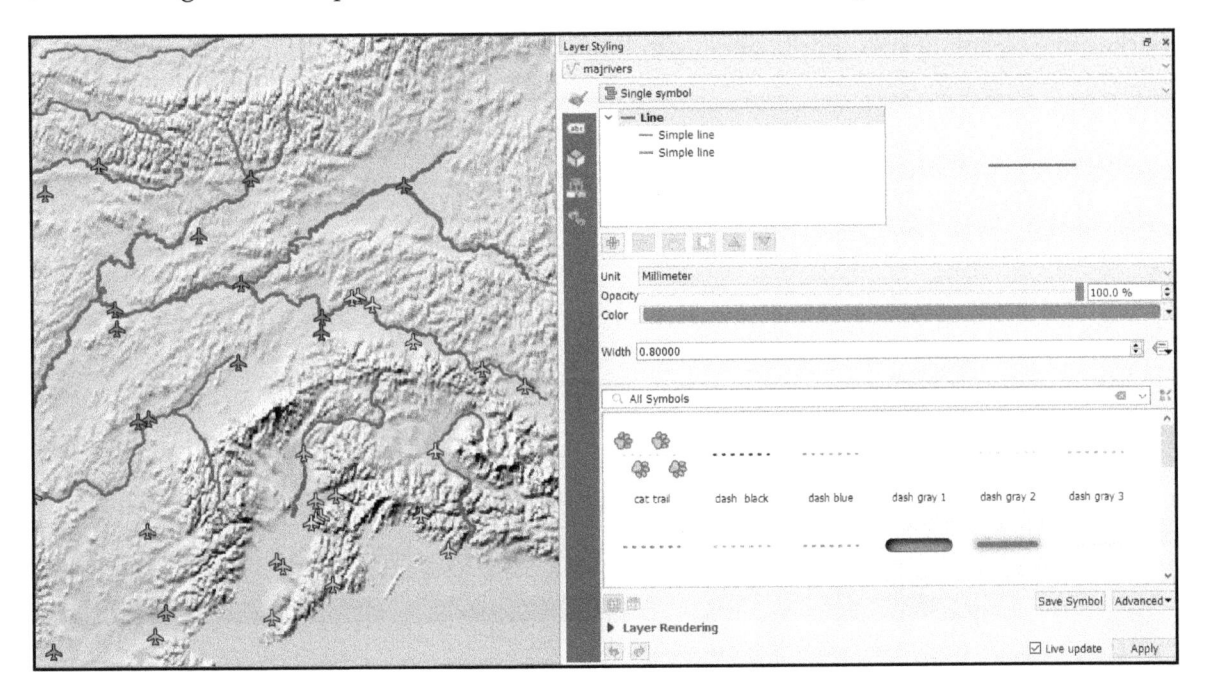

Adjusting the symbol levels

> **TIP**: Whenever we create a symbol that we might want to reuse in other maps, we can save it by clicking on the **Save** button under the symbol preview area. We can assign a name to the new symbol, and after we save it, it will be added to the saved symbols preview area on the right-hand side.

Before we move on to styling polygons, let's take a look at the other symbol layer types for lines, which include the following:

- **Simple line**: This is a solid or dashed line.
- **Marker line**: This line is made up of point markers located at line vertices or at regular intervals.
- **Geometry Generator**: This enables us to manipulate geometries and even create completely new geometries using the built-in expression engine.

Visualizing Data

A common use case for Marker-line symbol layers are train-track symbols. These often feature repeating perpendicular lines, which are abstract representations of railway sleepers. The following screenshot shows how we can create a style like this by adding a marker line on top of two simple lines with the **Layer Styling** panel:

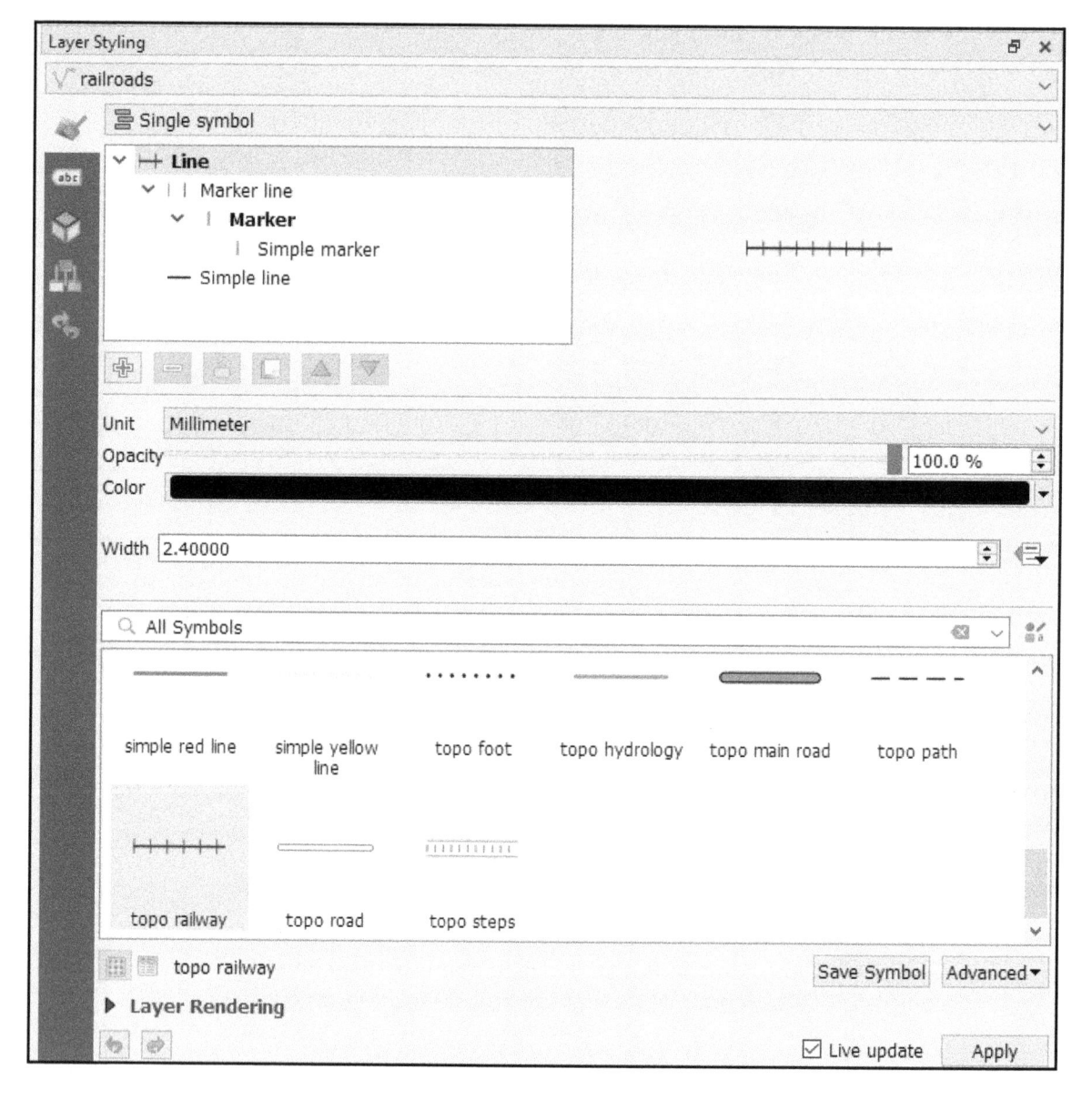

Layer styling for topo railway

Chapter 3

Creating polygon styles – an example of a landmass style

Load `alaska.shp` into QGIS and zoom to the extent of the polygon. Let's use this shapefile to create a boundary for Alaska. Open the **Layer Styling** panel and select Single symbol. Click on simple fill and set the fill color to transparent fill (this is a checkbox selection). Set the stroke width to `0.5` mm and the stroke style to dash line. Your screen should now look similar to the following screenshot:

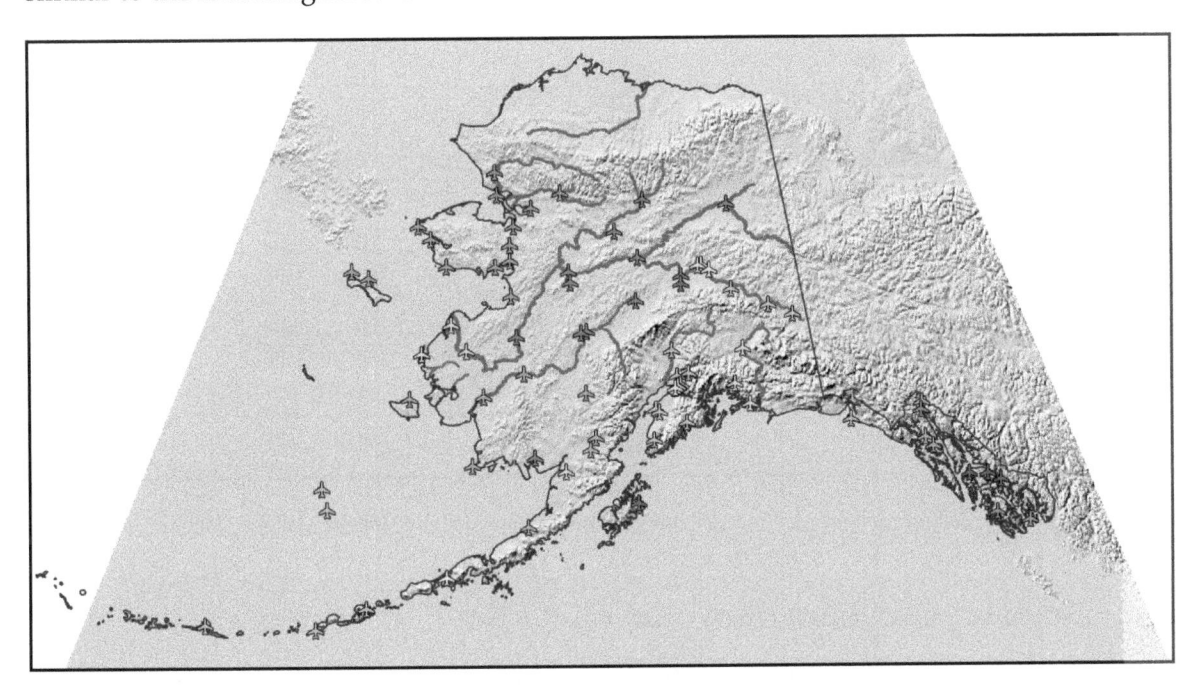

The view of all the styled data

[109]

Visualizing Data

Turn off the `SR_50M_alaska_nad` layer (Hillshade) and add `lakes.shp`, style them with **topo water**, then add in `trees.shp` and style them as **topo forest**. Now your map should look similar to the following screenshot:

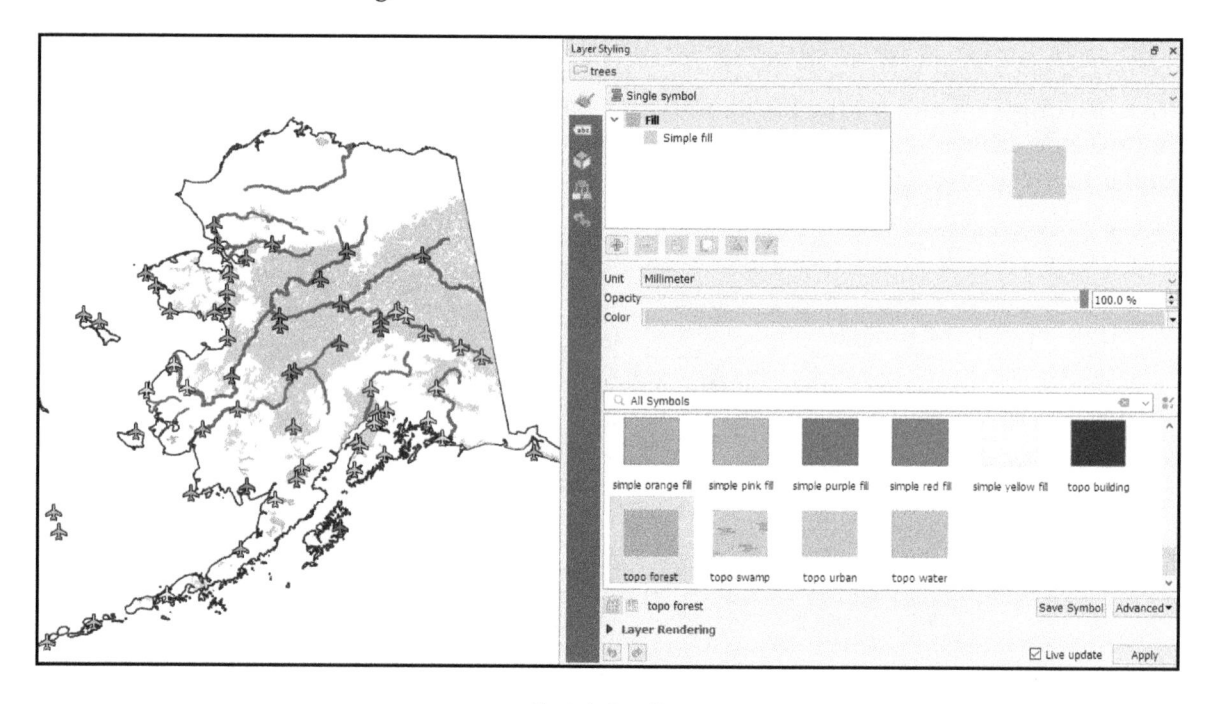

Fine tuning the styling

Now you can see the power of layers and layer control. Keep points at the top and lines next, followed by polygons and Raster datasets.

Finally, let's take a look at the other symbol layer types for polygons:

- **Simple fill**: This defines the fill and outline colors as well as the basic fill styles.
- **Centroid fill**: This allows us to put point markers at the centers of polygons.
- **Line/Point pattern fill**: This supports user-defined line and point patterns with flexible spacing.
- **SVG fill**: This fills the polygon using SVGs.
- **Gradient fill**: This allows us to fill polygons with linear, radial, or conical gradients.
- **Shapeburst fill**: This creates a gradient that starts at the polygon border and flows toward the center.

Chapter 3

- **Outline – Simple line or Marker line**: This makes it possible to outline areas using line styles.
- **Geometry Generator**: This enables us to manipulate geometries and even to create completely new geometries using the built-in expression engine.

Some examples of these are shown in the following screenshot.

The Point pattern fill is useful for showing different vegetation types. In the following example, the fill is a simple fill with a point pattern overlaid. To shortcut to this symbol type, locate the **pattern dot green** symbol in the symbols, as shown in the following screenshot:

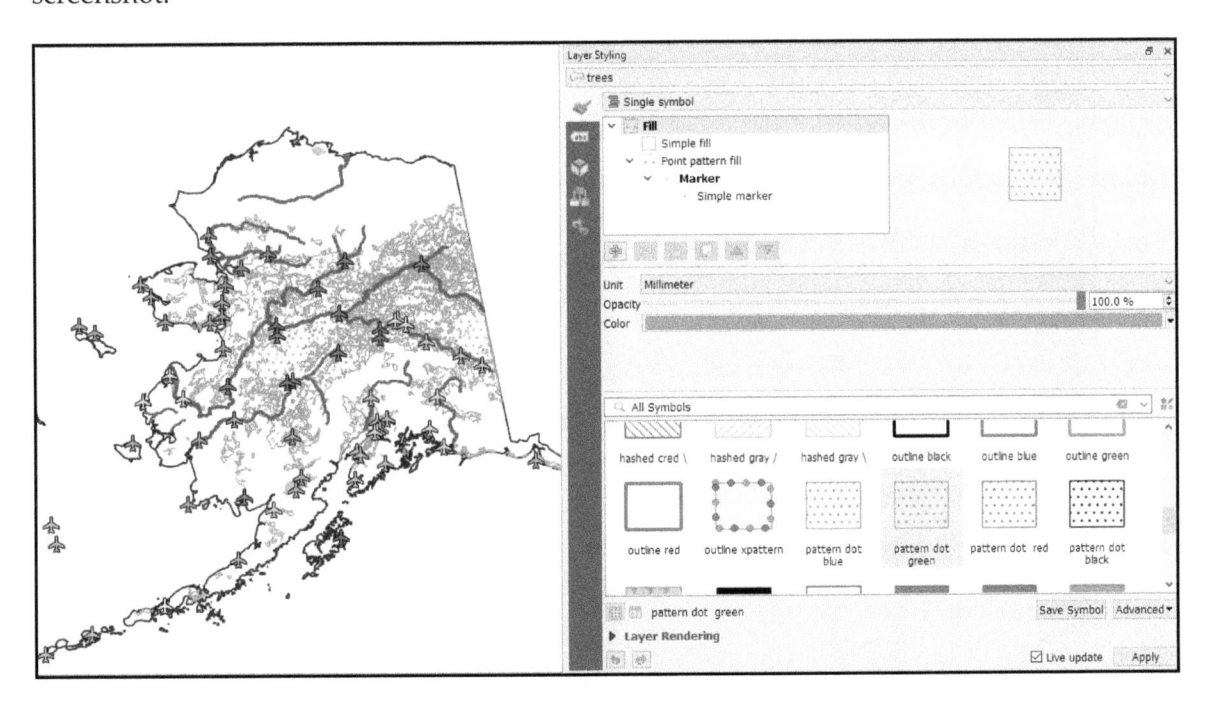

Point pattern styling

[111]

Visualizing Data

A point pattern fill can be customized using any of the marker types. For example, the following screen shows a cross from the icons in the SVG markers used for the pattern fill:

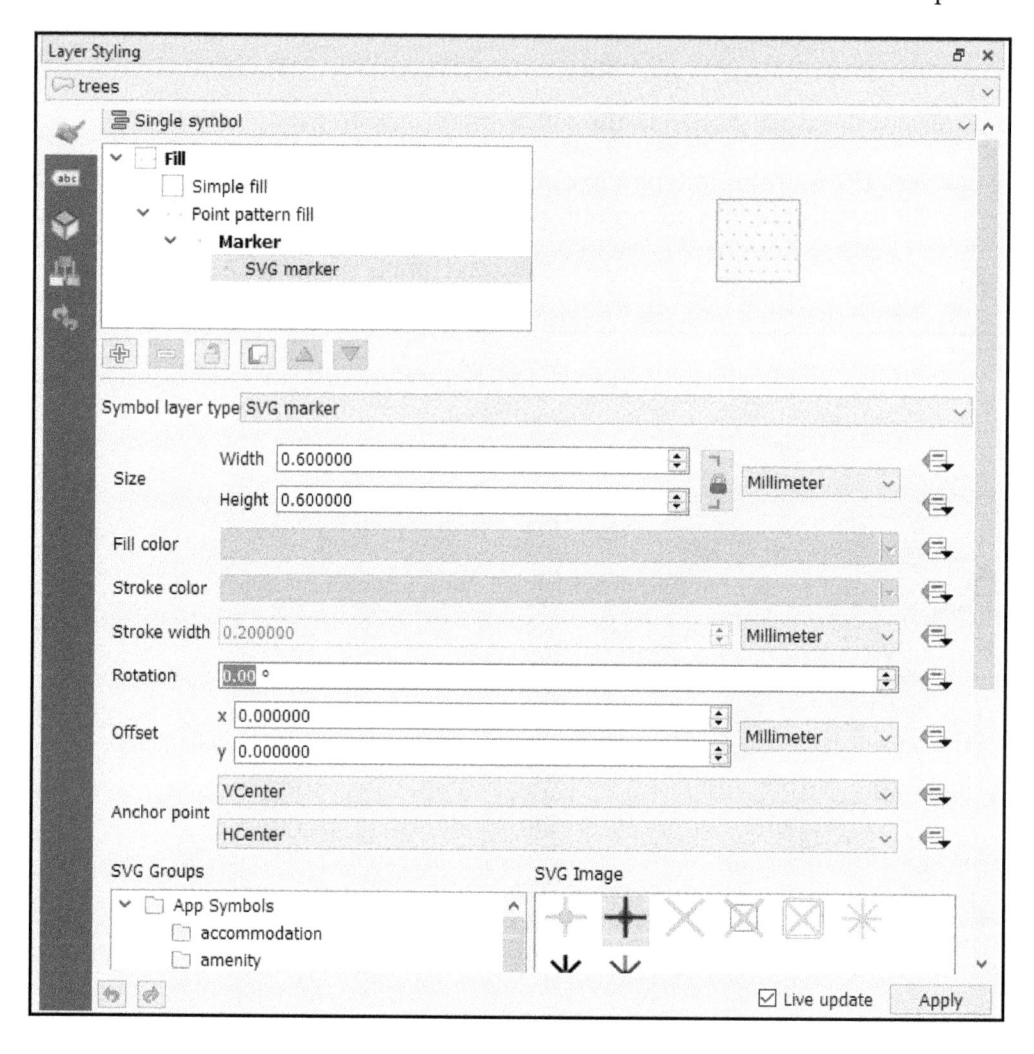

SVG markers for the pattern fill

The Shapeburst fill symbol layer type is good for symbolizing water bodies. It does this by using a gradient fill that flows from the polygon border inward. This option is shown for the lakes layer in the following screenshots:

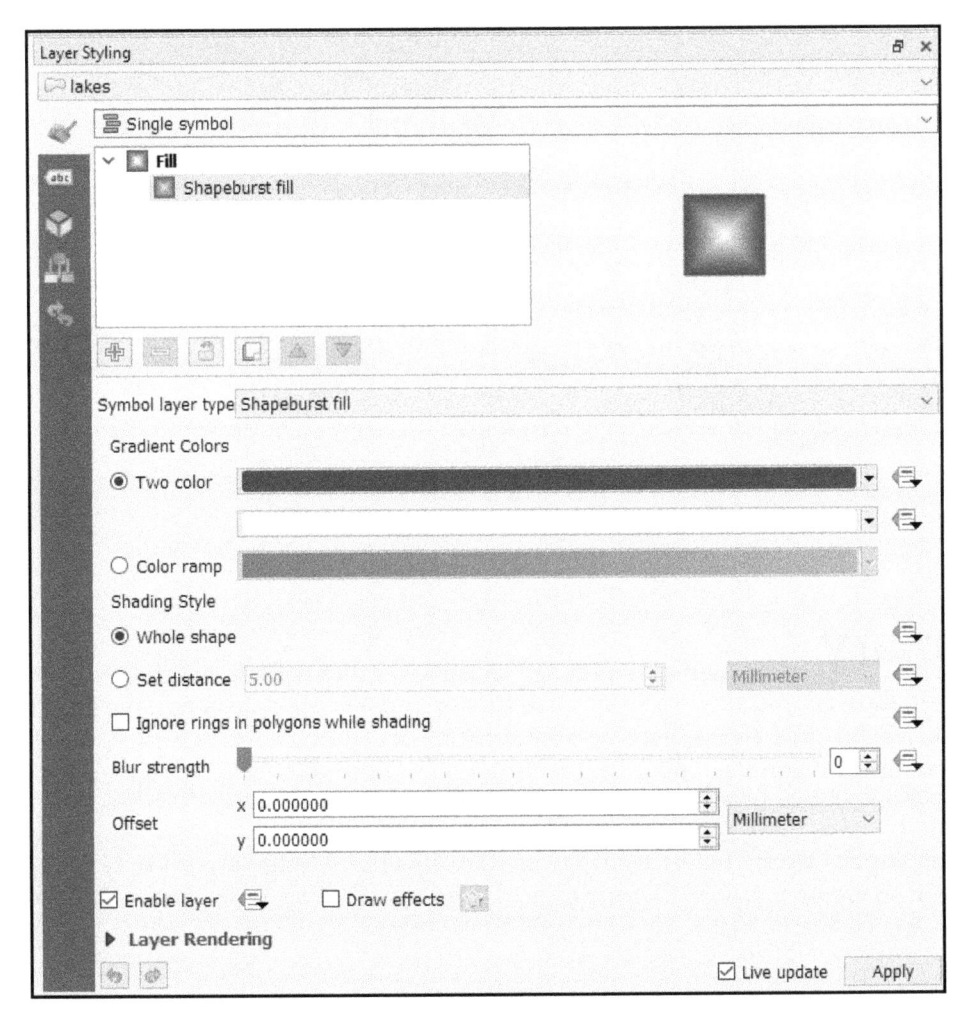

Shapeburst fill symbol layer styling

Visualizing Data

As always, choose the best option to visualize the data that you have, and then save the project. The result of the styling would be as follows:

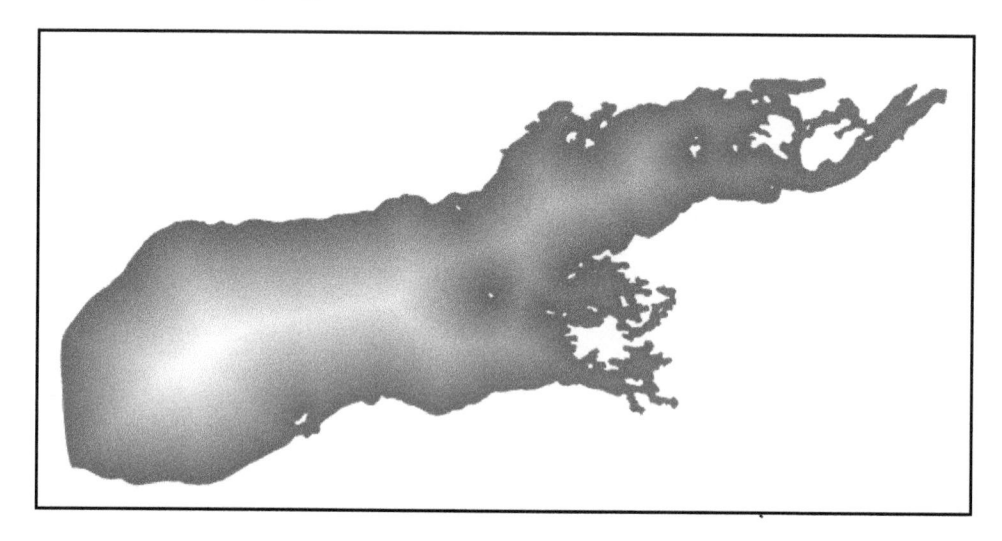

Result of the styling

Summary

This chapter showed you how to symbolize Raster and Vector data. We have progressed from quickly inspecting our data to presenting it in a way that adds meaning. We have also covered a range of examples, including styling GIS data in Alaska. The focus has been on building a series of layers that complement each other.

In the next chapter, we will look at bringing all of this knowledge together by using the Print Layout to create maps from your data.

4
Creating Great Maps

In this chapter, we will cover some of the important features of QGIS that enable us to create great maps. We will also learn how to label features, which can now be done interactively in QGIS 3. QGIS 3 has improved the way maps are created with new print layout tools. We will look at these in detail in the coming sections, before looking at ways of sharing data at the end of the chapter.

Topics covered in this chapter include the following:

- Communicating with data
- Labeling
- Creating maps
- Loading data
- Map outputs

> **TIP**
> QGIS 3 is used on a worldwide basis to produce stunning maps. To get an idea of the maps that QGIS is capable of producing, visit the following link: `https://www.flickr.com/groups/qgis/pool/`.

Communicating with data

Perhaps the most common reason that people use GIS is to create maps. We have already covered the creation of data, as well as the loading and basic styling of vector and raster data in previous chapters. In this section, we are going to be bringing this together to make a map. In the final two chapters of this book, the focus will shift to geoprocessing and some of the more advanced features in QGIS 3, but for now, let's lay the foundations to enable you to create beautiful maps, and where better to begin than with the newly updated labeling tools in QGIS 3?

Labeling

We already have a number of layers in the layer panel, including both Vector and Raster. There are seventy-six airport points, each of which has an attribute called **name**. We will use this to label our data.

The QGIS labeling toolbar is shown in the following screenshot:

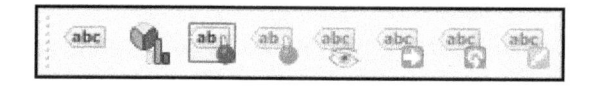

Labeling toolbar

If this is not shown in your QGIS project, navigate to **View** | **Toolbars** | **Label Toolbar**, and click to enable the toolbar. There are eight buttons on this toolbar. In order, these are as follows:

- Layer Labeling: Clicking on this will open the Layer Styling panel and the label tab by default.
- Layer Diagram properties: This is where we can control the input to our labels.
- Highlight pinned labels and diagrams.
- Pin/unpin labels and diagrams.
- Show/hide labels and diagrams.
- Move labels and diagrams.
- Rotate labels and diagrams.
- Change labels, used for label editing.

Chapter 4

We will use these tools to help us label the airport layer. Click on the first button in the toolbar called **layer labeling**. In the **Layer Styling** panel, select **show labels for this layer** and set the label to **Name**. Check the box next to **Draw text buffer**. Your screen should look similar to the following diagram:

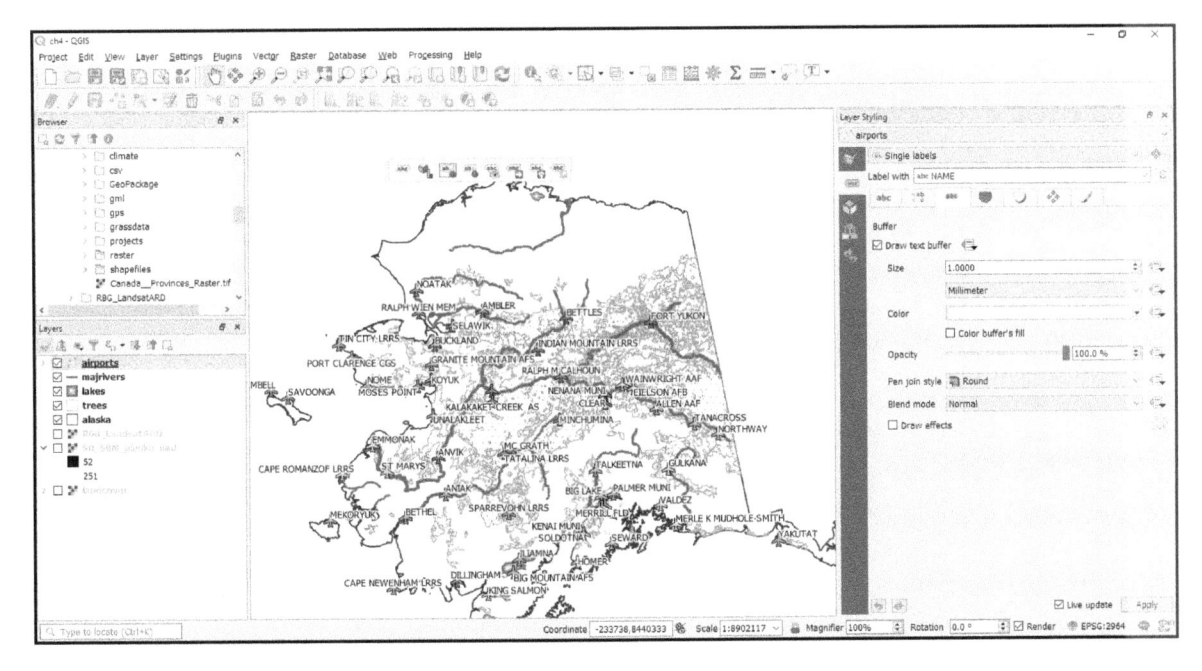

Labeling in the Layer Styling panel

Turn off every layer, apart from the **airports** and **alaska** layers, and navigate to your newly labeled data. Some labels conflict with each other. For example, turn on `majrivers` again and you will see that some of the labels are sitting over the rivers layer. To demonstrate this, **Tatalina LRRS** and **McGrath** airports in the following example are being displayed over the river:

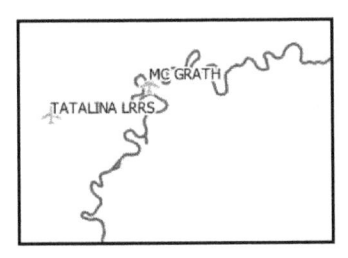

Labels over features

[117]

Creating Great Maps

Within the labels tab in the **Layer Styling** panel, we can set some placement rules with the **Placement** tab. In the following example, I have selected the **Offset from point** radio button and then selected the top-left quadrant to improve the placement:

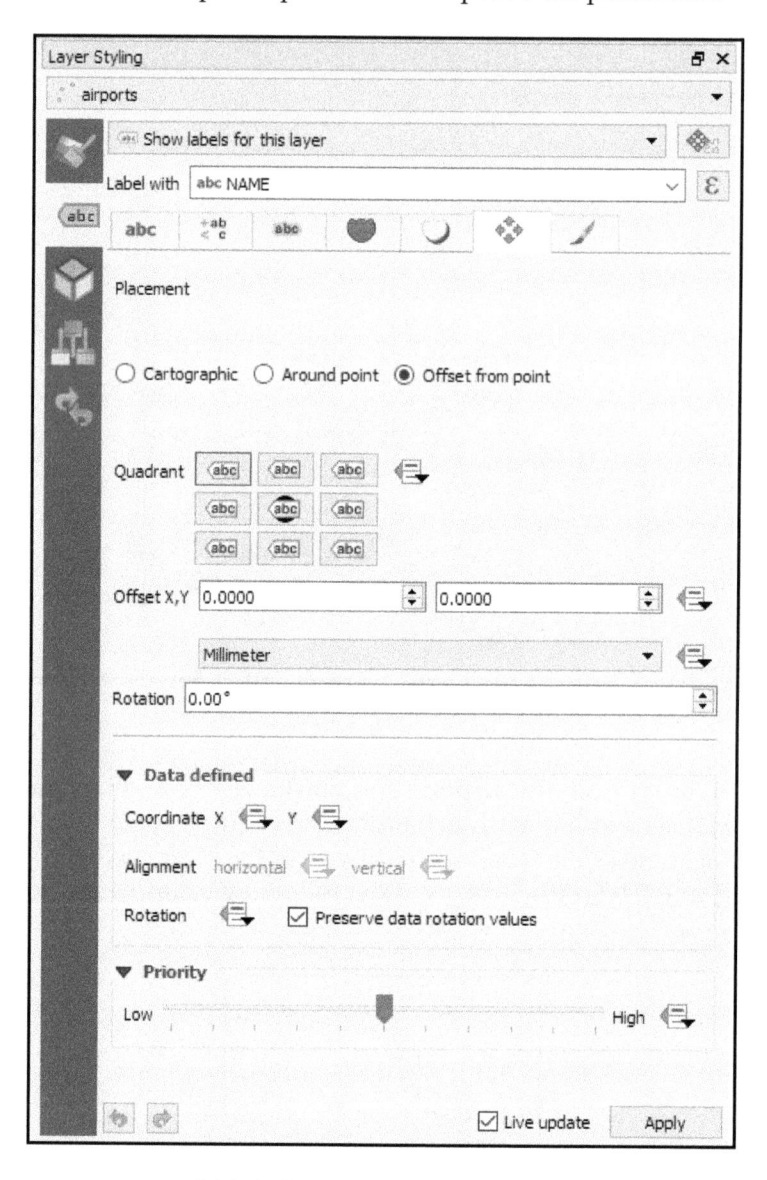

Defining the placement options in the Layer Styling panel

Chapter 4

This does improve the labeling, but it may need some manual adjustments. That is where manual interaction can help.

Interactively editing labels

A new feature in QGIS 3 is the ability to edit the labels interactively within the map using the label toolbar. Click on the move label and diagram button and accept **ID** as the primary key. This is shown in the following screenshot:

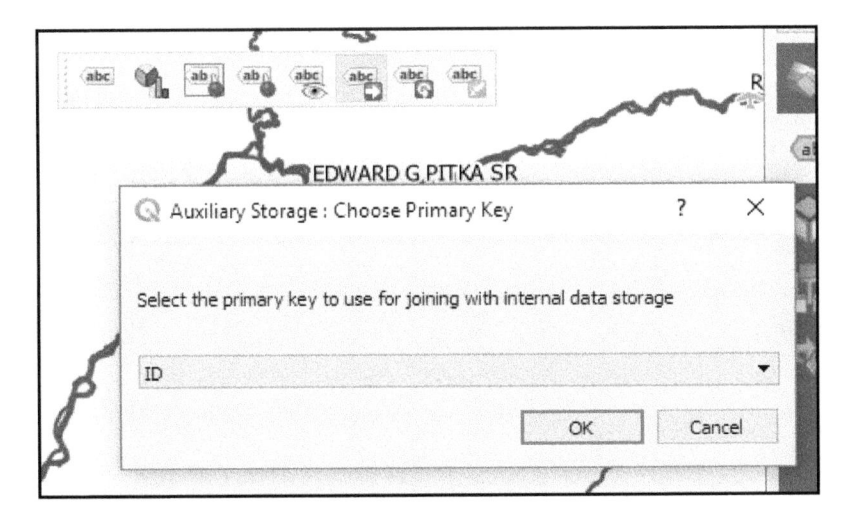

Defining the primary key

Now, click on a label and move it. As you click and drag a label, a placement box appears where the new location of the label will be. This is shown in the following screenshot:

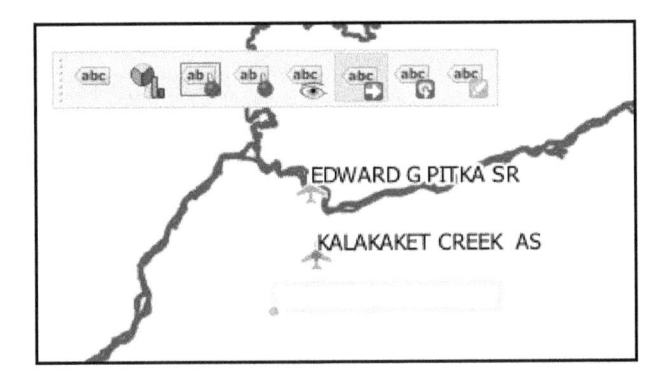

Adjusting the labeling placement

[119]

Creating Great Maps

As you drag the box to the new location, a red dot will appear on the point associated with the label. When you are happy with the new location, release the mouse-click. The label will be moved to the new location, as shown in the following screenshot:

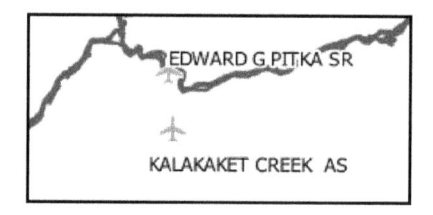

New label location

It is also possible to alter each label's properties. Click on the last button on the labeling toolbar and select the label you wish to edit. The **Label Properties** window will appear as follows:

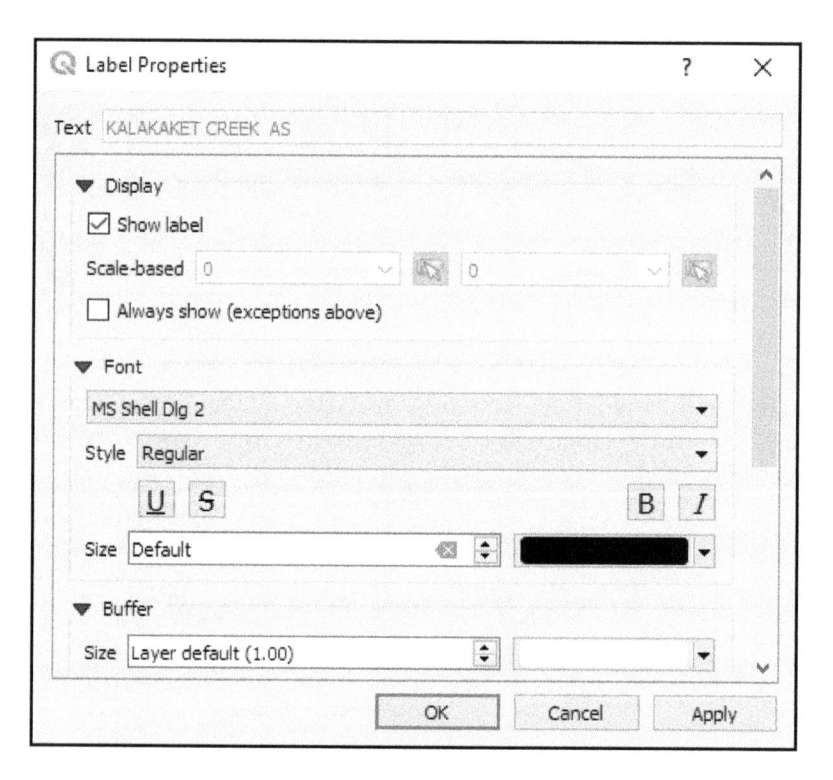

Label Properties

[120]

Change the label color to red, set it to bold, and click **OK**. This will just change the selected label. It should now look similar to the following screenshot:

Updated labels

Finally, in this section on interactive labels, click on the rotate button and rotate the label to show it so that it does not cross the river. This is shown in the following screenshot:

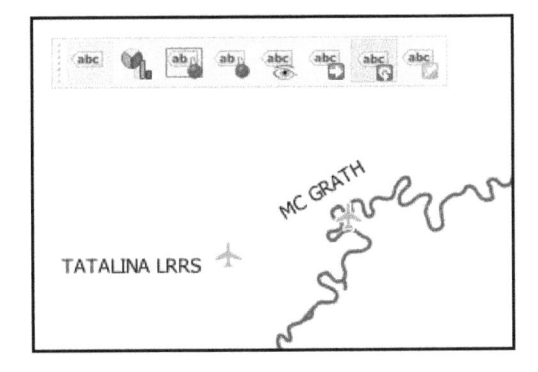

Rotating the labels

These may not be the optimum label placements, but they are fully customizable by the user, providing fast feedback.

Displaying more information using labels

It is possible to build expressions using labels. Using expressions (the button that is right beside the attribute drop-down list and looks like an E), we can format the label text. For example, the NAME field in our sample `airports.shp` file contains text in uppercase. To display the airport names in mixed case instead, we can set the `title(NAME)` expression, which will reformat the name text in the title case. We can also use multiple fields to create a label, for example, by combining the name and elevation in brackets using the concatenation operator (||), as follows:

```
title(NAME) || ' (' || "ELEV" || ')'
```

Creating Great Maps

Note the use of simple quotation marks around text such as ' (', and double quotation marks around field names, such as **"ELEV"**. The dialog will be the same as that shown in the following screenshot:

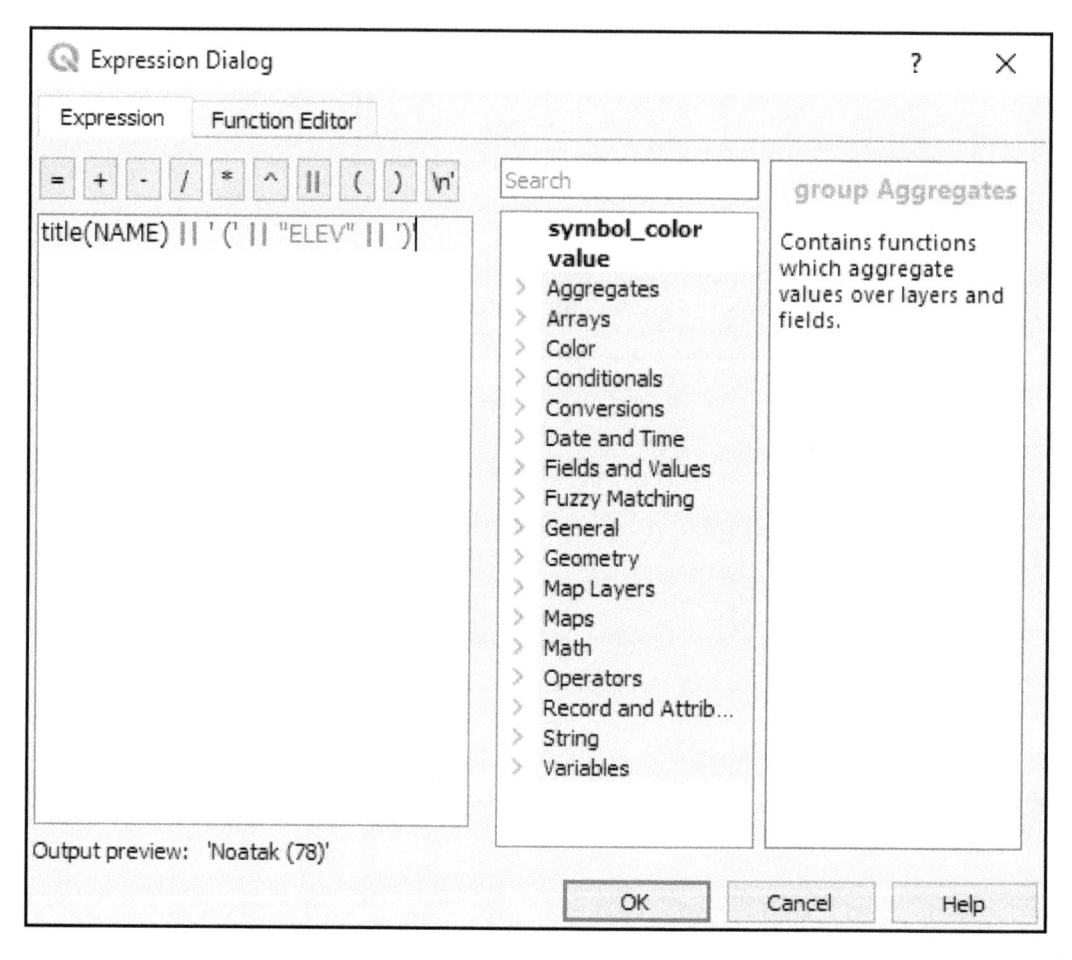

Expression Dialog window

Chapter 4

In the bottom left of the expression window, the output will be previewed. This is common throughout any expressions built in QGIS. The results map window will now look similar to the following screenshot:

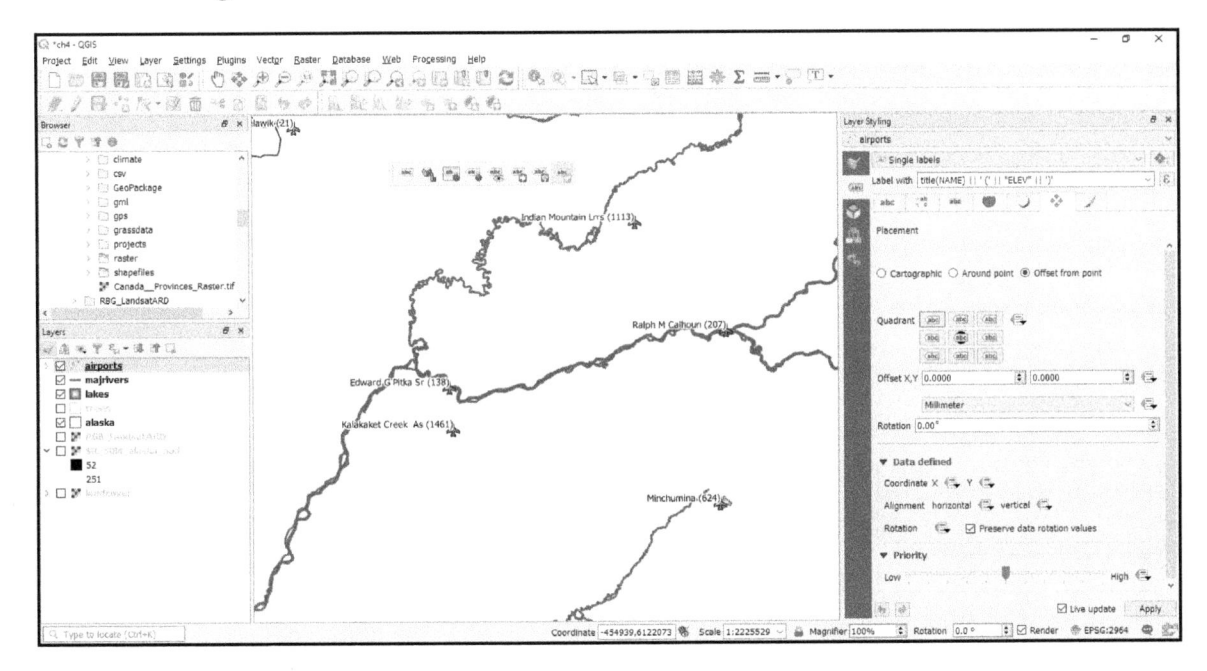

Labeling in the map window after setting an expression

Creating Great Maps

Similar to the styling that we saw in Chapter 3, *Visualizing Data*, the possibilities are endless when it comes to labeling. For a final example, I have reduced the font size to 8 mm and, on the background tab, I have selected a background to be drawn. This often proves to be an effective way of displaying a large number of labels. This is especially true when manually editing labels is time-consuming and it is difficult to find a placement rule that fits all. My final point labeled map window ends up looking like the following diagram:

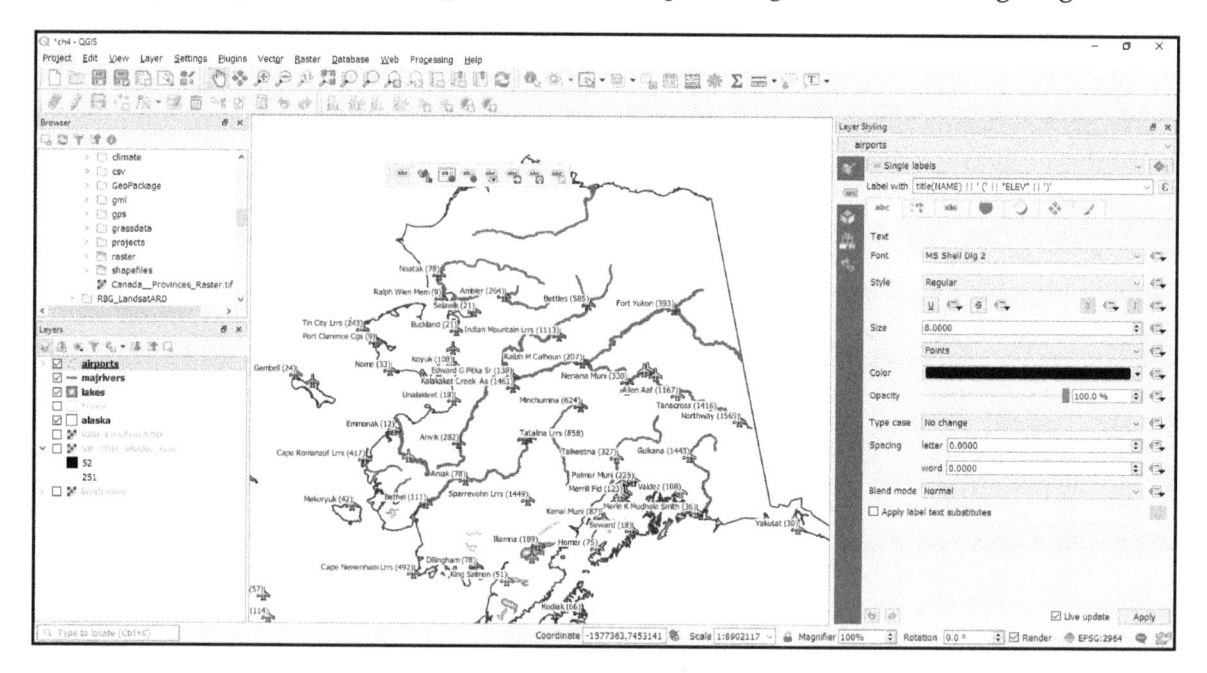

Final data after adding a buffer around the labels

Line labels

For line layers, we can choose from the following placement options:

- Parallel for straight labels that are rotated according to the line orientation
- Curved for labels that follow the shape of the line
- Horizontal for labels that keep a horizontal orientation, regardless of the line orientation

For further fine-tuning, we can define whether the label should be placed above the line, on the line, or below the line, and how far above or below it should be placed using label distance. We can also utilize a setting shown in the following in the rendering tab called **Merge connected lines to avoid duplicate labels**. This does a reasonable job of reducing the labels on `majrivers.shp`, but it is still very noisy, as shown in the following screenshot:

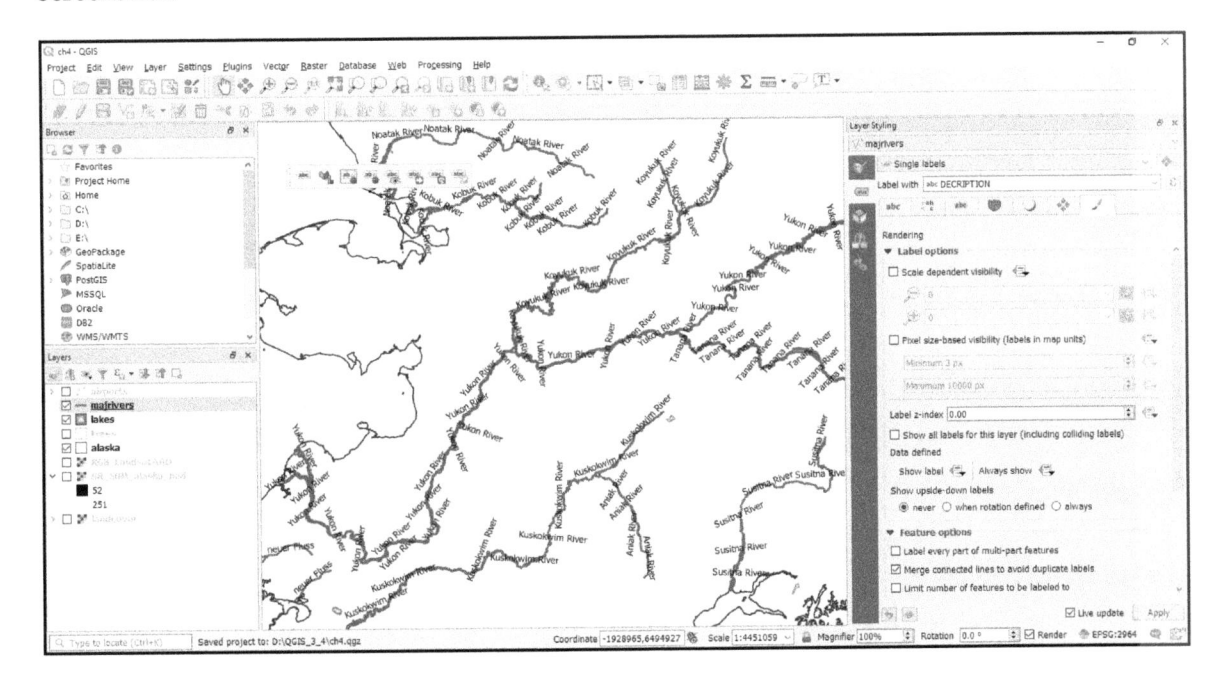

Labeling lines

Creating Great Maps

Ultimately, with this layer, which has five three-hundred and forty-five records in the attribute table, the best option is to dissolve the shapefile based on the description field. We do this to reduce each river to a single record and therefore a single label. This is a useful geoprocessing task and we will cover these more in the next chapter. Click **Processing | Toolbox** to bring up the processing tools. In the search bar, type `dissolve` and double-click on the dissolve process. In the **Unique ID** fields, select **DESCRIPTION** to dissolve based on the name of the river. After doing this, fill in the parameters shown in the following screenshot:

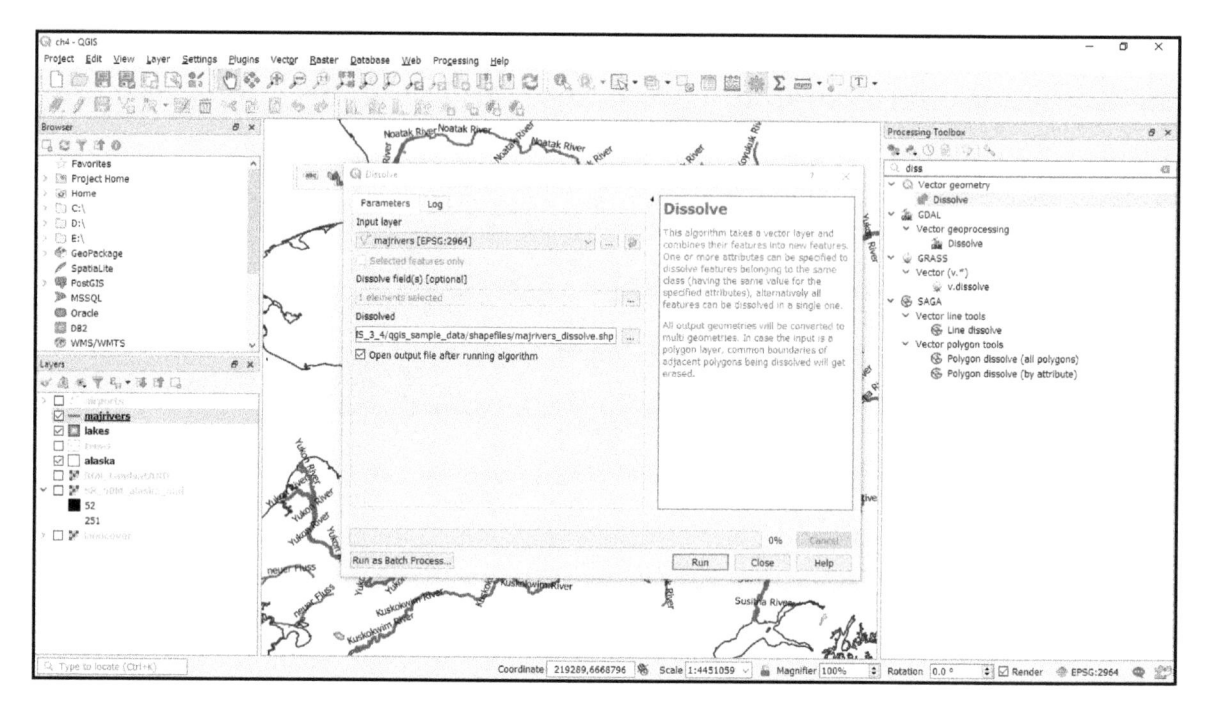

Using dissolve to make the labeling of the lines easier

Click on the **Run** button. Once complete, the newly created shapefile will appear in the map. It should now only have 12 features, and therefore only 12 labels to display.

Right-click on the **majrivers** layer, select **Style | Copy Style | All Style Categories,** and turn the layer off. Now, on the newly created dissolve layer, right-click and select **Style | Paste Style | All Style Categories** to take the layer styling across. Finally, click on the label toolbar's **label layering** button, turn labeling on for this layer, and select **Description** as the labeling field.

Use the same approach as used previously for labeling points. The following is a screenshot of the labels:

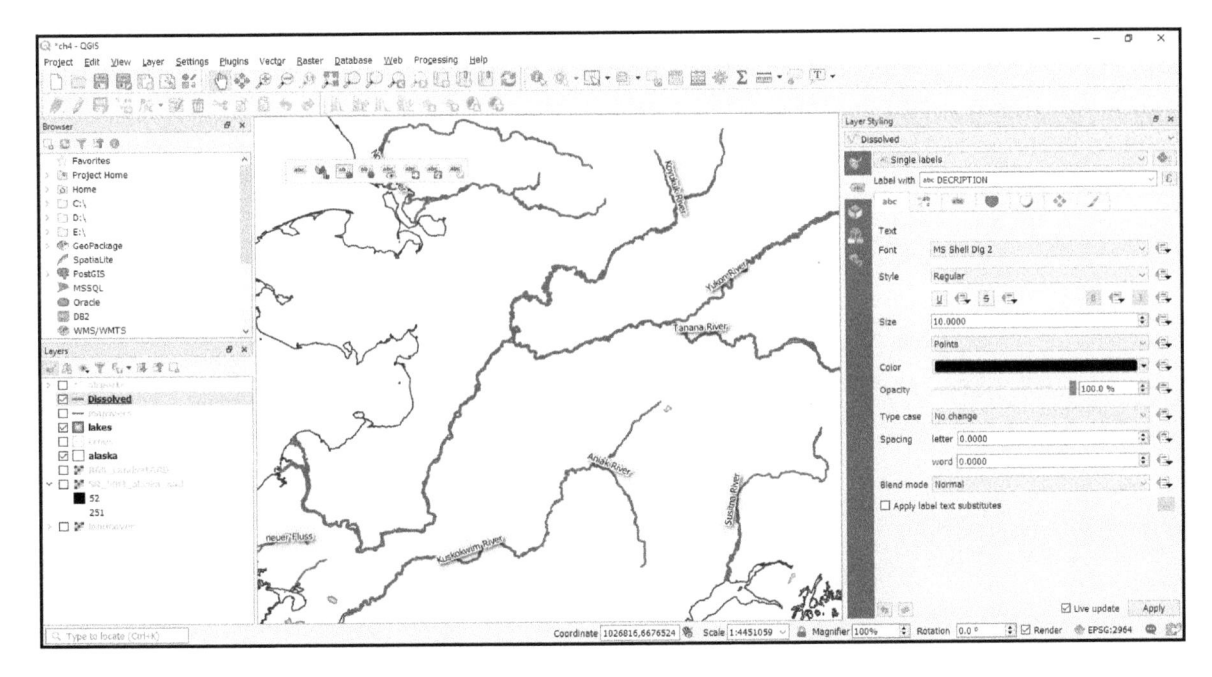

Post dissolve function labeling the lines

> **TIP**
> On a country scale, for the labels to follow the curve of the river better, it might be necessary to generalize the line to remove the nodes. Search for `v.generalise` in the **Processing Toolbox**. The **Processing Toolbox** is always worth exploring. Make adjustments to your layer based on the scale in which you wish to present your data.

Polygon labels

For polygon layers, the placement options are as follows:

- Offset from centroid uses the polygon centroid as an anchor and works like offset from point-for-point layers.
- Around centroid works in a manner similar to around point.
- Horizontal places a horizontal label somewhere inside the polygon, independent of the centroid.

[127]

Creating Great Maps

- Free fits a freely rotated label inside the polygon.
- Using perimeter places the label on the polygon's outline.

The following screenshot shows the **lakes** labels (`lakes.shp`) using the wrapping on the character as an empty space character (click and press the spacebar once), as well as center alignment, and, from the Placement tab, select positioning using the **Free** option. I have added a buffer to the label as well. This is shown in the following screenshot:

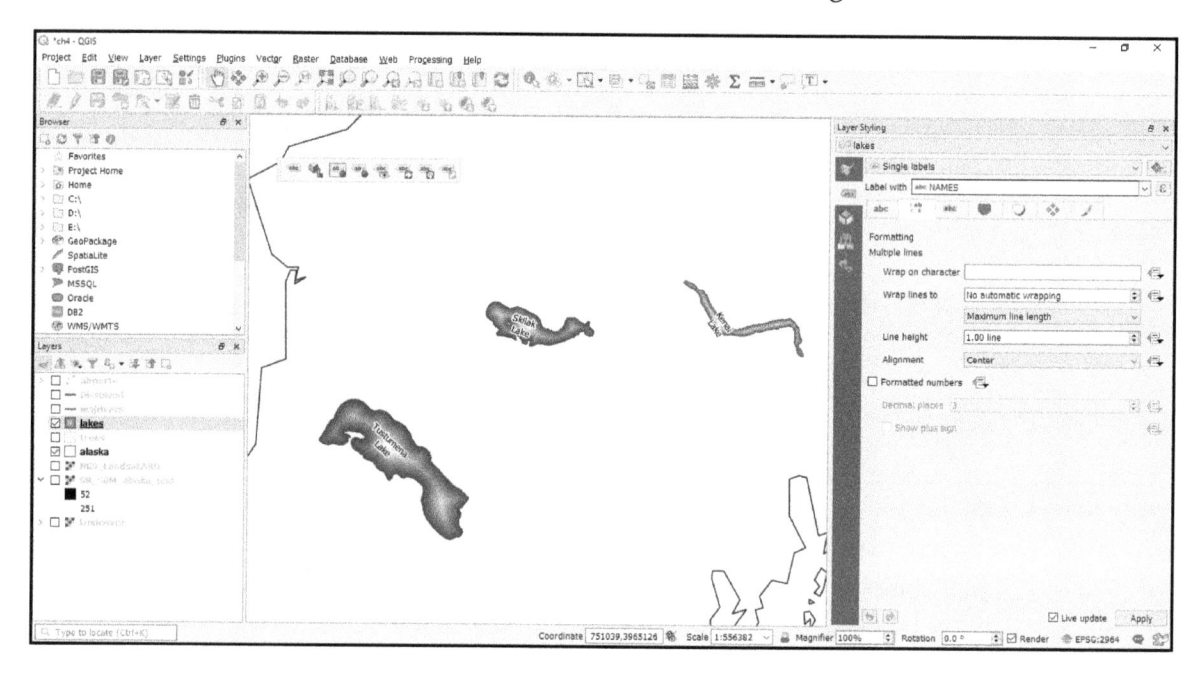

Polygon labels

[128]

Creating a map

So, we have loaded, styled, and labeled our data with the help of the Processing Toolbox. Now, it is finally time to make a map.

To begin, turn on the following layers:

- Dissolved
- Lakes
- Trees
- Alaska
- SR_50m_alsaka_nad

Right-click on **Dissolved** and rename it to **Major_Rivers**, then right-click on **SR_50m_alaska_nad** and rename it to **Hillshade**. Click on **Project | New Print Layout** (or click the corresponding button on the **Project** Toolbar). In the **Layer Styling** panel, change the **symbology** to **renderer** to **Single Band Psuedo Color** and select **Viridis** as the color ramp.

We are now ready to create a map. In the **Create print layout Title** dialog box give your new, empty map a title, and click **OK**. This is demonstrated as follows:

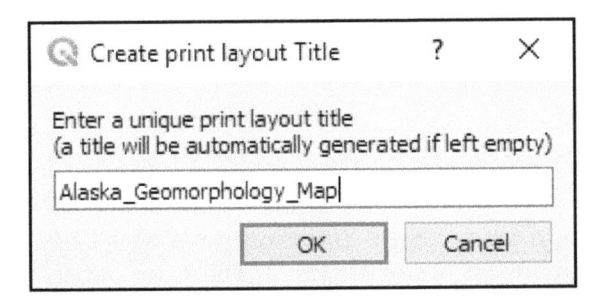

Creating a print layout Title

Creating Great Maps

You will now have an empty canvas on which we will build our first map. It will look like this:

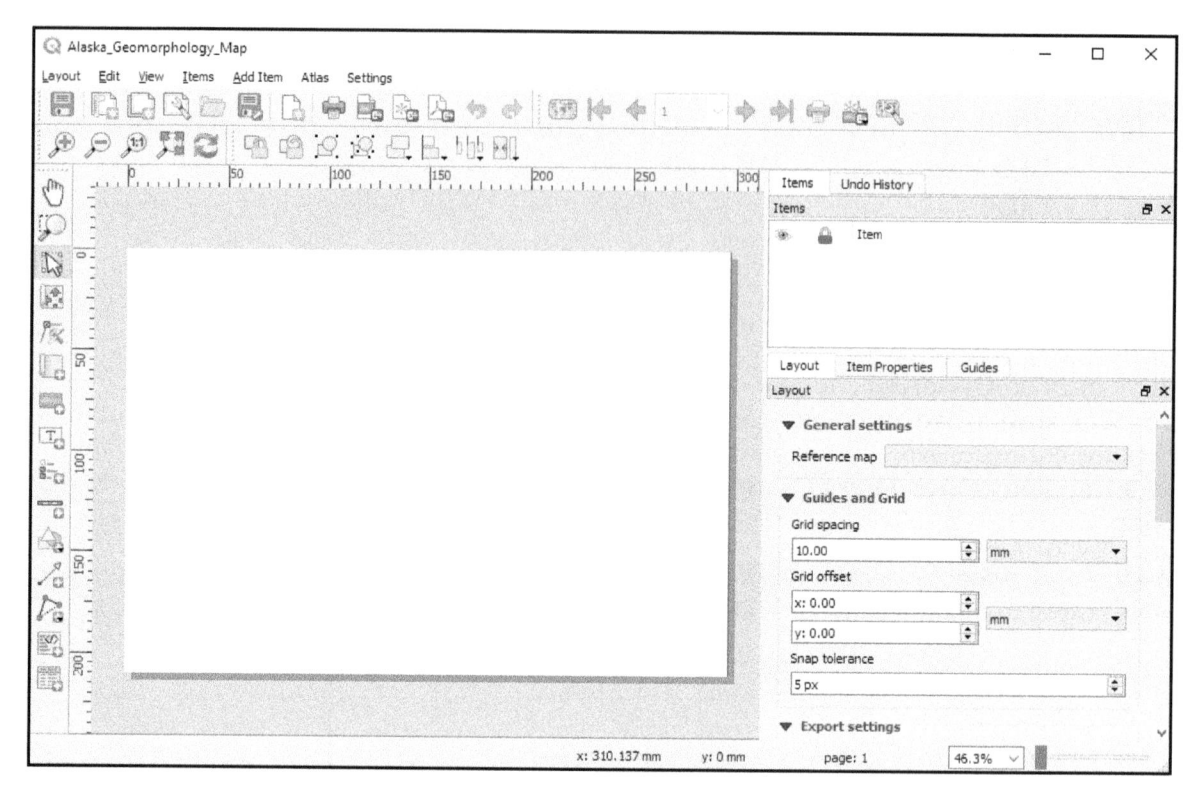

Starting with a blank map

There are many buttons and menus here. You can probably already tell that when creating maps, you can spend many hours adjusting them. There are panels for configuring layout, Item properties, and Atlas generation, as well as a command history panel for quick undo and redo actions. There are also toolbars designed to manage, save, and export layouts, navigate in the preview area, and add and arrange different layout items.

> **TIP**
> Once you have designed your print map the way you want it, you can save the template to a template .qpt file by going to **Layout | Save as template**. You can also reuse it in other projects by going to **Layout | Add Items** from Template.

Loading data

Now add your map. This is the view of the symbolized data created in the last chapter and the start of this one to the layout canvas. The layout canvas is your empty white page at present. To add a map select **Add Item** | **Add Map**. Then click and drag the mouse to draw on the canvas in the location you want to put your map. This is shown in the following screenshot:

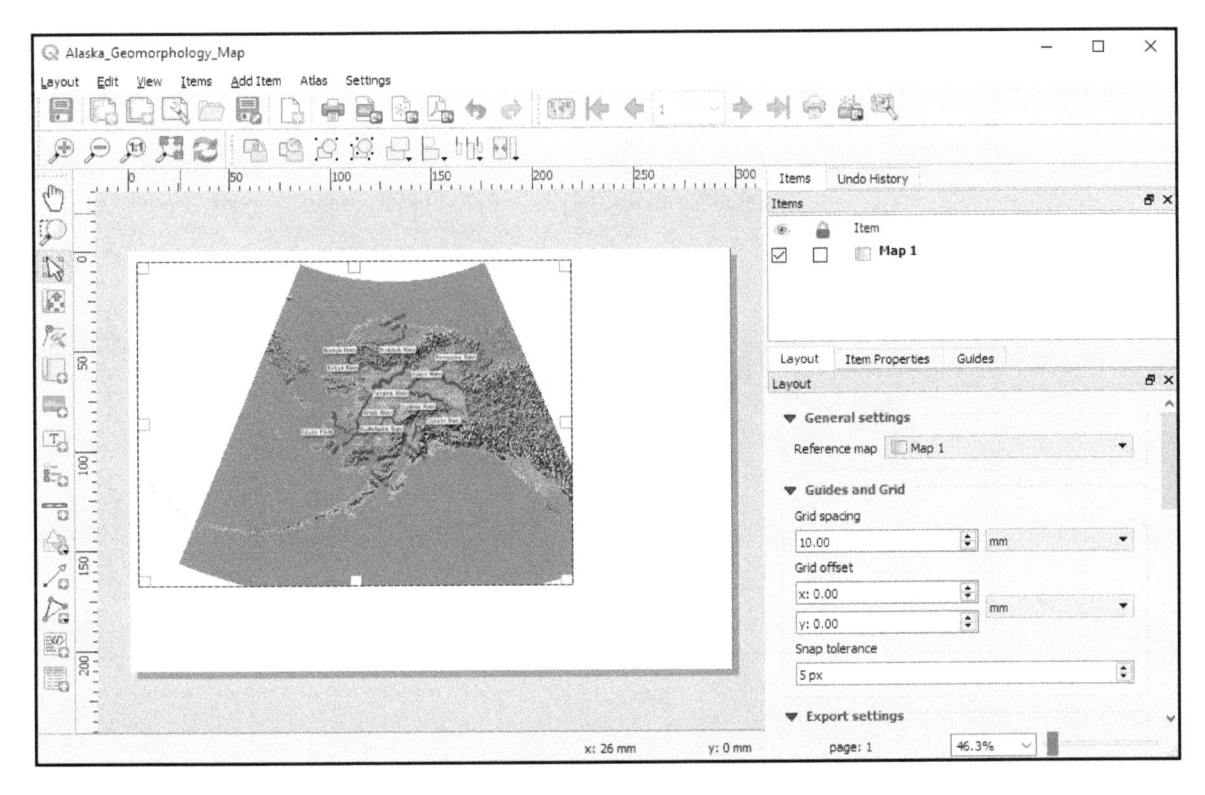

Adding the map to the layout canvas

Creating Great Maps

Use the move item tool to pan and zoom (using the mouse wheel) to adjust the map in your layout window. The Item properties panel's content depends on the currently selected layout item. If a map item is selected, we can adjust the maps **Scale** and **Extents**, as well as the position and size tool of the map item itself. Let's now set the scale to `10,000,000` (with the CRS set to EPSG:2964). The map now looks like the following screenshot:

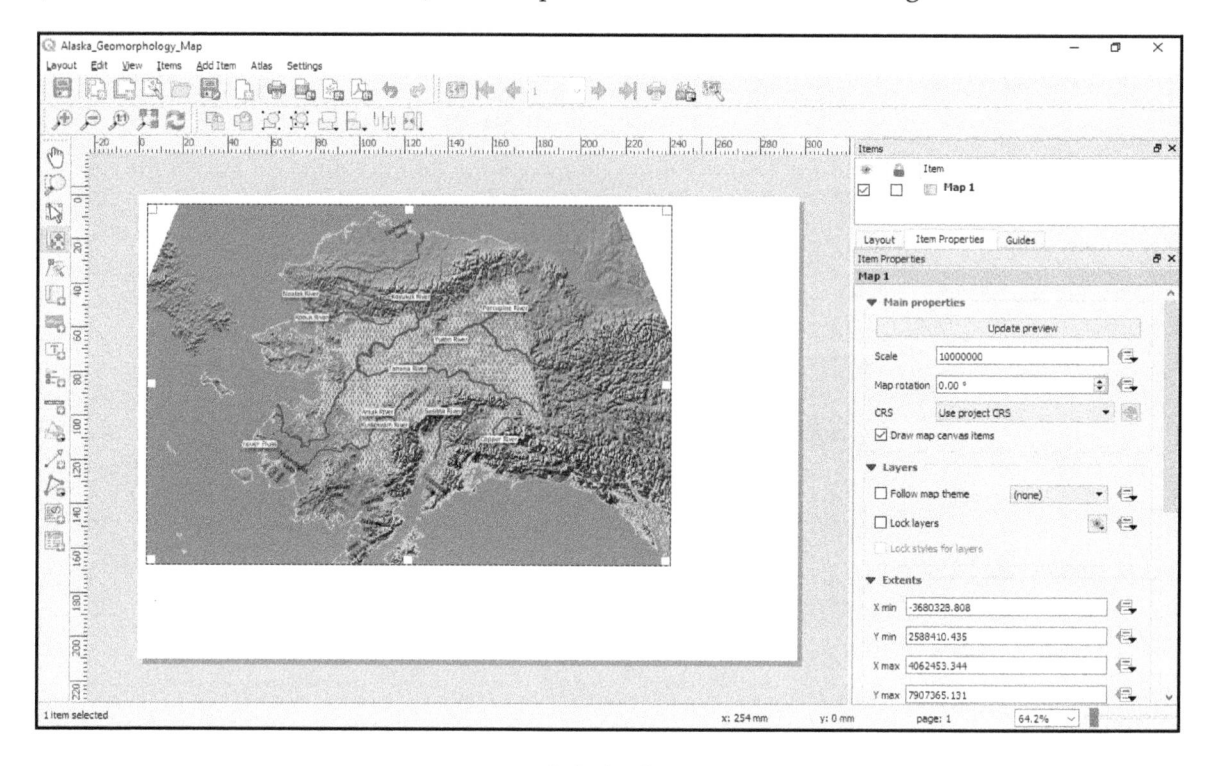

Setting the scale

Adding layout items

We can add a variety of other items to our canvas. Click on **Add Item** | **Add Legend** and draw the area that will contain the legend. Repeat the same steps for adding a scale bar, which we will look at shortly. You might find that your layout is now looking distinctively messy. Uncheck the auto update button in the **Legend Items Properties** window, as shown in the following screenshot:

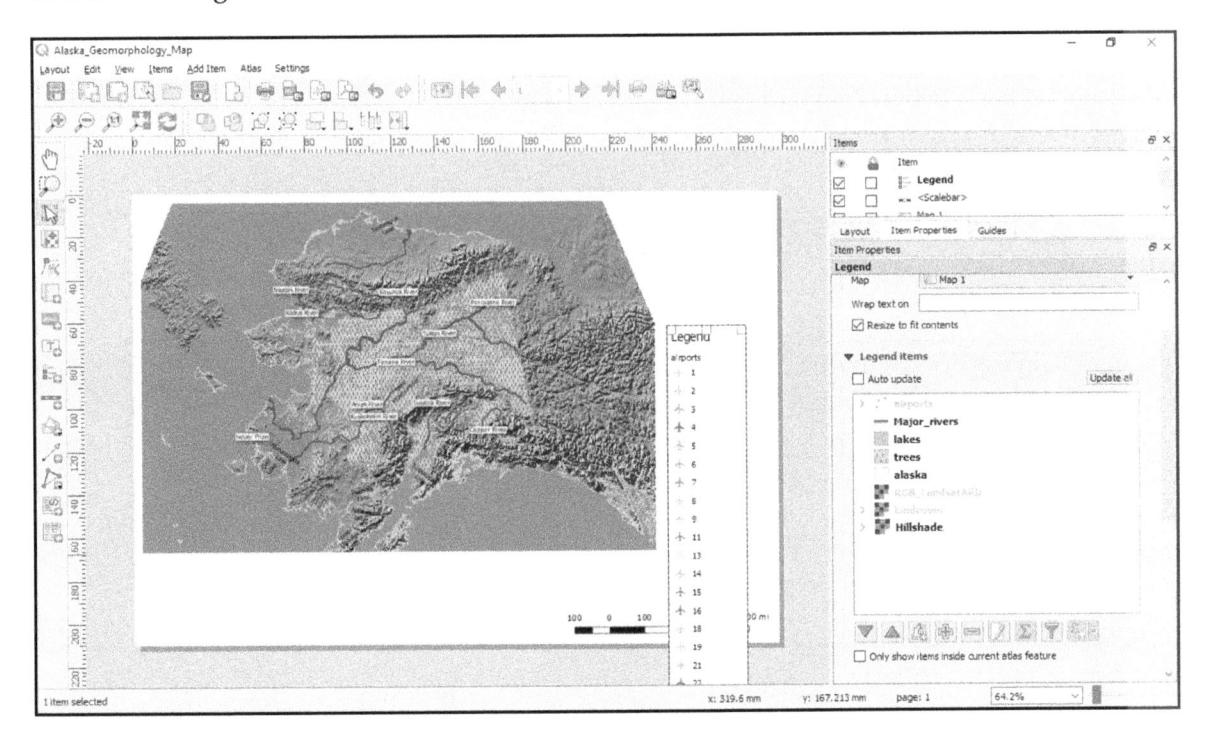

Adding a legend to the layout

By selecting a layer and then clicking on the red minus button, we can remove any layers that are not present in our final map. With this in mind, remove airports, `RGB_LandsatARD`, and `Landcover`. We still have a problem with the legend item for the Hillshade. Head back into the QGIS project and adjust the layer properties for the Hillshade, setting the **Mode** to **Quantile**. This will adjust the colors in the map as well. Back in the layout manager, click on **update all** and the legend will be updated.

In the fonts section, set all fonts to bold, set the background to gray, and update the map preview. Then select the scale bar and change the units to kilometers and the segments to **left 2** and **right 2**.

Creating Great Maps

Add a North arrow by clicking **Add Item** | **Add Picture** and drawing a box to contain your north arrow. Use the item properties to point to the location on your computer where the QGIS SVG files are stored. In this example, I am using
`.../apps/qgis/svg/arrows/NorthArrow_02.svg`, as shown in the following screenshot:

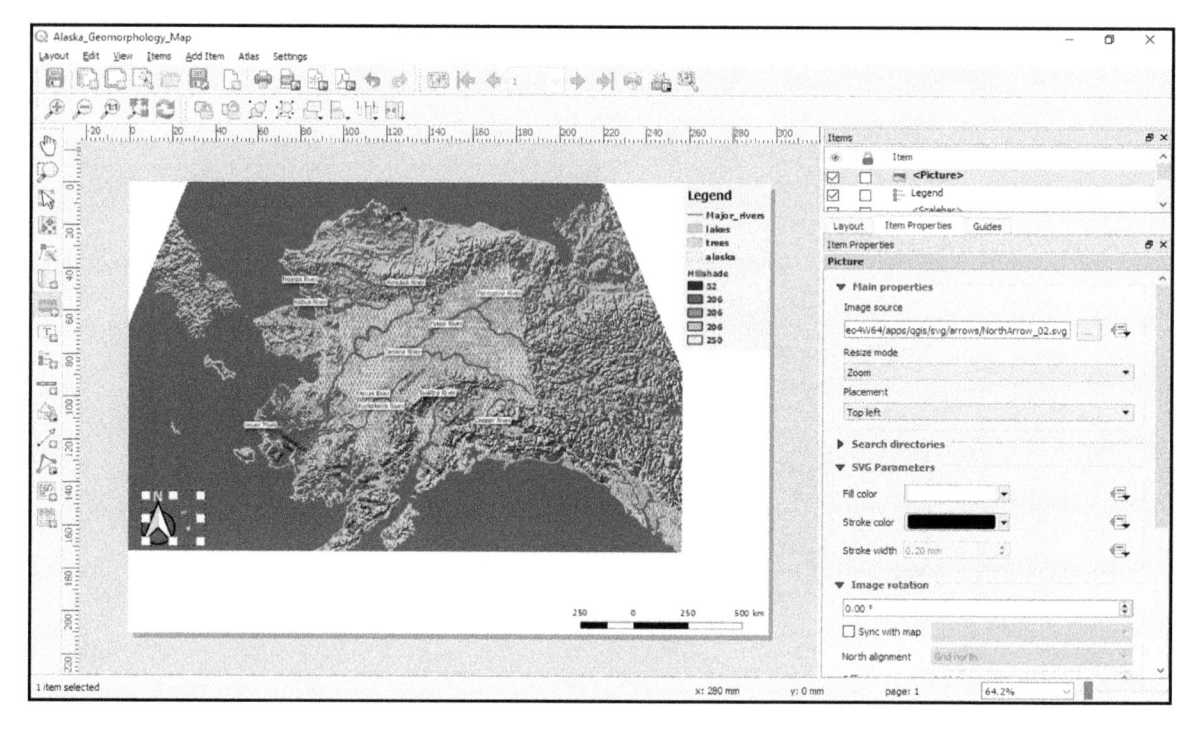

Changing the color scaling, and then adding a north arrow and scale bar

[134]

Add a title (or any text)

To add text to this map, select **Add Item | Add label**. Draw a box in the bottom-left corner and in the Item properties window, copy the following text:

```
<h1>My Geomorphology map of Alaska</h1>
<p>The name <i>"Alaska"</i> means "the mainland".</p>
<ul><li>The 12 main rivers are shown</li><li>Trees dominate central Alaska</li></ul>
<p style="font-size:70%;">[% format_date( $now ,'yyyy-mm-dd')%]</p>
```

Click on **render as HTML**. Your layout composer should now look similar to the following screenshot:

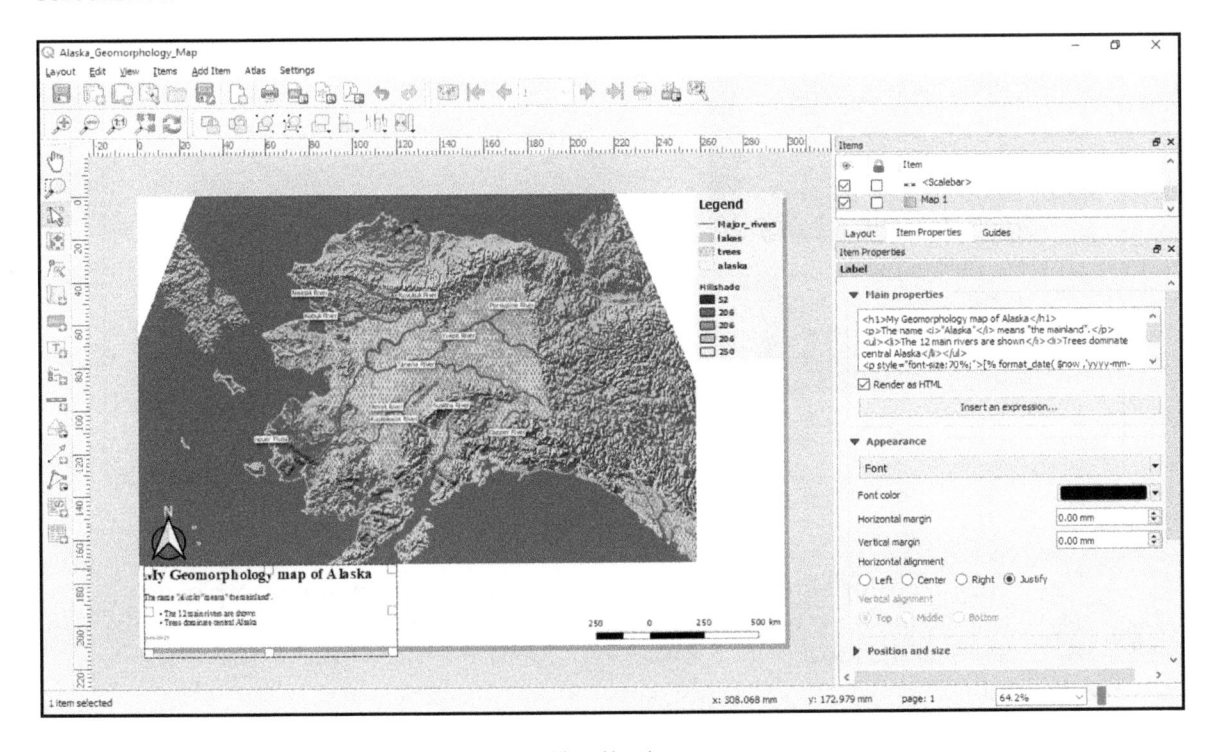

Adding a title to the map

Creating Great Maps

Set the background to the same color as the sea so that we can remove the white triangles in the top-left and top-right corners. To get the exact numbers to input, go back to the properties in the QGIS project window and make a note. The following is a screenshot to save you going back if you are following my map:

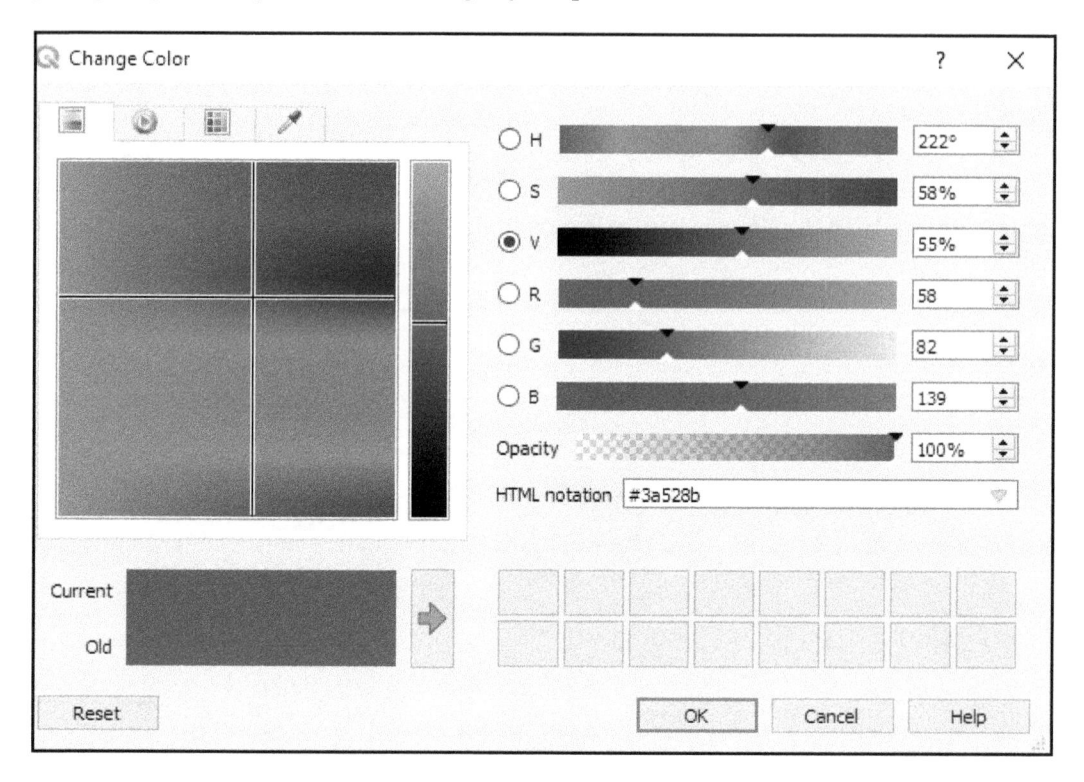

Color picker in QGIS

> **TIP**
> The preceding screenshot is the QGIS color picker. In our example, we were using it for matching colors. However, you can use the various tabs to select the ideal color for your requirements. More information can be found here: http://nyalldawson.net/2014/09/whats-new-in-qgis-2-6-tons-of-color-improvements/.

Your map should now be looking much closer to being complete; now it is a question of styling and personal preference. For example, your company logo could be added in the same way we added a north arrow, or more text could be added.

Chapter 4

In my final map shown here, I have added a rectangle (**Add Item** | **Add Shape** | **Add Rectangle**), colored it in with the same blue and used the items order to drag it to the back. The rectangle is added to ensure that the blue color is the same throughout the layout. It is another tool to help style and create beautiful maps. I have also added the QGIS logo in the bottom-right corner, as shown in the following screenshot:

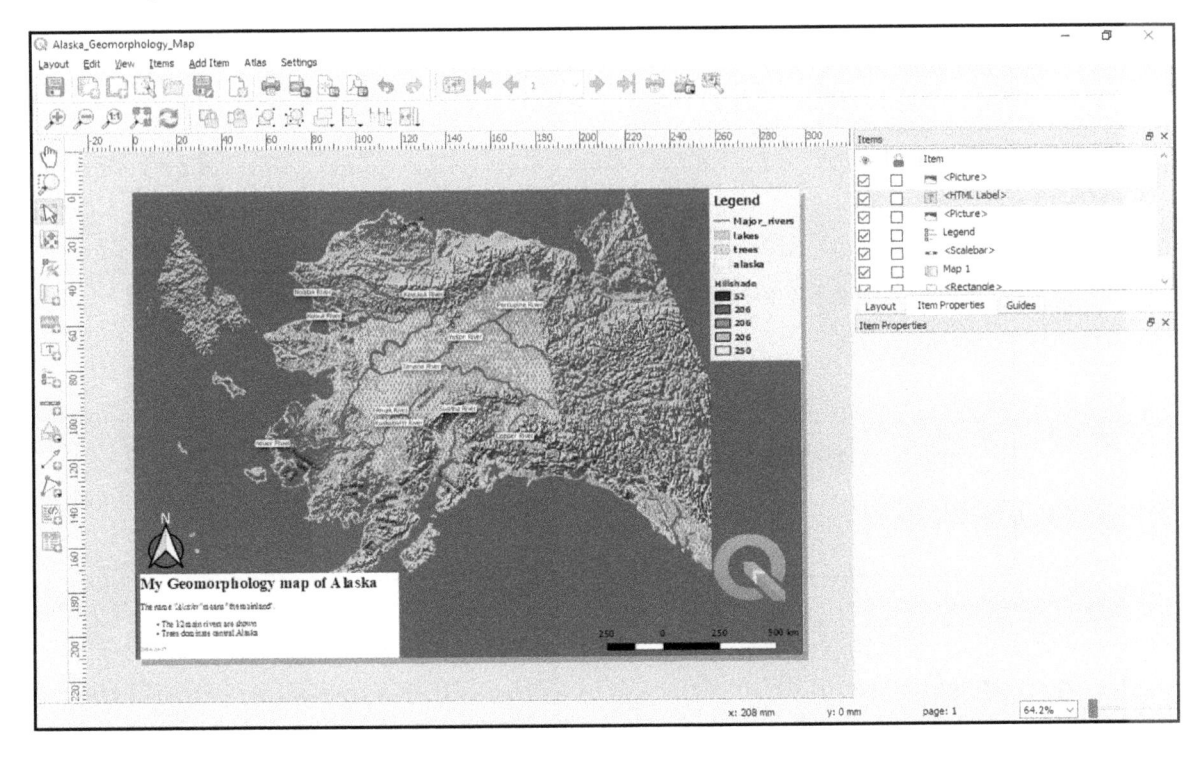

Final map created and styled

Further map creation options

Save your Geomorphology map and close the print layout. Back in the QGIS project, click **Project | Layout Manager,** and a new dialog box will appear as shown in the following screenshot:

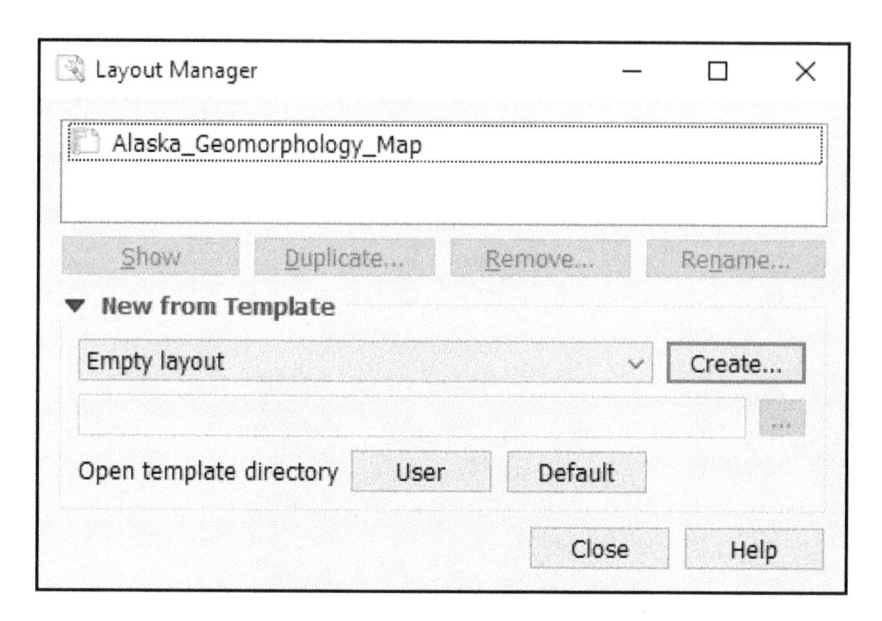

The **Layout Manager**, containing all your layouts and the ability to create a new one

The **Layout Manager** is useful for managing all your layouts in a project. It is very likely that you will have several maps you wish to create, perhaps with different designs or using different templates. The **Layout Manager** helps you to make sense of these.

Click on **Create** to build a new layout. This time we will look at some of the other capabilities in the print layout. I am using this map for further examples. In QGIS, zoom into an area near Skilak lake, turn on the **Airports** layer and the **landcover** layer, and turn off the Hillshade. I have made adjustments to my Airports layer, offsetting the labels to the right of the points, setting the symbols to the default **topo airport** style, and making them (and the label) size 10. Back in **Layout Manager**, I have also added a map item to the canvas.

Adding Grids

With the map item selected, add a grid. Every map item can have one or more grids. Click on the + button in the Grids section to do this. The **Interval** and **Offset** values have to be specified in map units. We can choose between the following grid options:

- A normal solid grid with customizable lines.
- Crosses at specified intervals with customizable styles.
- Customizable markers at specified intervals.
- Frame and annotation will hide the grid while still displaying the frame and coordinate annotations.

For Grid frame, we can select from the following frame styles:

- Zebra, with customizable line and fill colors, as shown in the next screenshot
- Interior ticks, Exterior ticks, or Interior and exterior ticks, for tick marks pointing inside the map, outside it, or in both directions
- Line border for a simple line frame

In the following example, I have made the following selections:

- Grid type = Solid
- Set the X and Y intervals to 10 cm
- Chosen the Zebra frame
- Checked the draw coordinates box (scroll down the dialog box to find this option)

Creating Great Maps

My print layout now looks like this:

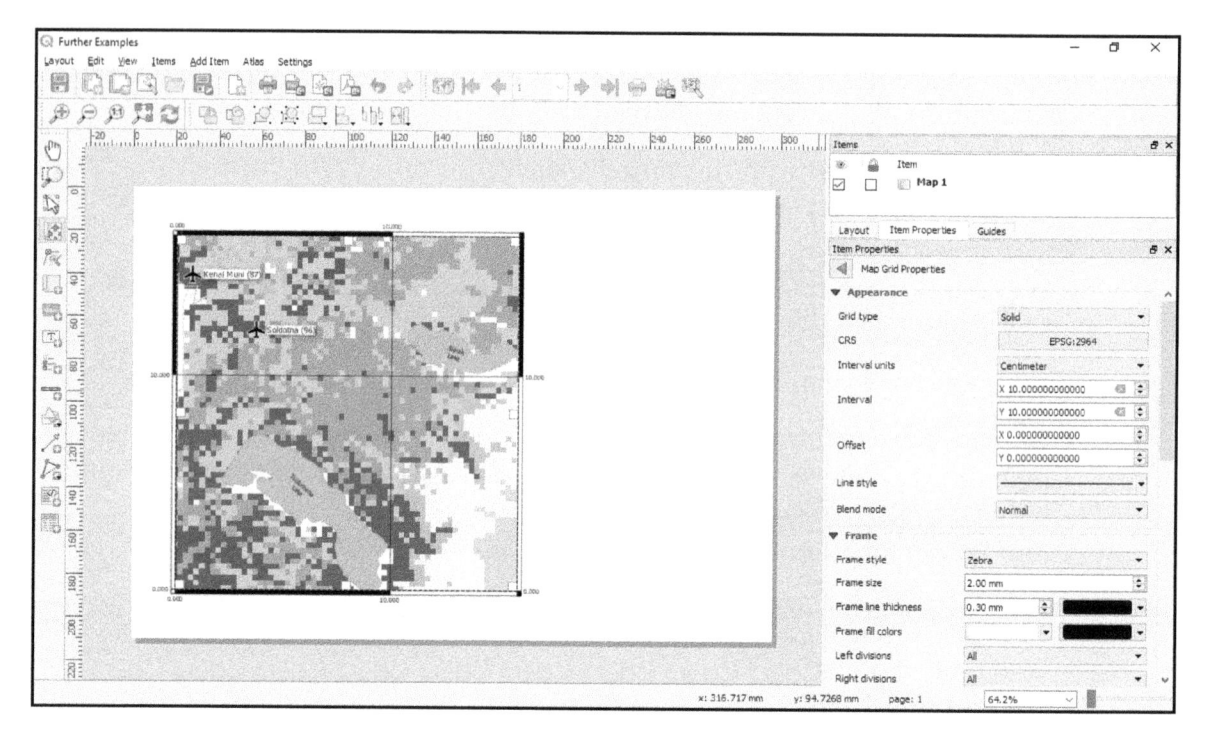

Adding a new grid

Adding an overview map

Maps that show an area up close are often accompanied by a second map that tells the reader where the area is located, helping to provide context to your map. To create such an overview map, we need to add a second map item, then make it an overview map by clicking on the + button in the Overviews section. By setting the Map frame, we can define the map extent and how it should be highlighted. The following screenshot shows an example of this using an overview map. In the main map, the area is highlighted in red. This relates to the corresponding area in the overview window. I have checked the center on canvas button on the toolbar on the left of the following screenshot. You may need to return to the QGIS project window and make adjustments to improve each added map:

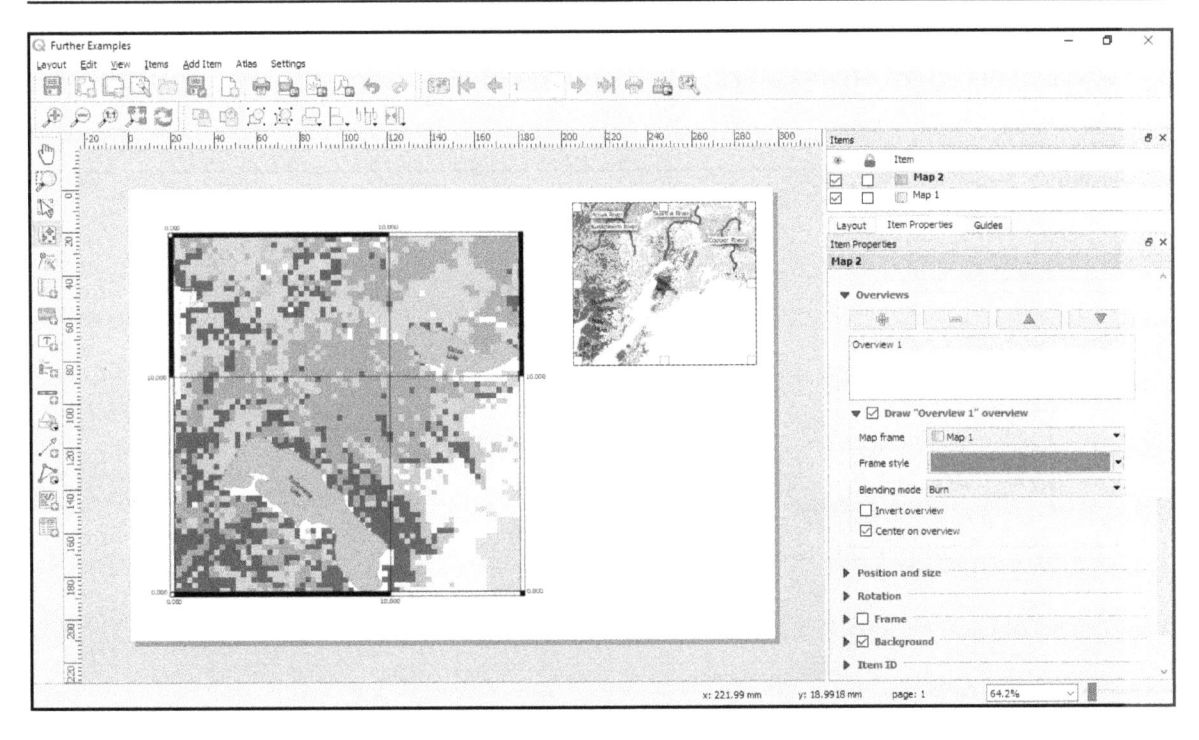

Adding an overview map

> **TIP**
> Every map item in a composition can display a different combination of layers. Generally, map items in a layout are synced with the map in the main QGIS window. So, if we turn a layer off in the main window, it is removed from the print composer map as well. However, we can stop this automatic synchronization by enabling Lock layers for a map item in the map item's properties.

Adding an attribute table

The final thing to add to this map is an attribute table. To do this, go to **Add Item** | **Add Attribute Table,** and then draw the bounding box on the canvas. Adjust the appearance first by clicking the **Attributes** button, renaming fields, and removing unnecessary ones. In the following example, I have selected the airport layer for my attribute layer, removed ID field, and changed the name of the other fields from **ELEV** to **Elevation**, and **fk_region** to **Region**.

Creating Great Maps

I have also added a purple frame to surround the table. Scroll down through the **Item Properties** until you find the **Frame** options. My final map looks like the following screenshot:

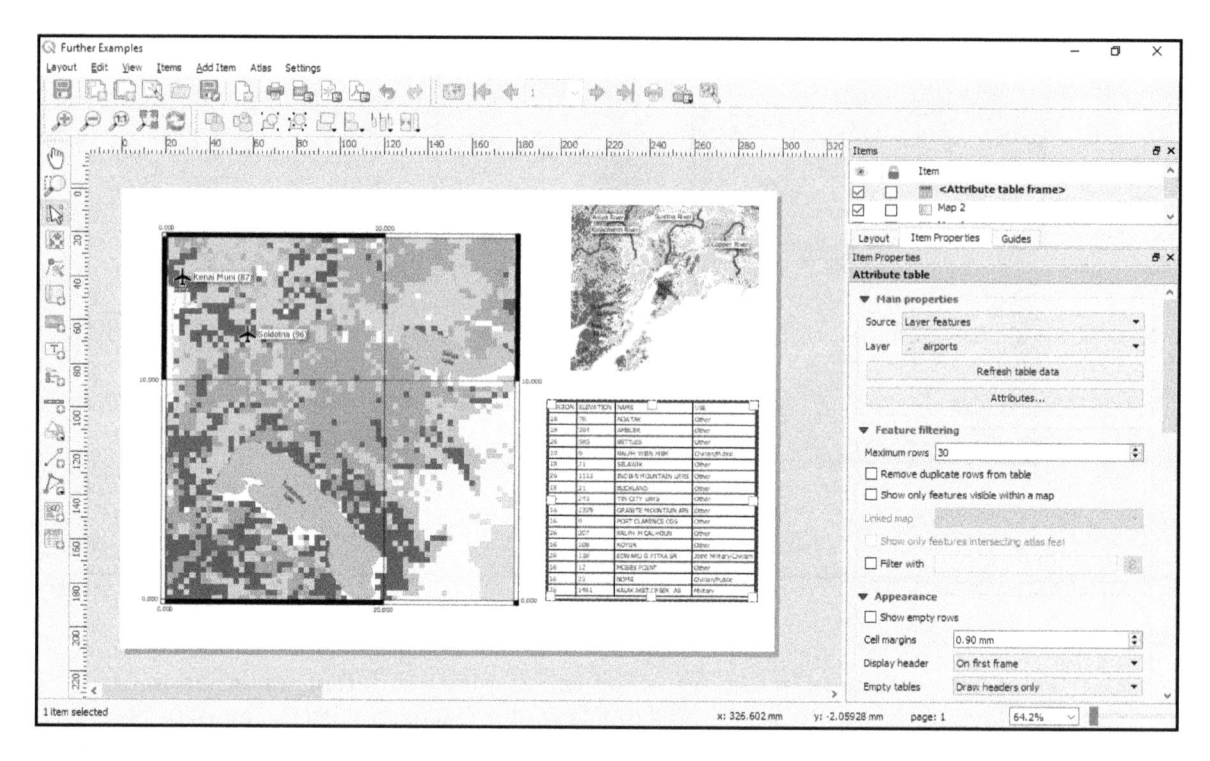

Adding an attribute table to the layout

Even more advanced content can be added using the **Add HTML frame** button. We can point the item's URL reference to any HTML page on our local machines or online, and the content (text and images as displayed in a web browser) will be displayed on the composer page. When you have done this, save your map.

Map outputs

Return to your Geomorphology map through the layout manager. You may have noticed that it looks a little different now. This is because we have made another map that has impacted this one. Reset the layers in the QGIS project to before (Major rivers, lakes, trees, alaska and Hillshade on – everything else off), check that your zoom level is still correct (scale: 10,000,000), and then, in the **Layers** section of the map item, click on **Lock Layers** and **Lock styles for layers**. This is shown in the following screenshot:

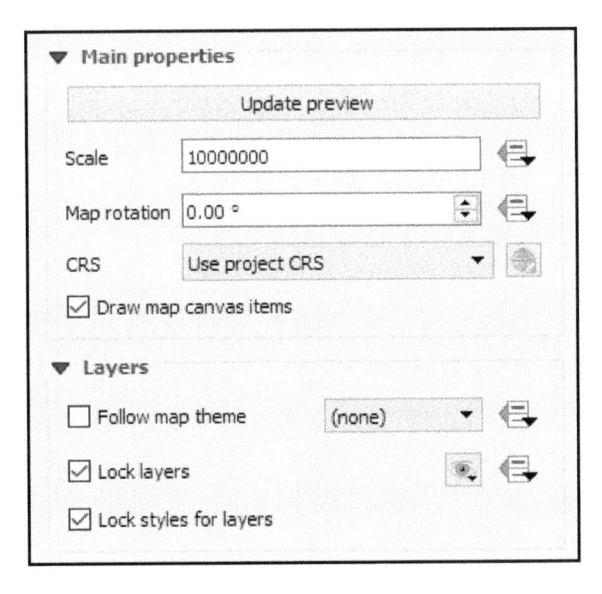

Changing the scale

We are now ready to create map outputs.

Saving maps to share

The simplest way to do this is to share the maps either to .pdf or .jpg, or to print them. This is all done through the Layout menu. For many of the processes in QGIS, once an operation has been performed, you will get a message at the top of your screen letting you know that it has been completed successfully. This is the case when saving your map to .pdf, for example.

Creating Great Maps

To adjust properties such as the dpi, or determine whether a world file is written or not, select the **Layout** tab and look for the **Export settings**, as shown in the following screenshot:

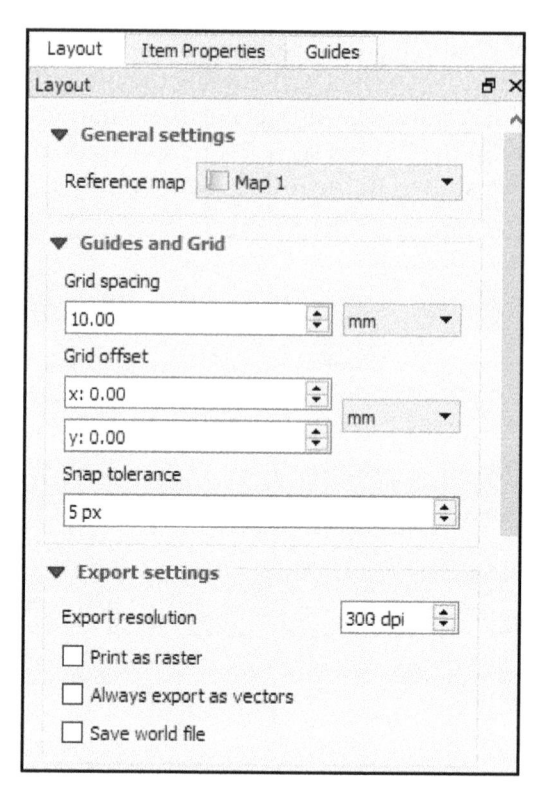

The export settings for the map prior to saving as an image

> **TIP**: So that it can be loaded to the correct location in QGIS, select the world file option if you wish to maintain a projection with the map.

Creating an Atlas

QGIS also has the ability to create an Atlas. An Atlas is a series of maps that could be based on information in a layer, such as the name of a river. To do this, create a new print layout and draw a new map item in the center of the canvas. From the Menu, select **Atlas | Atlas settings** and then check the box next to **Generate Atlas**. Now, select the **Coverage layer** as **Major_rivers** and the page name as **DESCRIPTION**.

[144]

This will tell the Atlas to create one page per river description. In the **Item Properties**, navigate to **Controlled by Atlas** and check the box. Click on the **preview** button in the Atlas toolbar and use the arrows to scroll through the proposed Atlas. This is shown in the following screenshot:

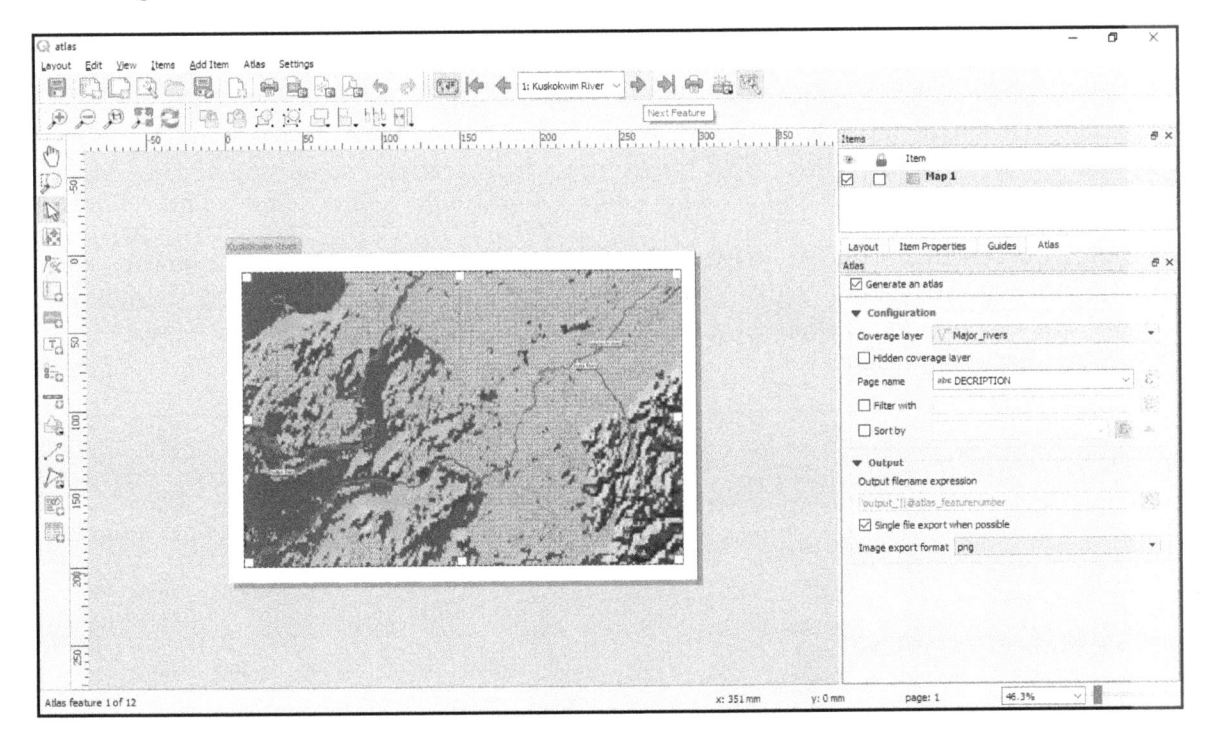

Creating an Atlas

Finally, select **Atlas | Export Atlas** from the menu as `.pdf` and save to it disk. This is a relatively simple example, but it shows the power behind creating an Atlas and you only need to build one layout in order to do it.

Presenting Maps online

Besides print maps, web maps are another popular way of publishing maps. In this section, we will use different QGIS plugins to create different types of web maps. Plugins can change rapidly (for the better). More functionality is added frequently and the appearance can change slightly. We present these two examples as they were at the time of writing.

Creating Great Maps

Exporting a web map

To create web maps from within QGIS, we can use the QGIS2Web plugin, which we have to install using the Plugin Manager. Once it is installed, go to **Web | qgis2web | Create web map** to start it. QGIS2Web supports the two most popular open source web mapping libraries: OpenLayers 3 and Leaflet.

I have created a new QGIS project and set the projection (in the bottom-right corner) to EPSG 3857. This is the web Mercator projection. I have loaded the `Airports` and `Alaska` shapefile and the OpenStreetMap XYZ tile (refer to data creation and editing in `Chapter 2`, *Data Creation and Editing*).

The following screenshot shows an example of our `airports` dataset. In this example, we are using the **OpenLayers** library (as configured in the bottom-left corner of the following screenshot). You could also choose Leaflet if you wish, which is a different JavaScript library for interactive maps:

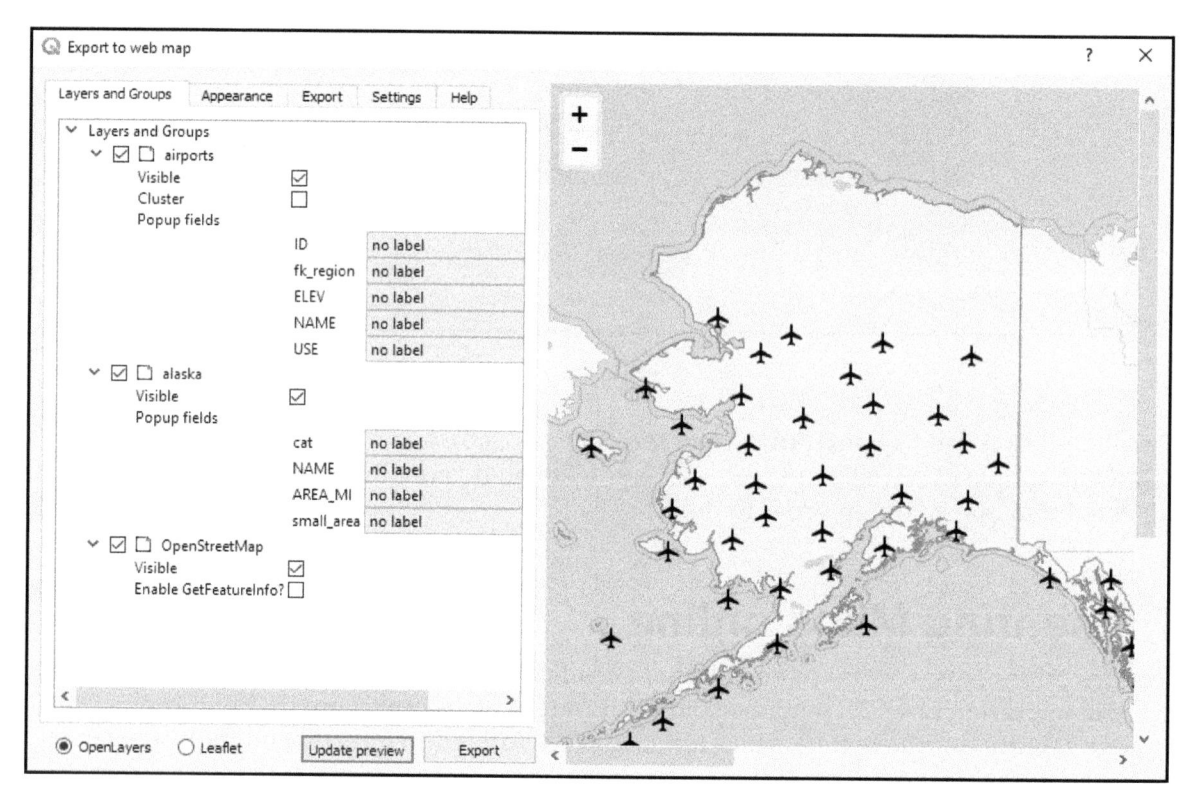

[146]

QGIS2Web – an excellent way to export your data in openlayers or leaflet

In the top-left corner, you can configure which layers from your project should be displayed on the web map, as well as the info pop-up content, which is displayed when the user clicks on, or hovers over, a feature (depending on the **Show popups on hover** setting).

Using the **appearance** tab, you can further configure the web map. All available settings are documented in the **Help** tab, so the content is not reproduced here. Again, don't forget to click on the **Update preview** button when you make changes.

When you are happy with the configuration, click on the **Export** button. This will save the web map at the location specified as the `Export` folder. Then open the resulting web map in your web browser. You can copy the contents in the `Export` folder to a web server to publish the map. The QGIS2Web plugin is a very efficient way of creating web maps.

Exporting a 3D web map

To create stunning 3D web maps, we need the Qgis2threejs plugin, which we can install using the **Plugin Manager**.

For example, we can use our `srtm_05_01.tif` elevation dataset to create a 3D view of that part of Alaska. The following screenshot shows the configuration of a DEM Layer in the Qgis2threejs dialog. From the scene menu, I have changed the vertical exaggeration to 10 times to highlight the elevations. Right-click on the `srtm_05_01.tif` layer to bring the layer properties box up.

Creating Great Maps

By selecting **Map canvas image** under **Display type**, we therefore define that the current map image will be draped over the 3D surface:

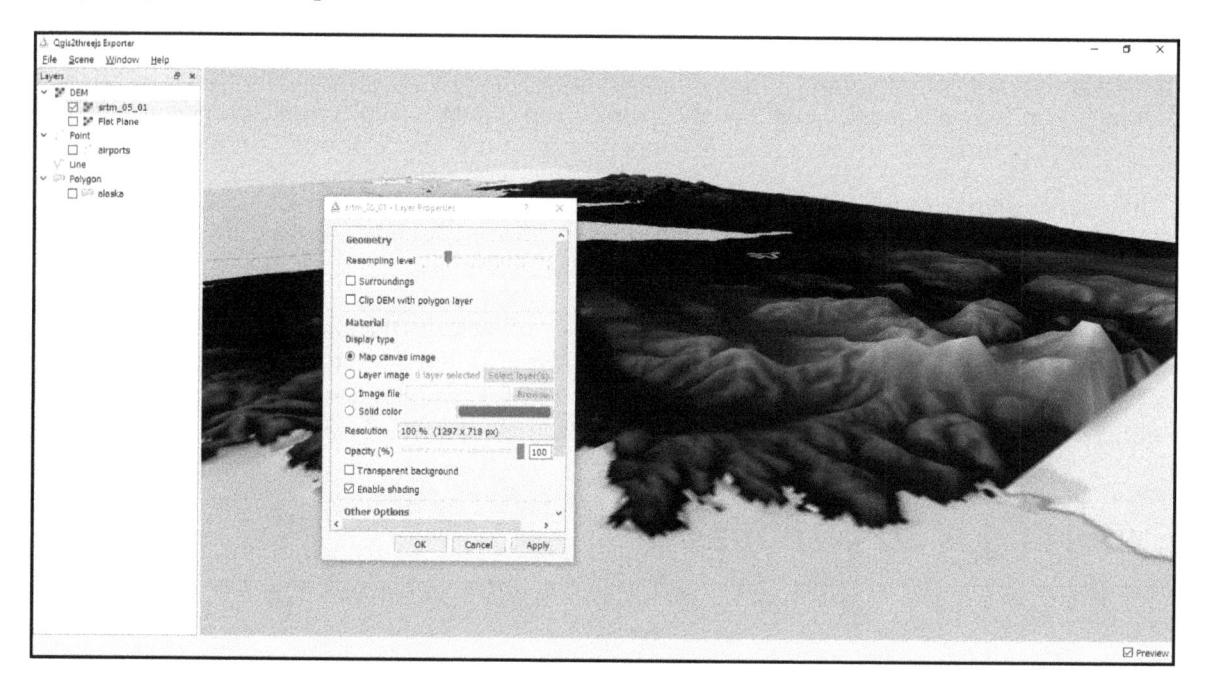

Setting up the elevation for a 3D view in the browser from QGIS with the Qgis2threejs plugin

Besides creating a 3D surface, this plugin can also label features. For example, we can add our **airports** and label them with their names. Right-click on the **airports** layer and select properties. Check the box next to **Export attributes** and choose **NAME** as the label field. The properties box should look like the following screenshot:

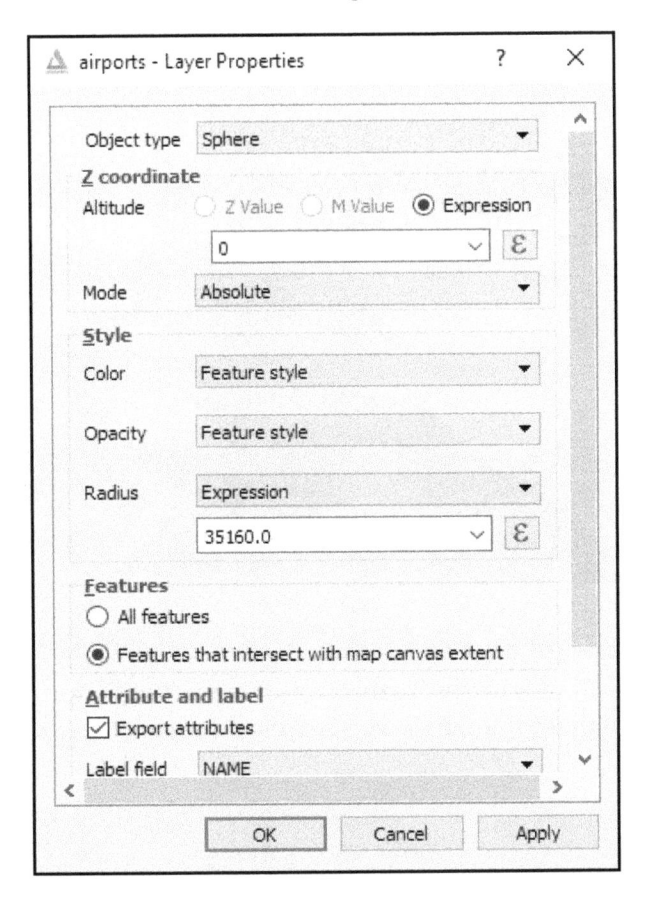

Labeling the airports in the 3D view

If you click on **File | Export to web,** the plugin will create the export and open the 3D map in your web browser. On the first try, it is quite likely that the surface will look too flat. Luckily, this can be easily changed by adjusting the Vertical exaggeration setting in the World section of the plugin configuration.

Creating Great Maps

The following example was created with a Vertical exaggeration of 10:

Final visualization of the data

`Qgis2threejs` exports all files to the location specified in the Output HTML file path. You can copy the contents in that folder on a web server to publish the map.

Summary

In this chapter, we looked at creating maps. Firstly, we studied labeling capabilities and then we moved on to map generation with the layout composer. There is a great deal of power in the layout composer and it is worth spending time exploring this in more detail in order to add more value to your maps.

We have now achieved a major milestone in this book: we have built familiarity with QGIS as a GIS, navigated how to load and create data, styled and presented our data, built maps, and created web maps as well as an Atlas.

In the final chapter of this book, we will look at extending and customizing QGIS 3. But first, in `Chapter 5`, *Spatial Analysis*, we will look at the processing toolbox. Let's become spatial scientists!

5
Spatial Analysis

In this chapter, we will use QGIS to perform many typical spatial analysis tasks. We will start with raster processing, using tools such as clipping and terrain analysis. We will also cover the essentials of converting between raster and vector formats. We will then continue with common vector processing tasks, such as generating heatmaps and calculating area shares within a region. We use the new Processing toolbox as well as the modeler to begin to build automated processing workflows.

Topics covered in this chapter include the following:

- Processing toolbox
- Analyzing raster data
- Converting between raster and vector
- Raster and vector statistics
- Heatmap from points
- Advanced raster and vector processing
- Batch processing
- Graphical modeler

Processing toolbox

The processing toolbox in QGIS 3.4 is accessed from **Processing | Toolbox**. In this chapter, we will utilize many tools via the processing toolbox. This has a fast search feature, which is the easiest method for finding a tool. If you are familiar with older versions of QGIS, you will still find many of the tools in the locations or menus where they were previously available. Many plugins often become core functions in QGIS. If you cannot find the plugin, try searching the toolbox first. Alternatively you can also search for tools in the information toolbar.

Analyzing raster data

Raster data, including, but not limited to, elevation models or remote sensing imagery, is commonly used in many workflows. The following exercises show common raster processing and analysis tasks such as clipping to a certain extent, creating relief, slope rasters from digital elevation models, and using the raster calculator.

Clipping rasters

To begin the process of clipping rasters, load the `SR_50M_alaska_nad.tif` raster and the `regions.shp` (both from our sample data) as the layer to be clipped. Now zoom to the extent of the `regions.shp` and select one region using the selection tools. In this example, we will clip the raster to a selected layer within the polygon shapefile. From the main menu, select **Processing | Toolbox**, and the new processing toolbox will appear. In the search bar, type in `clip raster by mask layer` and double-click on the associated toolbox. After doing this, fill in the parameters that are shown in the following screenshot:

![Clip raster by mask layer dialog box]

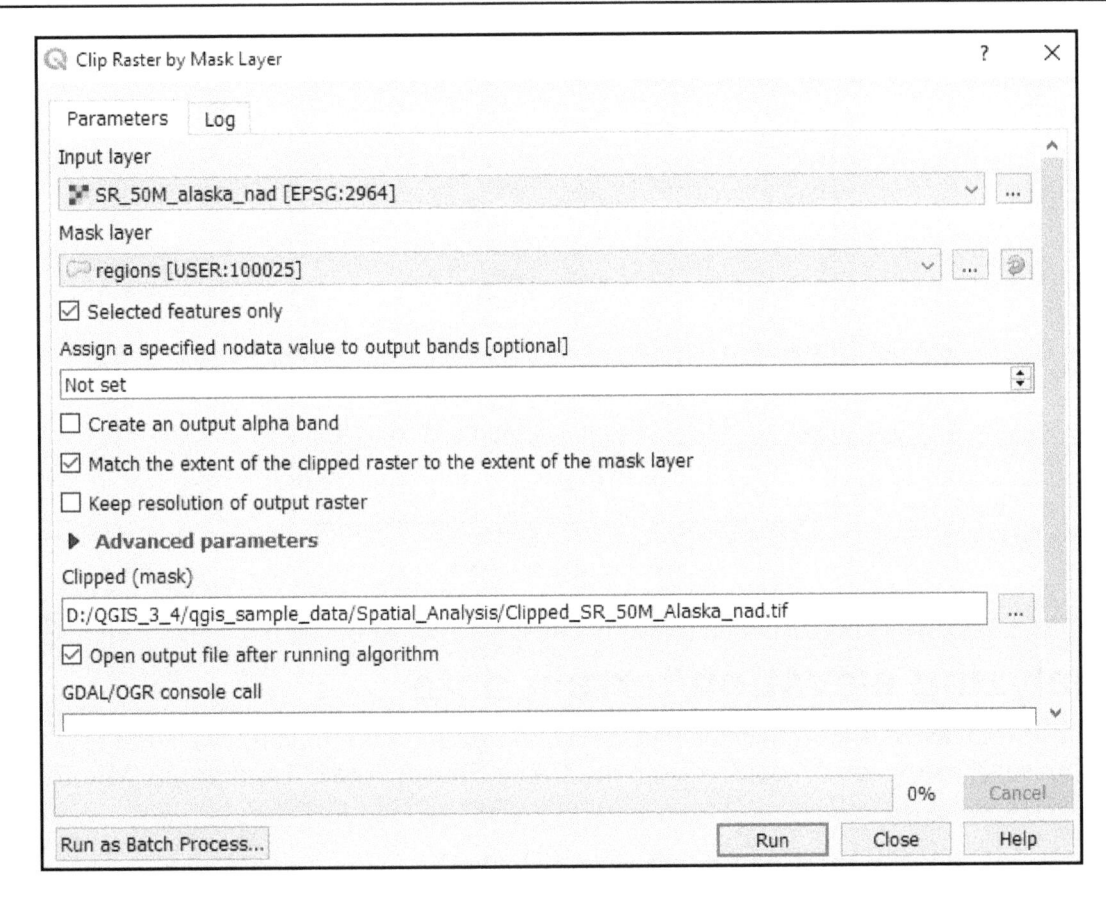

Clip raster by mask layer dialog box

Click on **Run**. In earlier versions of QGIS 3, this button was called **Run in background**, which is a new feature in QGIS 3. Previously, you would have had to wait for any processing to complete if you wanted to continue working in QGIS. However, this will now run in the background, making it possible for you to continue working with QGIS while tasks execute.

> In the GDAL/OGR console window, the raw `GDAL` command is displayed. You can copy this and paste it into a command prompt if you wish to perform this analysis outside of QGIS. In Python, it would also be possible to use the subprocess library to execute this command in a script.

Spatial Analysis

The resulting raster is loaded directly into QGIS and should appear similar to the following screenshot:

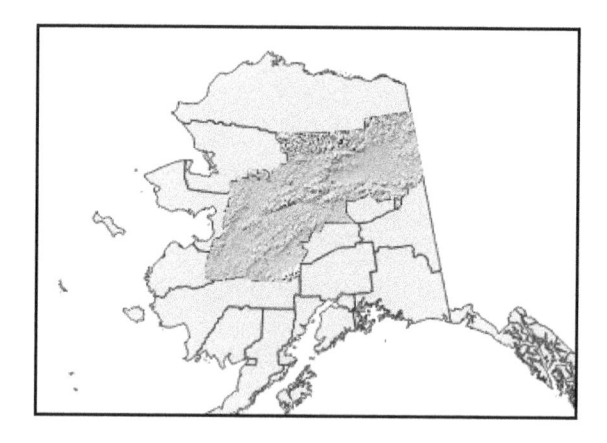

Result of the clip operation in QGIS

Analyzing elevation/terrain data

To use terrain analysis tools, we need an elevation raster. If you don't have a DEM to hand, you can simply download a dataset from the NASA **Shuttle Radar Topography Mission** (**SRTM**) using `http://dwtkns.com/srtm/` or any other SRTM download services.

> **TIP**
> If you want to replicate the results in the following exercise, then download the dataset called `srtm_05_01.zip`, which covers a small part of Alaska.

Raster terrain analysis can be used to calculate Slope, Aspect, Hillshade, Ruggedness Index, and Relief from elevation rasters. These tools are available from the processing toolbox.

Analysis includes some of the following tools:

- **Aspect**: This tool calculates the exposition (in degrees and counterclockwise, starting with 0 for north).
- **Hillshade**: This tool creates a basic Hillshade raster with lighted areas and shadows.
- **Hypsometric curves**: These will create `.csv` files that can be used for visualizing the DEM data in QGIS.

- **Relief**: This tool creates a shaded relief map with varying colors for different elevation ranges.
- **Ruggedness Index**: This tool calculates the ruggedness of a terrain, describing how flat or rocky an area is. The index is computed for each cell using the algorithm presented by Riley and others (1999) by summarizing the elevation changes within a 3 x 3 cell grid.
- **Slope**: This tool calculates the slope angle for each cell in degrees (based on the first-order derivative estimation).

The tools are shown in the following screenshot:

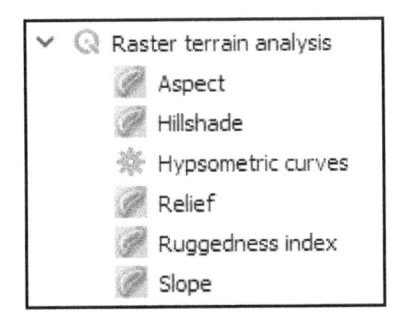

Raster terrain analysis tools

The results of terrain analysis depend on the resolution of the input elevation data. It is recommended using small-scale elevation data, with, for example, 30 meters x/y resolution, particularly when computing ruggedness.

An important element in all terrain analysis tools is the **Z factor**. The **Z factor** is used if the x/y units are different from the z (elevation) unit. For example, if we try to create a relief from elevation data where x/y are in degrees and z is in meters, the resulting relief will look grossly exaggerated. The values for the z factor are as follows:

- If x/y and z are either all in meters or all in feet, use the default **Z factor**, 1.0
- If x/y are in degrees and z is in feet, use the **Z factor** 370,400
- If x/y are in degrees and z is in meters, use the **Z factor** 111,120

Spatial Analysis

Since the SRTM rasters are provided in WGS84 EPSG:4326, we need to use a **Z factor** of `111,120` in our exercise. Let's create a Hillshade raster. The easiest way to find the tool is to search for **Hillshade** in the processing toolbox:

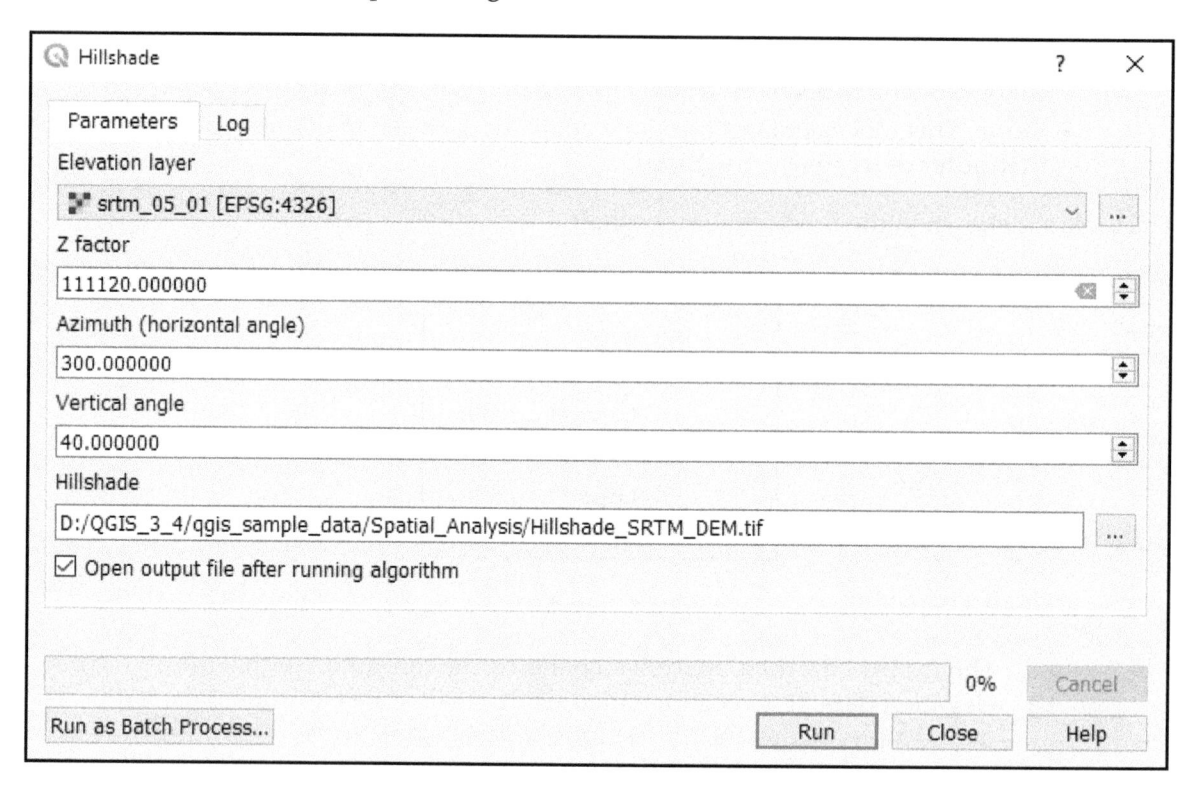

Hillshade dialog box

Chapter 5

Once the tool is run, close the window and you should see your data in the map, similar to the following diagram:

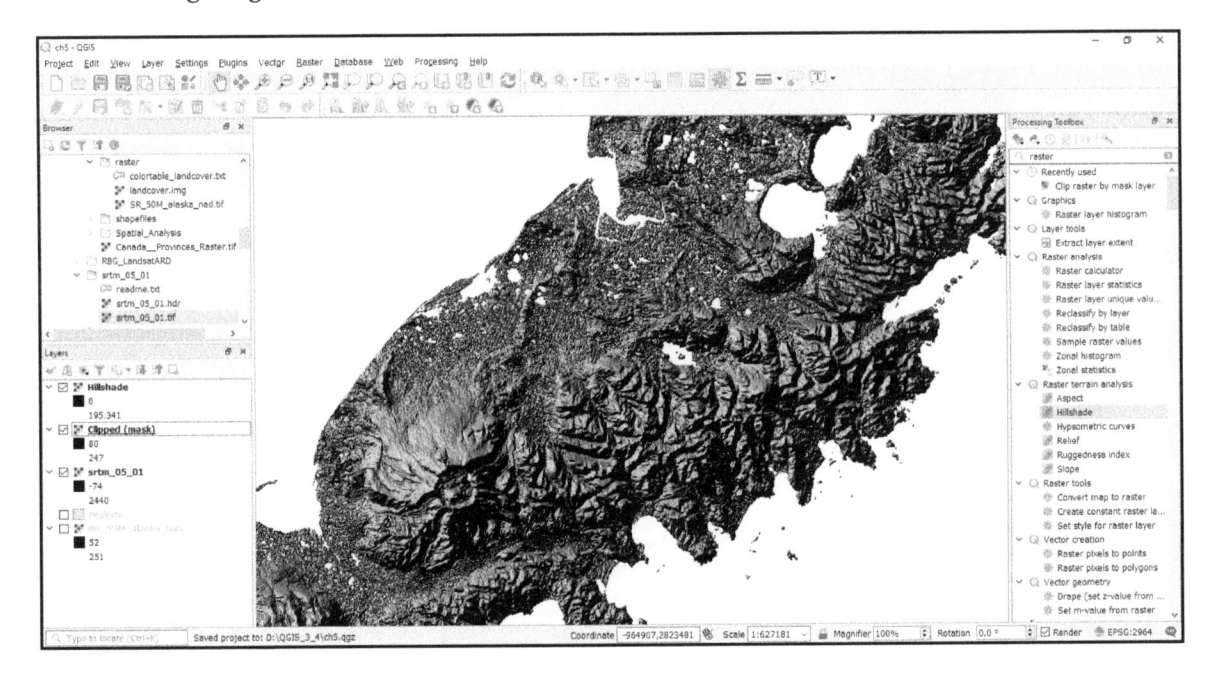

Result of the Hillshade operation

As we saw in `Chapter 3`, *Visualizing Data,* when creating our geomorphology map, hillshading can be used to great effect to visualize the terrain.

Terrain projections – slope maps

It is often best practice to convert the DEM data you are working with into the local projection, especially when deriving terrain products. In QGIS, right-click on the SRTM DEM layer and **Export** | **Save as**. Be sure to set the projection to EPSG:2964. The **Save Raster Layer as...** window should look similar to the following:

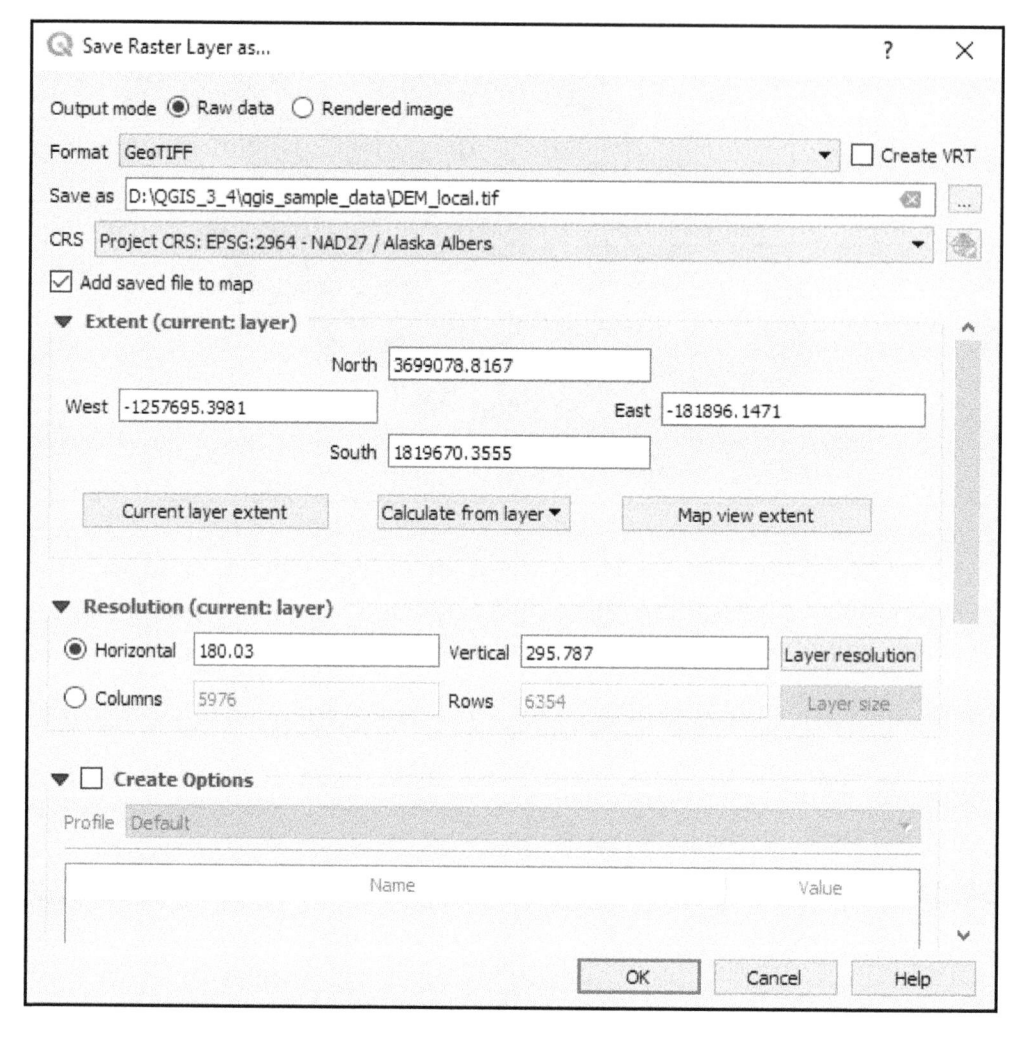

Saving the raster layer

Now that we have a local projection DEM, we can run the **Slope** tool. In the toolbox, search for **Slope**. Fill in the parameters (**Z factor** is 1) and click on the **run** button. You should now have a slope raster in the table of contents. We will use this raster for the next section, where we will introduce the raster calculator. Your slope raster will look similar to the following screenshot:

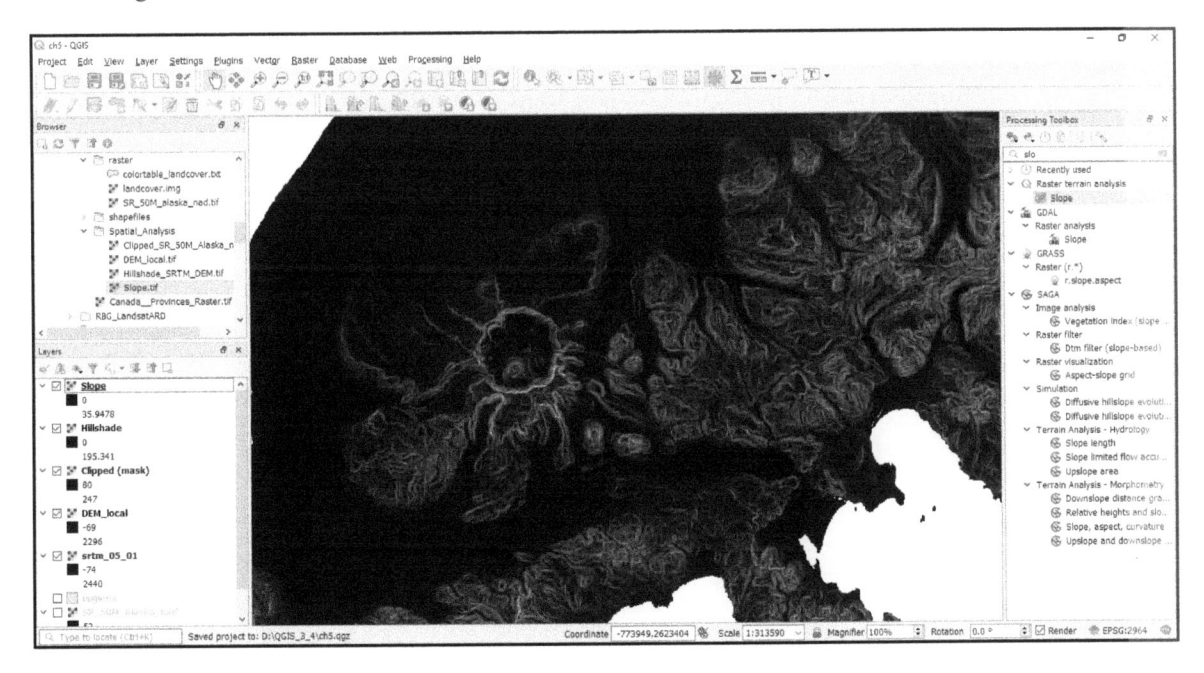

Building a slope map and displaying the result

> **TIP**: You could use a singleband pseudocolor render (green to red) and stretch the data to display the slope data clearer.

Using the raster calculator

With the raster calculator, we can create a new raster layer based on the values in one or more rasters that are loaded in the current QGIS project. To access this, go to **Raster** | **Raster Calculator**. All available **Raster Bands** are presented in a list in the top-left corner of the dialog using the `raster_name@band_number` format.

[161]

Spatial Analysis

Continuing from our previous exercise in which we created a slope raster, we can, for example, find areas at elevations above 1,000 meters and with a slope of less than 5 degrees using the following expression:

`"srtm_05_01@1" > 1000 AND "slope@1" < 5`

> **TIP**: You might have to adjust the values depending on the dataset you are using. Check out the *Accessing raster and vector layer statistics* section later in this chapter to learn how to find the minimum and maximum values in your raster.

The dialog box should look similar to the following:

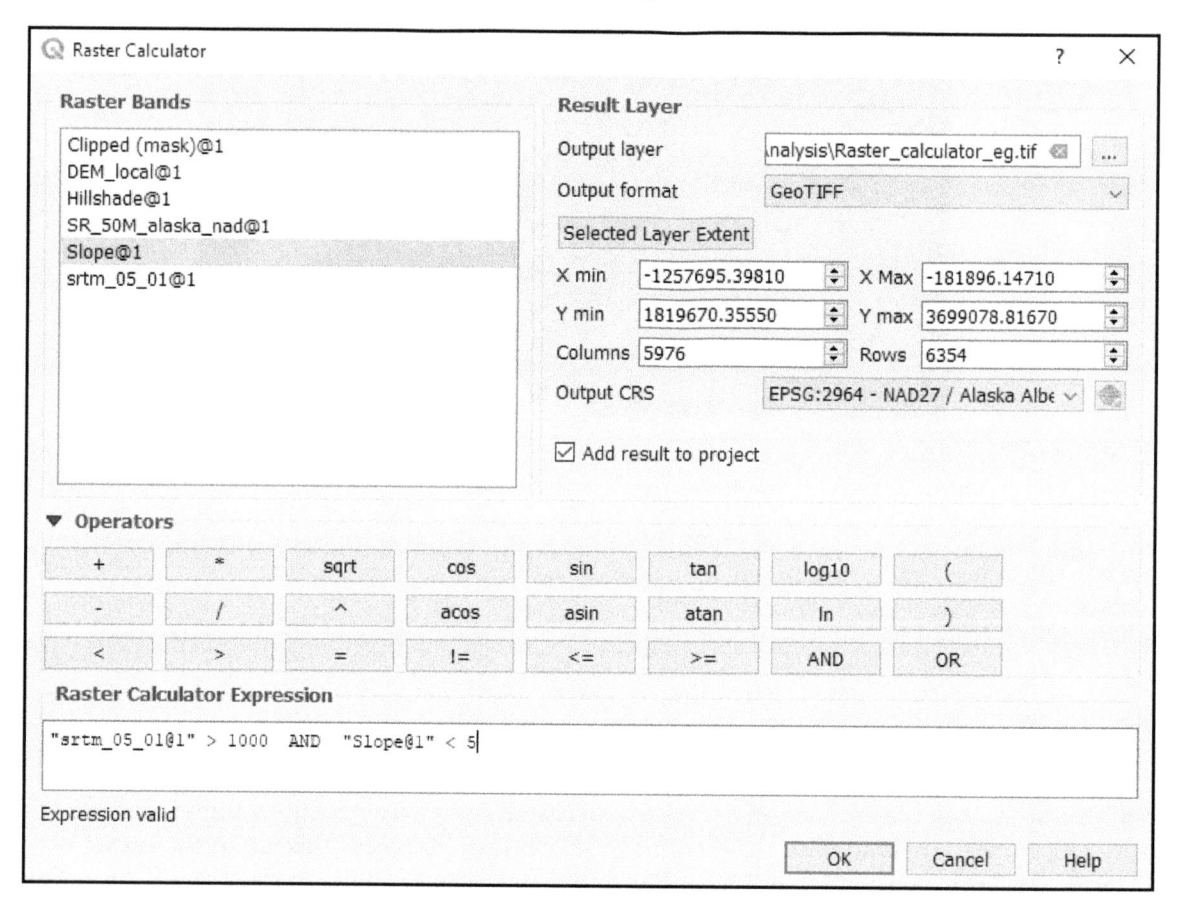

The raster calculator dialog box

Cells that satisfy both criteria in terms of high elevation and low slope will be assigned a value of **1** in the resulting raster, while cells that fail to meet even one criterion will be set to **0** (black). Areas with a value of **1** (white) are found in the southern part of the raster layer. You can see a section of the resulting raster in the following screenshot:

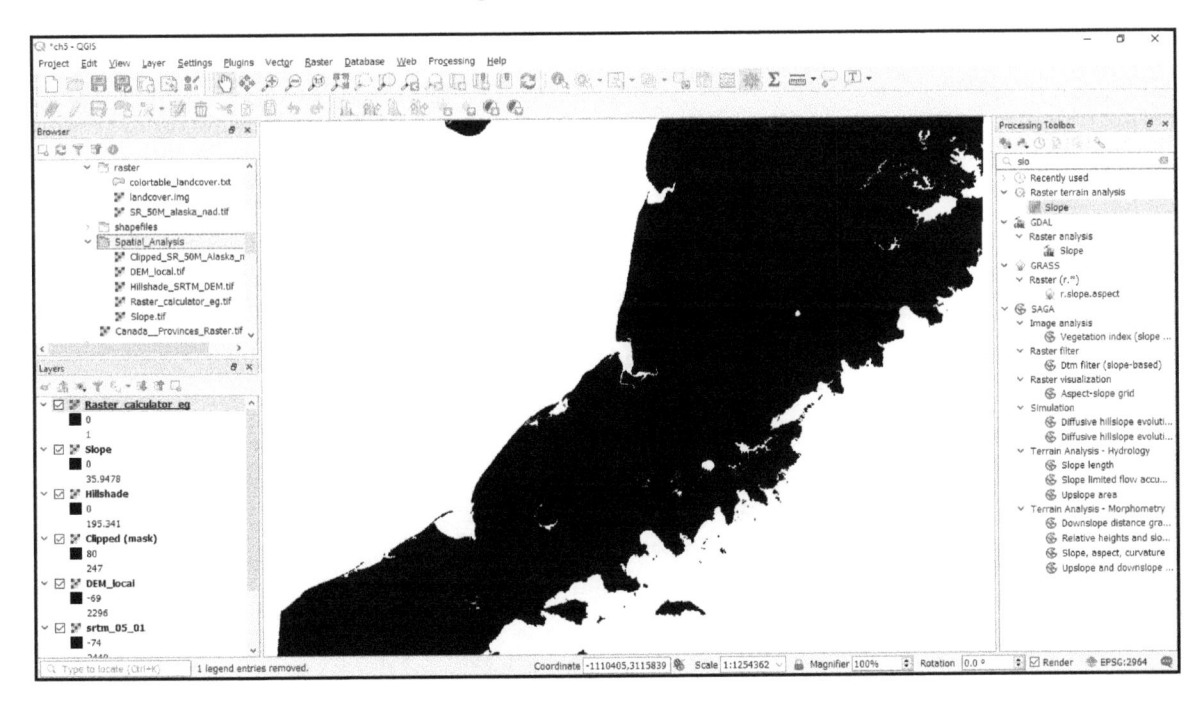

The result of the raster calculator

The raster calculator is useful for reclassifying a raster. For example, we might want to reclassify the `landcover.img` raster in our sample data so that all areas with a `landcover` class from 1 to 5 receive a value of 100, areas from 6 to 10 receive a value of 101, and areas over 11 get a new value of 102. Load the `landcover.img` into the **Layers** Panel. We will use the following in the raster calculator, the code for this being as follows:

```
("landcover@1" > 0 AND "landcover@1" <= 6 ) * 100
+ ("landcover@1" >= 7 AND "landcover@1" <= 10 ) * 101
+ ("landcover@1" >= 11 ) * 102
```

Spatial Analysis

This equation is shown in the following raster calculator:

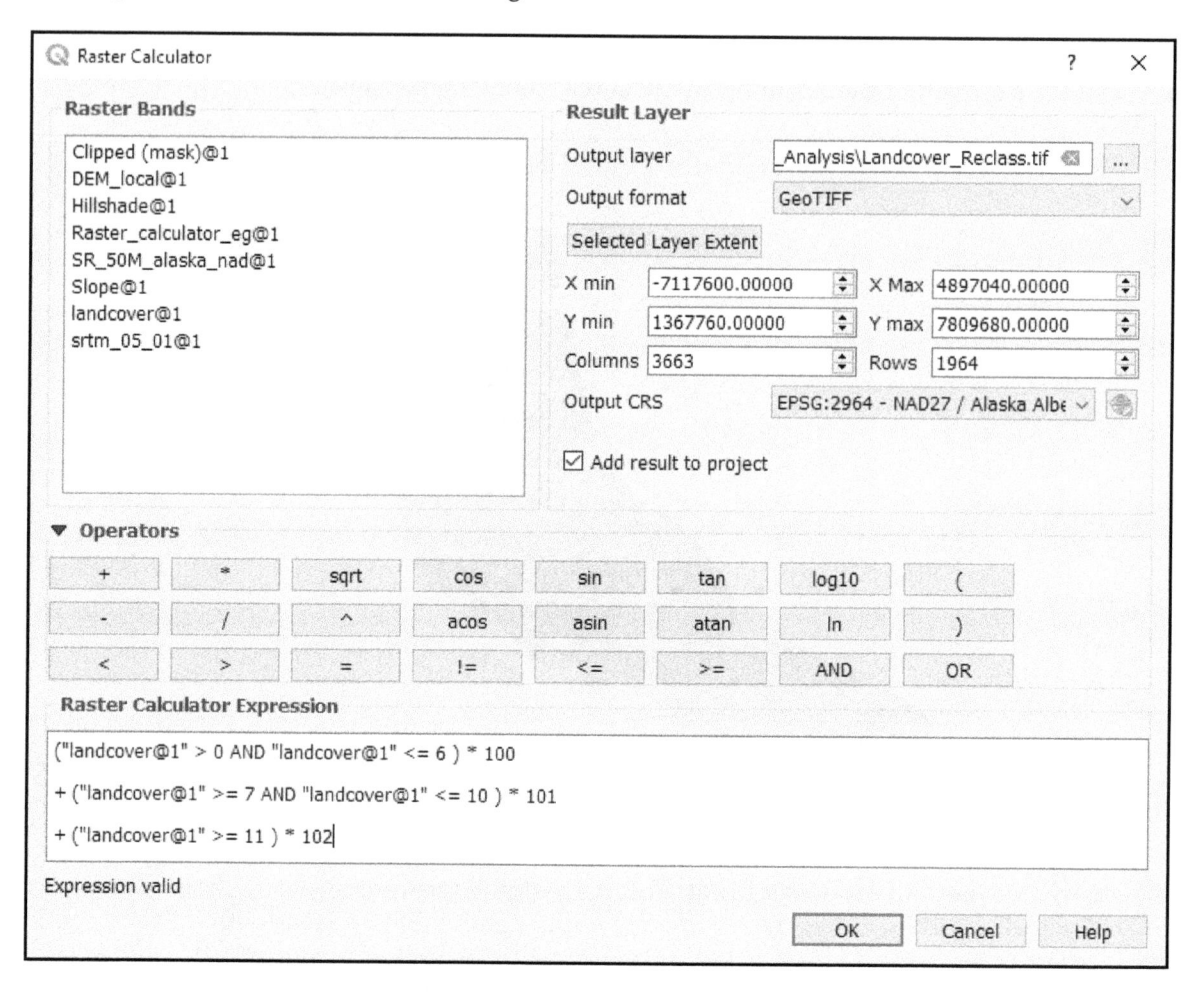

Raster Calculator

Raster Bands:
- Clipped (mask)@1
- DEM_local@1
- Hillshade@1
- Raster_calculator_eg@1
- SR_50M_alaska_nad@1
- Slope@1
- landcover@1
- srtm_05_01@1

Result Layer:
- Output layer: _Analysis\Landcover_Reclass.tif
- Output format: GeoTIFF
- Selected Layer Extent
- X min: -7117600.00000   X Max: 4897040.00000
- Y min: 1367760.00000   Y max: 7809680.00000
- Columns: 3663   Rows: 1964
- Output CRS: EPSG:2964 - NAD27 / Alaska Albe
- ☑ Add result to project

Operators: + * sqrt cos sin tan log10 (- / ^ acos asin atan ln) < > = != <= >= AND OR

Raster Calculator Expression:

```
("landcover@1" > 0 AND "landcover@1" <= 6 ) * 100
+ ("landcover@1" >= 7 AND "landcover@1" <= 10 ) * 101
+ ("landcover@1" >= 11 ) * 102
```

Expression valid

The resulting raster will look similar to the following with the render as paletted/unique values:

Reclassing the landcover

Reclassifying rasters is a really useful function in GIS. It allows us to perform fast calculations on raster datasets to generate informed answers.

> You can use the processing toolbox to reclassify raster data as well as the raster calculator.

Combining raster and vector data

As discussed in Chapter 2, *Data Creation and Editing*, raster and vector data are the main sources of GIS data. These are often analyzed separately. However, more complex analyses sometimes require a combination of raster and vector data. We often need to convert raster data to vector data and vice versa. QGIS has this ability and uses GDAL calls (Polygonize and Rasterize) respectively. In the following exercises, we will use both raster and vector datasets to explain how to convert between these different data types. We will also look at how to access layer and zonal statistics, and finally, how to create a raster heatmap from point data.

Converting between rasters and vectors

Tools for converting between raster and vector formats can be accessed by going to **Raster | Conversion**. The GDAL command is displayed at the bottom of the dialog box when you run these functions. In QGIS 2.x, there was the ability to edit these GDAL calls manually, but that functionality is not present in Version 3.4. However, it is possible to copy and paste a GDAL command to the command line and adjust the command there instead.

Raster to vector

Polygonize converts a raster into a polygon layer. Depending on the size and complexity of the raster, the conversion may take some time. Let's convert the reclassified landcover raster to polygons. From the **Raster** menu, select **Conversion | Polygonize (Raster to Vector)**. The resulting vector polygon layer contains multiple polygonal features with a single attribute. We have named this lc, based on the original raster value. Polygonize's output format is the GeoPackage format (the default in QGIS 3).

The dialog box should look similar to the preceding screenshot:

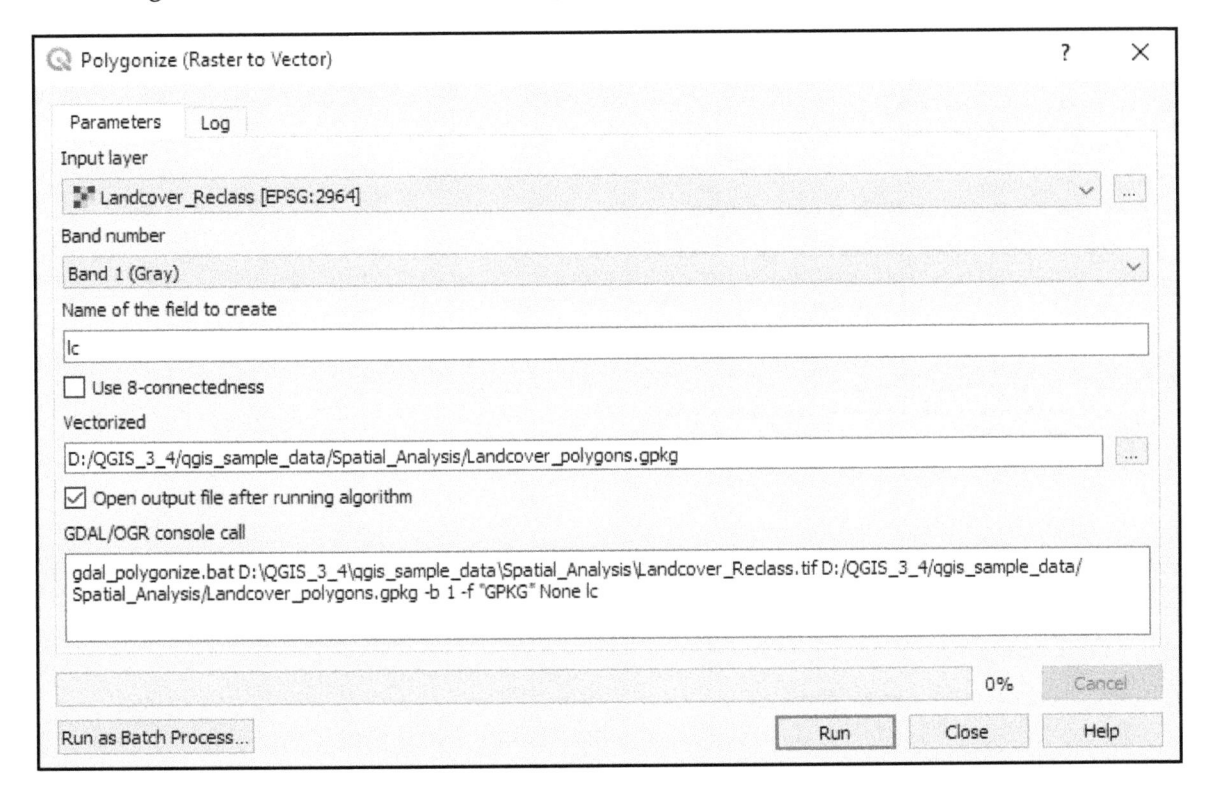

Polygonize raster-to-vector dialog box

Spatial Analysis

Once this process is complete, you will get a report. This is shown in the following screenshot:

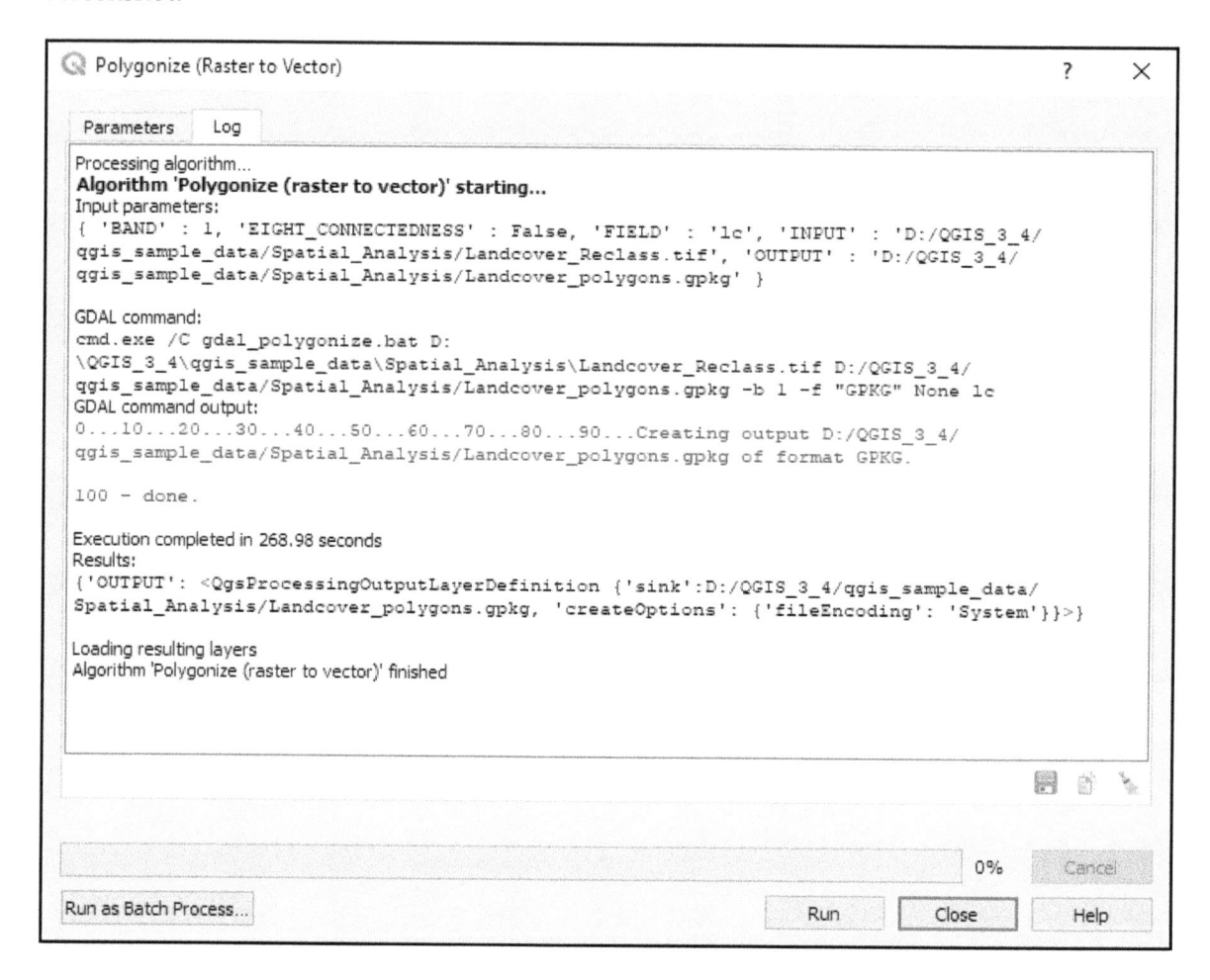

Resulting log file from the polygonize function

The resulting vector file is shown as follows. I have colored the **lc** field and clicked on the layer in QGIS to show its attributes:

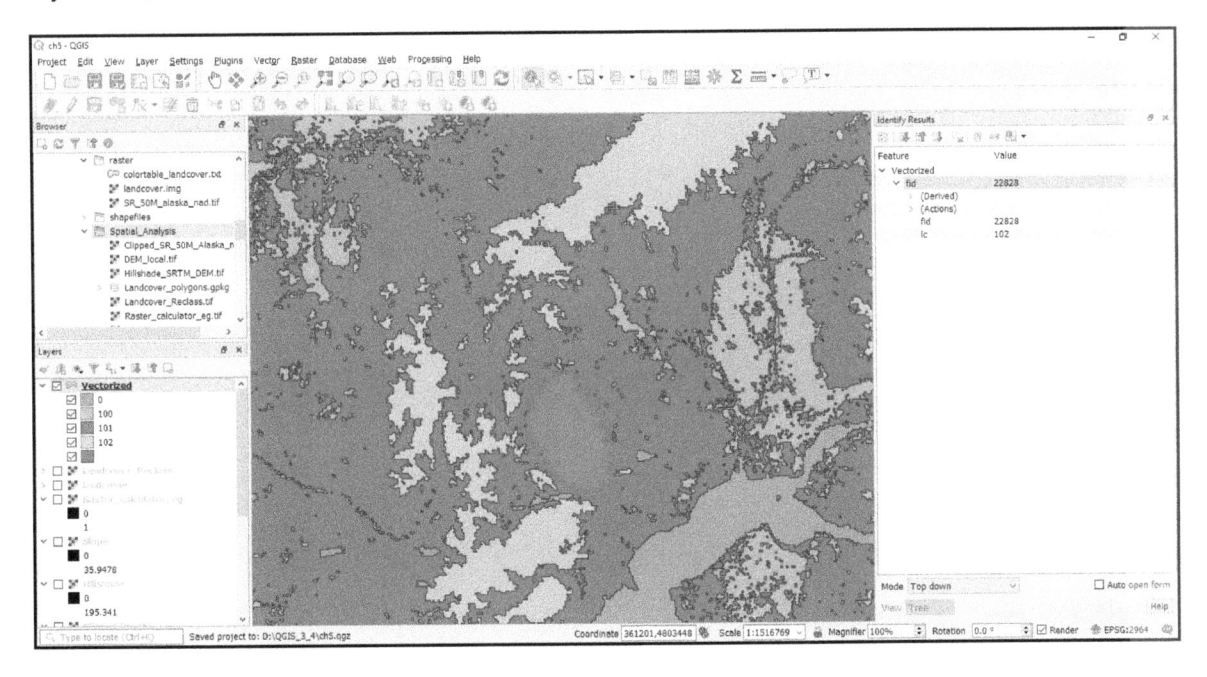

The vectorized layer from the polygonize function

Vector to raster

Using the **Rasterize** tool is very similar to using the **Polygonize** tool. The only difference is that we get to specify the size of the resulting raster in pixels/cells. We can also specify the attribute field, which will provide input for the raster cell value, as shown in the next screenshot. Load `alaska.shp` into the **Layers** panel and, from the **Raster** menu, select **Conversion** | **Rasterize** (**Vector to Raster**). In this case, the `cat` attribute of our `alaska.shp` dataset is rather meaningless.

[169]

Spatial Analysis

Make sure you set the **Output extent** to the alaska layer. Otherwise, leave the other values as their defaults, as shown in the following screenshot:

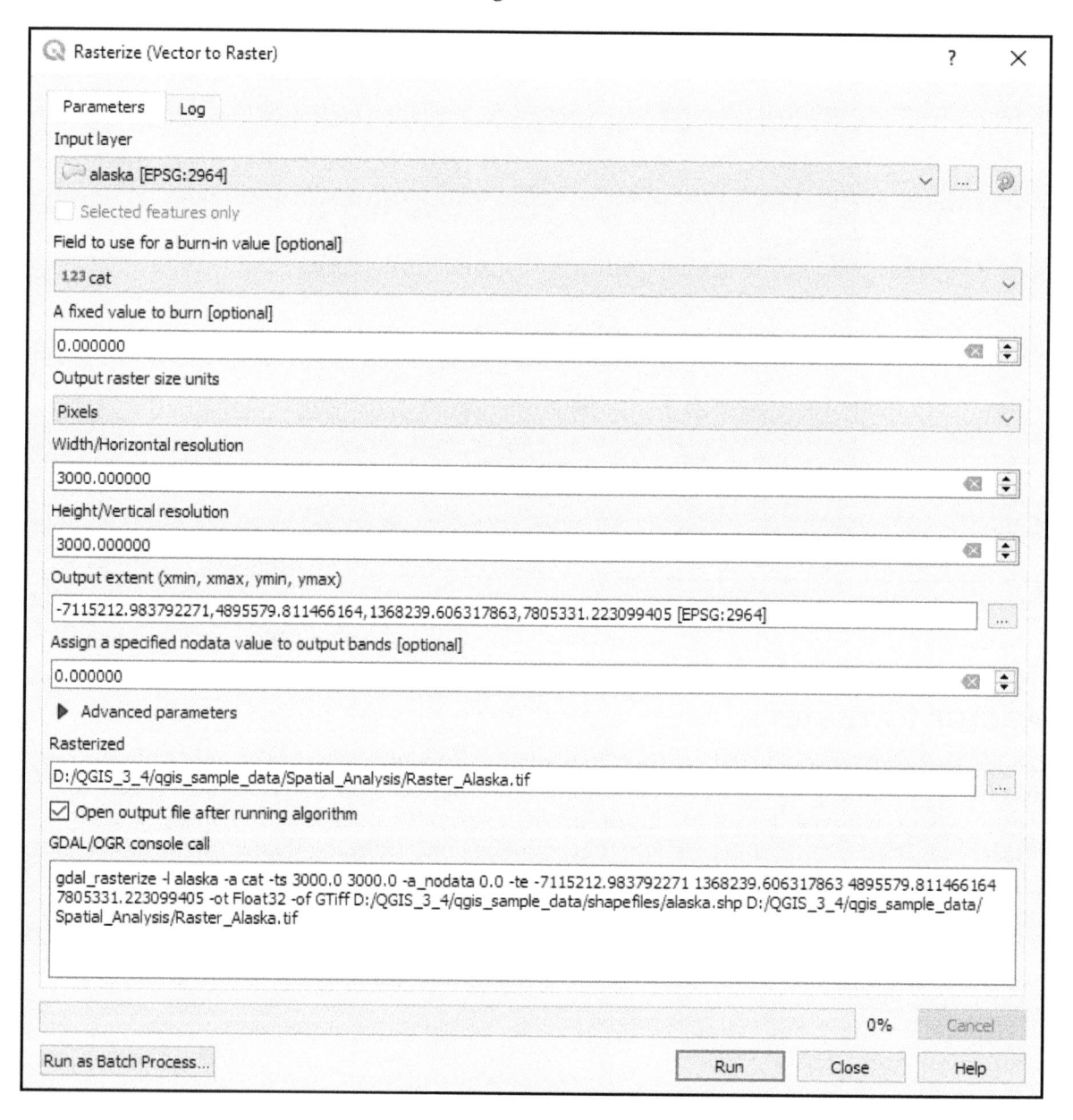

Rasterize function dialog box

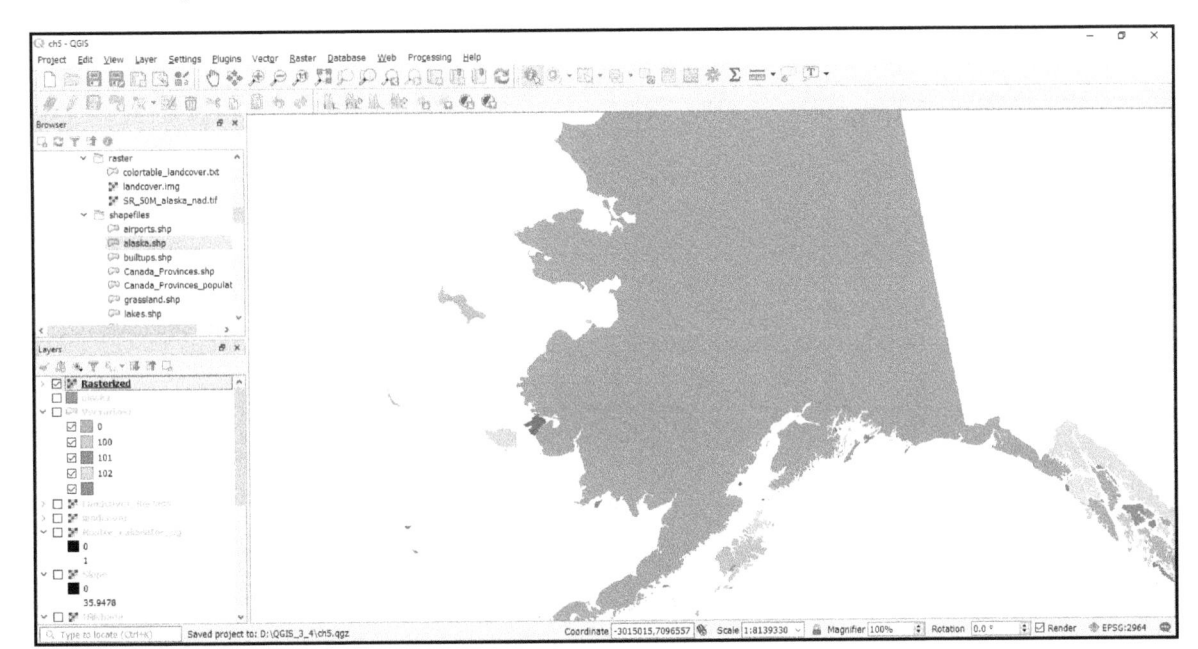

The resulting raster file should appear similar to the following screenshot:

Resulting raster created from the polygon layer

> **TIP**: Converting between raster and vector format can mean that information can be lost. Review what you are trying to achieve before entering values. If you want a detailed raster to make the pixel size smaller, this change will impact the file size and the speed at which the raster is generated.

Accessing raster and vector layer statistics

Whenever we get a new dataset, it is useful to examine the layer statistics to get an idea of the data it contains. This includes, for example, the minimum and maximum values and the number of features. QGIS offers a variety of tools to explore these values.

Raster layer statistics are readily available in the **Layer Properties** dialog, specifically in the following tabs:

- **Metadata**: This tab shows the minimum and maximum cell values, as well as the mean and the standard deviation of the cell values.

Spatial Analysis

- **Histogram**: This tab presents the distribution of raster values. Use the mouse to zoom into the histogram to see the details. For example, the following screenshot shows the zoomed-in version of the histogram for our `landcover` dataset:

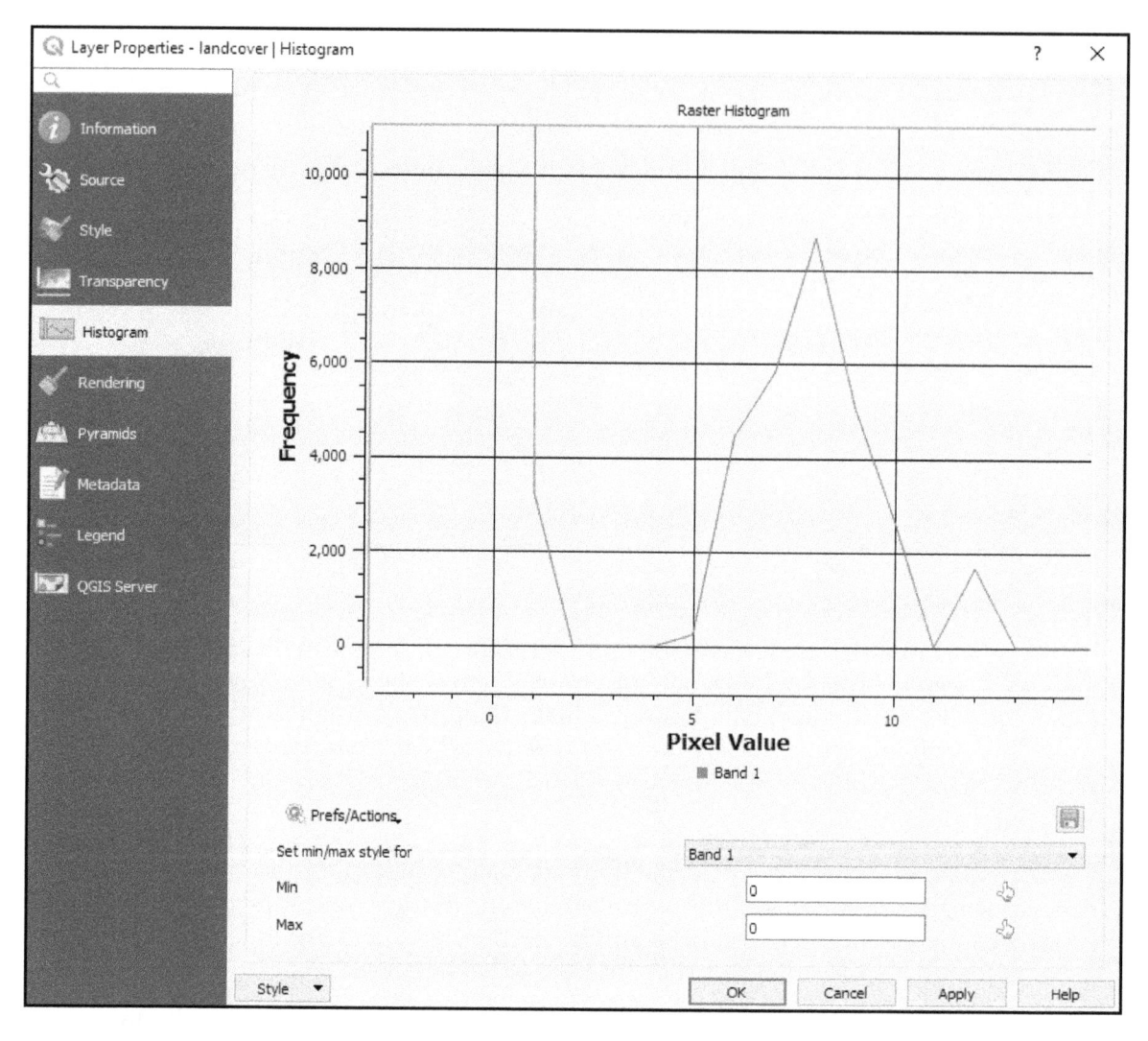

Layer Properties dialog box

For vector layers, we can get summary statistics using two tools in **Vector | Analysis Tools**:

- Basic statistics is very useful for numerical fields. It calculates mean and median, min and max, for all features of a layer or for a selection.
- Listing unique values is useful for getting all unique values of a certain field.

The following screenshot shows an example of exploring the contents of our `airports.shp` layer, looking at the `ELEV` field as the sample dataset. Load the `airports.shp` layer and run the **Basic Statistics for Fields** tool, as shown in the following screenshot:

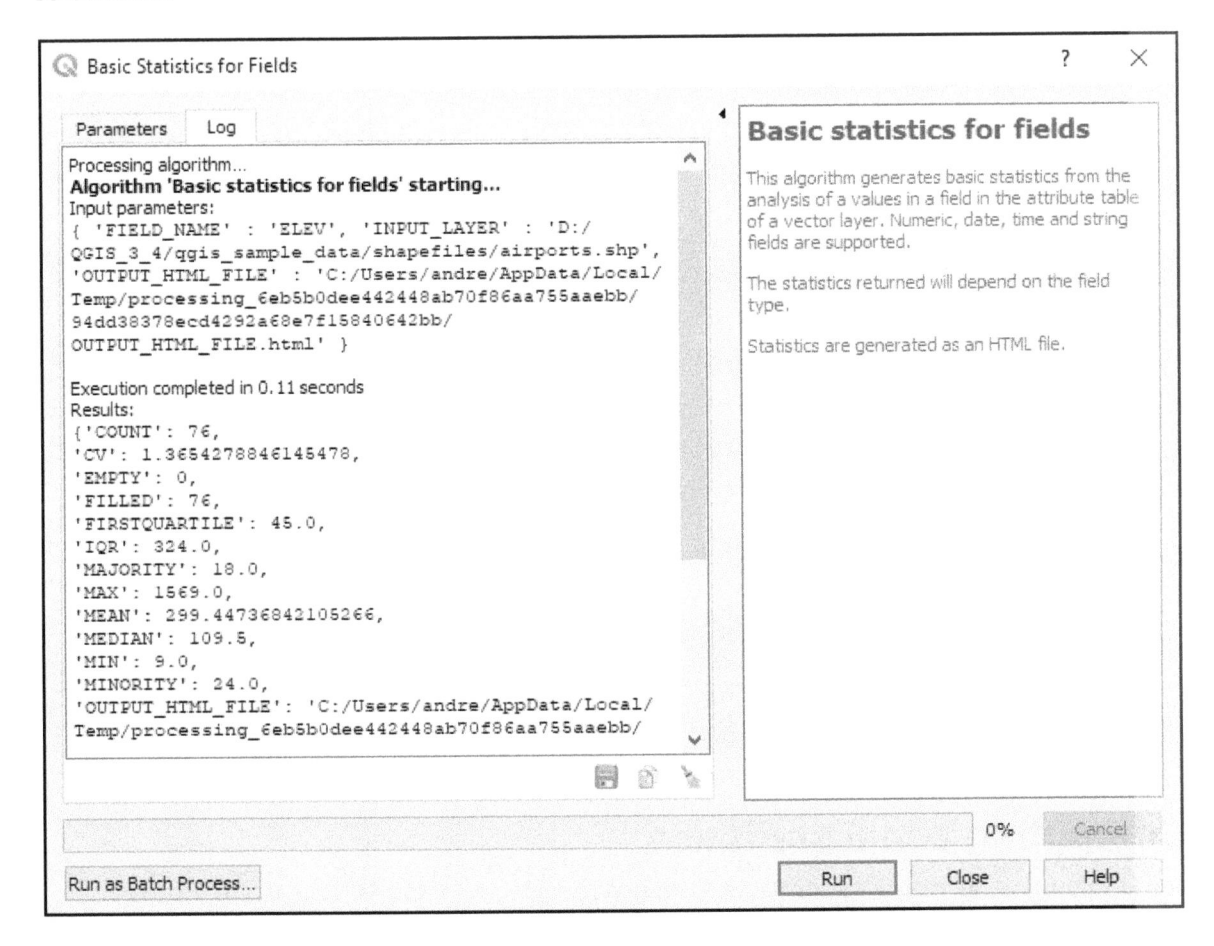

Basic statistics for the airports dataset

Spatial Analysis

A results panel will appear in QGIS containing the results which, when clicked, will open your browser with the statistics inside. An alternative to the **Basics statistics for fields** tool is the **Statistics** panel, which you can activate by going to **View** | **Panels** | **Statistics**, as shown in the following screenshot for the same data:

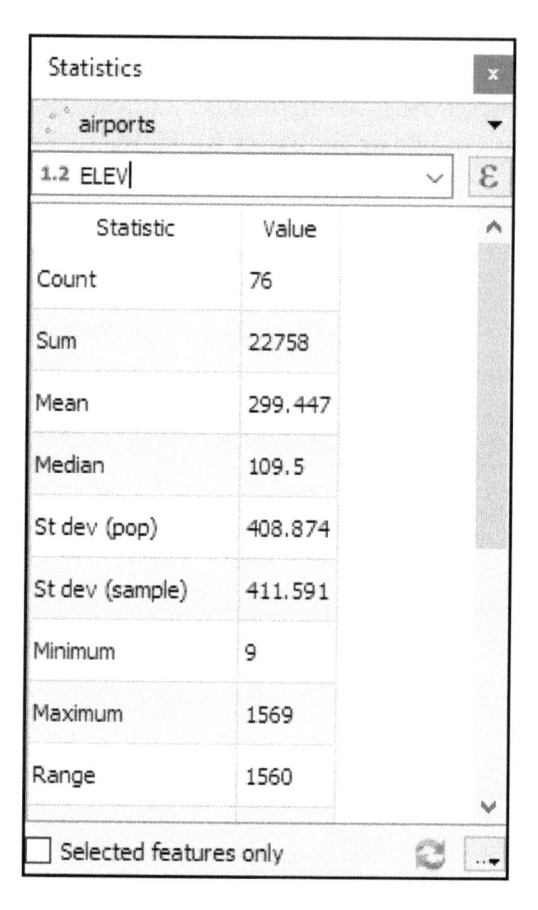

Statistic	Value
Count	76
Sum	22758
Mean	299.447
Median	109.5
St dev (pop)	408.874
St dev (sample)	411.591
Minimum	9
Maximum	1569
Range	1560

Statistics panel

Computing zonal statistics

Sometimes, it is necessary to compute statistics for selected regions. This is what the zonal statistics does in the raster processing toolbox. For example, we can compute landcover class statistics areas around each airport using `landcover.img` and `airports.shp` from our sample data. This is useful when it comes to finding the most commonly occurring terrain type, in other words, the median value.

First, we create the analysis areas around each airport using the **Vector** | **Geoprocessing Tools** | **Buffer(s)** tool and a buffer size of `100,000` **feet**, as demonstrated in the following screenshot:

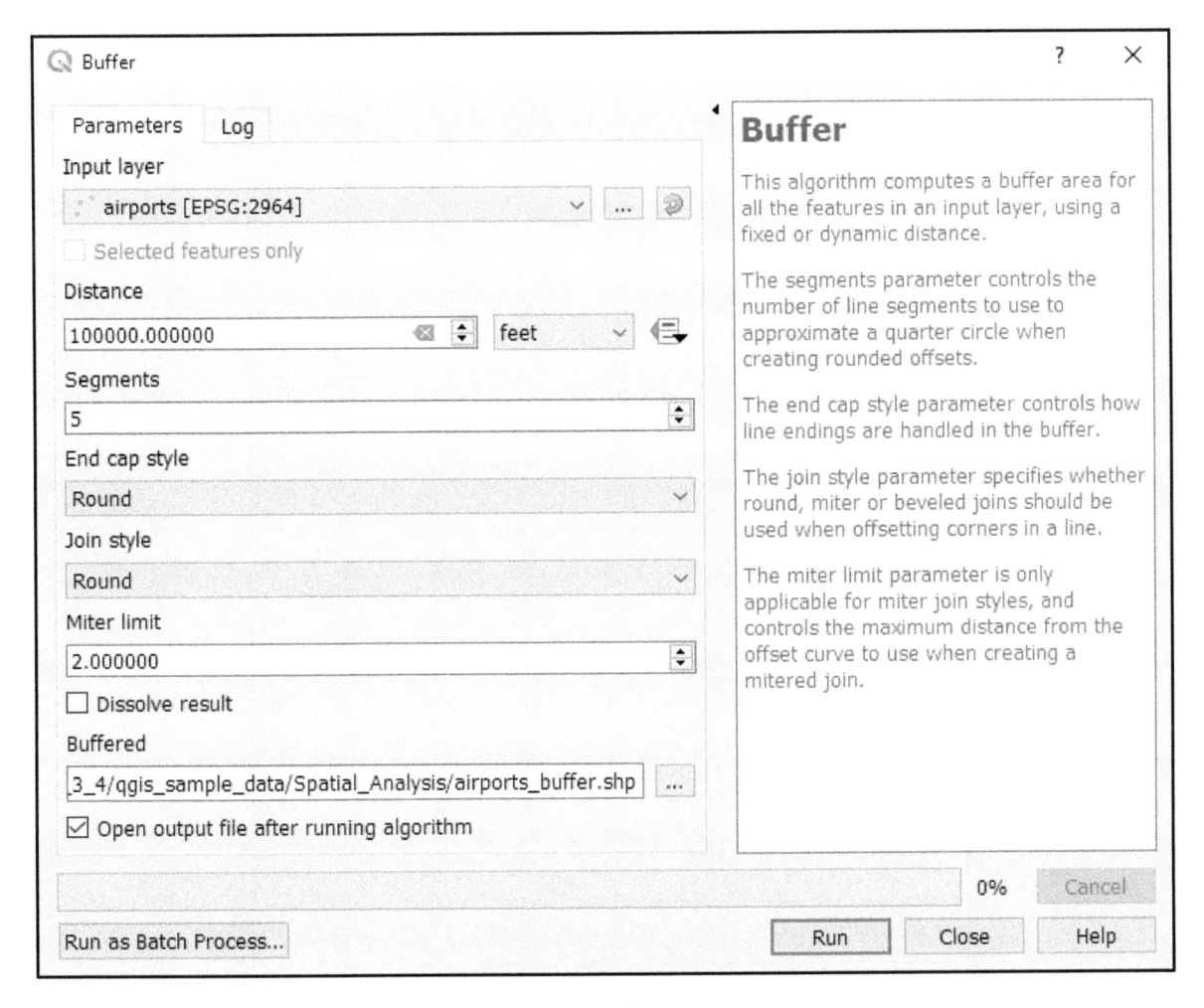

The buffer tool dialog box

Spatial Analysis

Now we can compute the statistics for the analysis areas using the **Zonal Statistics** tool. To do this, search for **Zonal Statistics** in the processing toolbox. We use the statistics to calculate the **Median** value to show the most common landcover type. This is shown in the following screenshot:

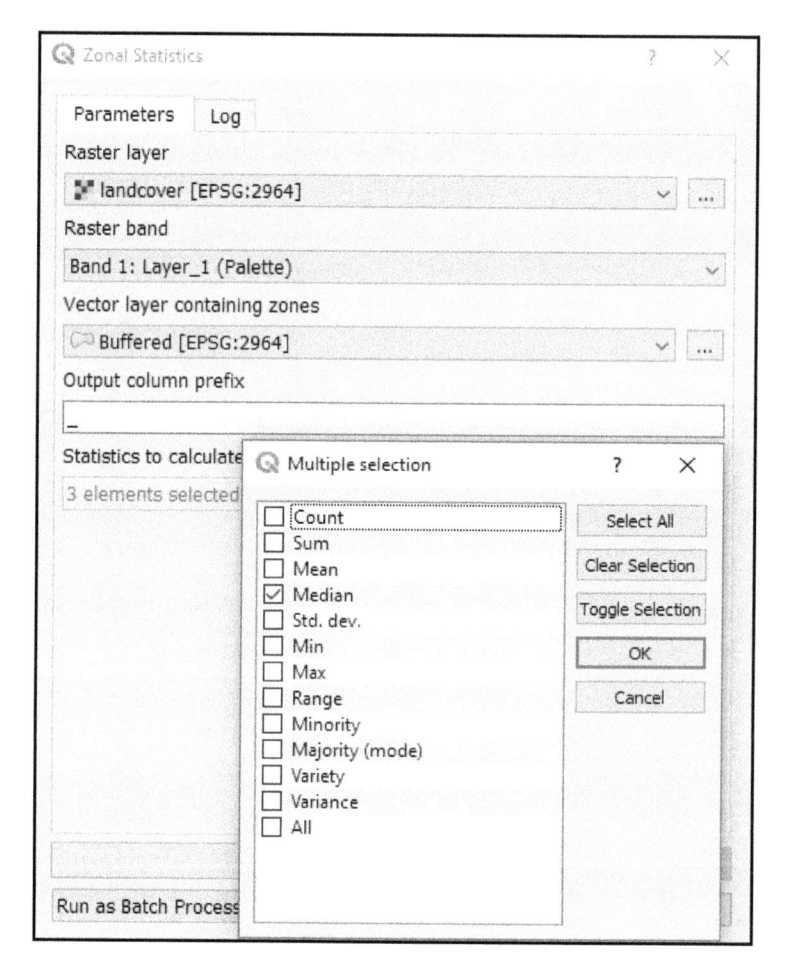

Using the zonal statistics tool

After you click on the **Run** button, the selected statistics are appended to the polygon layer attribute table, as shown in the following screenshot:

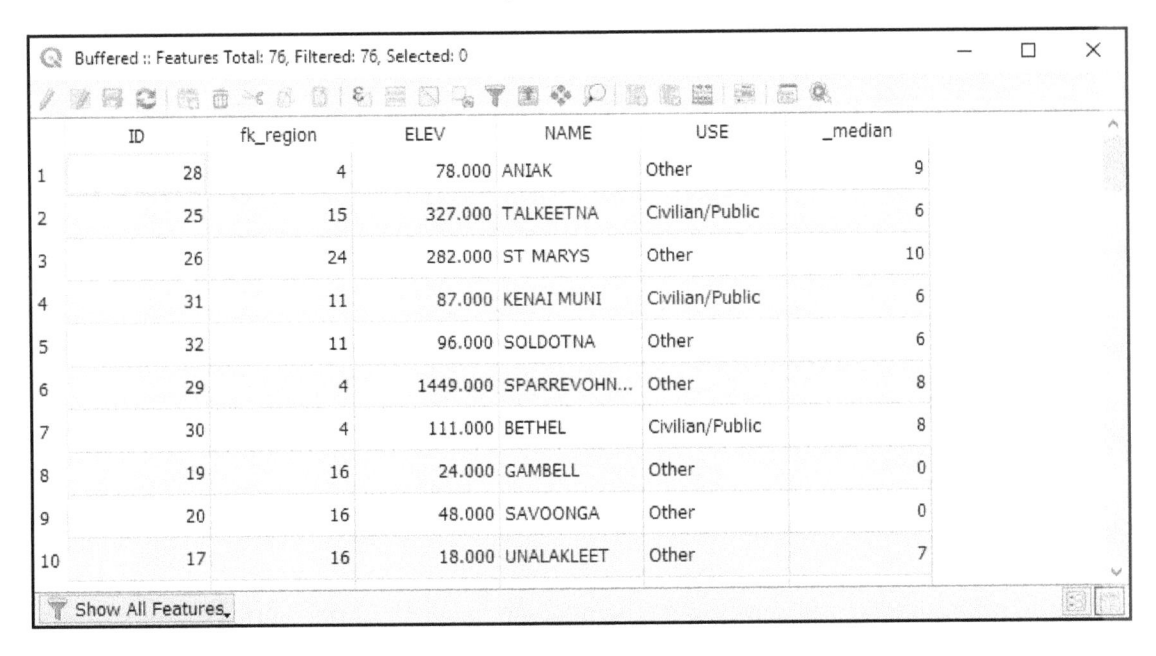

ID	fk_region	ELEV	NAME	USE	_median
28	4	78.000	ANIAK	Other	9
25	15	327.000	TALKEETNA	Civilian/Public	6
26	24	282.000	ST MARYS	Other	10
31	11	87.000	KENAI MUNI	Civilian/Public	6
32	11	96.000	SOLDOTNA	Other	6
29	4	1449.000	SPARREVOHN...	Other	8
30	4	111.000	BETHEL	Civilian/Public	8
19	16	24.000	GAMBELL	Other	0
20	16	48.000	SAVOONGA	Other	0
17	16	18.000	UNALAKLEET	Other	7

Attribute table created with the statistics added

If you knew what the corresponding terrain codes related to, then you could add another field in the table and use the field calculator to look up the terrain name.

Creating a heatmap from points

In Chapter 3, *Visualizing Data*, we showed how points can be symbolized on the fly as a **Heatmap**. Now, let's take a look at how to create a **Heatmap** and save it as a permanent raster dataset. In the processing toolbox, search for **Heatmap** and double-click on the corresponding result: **Heatmap** (**Kernel Density Estimation**).

[177]

Spatial Analysis

Complete the dialog box as shown as follows with a kernel **radius** of 300,000 layer units, which, in the case of our airport data, is displayed in feet. In QGIS 3.4, you can adjust the measurement unit in the tool, so, if you prefer, you could calculate in meters. I have set the pixel size to 10000 by 10000:

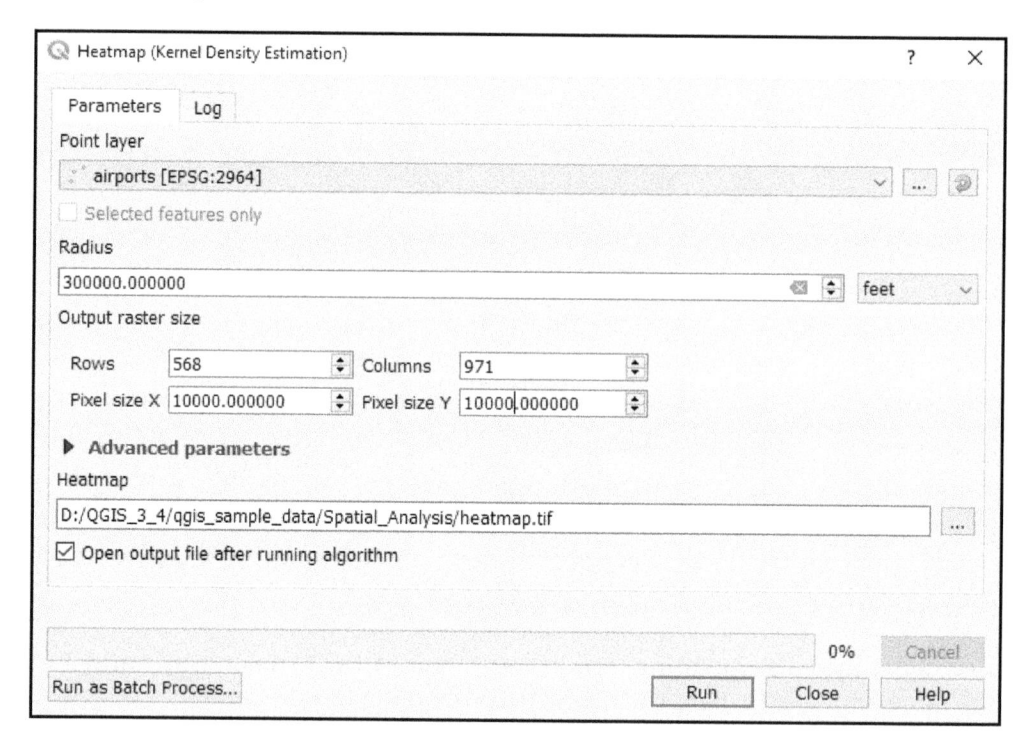

Heatmap dialog box

> Radius determines the distance around each point at which the point will have an influence. Therefore, smaller radius values result in heatmaps that show finer and smaller details, while larger values result in smoother heatmaps with fewer details.
>
> Additionally, the Kernel shape controls the rate at which the influence of a point decreases as the distance from the point increases. The kernel shapes that are available in the **Heatmap** plugin are listed in the following screenshot. For example, a **Triweight** kernel creates a smaller hotspot than the **Epanechnikov** kernel. For formal definitions of the kernel functions, refer to https://ipfs.io/ipfs/QmXoypizjW3WknFiJnKLwHCnL72vedxjQkDDP1mXWo6uco/wiki/Kernel_(statistics).html.

[178]

By default, the heatmap output will be rendered using the singleband gray render type (with low raster values in black, and high values in white). As we saw in `Chapter 3`, *Visualizing Data,* the resulting raster can be styled to show the areas with the highest density using the Layer Styling panel. An example of this is shown in the following screenshot:

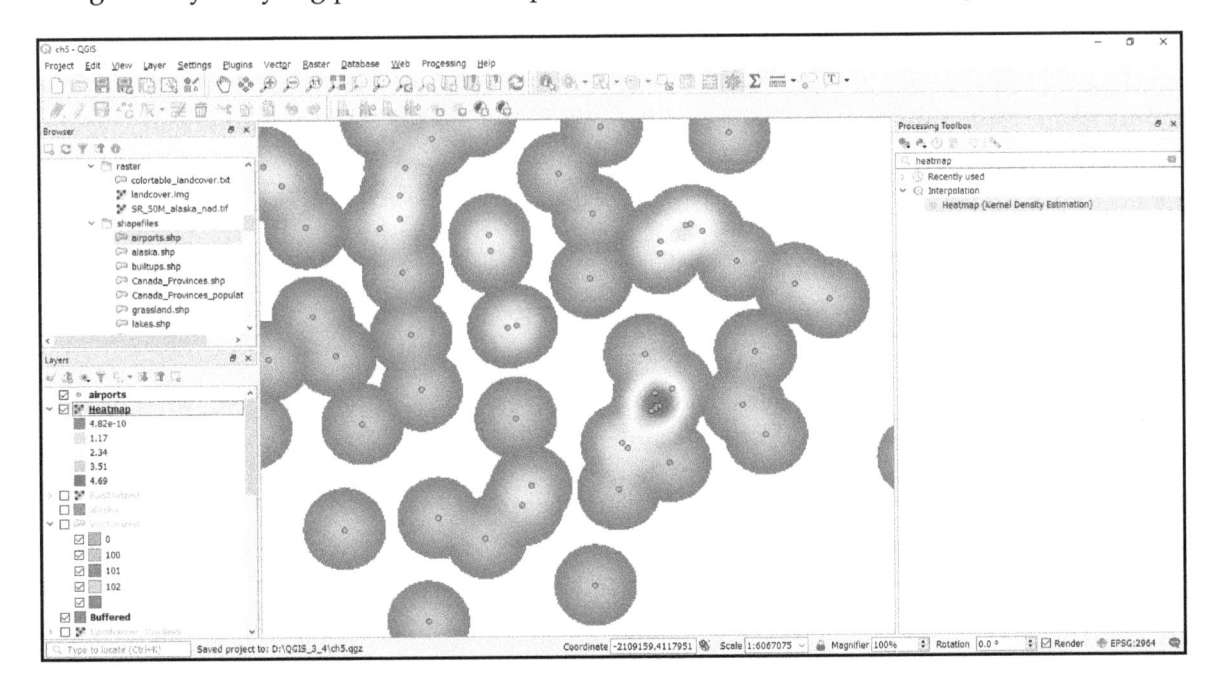

The resulting raster heatmap

Advanced vector and raster analysis with processing

In the following sections, we will cover more advanced processing tools and see how we can use the modeler to automate our tasks.

Finding nearest neighbors

Finding nearest neighbors – for example, the airport nearest to a populated place – is a common task in geoprocessing.

Spatial Analysis

To do this, load the `popp.shp` into QGIS as well as the `airports.shp`, if this is not already loaded. Then search for the **Distance to Nearest Hub** tool (**Line to Hub**) in the toolbox. You should use the `popp.shp` as the **Source points layer** and the airports as the **Destination hubs layer**. The **Hub layer name attribute** will be added to the results attribute table to identify the nearest feature. Select **NAME** to add the airport name to the populated places.

It is recommended that you use the **Layer units** as **Measurement units** to avoid potential issues with incorrect measurements, as seen in the following screenshot:

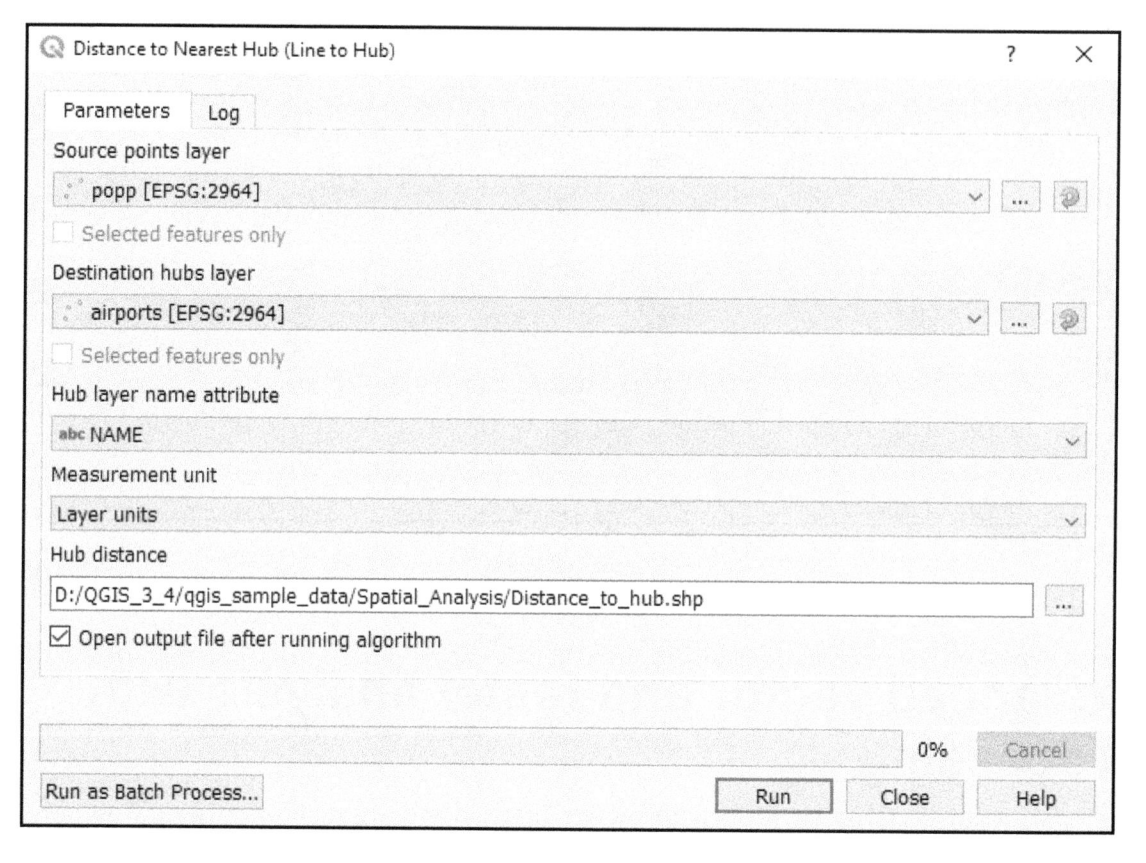

Distance to nearest hub (line to hub) dialog box

The resulting `Distance_to_hub` layer is added to the map as the **Open output file after running algorithm** checkbox has been left checked. Using the knowledge gained in Chapter 3, *Visualizing Data,* shade the resulting lines based on distance from the hub using a Graduated render. This will look similar to the following screenshot:

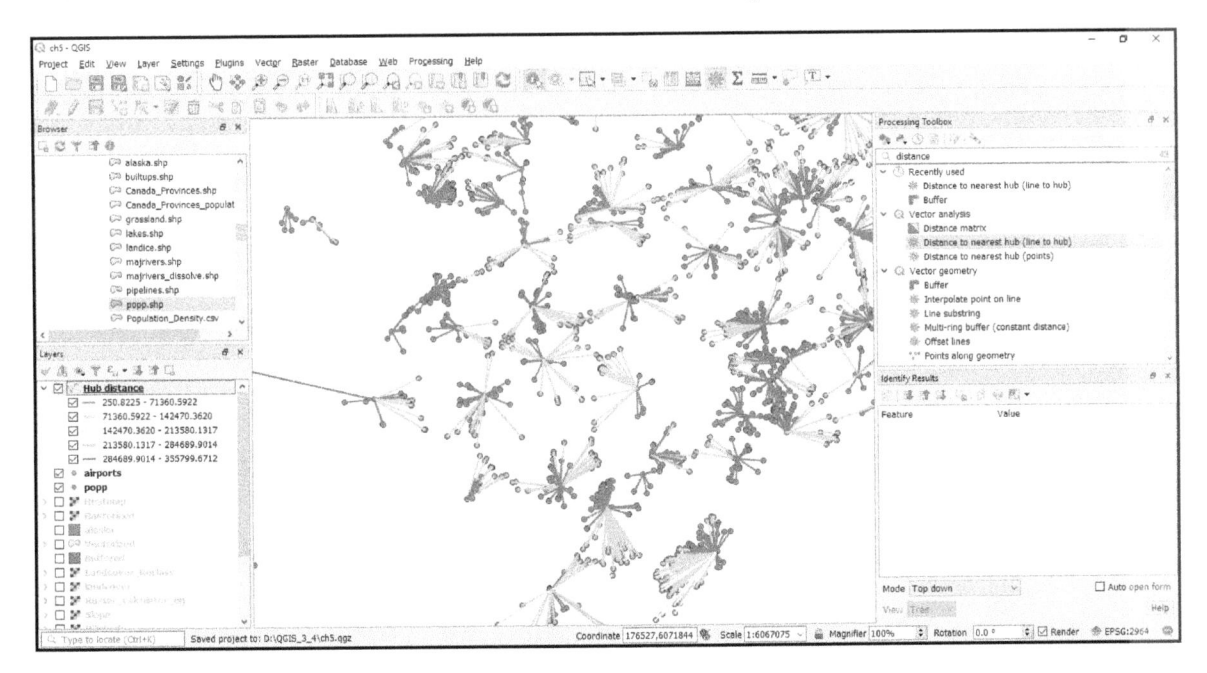

Hub distance layer added to map

Converting between points, lines, and polygons

It is often necessary to be able to convert between points, lines, and polygons, for example, to create lines from a series of points, or to extract the nodes of polygons and create a new point layer out of them. There are many tools that cover these different use cases.

Spatial Analysis

The following table provides an overview of the tools that are available in the processing toolbox for conversion between points, lines, and polygons:

	To points	To lines	To polygons
From points	-	Points to path	Convex hull Concave hull
From lines	Extract nodes	-	Lines to polygons Convex hull
From polygons	Extract nodes Polygon centroids (Random points inside a polygon)	Polygons to lines	-

In general, it is easier to convert more complex representations into simpler ones (polygons to lines, polygons to points, or lines to points) than to convert in the other direction (points to lines, points to polygons, or lines to polygons). Here is a short overview of these tools:

- **Extract nodes**: This takes one input layer with lines or polygons and creates a point layer that contains all the input geometry nodes. The resulting points contain all the attributes of the original line or polygon feature.
- **Polygon centroids**: This tool creates one centroid per polygon or multipolygon. It is worth noting that this does not ensure that the centroid falls within the polygon.
- **Random points inside polygon**: This tool creates a certain number of points at random locations inside the polygon.
- **Points to path**: To be able to create lines from points, the point layer needs attributes that identify the line (Group field) and the order of points in the line (Order field).
- **Minimum bounding geometry – Convex hull**: This tool creates a convex hull around the input points or lines. The convex hull can be imagined as an area that contains all the input points as well as all the connections between the input points.
- **Concave hull**: This tool creates a concave hull around the input points. The concave hull is a polygon that represents the area occupied by the input points. The concave hull is equal to, or smaller than, the convex hull. In this tool, we can control the level of detail of the concave hull by changing the Threshold parameter between 0 (very detailed) and 1 (equivalent to the convex hull).
- **Lines to polygon**: Finally, this tool can create polygons from lines that enclose an area. Make sure that there are no gaps between the lines.

The difference between a convex hull and a concave hull on some selected points from the popp layer is shown as follows:

Difference between a convex hull (inner polygon) and a concave hull (outer polygon)

Building workflows with processing tools

Spatial processing or geoprocessing tools are often used in either batch (the same function performed several times over several layers), or in combination with one or more tools. As the level of complexity increases, there are tools that simplify the workflows.

In this section, we will look at the increasing complexity of tools using examples. In the following section, we will look at batch processing and model creation.

Spatial Analysis

Identifying features in the proximity of other features

One common spatial analysis task is to identify features in the proximity of certain other features. One example would be to find all airports near rivers. Using `airports.shp` and `majrivers.shp` from our sample data, we can find airports within 5,000 feet of a river by using a combination of the **Fixed distance buffer** and **Select by Location** tools. Use the search box to find the tools in the **Processing Toolbox**. The tool configurations for this example are shown in the following screenshot:

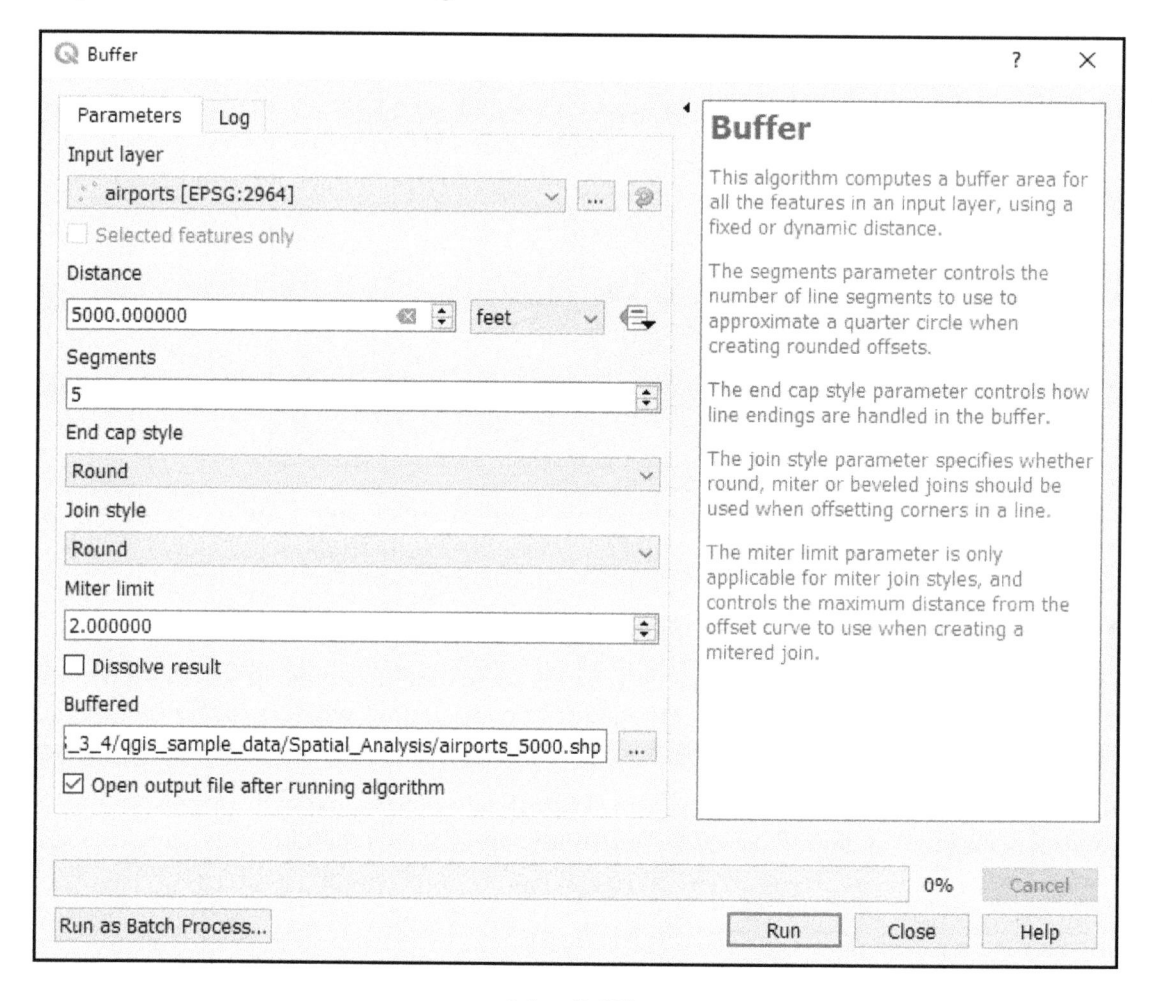

Buffer tool in QGIS

Chapter 5

After buffering the airport point locations, the **Select by Location** tool selects all the airport buffers that intersect a river. This is shown in the following screenshot:

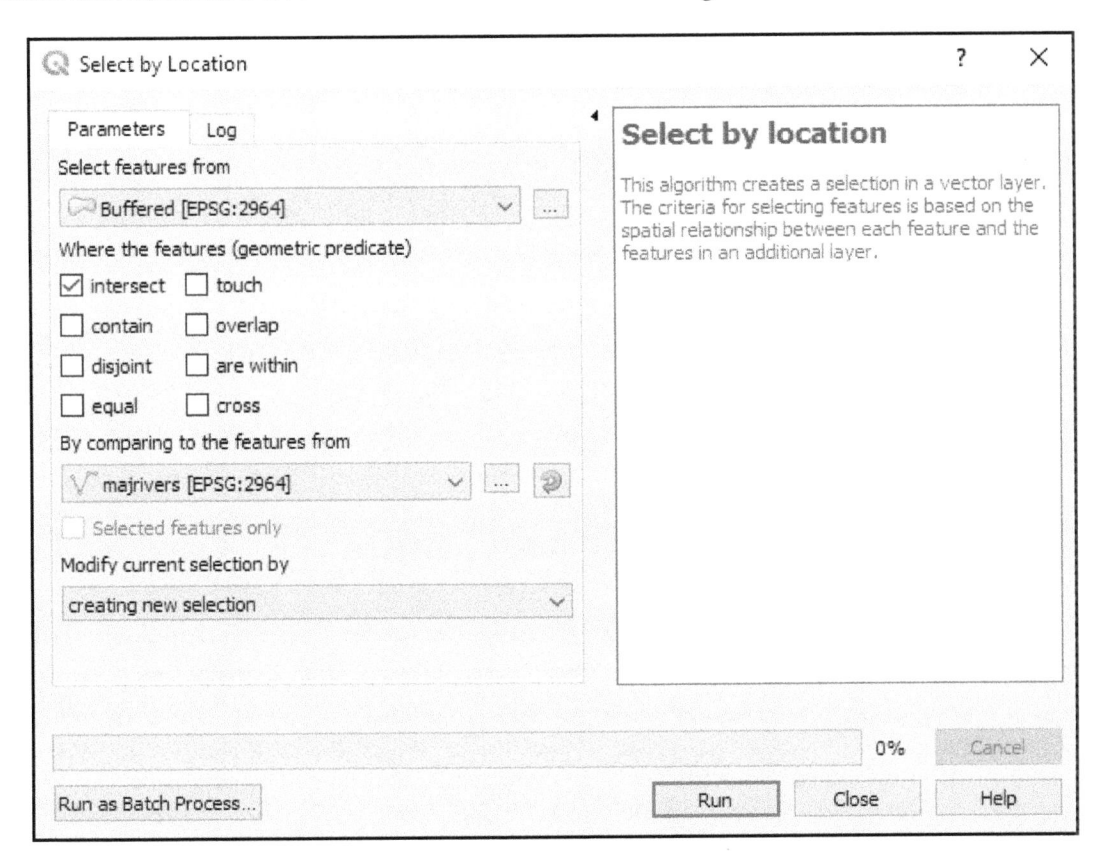

Spatial Analysis

As a result, **14** out of the **76** airports are selected, as shown in the following screenshot:

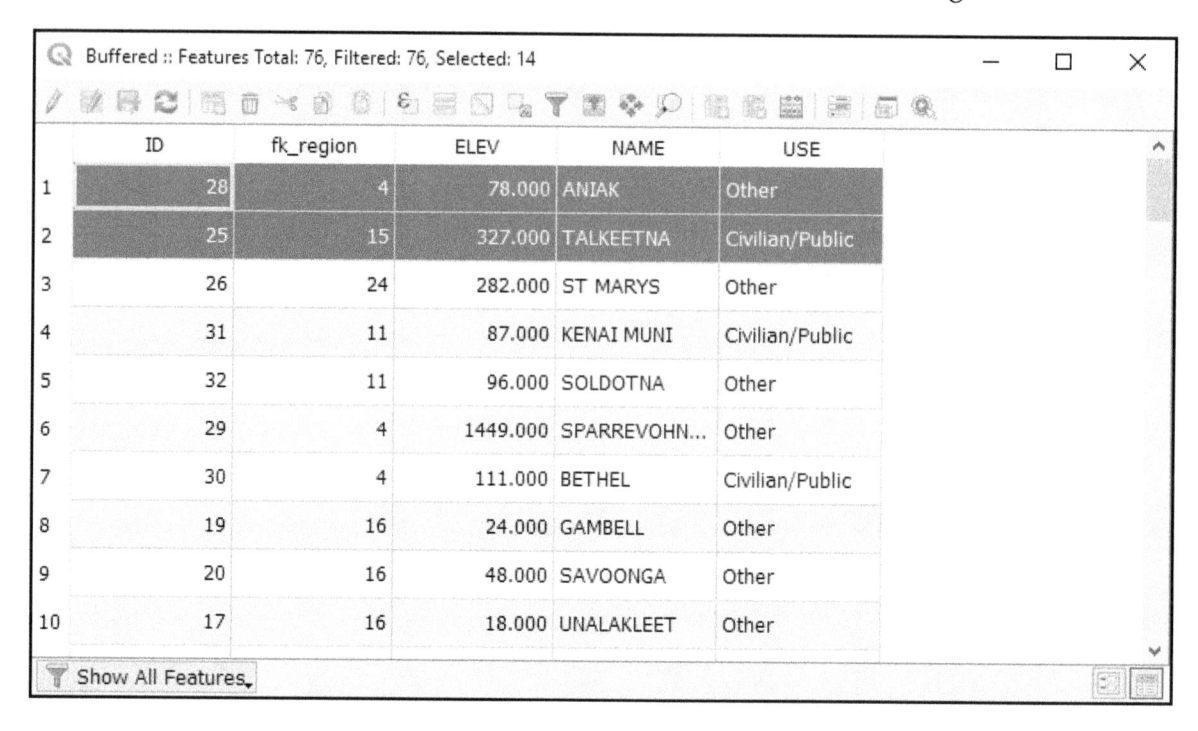

	ID	fk_region	ELEV	NAME	USE
1	28	4	78.000	ANIAK	Other
2	25	15	327.000	TALKEETNA	Civilian/Public
3	26	24	282.000	ST MARYS	Other
4	31	11	87.000	KENAI MUNI	Civilian/Public
5	32	11	96.000	SOLDOTNA	Other
6	29	4	1449.000	SPARREVOHN...	Other
7	30	4	111.000	BETHEL	Civilian/Public
8	19	16	24.000	GAMBELL	Other
9	20	16	48.000	SAVOONGA	Other
10	17	16	18.000	UNALAKLEET	Other

All the buffered points that are intersecting the river lines

> **TIP**: If you ever forget which settings you used, or if you need to check whether you have used the correct input layer, you can go to **Processing** | **History**. The **ALGORITHM** section lists all the algorithms that we have been running as well as the settings used.

Sampling a raster at point locations

You may have noticed that there are not just QGIS processing tools available in the toolbox. GRASS and SAGA GIS also have tools available. If you cannot see them in your toolbox, check the installation of QGIS and the version you are running. There is an option to run QGIS with GRASS when you install via OSGeo4W. In the following examples, open a new QGIS project with GRASS enabled (GRASS 7.4.2 at the time of writing). Load the `aiports.shp` and `landcover.img` layers into the **Layers** panel.

The GRASS tool **v.sample** allows us to sample a raster at specific point locations. Search for **v.sample** (the **v** stands for **vector**) in the toolbox. Let's sample the **landcover** layer at the airport locations. All we have to do here is specify the vector layer containing the sample points and the raster layer that should be sampled. For this example, we can leave all other settings at their default values, as shown in the following screenshot. This tool not only samples the raster, but also compares point attributes with the sampled raster value:

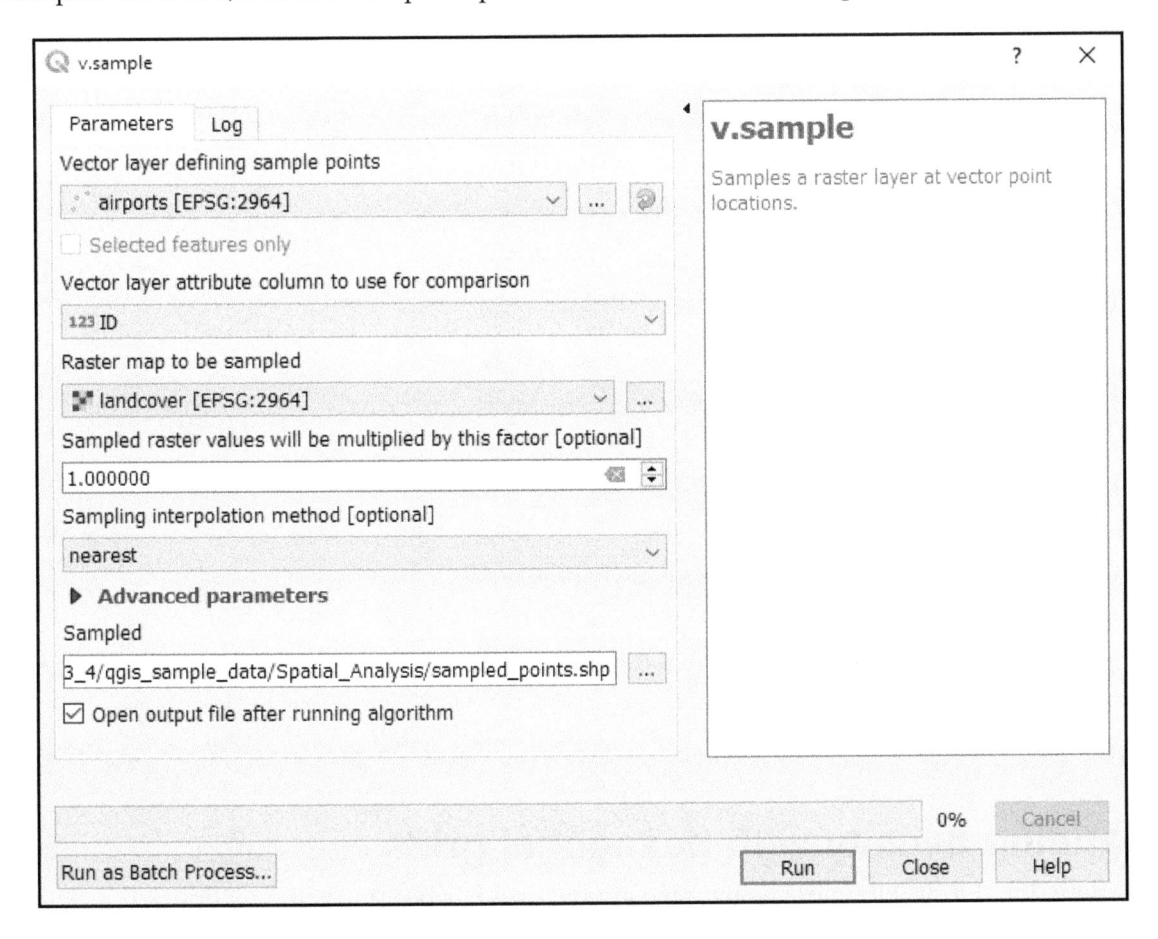

Sampling the raster tool at given locations, in this case airports

Spatial Analysis

The resulting layers attribute table looks similar to the following:

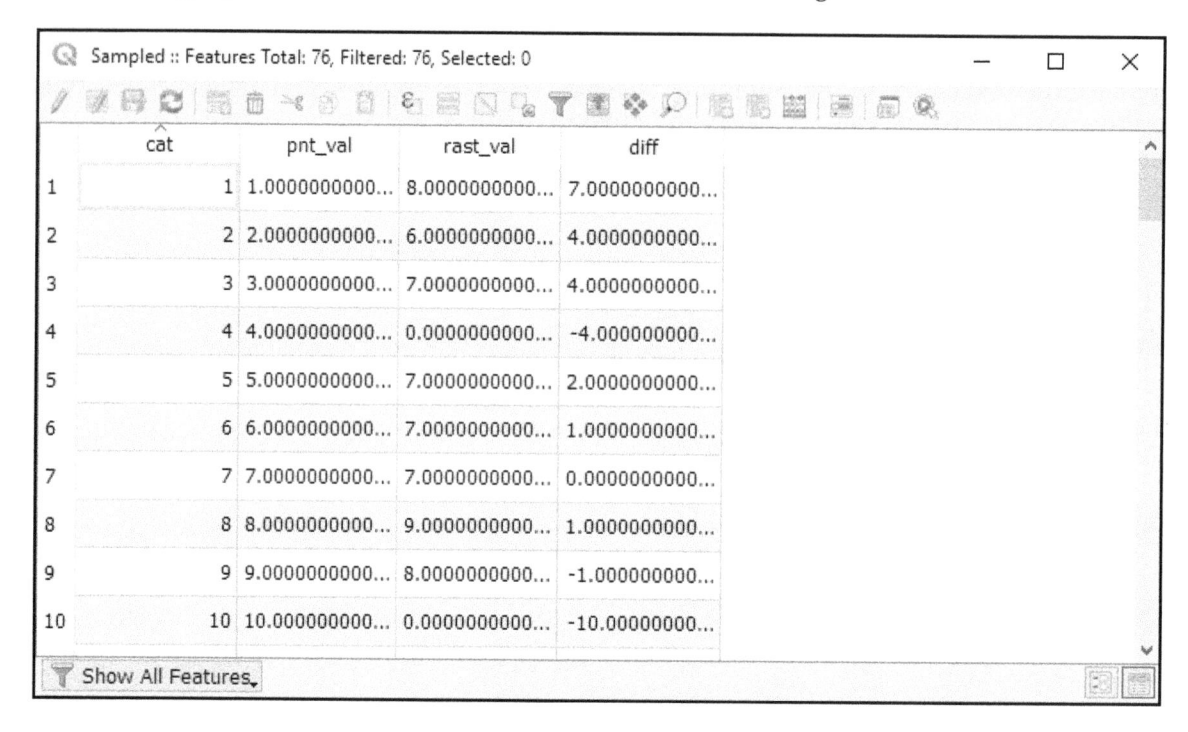

	cat	pnt_val	rast_val	diff
1	1	1.0000000000...	8.0000000000...	7.0000000000...
2	2	2.0000000000...	6.0000000000...	4.0000000000...
3	3	3.0000000000...	7.0000000000...	4.0000000000...
4	4	4.0000000000...	0.0000000000...	-4.000000000...
5	5	5.0000000000...	7.0000000000...	2.0000000000...
6	6	6.0000000000...	7.0000000000...	1.0000000000...
7	7	7.0000000000...	7.0000000000...	0.0000000000...
8	8	8.0000000000...	9.0000000000...	1.0000000000...
9	9	9.0000000000...	8.0000000000...	-1.000000000...
10	10	10.000000000...	0.0000000000...	-10.00000000...

Attribute table from the sampled points

> **TIP:** The SAGA GIS tool **Add raster values to Points** will perform the same process.

Mapping density with hexagonal grids

Mapping the density of points using a hexagonal grid has become quite a popular alternative to creating heatmaps. Load the `popp.shp` layer into the **Layers** panel. We will build a grid based on the extent of the `landcover.img` layer. Each cell in the grid will ultimately contain a count of points that fall in each cell. Processing offers us a fast way to create such an analysis. To create a grid, search **Create Grid** in the **Processing Toolbox**. After doing this, fill in the dialog box as follows and select **Hexagon (polygon)** as the **Grid type**:

[188]

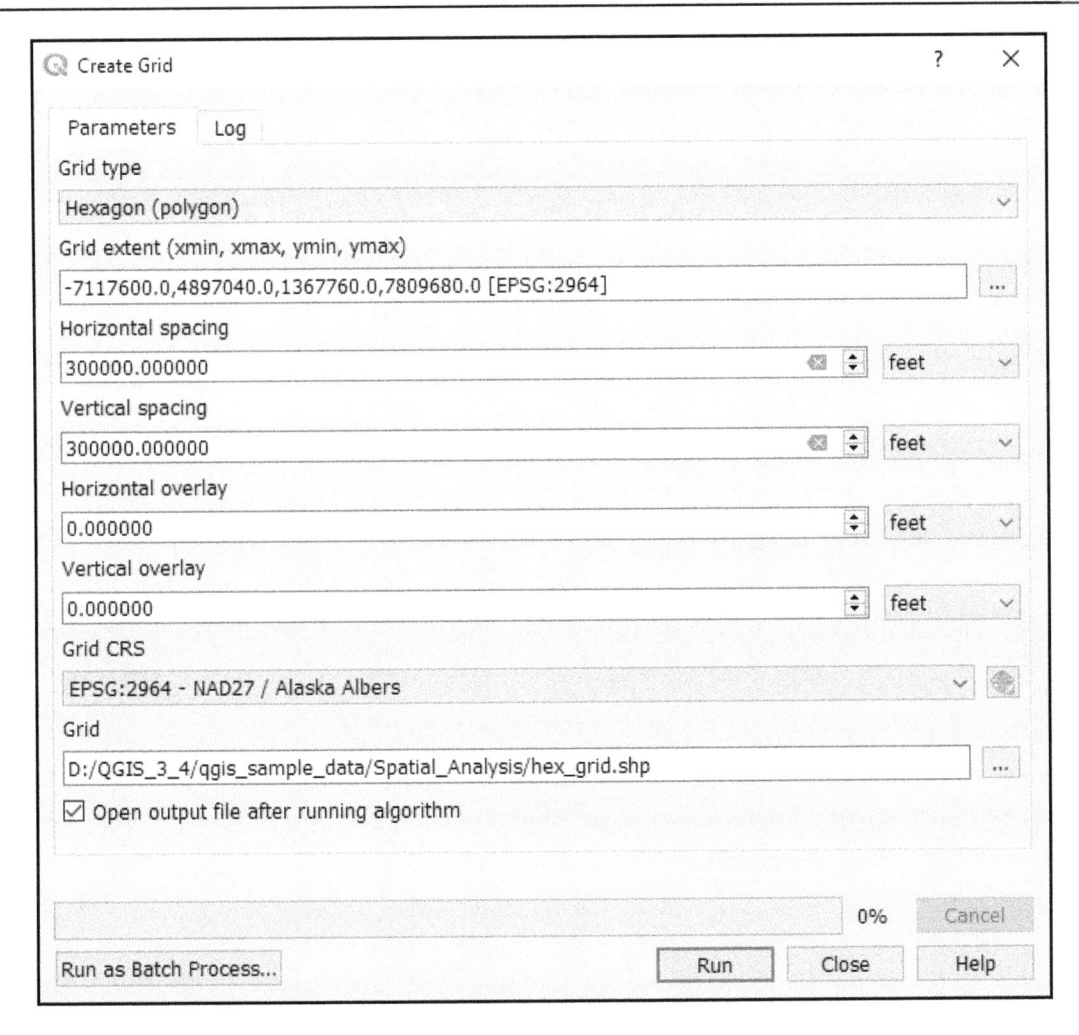

Creating a hexagonal grid

Spatial Analysis

Search for **Count Points in Polygon** in the toolbox to calculate the number of points in each hexagonal grid. The number of points will be stored in the NUMPOINTS column if you use the settings shown in the following screenshot:

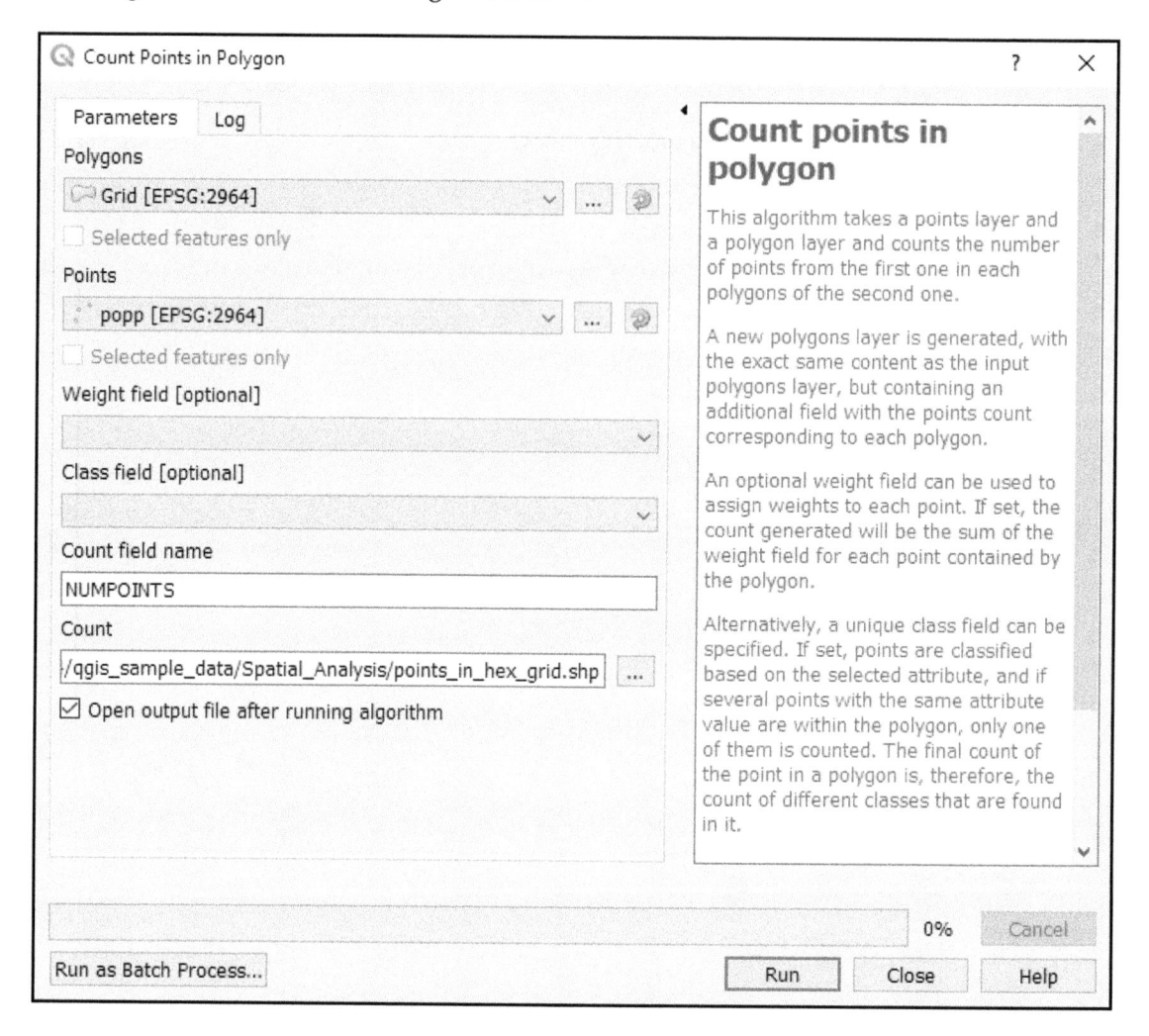

Counting the number of points within each hexagonal polygon

Chapter 5

Use a graduated color scheme to shade the hexagons based on the NUMPOINTS field. An example of this is shown in the following screenshot using the red color ramp:

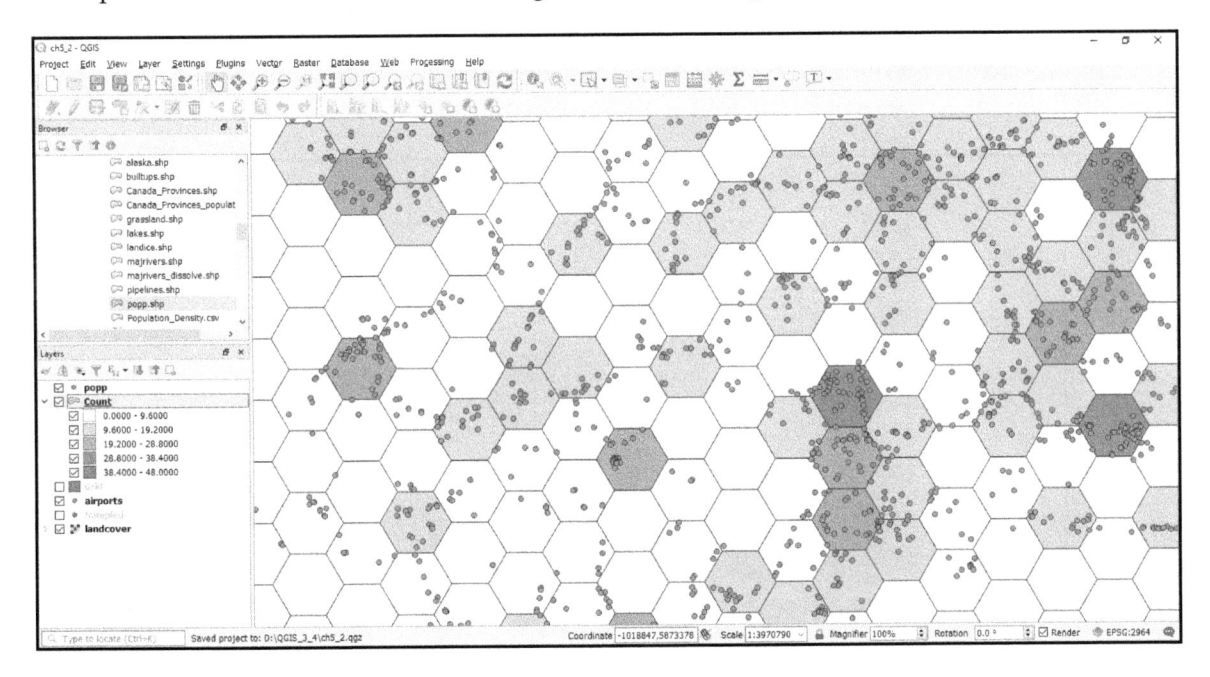

The result of the hexagonal grid

[191]

Spatial Analysis

Calculating area shares within a region

Calculating area shares within a certain region is another common workflow, for example, landcover shares along one specific river. Using `majrivers.shp` and `trees.shp`, we can calculate the share of wooded area in a 10,000 feet-wide strip of land along the Susitna River. Both layers are shown in the following screenshot:

The river and tree layers

Before starting, please run the **Fix Geometries** tool on the `trees.shp` layer. **You will only need to do this once**. I have found this layer to have several geometry errors. Search for **Fix Geometries** in the toolbox and fill in the tool as shown in the following screenshot:

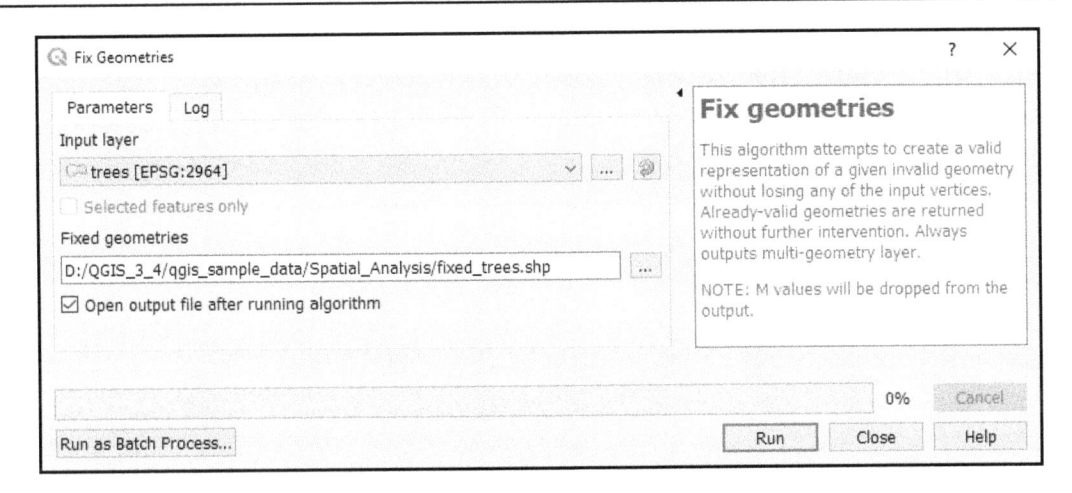

Fix Geometries

We first define the analysis region by selecting the river and buffering it. To select the **Susitna River**, we use the **Select by attribute** tool and search for it in the **Processing Toolbox**. After running the tool, you should see that our river of interest is selected and highlighted. The tool looks like this:

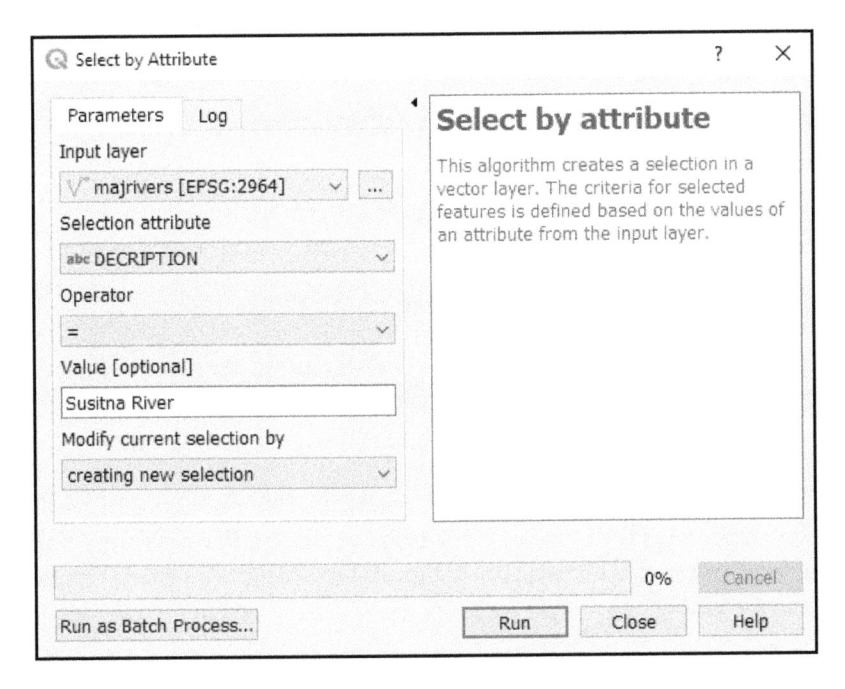

Select by attribute

Spatial Analysis

We can then use the fixed distance buffer tool to get the area within 5,000 feet along the river. Note that the **Dissolve result** option should be enabled to ensure that the buffer result is one continuous polygon. The buffer tool is checked for **Selected features only**, as shown in the following screenshot:

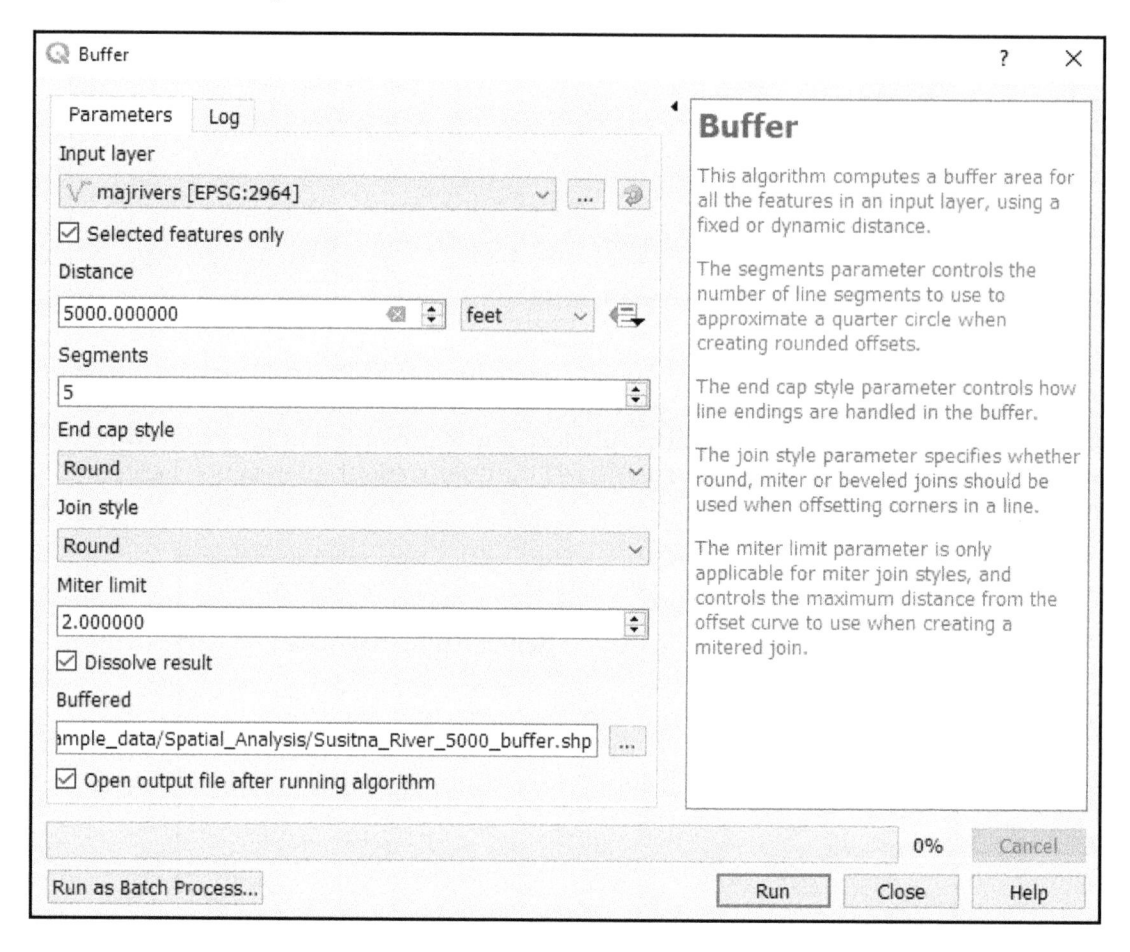

Buffering the river layer by 5,000 feet

Next, we calculate the size of the strip of land around our river. This can be done by using the **Add geometry attributes** tool – search for this tool in the **Processing Toolbox**. This will add the area and perimeter to the attribute table. After doing this, fill in the table as shown in the following screenshot:

[194]

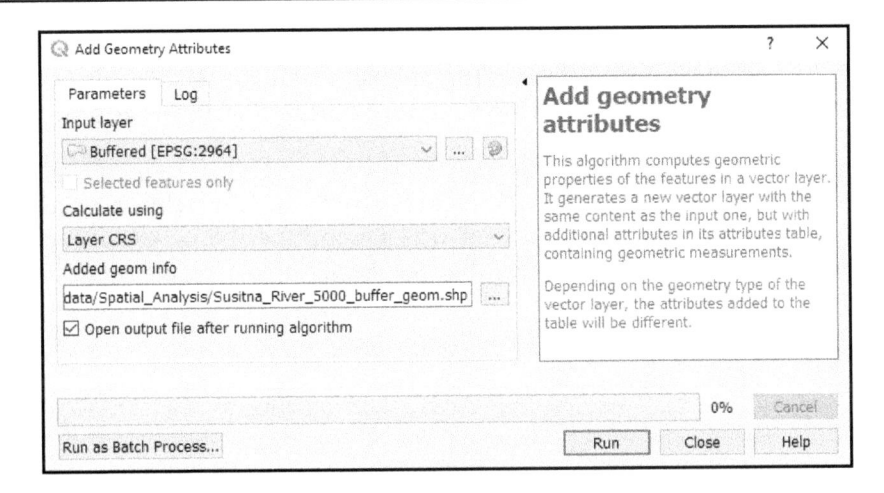

Export geometry columns dialog

We can then calculate the **Intersection** between the area along the river and the wooded areas in `trees.shp`. Search for **Intersection** in the **Processing Toolbox** and fill in the dialog box as shown in the following screenshot. The result of this operation is a layer that contains only those wooded areas within the river buffer:

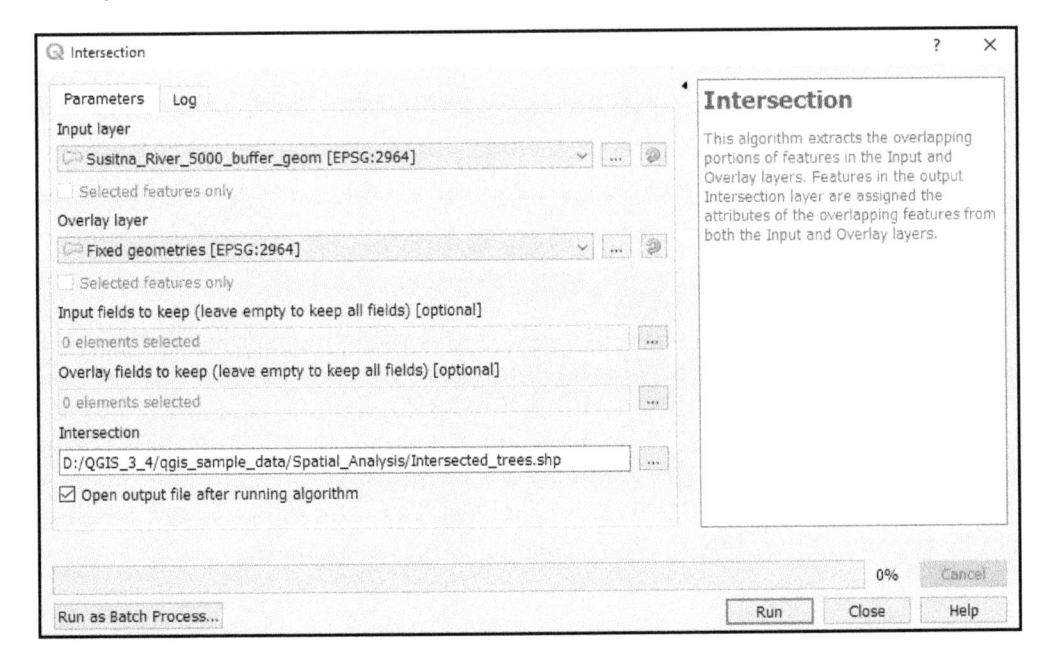

Intersection dialog box

Spatial Analysis

> **TIP:** You may get an error regarding invalid geometries. If this happens, go to **Settings | Options | Processing** and select **General dropdown**. Change the **Invalid features** filtering to **ignore features with invalid geometries**.

Using the **Dissolve** tool, we can recombine all areas from the intersection results into one big polygon that represents the total wooded area around the river. Search for **Dissolve** in the **Processing Toolbox**. Note how we use the Unique ID field VEGDESC to only combine areas with the same vegetation in order not to mix deciduous and mixed trees. The dialog box should look like the following screenshot:

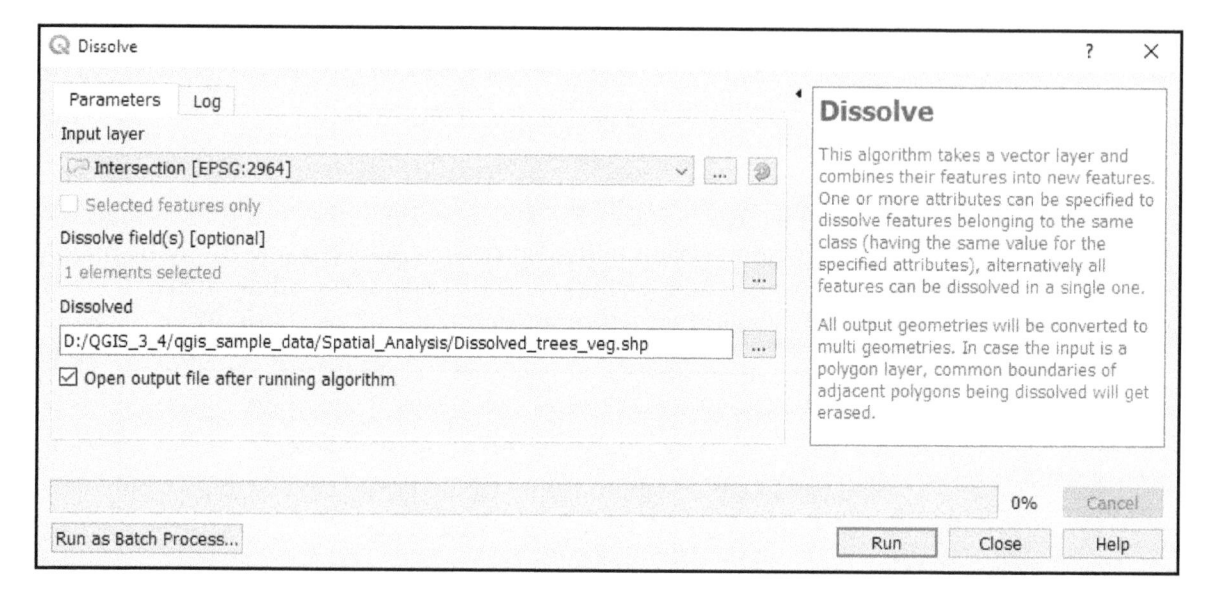

Dissolve the intersection layer

Finally, we can calculate the final share of wooded area using the **Advanced Python Field Calculator**. Again, search for this tool in the **Processing Toolbox**. The formula `value = $geom.area()/<area>` divides the area of the final polygon (`$geom.area()`) by the value in the area attribute (`<area>`), which we created earlier by running **Export/Add geometry columns**. As shown in the following screenshot, this calculation results in a wood share of 0.316 for deciduous and 0.096 for mixed trees. Consequently, we can conclude that a total of 41.2 percent of the land along the Susitna River is wooded:

Chapter 5

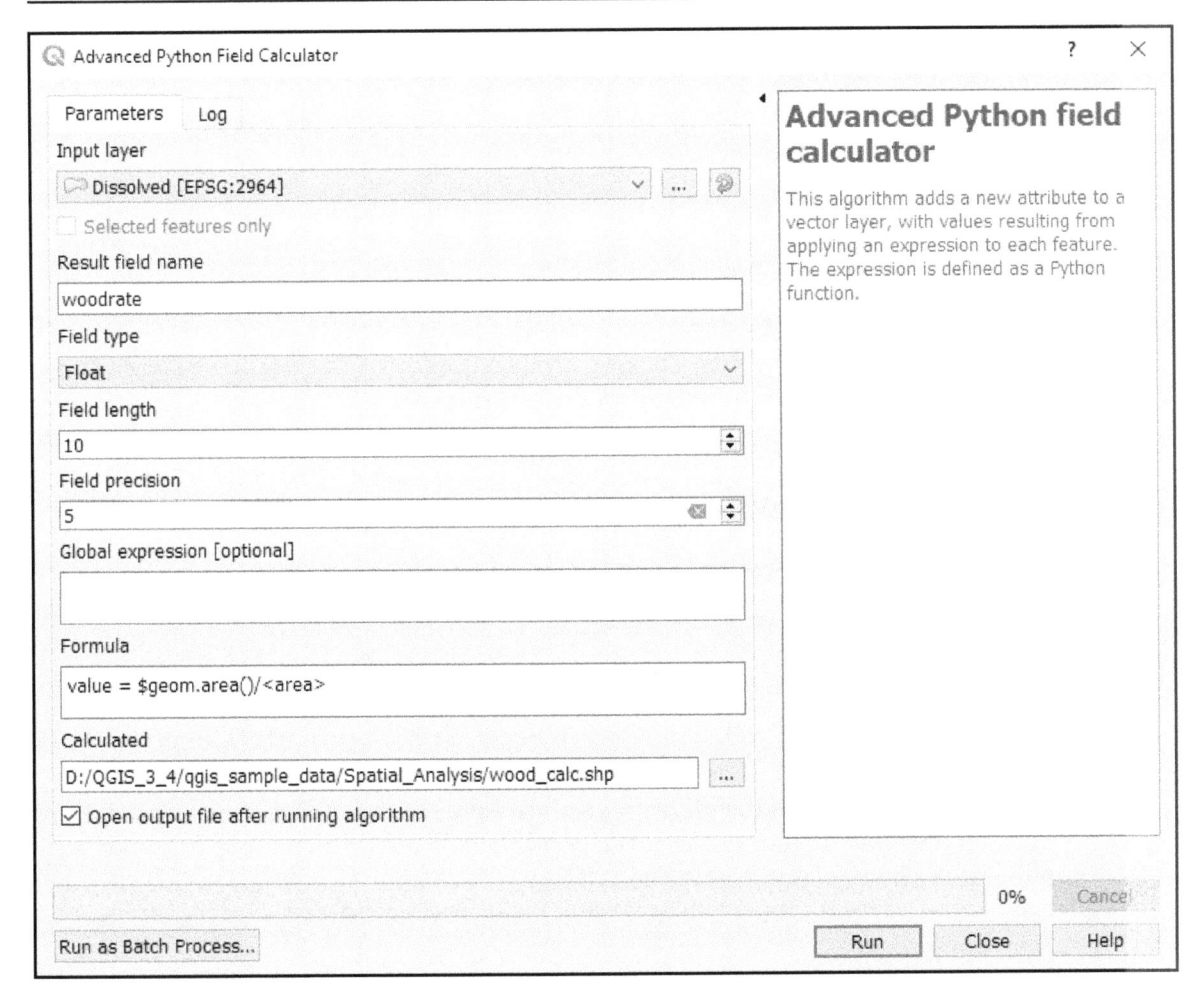

Advanced Python Field Calculator	? ×
Parameters Log	**Advanced Python field calculator**
Input layer	
Dissolved [EPSG:2964]	This algorithm adds a new attribute to a vector layer, with values resulting from applying an expression to each feature. The expression is defined as a Python function.
☐ Selected features only	
Result field name	
woodrate	
Field type	
Float	
Field length	
10	
Field precision	
5	
Global expression [optional]	
Formula	
value = $geom.area()/<area>	
Calculated	
D:/QGIS_3_4/qgis_sample_data/Spatial_Analysis/wood_calc.shp	
☑ Open output file after running algorithm	
0% Cancel
Run as Batch Process...	Run Close Help

Calculating the wood share across the Susitna River

In total, this took six different tools to get to the final result. When workflows are developed, they can be converted into models. Later on, we will see that processing tools can be incorporated into the model builder to create one-click workflows with a simple example.

[197]

Spatial Analysis

Batch processing multiple datasets

Sometimes, we want to run the same tool repeatedly, but with slightly different settings. For this use case, processing offers the **Batch Processing** functionality.

Use this tool to extract some samples from our airports layer using the **Random extract** tool (search for the tool in the processing toolbox). To do this, click on the **Run** button as **Batch Process**; this will open the **Batch Processing** dialog box. From here, you should observe the following steps:

1. Configure the **Input layer** by clicking on the **...** button and selecting **Select from Open Layers**, as shown in the following screenshot:

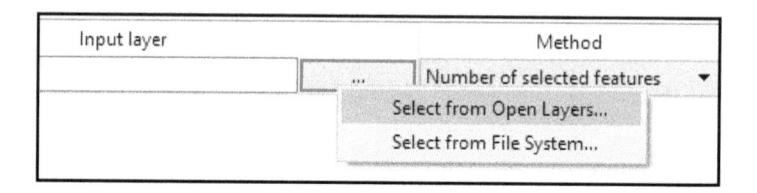

Batch processing

2. This will open a small dialog in which we can select the airports layer and click the **OK** button.
3. To automatically fill in the other rows with the same input layer, we can double-click on the table header of the corresponding column (which reads Input layer).
4. Next, we configure the method by selecting the **Percentage of selected features** option and again double-clicking on the respective table header to autofill the remaining rows.
5. The next parameter controls the **Number/percentage of selected features**. For our exercise, we will configure 10, 20, and 30 percent.
6. Lastly, we need to configure the output files in the **Extracted (random)** column. Click on the **...** button, which will open a file dialog. There, you can select the save location and filename (for example, data) and click on the **Save** button.

This will open the **Autofill** settings dialog, which helps us to create distinct filenames for each run automatically. Using the **Fill with numbers** mode will automatically append our parameter values (1,2,3) to the filename. This will result in data1, data2, and data3, as shown in the following screenshot:

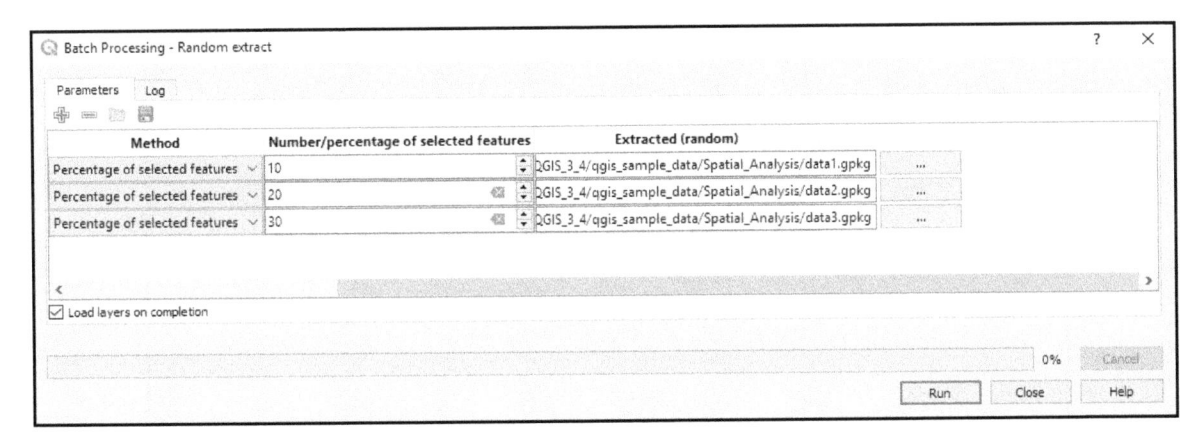

Batch processing example

Once everything is configured, click on the **Run** button and then wait for all the batch instructions to be processed and the results to be loaded into the project.

Batch running is very useful, especially if you have tens of layers to run the same operation on. Save yourself time by using these types of tools.

Automated geoprocessing with the graphical modeler

Using the graphical modeler, we can turn entire geoprocessing and analysis workflows into automated models. We can then use these models to run complex geoprocessing tasks that involve multiple different tools in one go. To create a model, we go to **Processing** | **Graphical modeler** to open the modeler, where we can select from different **Inputs** and **Algorithms** for our model.

Spatial Analysis

The Graphical modeler is shown in the following screenshot:

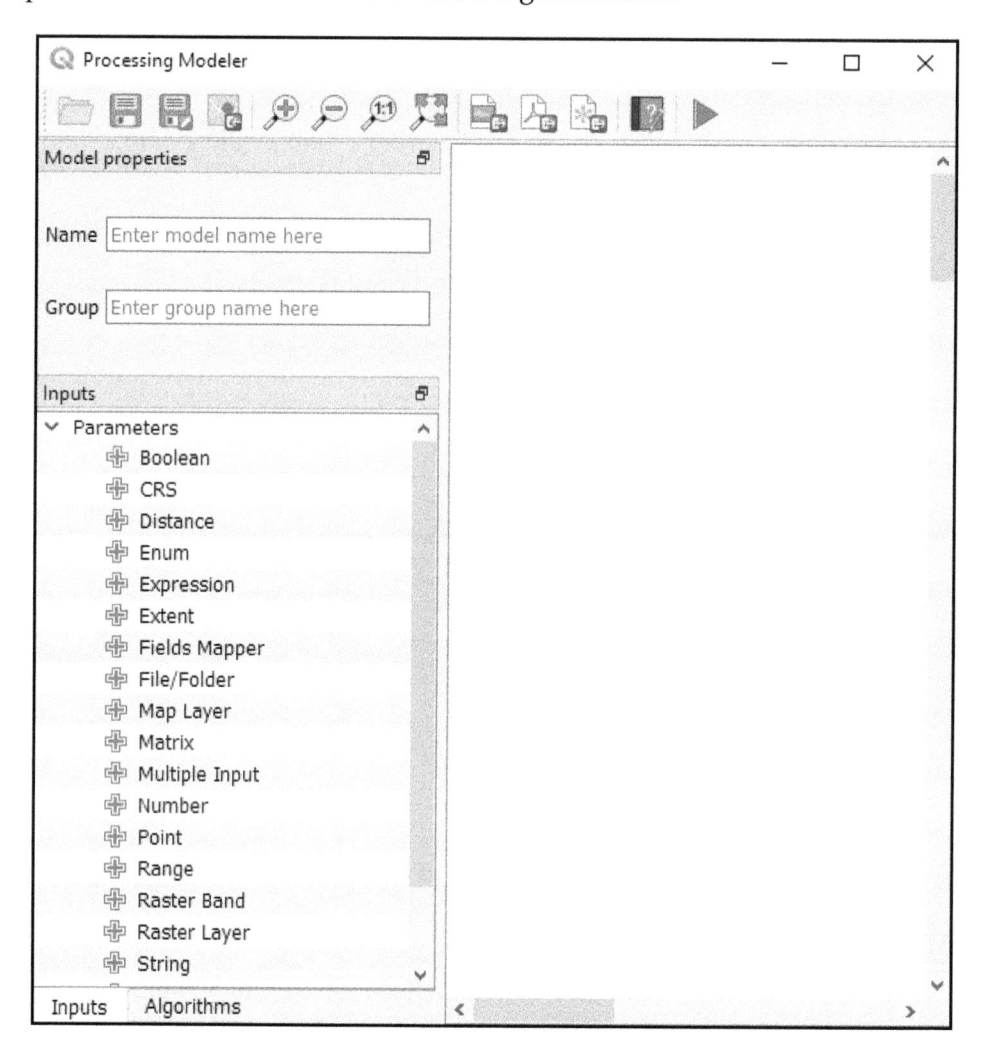

The default layout of the Processing Modeler

Create a model that automates the creation of hexagonal heatmaps

By double-clicking on the **Vector layer** entry in the **Inputs** list, we can add an input field for the point layer. It's a good idea to use descriptive parameter names so that we can recognize which input comes first and which comes later in the model. It is also useful to restrict the Shape type field wherever appropriate. In our example, we restrict the input to **Point** layers. This will enable Processing to prefilter the available layers and present us with just the layers of the correct type:

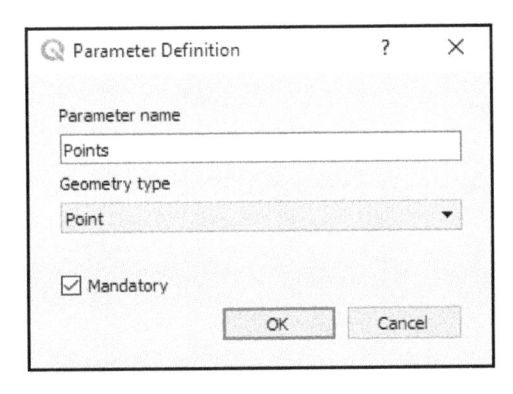

Setting a parameter as Points with a Point geometry type

The second input that we need is a Number field to specify the desired hexagonal cell size, as shown in the following screenshot:

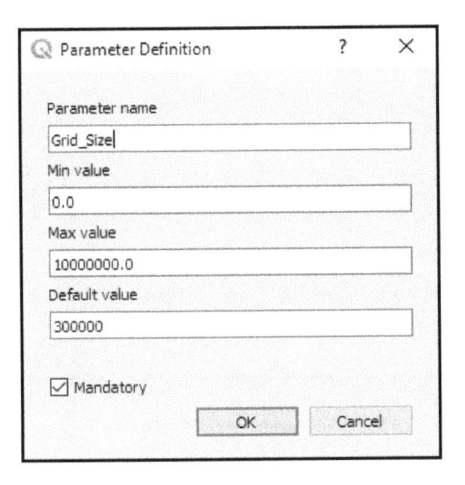

Setting another parameter

Spatial Analysis

In the **Algorithms** tab, we can use the filter at the top to narrow down our search for the correct algorithm. Search from **Create Grid** and double-click to open the algorithm. Set the **Horizontal spacing** and **Vertical spacing** to `Grid_Size`. Set the **Grid Extent (xmin, xmax, ymin, ymax)** to the **Extent of Points** and give the Grid output a name in the case, below `Hex_Grid`. This means that your model has an output. Your algorithm should look similar to what we can see in the following screenshot:

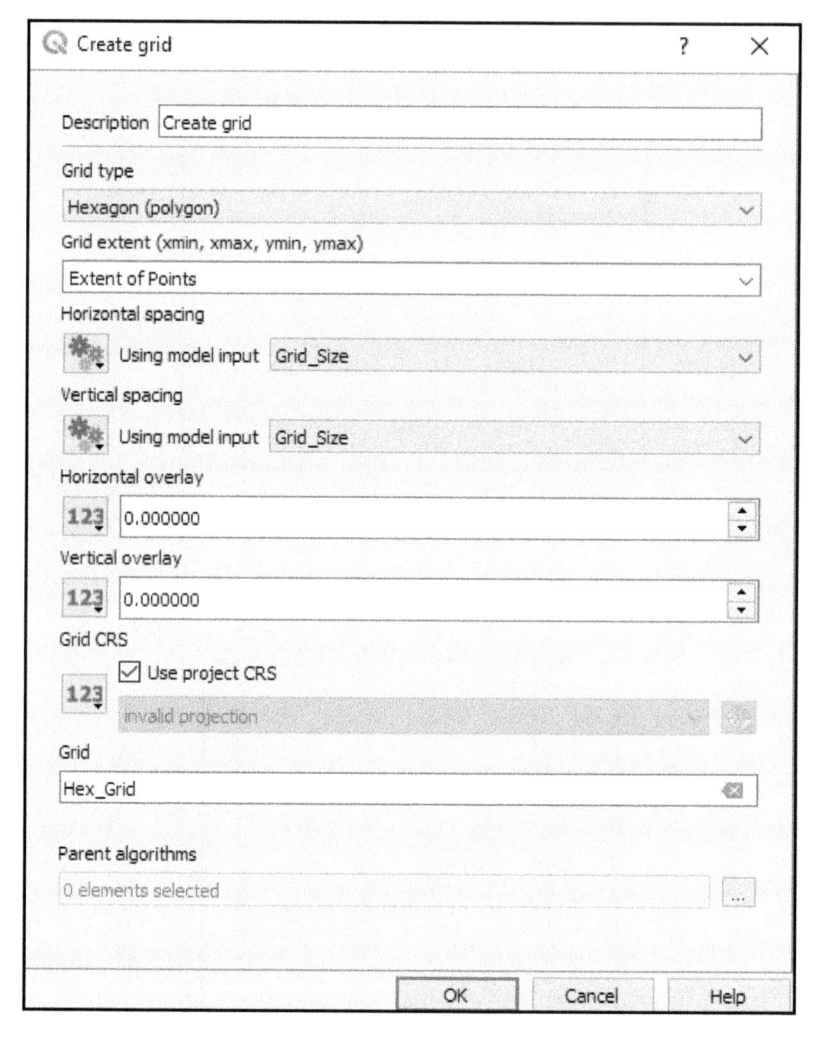

Setting up the Create Grid algorithm

Chapter 5

To finish the model, we need to enter a model name (`Create_hexagonal_grid`) and a group name (`Learning QGIS`). Processing will use the group name to organize all the models that we create into different toolbox groups. The finished model will look as follows:

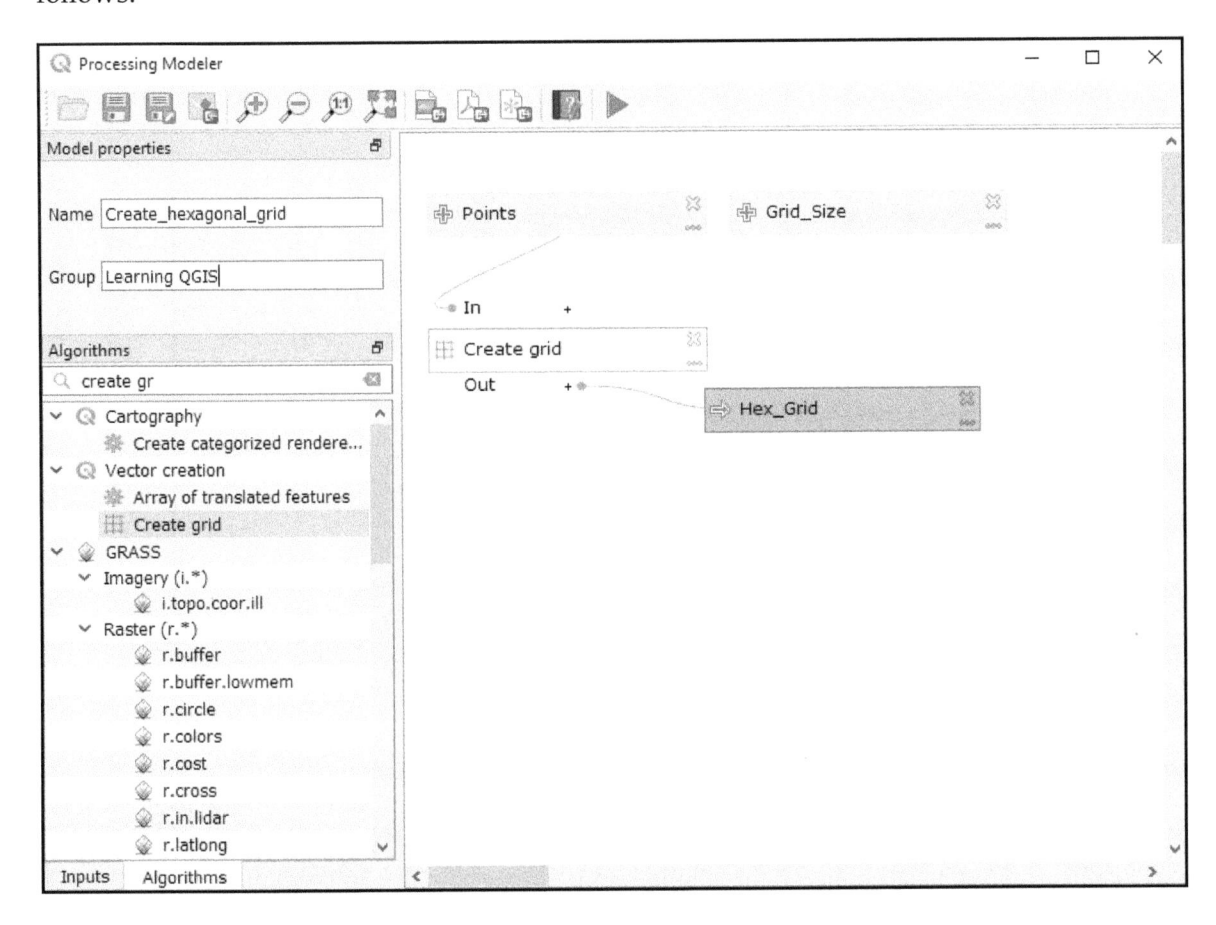

Finished model

Spatial Analysis

Click the save icon and save as `hex_model.model3`. In QGIS 3.4, a button was added to save the model to a project. This is the fourth button from the left on the menu bar in the previous diagram. Click on the green triangle or press *F5* to run the model. A dialog box should appear as shown in the following screenshot:

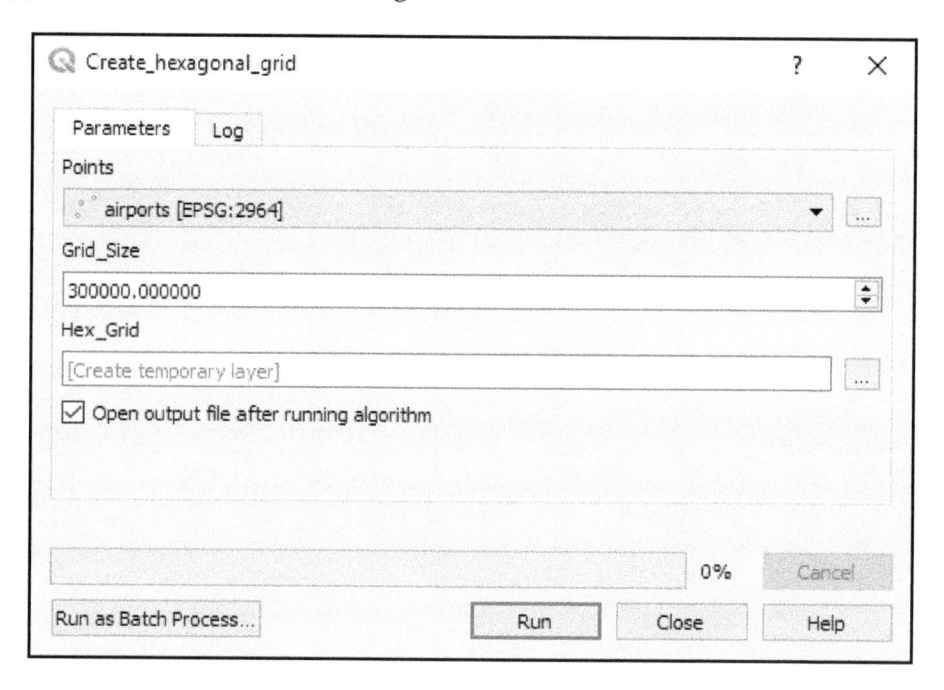

Final model dialog box when the run button is clicked

Click on the **Run** button and you should see a newly created Hexagonal Grid in the QGIS map window. After closing the modeler, we can run the saved models from the toolbox like any other tool. Look in the **Processing Toolbox** under models. This newly created model will appear there, as shown in the following screenshot. It is even possible to use one model as a building block for another model:

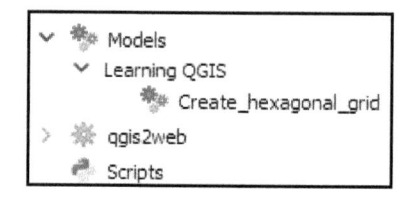

Model Processing Toolbox

[204]

Another useful feature is that we can specify a layer style that needs to be applied to the processing results automatically. This default style can be set using Edit, rendering styles for outputs in the context menu of the model created in the toolbox. This means that you can model building maps to an extent.

Documenting and sharing models

Models can easily be copied from one QGIS installation to another and shared with other users. To ensure the usability of the model, it is a good idea to write a short document. Processing provides a convenient **Help Editor** that can be accessed
by clicking on the **Edit model help button** in the Processing Modeler, as shown in the following screenshot:

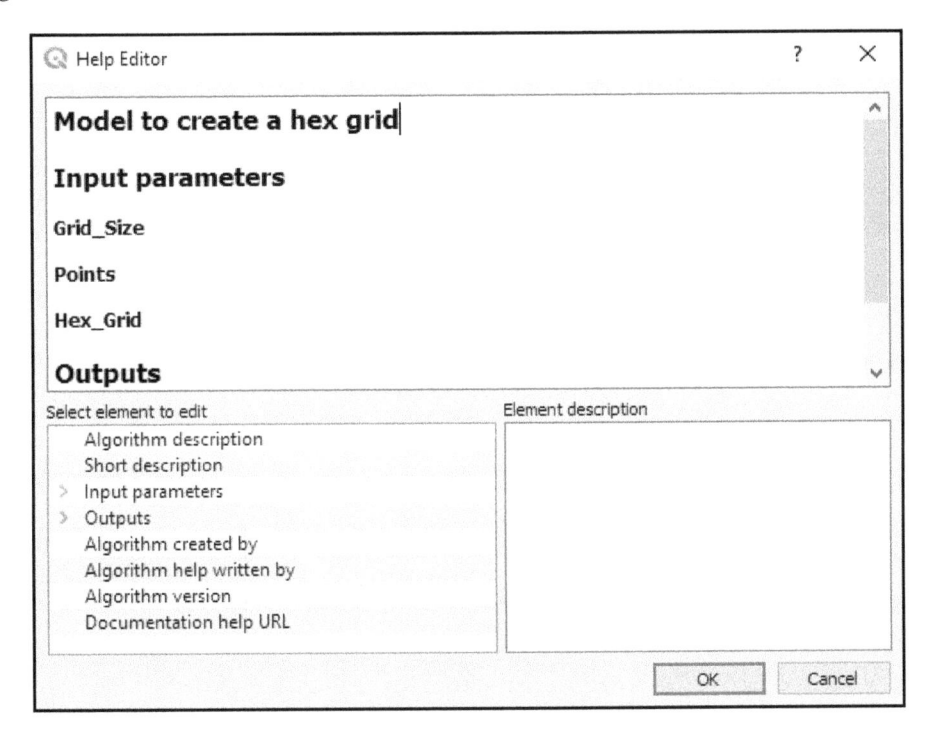

Setting any help for the user

By default, the `.model` files are stored in your user directory. On Windows, this is `C:\Users\AppData\Roaming\QGIS\QGIS3\profiles\default\processing\models`. If you are unsure where they are stored on your configuration, search for `.model3`.

Spatial Analysis

You can copy these files and share them with others. To load a model from a file, use the loading tool by going to **Models | Tools | Add model from the file** in the **Processing Toolbox**.

> QGIS 2 models with the `.model` extension cannot be used in the QGIS 3 model builder.

Summary

In this chapter, we covered various raster and vector geoprocessing and analysis tools and looked at how to apply these in common tasks. We saw how to use the processing toolbox to run individual tools, as well as the modeler to create complex geoprocessing models from multiple tools. Using the modeler, we can automate our workflows and increase our productivity, especially with respect to recurring tasks.

In the final chapter of this book, we will look at how to extend QGIS further using Python and explore some of the new features in QGIS 3, including 3D visualization.

6
Extending QGIS with Python

In our final chapter, we will be using Python to extend QGIS 3.4 Python is a very accessible programming language even for beginners. It is used extensively in both the open source and proprietary GIS world. QGIS 3.4 uses Python 3, whereas QGIS 2.x uses Python 2.7. Care should be taken when migrating any existing scripts, since the API has been updated. We will start with an introduction to actions and then move on to the QGIS Python Console before we go into more advanced development of custom tools for the Processing Toolbox. This will be followed by a guide on how to create your own basic plugin. The final topic that we will cover in this chapter is viewing data in 3D.

Topics covered in this chapter include the following:

- Adding functionality using actions
    - Opening files using actions
    - Opening a web browser using actions
- Getting to know the Python Shell in QGIS 3
- Creating custom geoprocessing scripts using Python
- Guide to building and deploying plugins
- A word on 3D views

Adding functionality using actions

If you need to add custom functionality to QGIS, then actions are the simplest way of achieving this. The different types of actions are listed as follows:

- **Generic actions**: These start external processes. For example, you can run command-line applications such as ogr2ogr.
- **Python actions**: These execute Python scripts.

Extending QGIS with Python

- **Open actions**: These open a file using your computer's configured default application; for example, your PDF viewing application for `.pdf` files or your browser for websites.
- **Operating system actions**: These work like generic actions, but are restricted to the respective operating system you are running.

Configuring your first Python action

Open QGIS and load in the `popp.shp` from the `Shapefile` folder in the QGIS sample data that we downloaded previously. Right-click on the layer in the layer panel. Select **Properties** and then the **Actions** tab, as shown in the following screenshot:

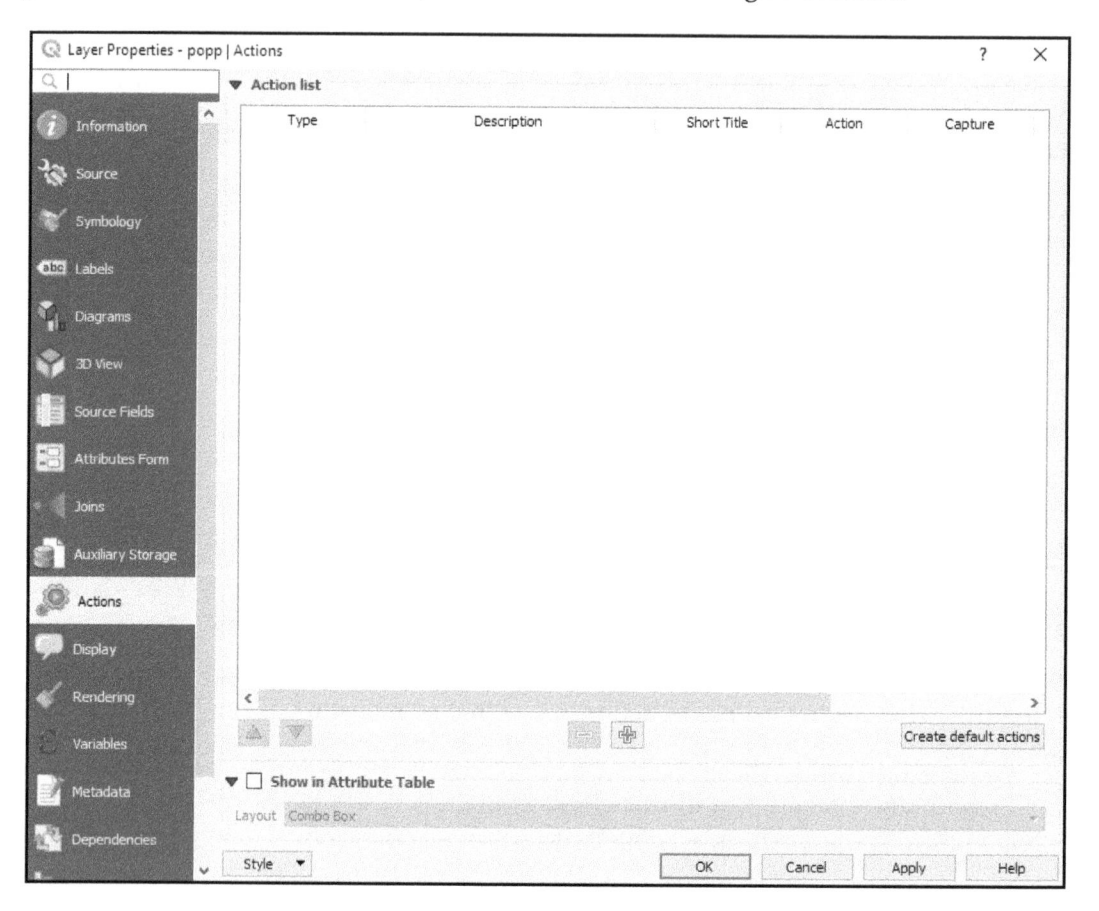

Actions tab

[208]

Click on the **Create Default Actions** button on the right-hand side of this window. It will then show some default behaviors that we can use. Double-click on the row that has a **Description** called **Selected field's value (Identify feature tool)**, as shown in the following screenshot:

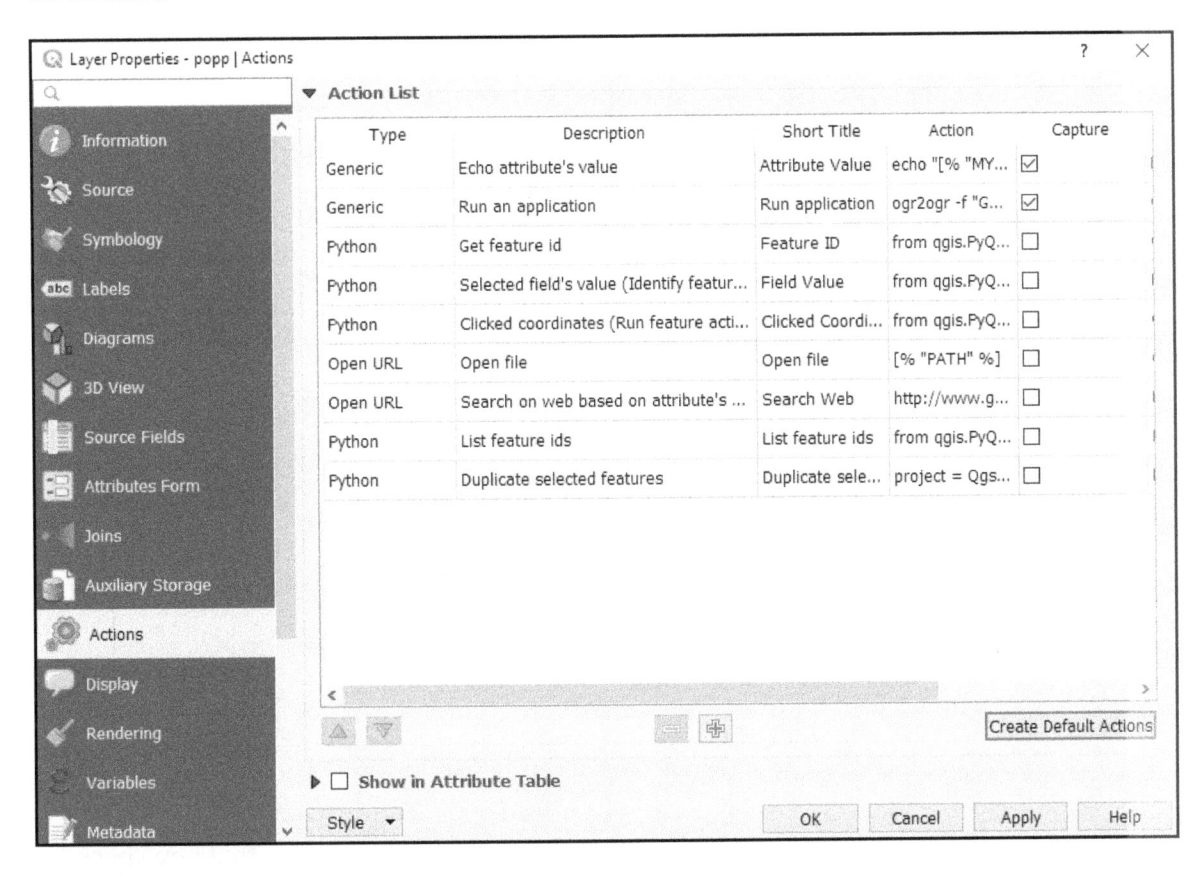

Action list

A new window will appear that we will configure just show the field type when this tool is selected. Change the code block to the following:

```
from qgis.PyQt import QtWidgets

QtWidgets.QMessageBox.information(None, "Current field's value",
"[%TYPE%]")
```

In the **Action Scopes**, select the **Canvas** checkbox and deselect the **Field Scope** checkbox. Finally, change the **Short Name** textbox to Show field type.

Extending QGIS with Python

Your inputs should look similar to the following screenshot:

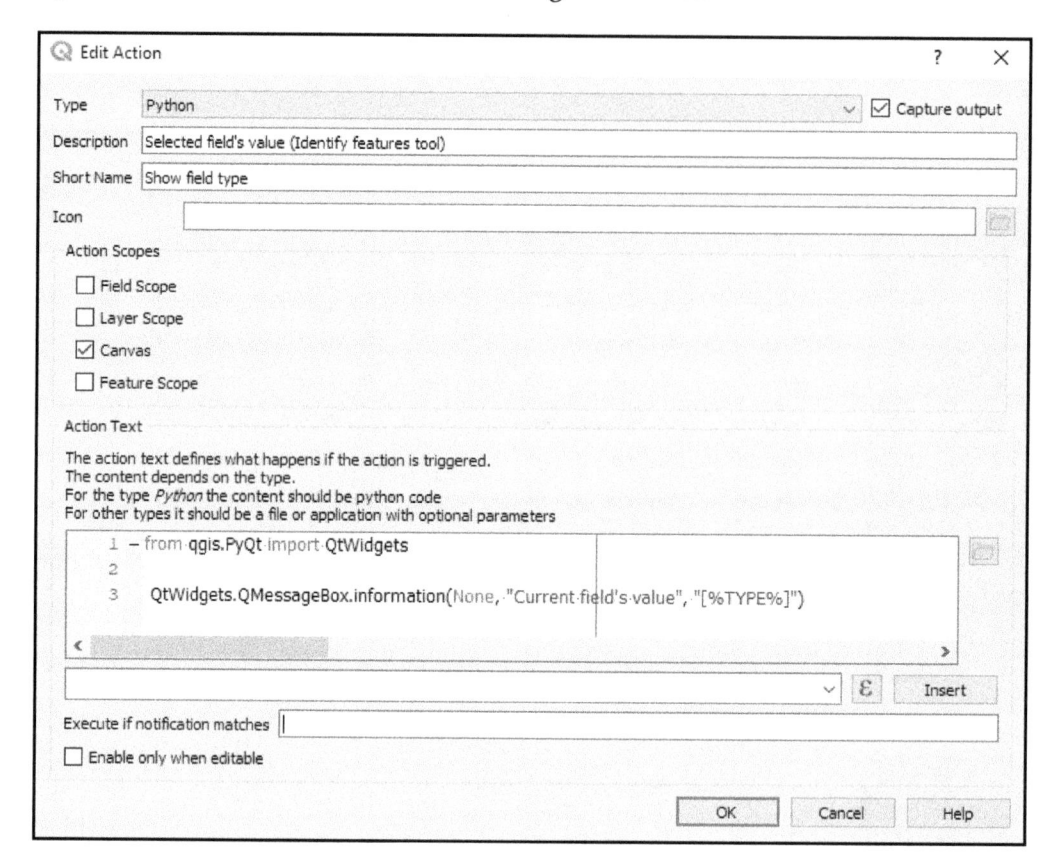

Creating and editing an action

Click on **OK** to return to the list of default actions. In this window, ensure that you check the box in the **Capture** column in order to enable the tool. With the layer selected in the layers panel, click on the down arrow button next to identify, as shown in the following screenshot:

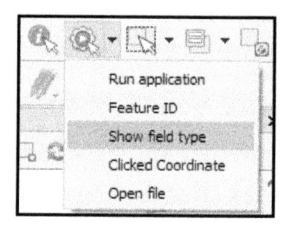

The new action appears in the menu

The newly created **Show field type** action should now be displayed. Select this and click on a point in the map panel. The data associated with the field type will be displayed.

Opening files using actions

To open files directly from within QGIS 3.4, we use the **Open actions** option. Right-click on the **popp** layer and select **Properties**. Then choose **Actions**. This time, pick the **Open URL** action. Select the checkbox next to **Capture** and then double-click the selected blue layer, as shown in the following screenshot:

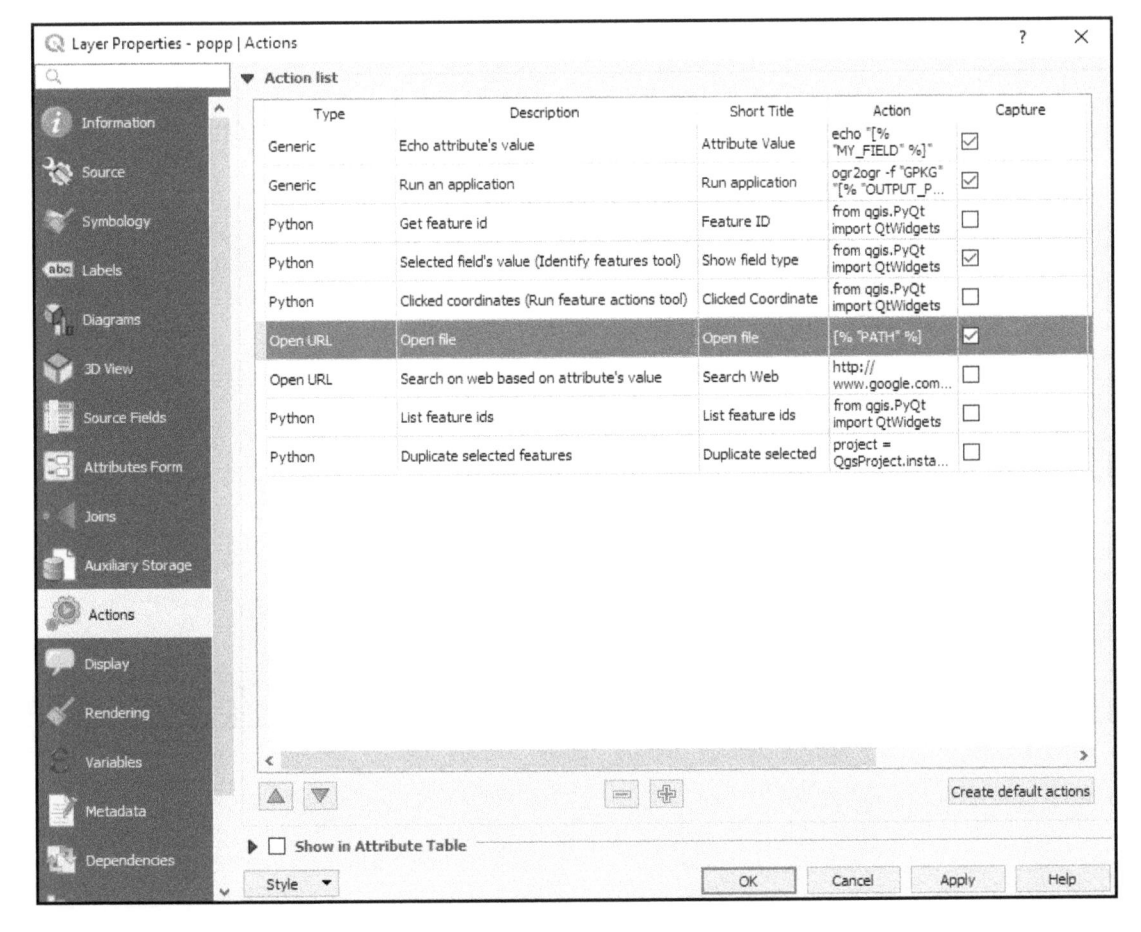

Creating an open file action

Extending QGIS with Python

In the resulting window, select the **Canvas** option in the **Action** scopes, as shown in the following screenshot:

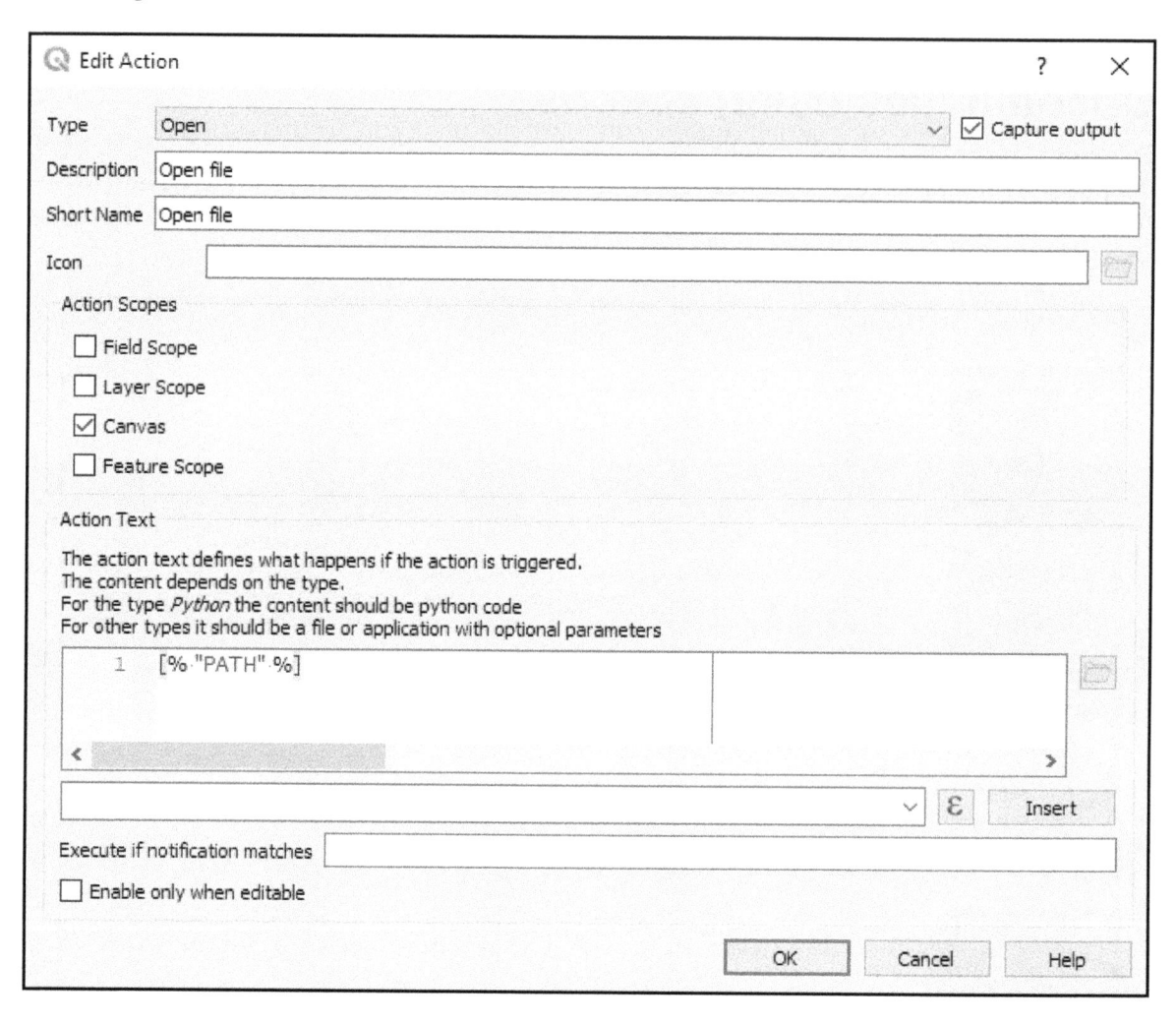

Editing the action

Click on **OK**, and then **OK** in the **Properties** dialog. After doing this, create a new field in your **popp** layer. Do this by opening the attribute table and start editing. Then, create a new field called PATH as text with a width of 250. Select a feature and, in this new field, add a path to a .png or .jpg file that exists and save your edits. Your table should now look similar to the following screenshot:

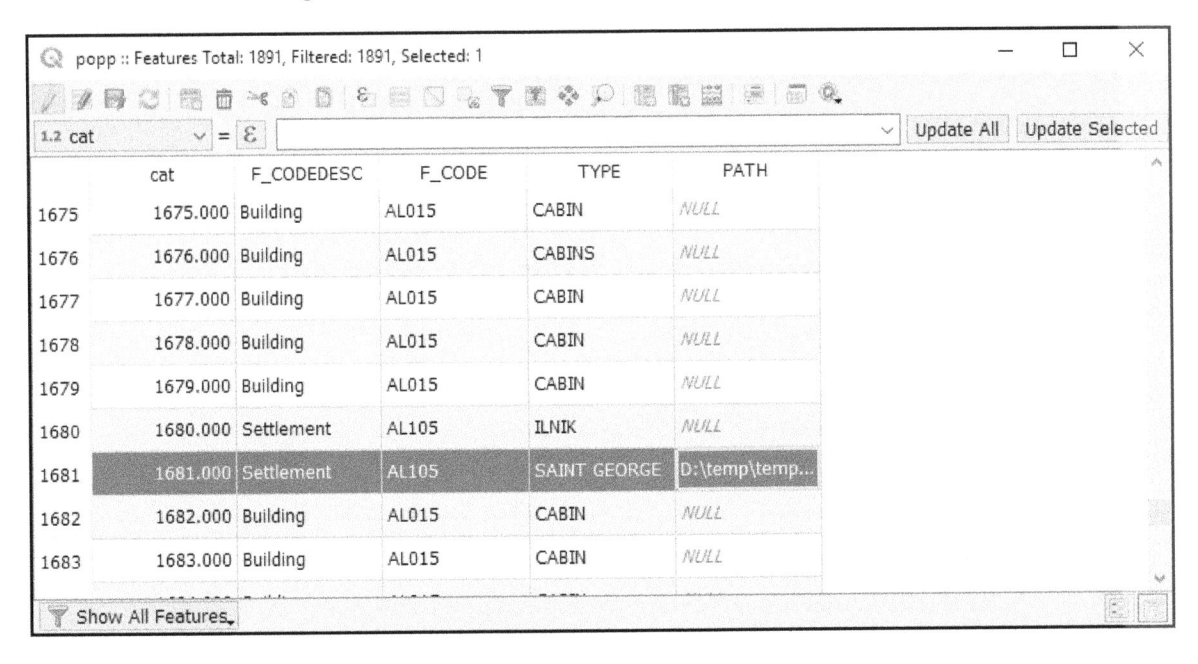

Assigning a filename and path to the PATH field for the open action

Make a note of where this point is, either by selecting it as I have done in the preceding table, or by zooming to the point. With the layer selected in the layers panel, click on the down arrow button next to identify, as in the following screenshot:

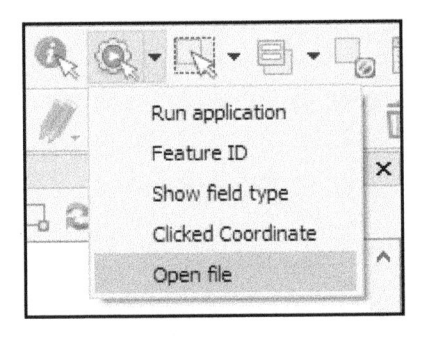

The Open file action appears in the menu

Extending QGIS with Python

Click on the point with the link associated with it (as shown in the preceding screenshot) and the image/document/file should now open in your default viewer.

Opening a web browser using actions

Another type of useful open action is to open the web browser and access certain websites. For example, consider the following action:

```
http://www.google.com/search?q=[% "TYPE" %]
```

Getting to know the Python console

The most direct way to interact with the QGIS **application programming interface** (**API**) is through the Python console, which can be opened by going to **Plugins** | **Python Console**. Alternatively, this can be done by clicking on the Python icon in the plugins toolbar. The **Python Console** is displayed within a new panel below the map, as demonstrated in the following screenshot:

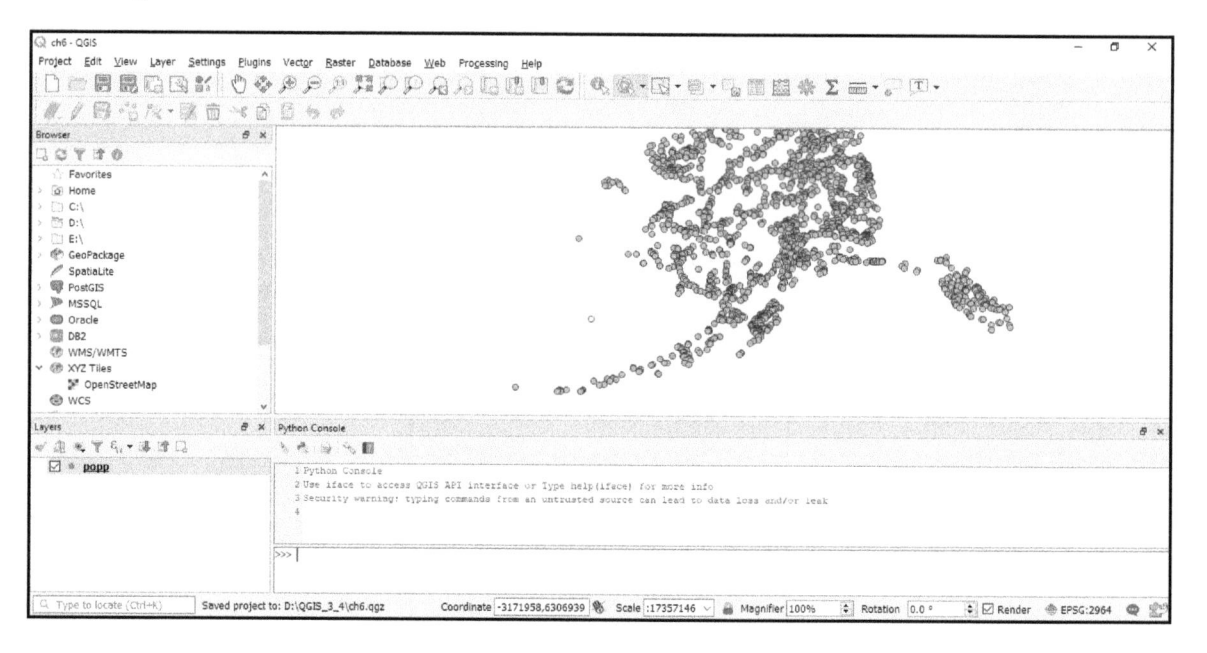

The Python Console

Chapter 6

The access point for interaction with the application, project, and data is the `iface` object. To get a list of all the functions available for `iface`, type `help`(iface).

> **TIP**
> This information is available online in the API documentation at http://qgis.org/api/classQgisInterface.html. Please also visit the dedicated Python API documentation at https://qgis.org/pyqgis/.

Loading and exploring datasets – vector data

One of the first things we will want to do is to load some data. For example, to load a vector layer, we use the `addVectorLayer()` function of `iface`. In the following example, I am adding the `airport.shp`. This is shown in a single line of code as follows:

```
v_layer = 
iface.addVectorLayer('D:/QGIS_3_4/qgis_sample_data/shapefiles/airports.shp'
,'airports','ogr')
```

When we execute this command, `airports.shp` will be loaded using the `ogr` driver and added to the map under the layer name of airports. Additionally, this function returns the created layer object. Using this layer object that we stored in `v_layer`, we can access vector layer functions such as `name()`. This returns the layer name and is displayed in the **Layers** list, as follows:

```
v_layer.name()
```

The output is as follows:

```
airports
```

The number of features can be accessed using `featureCount()`:

```
v_layer.featureCount()
```

The output is as follows:

```
76
```

[215]

Extending QGIS with Python

This shows us that the airport layer contains 76 features. In our next step, we will access these features. The `getFeatures()` function gives access to the features. This will return a `QgsFeatureIterator` object. Using a conditional iteration also known as a `for` loop, we can then print the attributes() of all features in our layer:

```
my_features = v_layer.getFeatures()
for feature in my_features:
    print (feature.attributes())
```

These are the first three records in the output:

```
[1, 18, 78.0, 'NOATAK', 'Other']
[2, 18, 264.0, 'AMBLER', 'Other']
[3, 26, 585.0, 'BETTLES', 'Other']
```

> **TIP**
> In a `for` loop, you must remember to indent the next line (the `print` statement). The console will prompt you with three dots (...), indicating that you are in a loop. Once the loop is finished, press return and the features will be iterated over.

To get the field names, we use this code:

```
for field in v_layer.fields():
 print (field.name())
```

The output is as follows:

```
ID
fk_region
ELEV
NAME
USE
```

If we know the field names, we can access specific feature attributes, for example, NAME:

```
for feature in v_layer.getFeatures():
    print (feature.attribute('NAME'))
```

This is the output showing (just) the first three records:

NOATAK
AMBLER
BETTLES

It is possible to perform queries on your data. For example, to sum up the elevation values in the airports' ELEV field, use the `sum` command, as in the following screenshot:

sum([feature.attribute('ELEV') for feature in v_layer.getFeatures()])

Chapter 6

The output is as follows:

```
22758.0
```

> **TIP**
> In the previous example, we took advantage of the fact that Python allows us to create a list by writing a `for` loop inside square brackets. This is called **list comprehension**, and you can read more about it at https://docs.python.org/2/tutorial/datastructures.html#list-comprehensions is better as its for Python3.

Loading and exploring datasets – raster data

Loading raster data is very similar to loading vector data, and this is done using the `addRasterLayer()` command, as in the following example:

```
r_layer = iface.addRasterLayer('D:/QGIS_3_4/qgis_sample_data/raster/SR_50M_alaska_nad.tif','Hillshade')
```

To show the name of the raster, use the following:

```
r_layer.name()
```

The output is as follows:

```
Hillshade
```

To get the raster layer's size in pixels, we can use the `width()` and `height()` functions, as follows:

```
r_layer.width(), r_layer.height()
```

The output is as follows:

```
(1754, 1394)
```

If we want to know more about the raster values, we use the layer's data provider object. This provides access to the raster band statistics. To get the maximum value of the raster, use the following:

```
r_layer.dataProvider().bandStatistics(1).maximumValue
```

The output is as follows:

```
251.0
```

[217]

Extending QGIS with Python

We have to use `bandStatistics(1)` instead of `bandStatistics(0)` to access the statistics of a single-band raster. Normally, Python items are 0,1,2,3, and so on, but bands are always 1,2,3, and so on. You can find out more about band statistics using the `help` command. This will display additional information about how QGIS performs the band statistics calculation. The command is in the following screenshot:

```
help(r_layer.dataProvider().bandStatistics(1))
```

Styling layers

Since we now know how to load data, we can continue by styling the layers. The simplest option here is to load a premade style (`.qml` file):

```
v_layer.loadNamedStyle('D:/QGIS_3_4/airports_style.qml')
```

This will return `True` if the `.qml` file is found:

```
('', True)
```

Use the following command to set the market style:

```
v_layer.triggerRepaint()
```

Make sure that you call `triggerRepaint()` to ensure that the map is redrawn to reflect your changes.

> **TIP**: You can create `airport_style.qml` by saving the airport style you created in Chapter 3, *Visualizing Data*. This can be done by going to **Layer Properties | Style | Save Style | QGIS Layer Style File**, or, alternatively, you can use any other style you like.

We can also create a QGIS style using the console. Let's take a look at a basic single symbol renderer. We create a simple symbol with one layer, for example, a yellow circle:

```
from PyQt5.QtGui import QColor

symbol = QgsMarkerSymbol()

symbol.symbolLayer(0).setSize(10)

symbol.symbolLayer(0).setColor(QColor('#ffff00'))

v_layer.renderer().setSymbol(symbol)

v_layer.triggerRepaint()
```

Typing this directly into the Python console can be confusing. Instead, use the code editor via the show editor button, and ensure that you save your scripts as you write them. To run the script, click on the Run script button at the bottom of the editor toolbar. The code editor is in the following screenshot:

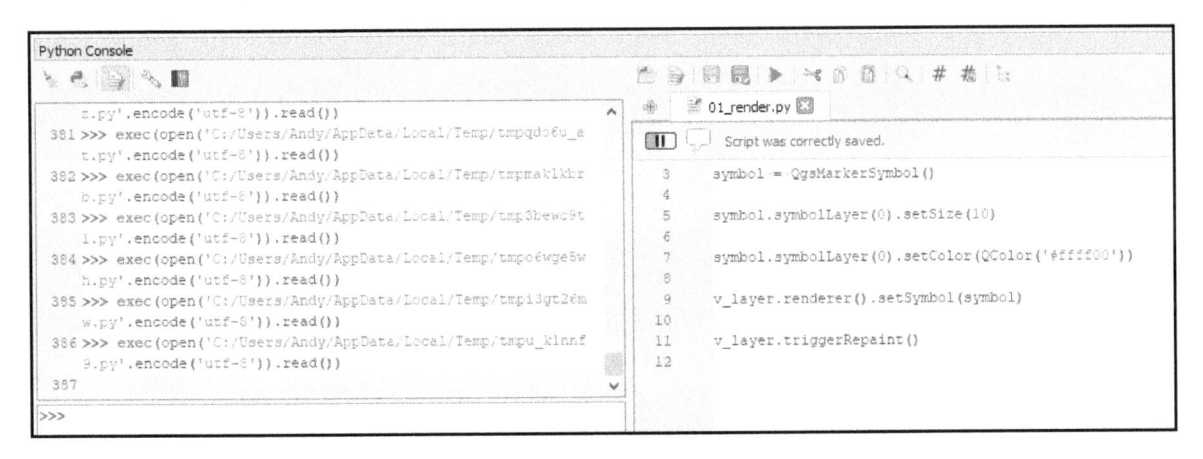

The Python console and script editor

A much more advanced approach is to create a rule-based renderer. We discussed the basics of rule-based renderers in `Chapter 4`, *Creating Great Maps*. The following example creates two rules: one for civil use airports and one for all other airports. Each rule in this example has a name, a filter expression, and a symbol color. Create a new script by clicking on the plus button in the code editor to create a new editor. Note how the rules are appended to the renderer's root rule:

```
from PyQt5.QtGui import QColor

rules = [['Civil','USE LIKE \'%Civil%\'','green'], ['Other','USE NOT LIKE \'%Civil%\'','red']]

symbol = QgsSymbol.defaultSymbol(v_layer.geometryType())

renderer = QgsRuleBasedRenderer(symbol)

root_rule = renderer.rootRule()

for label, expression, color_name in rules:

    rule = root_rule.children()[0].clone()

    rule.setLabel(label)
```

Extending QGIS with Python

```
        rule.setFilterExpression(expression)
        rule.symbol().setColor(QColor(color_name))
        root_rule.appendChild(rule)
    root_rule.removeChildAt(0)
    v_layer.setRenderer(renderer)
    v_layer.triggerRepaint()
```

Filtering data

To filter vector layer features programmatically, we can specify a subset string. This is the same as defining a feature subset query in the **Layer Properties** | **General section**. For example, we can choose to display airports only if their names start with an A:

```
v_layer.setSubsetString("NAME LIKE 'A%'")
```

This will return `true` in the Python Console. Open the attribute table to see the results of the filter. This is demonstrated in the following screenshot:

	ID	fk_region	ELEV	NAME	USE
1	76	19	108.000	ANNETTE ISL...	Other
2	49	3	129.000	ANCHORAGE I...	Civilian/Public
3	2	18	264.000	AMBLER	Other
4	40	22	1167.000	ALLEN AAF	Military
5	66	2	51.000	ATKA	Other
6	24	26	282.000	ANVIK	Other
7	28	4	78.000	ANIAK	Other

The attribute table post filtering

To remove the filter, just set an empty subset string as follows:

```
v_layer.setSubsetString("")
```

Creating a memory layer

A great way to create a temporary vector layer is by using so-called **memory layers**. Memory layers are a good option for temporary analysis output or visualizations. They are the scripting equivalent of temporary scratch layers, which we used in Chapter 2, *Data Creation and Editing*. Like temporary scratch layers, memory layers exist within a QGIS session and are destroyed when QGIS is closed. In the following example, we create a memory layer and add a polygon feature to it.

Basically, a memory layer is a QgsVectorLayer like any other. However, the provider (the third parameter) is not ogr as in the previous example of loading a file, but memory. Instead of a file path, the first parameter is a definition string that specifies the geometry type, the CRS, and the attribute table fields. In this case, this is one integer field called MYNUM and one string field called MYTXT. Create a new script by clicking on the plus button in the code editor to create a new editor. The code is in the following screenshot:

```
from qgis.core import QgsProject
mem_layer =
QgsVectorLayer("Polygon?crs=epsg:4326&field=MYNUM:integer&field=MYTXT:strin
g", "temp_layer", "memory")

if not mem_layer.isValid():

    raise Exception("Failed to create memory layer")

mem_layer_provider = mem_layer.dataProvider()

my_polygon = QgsFeature()

my_polygon.setGeometry(
  QgsGeometry.fromRect(QgsRectangle(16,48,17,49)))

my_polygon.setAttributes([10,"hello world"])
mem_layer_provider.addFeatures([my_polygon])

QgsProject.instance().addMapLayer(mem_layer)
```

Extending QGIS with Python

> **TIP:** Note how we first create a blank `QgsVectorLayer`, to which we then add geometry and attributes using `setGeometry()` and `setAttributes()` respectively. When we add the layer to `QgsProject`, the layer is rendered on the map.

Exporting map images

The simplest option for saving the current map is by using the scripting equivalent of **Save as Image** (under Project). This will export the current map to an image file in the same resolution as the map area in the QGIS application window:

```
iface.mapCanvas().saveAsImage('D:/temp/simple_export.png')
```

If we want more control over the size and resolution of the exported image, we need a few more lines of code. The following example shows how we can create our own `QgsMapRendererCustomPainterJob` object and configure to our own liking using a custom **QgsMapSettings** for size (`width` and `height`), resolution (`dpi`), map `extent`, and map `layers`. Create a new script by clicking on the plus button in the code editor to create a new editor. The code is contained in the following screenshot:

```
from PyQt5.QtGui import QImage, QPainter

from PyQt5.QtCore import QSize

# configure the output image

width = 800

height = 600

dpi = 92

img = QImage(QSize(width, height), QImage.Format_RGB32)

img.setDotsPerMeterX(dpi / 25.4 * 1000)

img.setDotsPerMeterY(dpi / 25.4 * 1000)

# get the map layers and extent

layers = [ layer for layer in iface.mapCanvas().layers() ]

extent = iface.mapCanvas().extent()
```

```
# configure map settings for export

mapSettings = QgsMapSettings()

mapSettings.setExtent(extent)

mapSettings.setOutputDpi(dpi)

mapSettings.setOutputSize(QSize(width, height))

mapSettings.setLayers(layers)

mapSettings.setFlags(QgsMapSettings.Antialiasing |
QgsMapSettings.UseAdvancedEffects |
QgsMapSettings.ForceVectorOutput | QgsMapSettings.DrawLabeling)

# configure and run painter

p = QPainter()

p.begin(img)

mapRenderer = QgsMapRendererCustomPainterJob(mapSettings, p)

mapRenderer.start()

mapRenderer.waitForFinished()

p.end()

# save the result

img.save("D:/temp/custom_export.png","png")
```

Creating custom geoprocessing scripts using Python

In `Chapter 5`, *Spatial Analysis*, we used the tools of **Processing Toolbox** to analyze our data. We are not limited to these tools, however, as we can also write our own. We can expand processing with our own scripts. The advantages of processing scripts over normal Python scripts, such as the ones we saw in the previous section, are as follows:

- Processing automatically generates a graphical user interface for the script to configure the script parameters
- Processing scripts can be used in Graphical modeler to create geoprocessing models

Writing your first processing script

We will now create our first script that fetches some layer information. The processing has been completely overhauled in QGIS 3. Start by opening the **Processing Toolbox**, click on the Python button, and select **Create New Script from Template...**, as shown in the following screenshot:

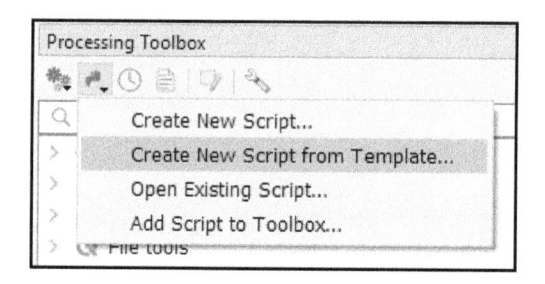

Creating a new script from a template in the processing toolbox

This opens a script template in the editor dialog.

Save this script as `my_first_script.py`. When you run this script, it will open a dialog box where you can select any layer and save it to either a temporary layer or a new layer. To run the script, click the green triangle as shown in the following screenshot:

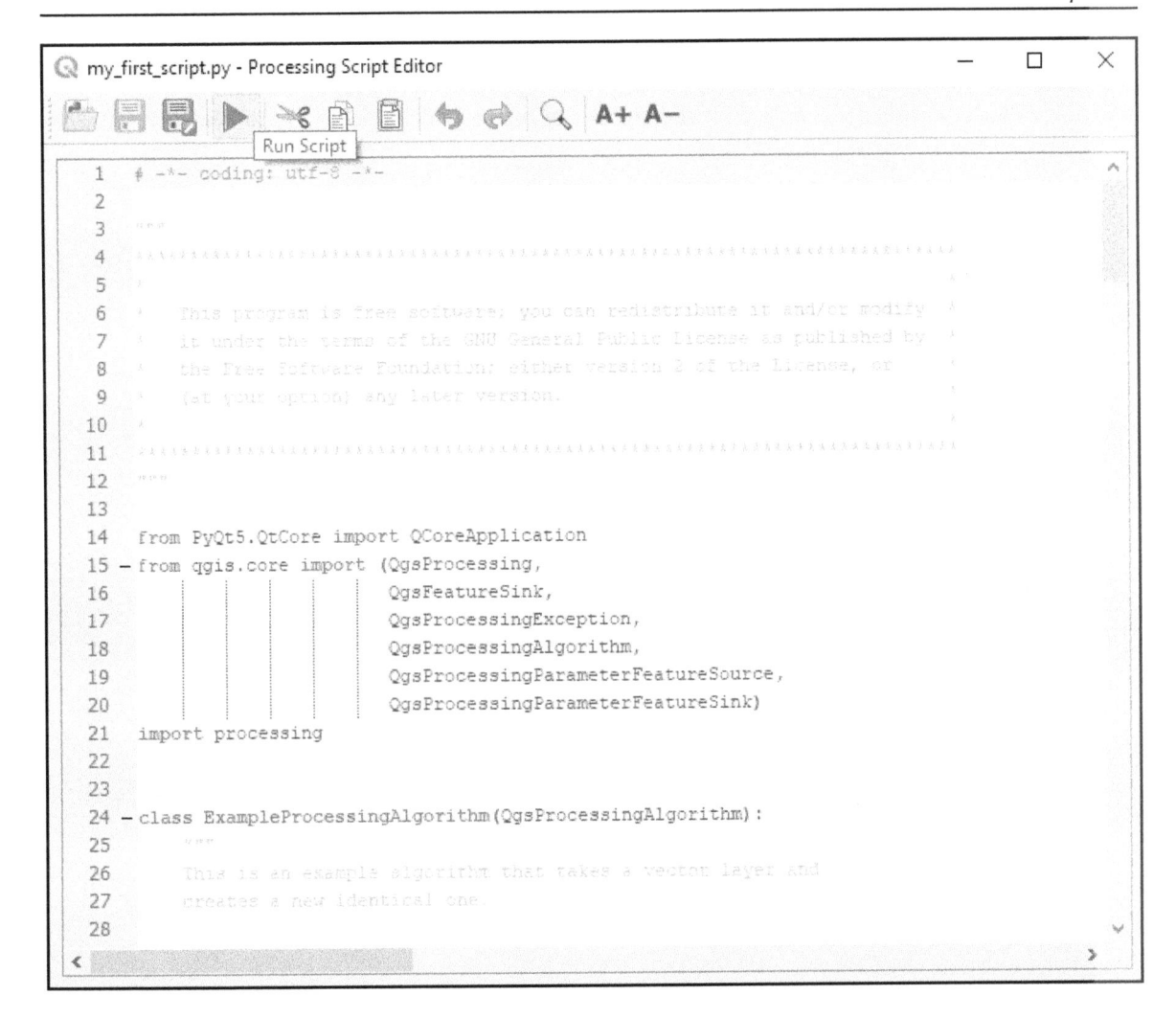

Default processing template

This example processing template will make a copy of the input layer, create it in memory, and add it to the map. In the next section, we will build our own simple script for a buffer.

Extending QGIS with Python

Building a basic buffer script

From the **Processing Toolbox**, click on the Python button and select **Create New Script...**, as shown in the following screenshot:

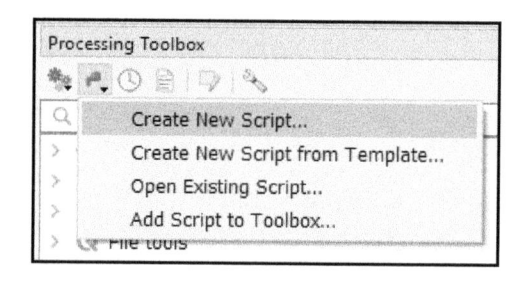

Create a new script

In a blank script, copy the following code:

```
import processing
from qgis.PyQt.QtCore import QCoreApplication
from qgis.core import QgsProcessingAlgorithm, QgsProcessing,
QgsProcessingParameterFeatureSink,QgsProcessingParameterFeatureSource

class testAlg(QgsProcessingAlgorithm):
 OUTPUT = 'OUTPUT'
 INPUT = 'INPUT'

 def tr(self, text):
     return QCoreApplication.translate('testalg', text)

 def createInstance(self):
     return type(self)()

 def group(self):
     return self.tr('Test')

 def groupId(self):
     return 'test'

 def __init__(self):
     super().__init__()

 def initAlgorithm(self, config=None):
     self.addParameter(
         QgsProcessingParameterFeatureSource(
             self.INPUT,
             self.tr('Input layer'),
```

```
                    [QgsProcessing.TypeVectorAnyGeometry]
                )
        )

        self.addParameter(
            QgsProcessingParameterFeatureSink(
            self.OUTPUT,
            self.tr('Output'),
            QgsProcessing.TypeVectorPolygon
            )
        )

    def name(self):
        return 'testalg'

    def displayName(self):
        return self.tr('Test Algorithm')

    def processAlgorithm(self, parameters, context, feedback):

        output = processing.run("native:buffer", {
        'INPUT': parameters['INPUT'],
        'DISTANCE': 100,
        'SEGMENTS': 5,
        'END_CAP_STYLE': 0,
        'JOIN_STYLE': 0,
        'MITER_LIMIT': 2,
        'DISSOLVE': False,
        'OUTPUT': parameters['OUTPUT']

        }, context=context, feedback=feedback)['OUTPUT']

        return {self.OUTPUT: output}
```

In this code, we are building a test algorithm. This will take an input as either a point/line/polygon layer and create a buffer of 10 units with no dissolve. We have created a class called `testAlg` and this implements the `QgsProcessingAlgorithm`. We have one input and one output in this class. To understand the various different functions in the script, please review the comments in the template shown in the previous section.

Extending QGIS with Python

Let's take a look at the two functions that will perform the processing. First of all, we need to assign the input and output. This is done with the def `initAlgorithm` method. In here, we have two parameters added. The first one is the `INPUT` parameter, which is set as `QgsProcessingParameterFeatureSource`. This can have <u>any geometry</u>. The second one is the `OUTPUT` parameter, which is set as `QgsProcessingParameterFeatureSink`. This can only have a polygon as an output, which is set as `QgsProcessing.TypeVectorPolygon`.

The second function is a call to the QGIS processing. This function is called `def processAlgorithm`. With this function, parameters, context, and feedback are parsed. This allows us to interact with the other functions and variables in this class.

The command to run any processing tool is `processing.run`. The following is the command to run the *buffering a processing* tool:

```
output = processing.run("native:buffer"{
        'INPUT': parameters['INPUT'],
        'DISTANCE': 10,
        'SEGMENTS': 5,
        'END_CAP_STYLE': 0,
        'JOIN_STYLE': 0,
        'MITER_LIMIT': 2,
        'DISSOLVE': False,
        'OUTPUT': 'memory:' ## changed to memory
```

Be sure to include all the parameters for the processing tool. To find out the parameters for each tool in the Python console, type the following:

```
processing.algorithmHelp("qgis:buffer")


for alg in QgsApplication.processingRegistry().algorithms():
print(alg.id())
```

Processing models will probably have an input and an output. In this function, the input is set to `Parameters ['INPUT']`, and the output is set to `Parameters ['OUTPUT']`. These input and output variables will match what the user puts as input to the script when it is run.

Running the script

To run the preceding script, click on the green triangle in the following screenshot:

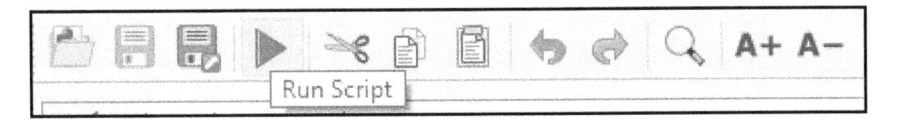

Running the script

This will call the GUI (graphical user interface), which looks like the following screenshot:

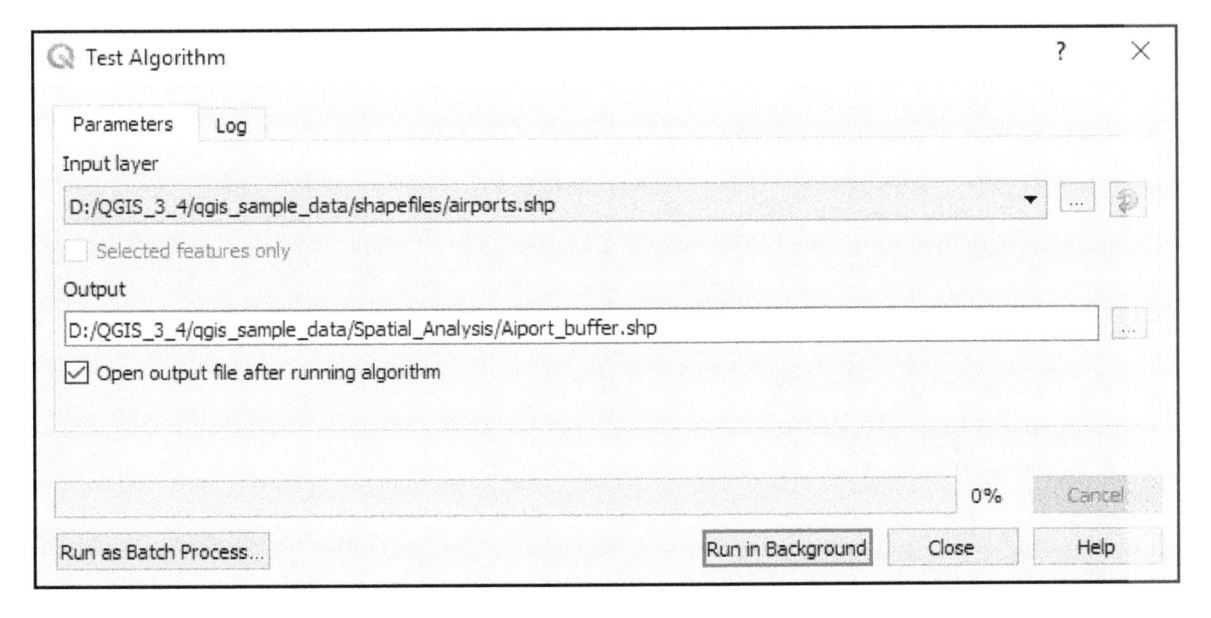

The GUI built by default

Once run, you will get a feedback log in the same GUI. The resulting buffered layer will appear in QGIS as a new layer.

Extending the script

It is more likely that you will wish to extend your scripts to include multiple processing and potential multiple inputs and outputs. In this example, we will build on the buffer example and convert this result back to centroids. The following is the new code:

```python
import processing
from qgis.PyQt.QtCore import QCoreApplication
from qgis.core import QgsProcessingAlgorithm, QgsProcessing,
QgsProcessingParameterFeatureSink,QgsProcessingParameterFeatureSource

class testAlg(QgsProcessingAlgorithm):
    OUTPUT = 'OUTPUT'
    INPUT = 'INPUT'

    def tr(self, text):
        return QCoreApplication.translate('testalg', text)

    def createInstance(self):
        return type(self)()

    def group(self):
        return self.tr('Test')

    def groupId(self):
        return 'test'

    def __init__(self):
        super().__init__()

    def initAlgorithm(self, config=None):
        self.addParameter(
            QgsProcessingParameterFeatureSource(
                self.INPUT,
                self.tr('Input layer'),
                [QgsProcessing.TypeVectorAnyGeometry]
            )
        )
        self.addParameter(
            QgsProcessingParameterFeatureSink(
                self.OUTPUT,
                self.tr('Output'),
                QgsProcessing.TypeVectorPoint ### changed
            )
        )

    def name(self):
        return 'testalg'
```

```python
    def displayName(self):
        return self.tr('Test Algorithm')

    def processAlgorithm(self, parameters, context, feedback):

        output = processing.run("native:buffer", {
            'INPUT': parameters['INPUT'],
            'DISTANCE': 10,
            'SEGMENTS': 5,
            'END_CAP_STYLE': 0,
            'JOIN_STYLE': 0,
            'MITER_LIMIT': 2,
            'DISSOLVE': False,
            'OUTPUT': 'memory:' ## changed to memory
        }, context=context, feedback=feedback)['OUTPUT']
        ### new process
        output2 = processing.run("native:centroids", {
            'INPUT': output,
            'ALL_PARTS': False,
            'OUTPUT': parameters['OUTPUT']
        }, context=context, feedback=feedback)['OUTPUT']
        return {self.OUTPUT: output2} ### a different output (output2 is now returned)
```

I have added the ## to show where new code has been entered and/or changed. The INPUT and OUTPUT variables remain the same. The output is now set as a point geometry. The buffer process is held in memory and the centroids are written out in output2.

> **TIP**
> The processing script part of QGIS is brand new and updated in QGIS 3. At the time of writing, https://github.com/qgis/QGIS/tree/master/python/plugins/processing/algs/qgis contains example scripts but not all will work in QGIS 3. Use the *Help* section in Chapter 1, *Where do I start?* to get help with this feature.

Extending QGIS with Python

Developing your first plugin

If you want to implement interactive tools or very specific graphical user interfaces, you will need to build a plugin. In the previous exercises, we introduced the QGIS Python API. Now we will focus on the necessary steps to get our first QGIS plugin built. The great thing about creating plugins for QGIS is that there is a plugin called **Plugin Builder**. Plugin Builder allows you to build the framework for a plugin. Also ensure that you install Plugin Reloader, since this is very useful for plugin development. It lets you reload your plugin without restarting QGIS every time you make changes to the code. When you have installed both plugins, your Plugins toolbar will look similar to this:

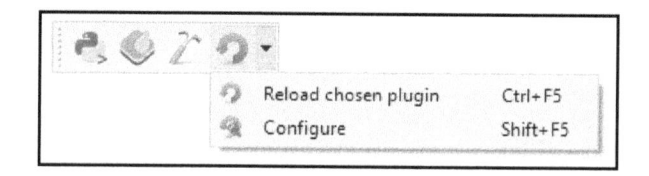

The plugin reloader

The simplest way to create plugins using Windows 10 is by using a version of QGIS installed via OSGeo4W. The plugin described here will assume you have installed QGIS using this method. If you are running a standalone version of QGIS, ensure that you review the paths to the installation. This will be required when you come to deploy (activate) your plugin.

QGIS 3.4 comes with Qt Designer. We will be using Qt Designer to make the GUI for our plugin. If you do not have this installed, please go back to either the OSGeo4W setup or download it from https://qgis.org/en/site/

> **TIP**
> You will need to be able to access the QGIS libraries on the command line in Python. For a detailed overview on how to do this, please refer to this link: http://spatialgalaxy.net/2018/02/13/quick-guide-to-getting-started-with-pyqgis3-on-windows/.

Creating the plugin template with Plugin Builder

The Plugin Builder plugin will create a template that will hold all the files that we need for our plugin. To create a plugin template, follow these steps:

1. Start Plugin Builder and input the basic plugin information, including the following:
    - **Class name** (one word in camel case. This means that each word starts with an upper case letter.)
    - **Plugin name** (a short description.)
    - **Module name** (the Python module name for the plugin.)

When your mouse hovers over the input fields in the Plugin Builder dialog, it displays help information, as shown in the following screenshot:

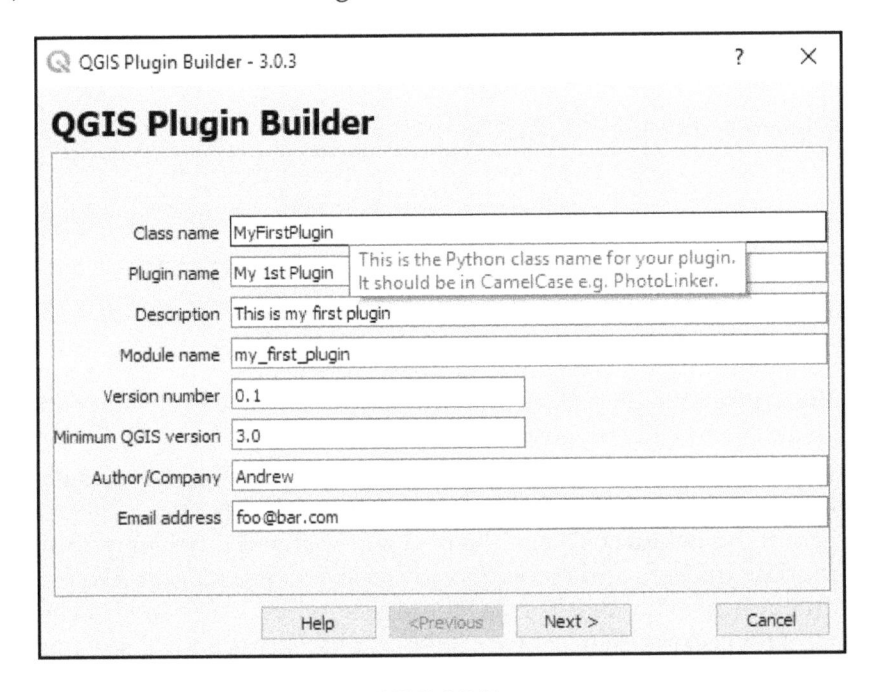

QGIS Plugin Builder

2. Click on **Next** to get to the **About** dialog, where you can enter a more detailed description of what your plugin does. Since we are planning to create the first plugin for learning purposes only, leave this blank and click on **Next**.

[233]

Extending QGIS with Python

3. Now we can select a plugin template and specify the **Text for the menu item**. This step allows us to choose which menu the plugin should be listed in, as shown in the following screenshot. The available templates include **Tool button with dialog**, **Tool button with dock widget**, and **Processing provider**. In this exercise, we'll create a **Tool button with dialog**. After this is selected, click on **Next**:

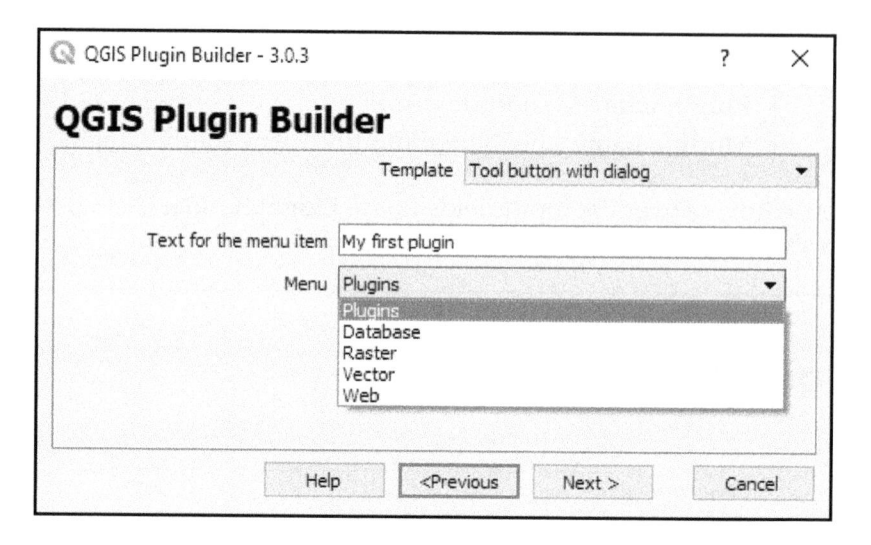

Choose what type of plugin

4. The following dialog presents a number of checkboxes where we can choose which nonessential plugin files should be created. For this demonstration, accept the defaults and click on **Next**.

5. In the next dialog, we need to specify the plugin **Bug tracker** and the code **Repository**. Again, since we are creating this plugin for learning purposes only, just accept the default URLs in the next screenshot. However, you should use the appropriate trackers and code repositories if you are planning to make your plugin publicly available. This is the stage at which you can also check the box if your plugin is experimental we will leave this unchecked. The screenshot will look similar to the following:

Chapter 6

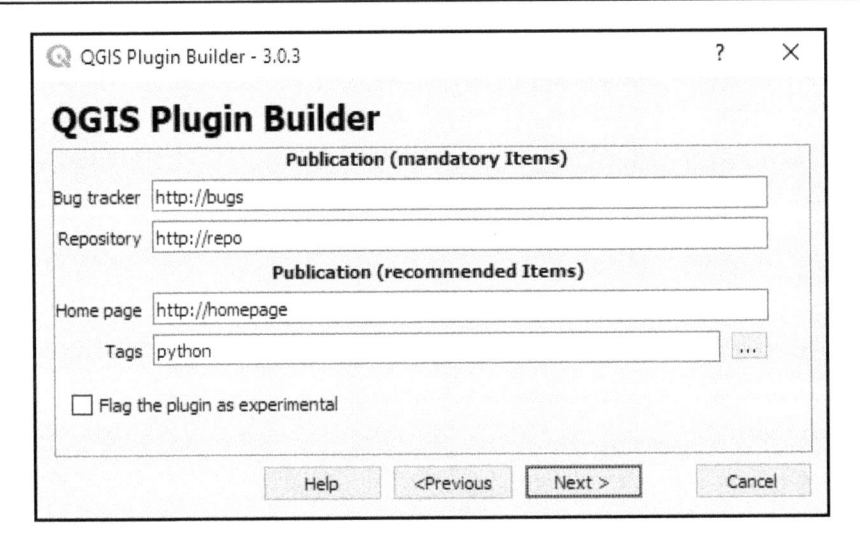

Defining the tracking

6. Once you click on **Next**, you will be asked to select a folder to store the plugin. Ideally, you will save this to the plugin folder. You can find this folder in QGIS by going to **Settings | User Profiles | Open Active Profile Folder** and then navigating to the `Python/plugins` folder. However, you can save to any location. In the following screenshot, I am saving to my `plugin` folder:

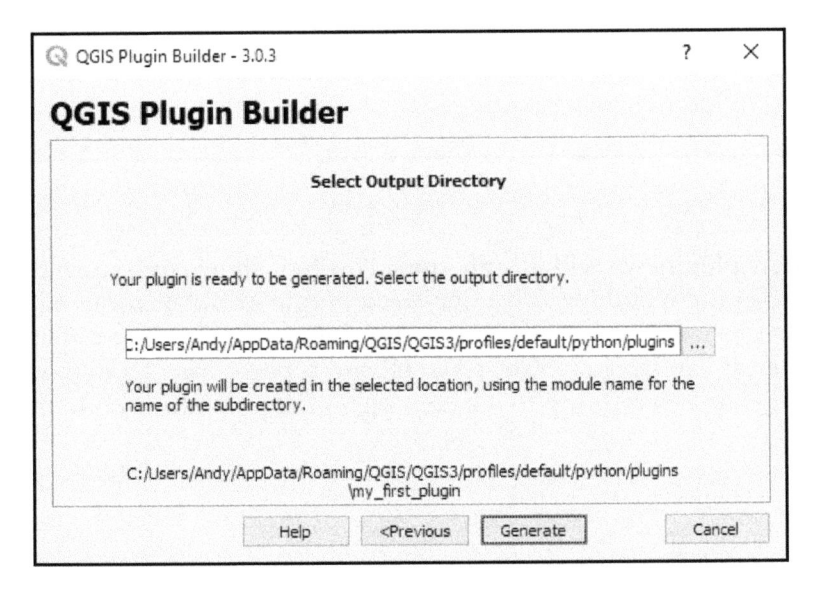

Saving your plugin

Extending QGIS with Python

7. Click on **Generate**. This displays a Plugin Builder results confirmation dialog, which confirms the location of your plugin folder as well as the location of your QGIS plugin folder. It also gives you details about what to do next. This is shown in the following screenshot:

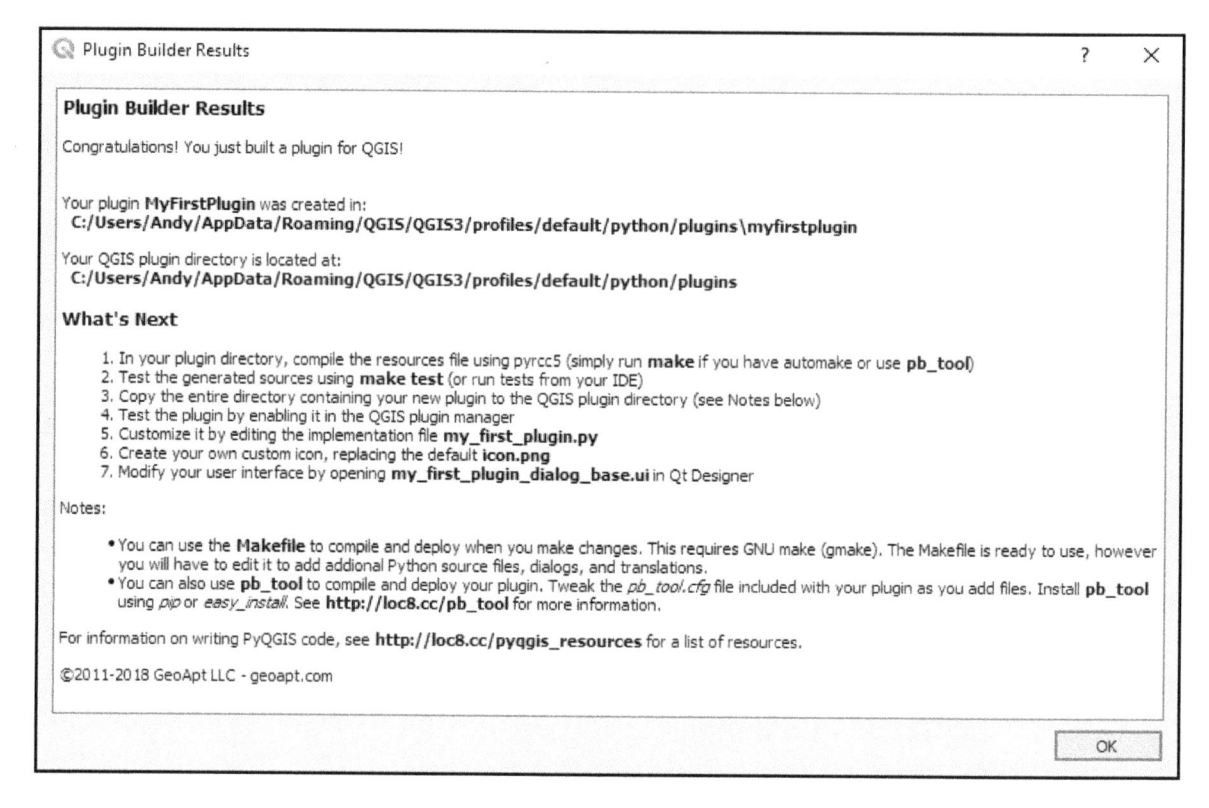

Plugin Builder Results

Congratulations! You just built a plugin for QGIS!

Your plugin **MyFirstPlugin** was created in:
C:/Users/Andy/AppData/Roaming/QGIS/QGIS3/profiles/default/python/plugins\myfirstplugin

Your QGIS plugin directory is located at:
C:/Users/Andy/AppData/Roaming/QGIS/QGIS3/profiles/default/python/plugins

What's Next

1. In your plugin directory, compile the resources file using pyrcc5 (simply run **make** if you have automake or use **pb_tool**)
2. Test the generated sources using **make test** (or run tests from your IDE)
3. Copy the entire directory containing your new plugin to the QGIS plugin directory (see Notes below)
4. Test the plugin by enabling it in the QGIS plugin manager
5. Customize it by editing the implementation file **my_first_plugin.py**
6. Create your own custom icon, replacing the default **icon.png**
7. Modify your user interface by opening **my_first_plugin_dialog_base.ui** in Qt Designer

Notes:

- You can use the **Makefile** to compile and deploy when you make changes. This requires GNU make (gmake). The Makefile is ready to use, however you will have to edit it to add addional Python source files, dialogs, and translations.
- You can also use **pb_tool** to compile and deploy your plugin. Tweak the *pb_tool.cfg* file included with your plugin as you add files. Install **pb_tool** using *pip* or *easy_install*. See http://loc8.cc/pb_tool for more information.

For information on writing PyQGIS code, see http://loc8.cc/pyqgis_resources for a list of resources.

©2011-2018 GeoApt LLC - geoapt.com

Plugin results and next steps

To deploy our new plugin, we will use **pb_tool**. This tool allows us to turn the plugin we have created in the plugin builder into a deployed plugin available for us to use in QGIS. Before we can do this we need to make sure we can access `qgis.core` outside of QGIS in a Python interpreter. If you start a OSGeo4W shell and type `Python3` and then type `qgis.core` and get no errors, jump to the next section. If not, follow on to the next section.

Accessing qgis.core from the command line external to Python

To access `qgis.core` in a Python interpreter, we need to configure the paths to the Python libraries. At the start of this section, I recommended you use OSGeo4W to install QGIS. If you have done this, then the following script will work. If not, then you will need to review the paths in the following screenshot carefully.

Create a new file in a text editor and call it `pyqgis.cmd`. Save this in the save location as your QGIS installation (or wherever it is easiest to find it).

Now, type the following lines and then perform a save as follows:

```
@echo off
SET OSGEO4W_ROOT=C:\OSGeo4W64
call "%OSGEO4W_ROOT%"\bin\o4w_env.bat
call "%OSGEO4W_ROOT%"\apps\grass\grass-7.4.2\etc\env.bat
@echo off
path %PATH%;%OSGEO4W_ROOT%\apps\qgis\bin
path %PATH%;%OSGEO4W_ROOT%\apps\grass\grass-7.4.2\lib
path %PATH%;C:\OSGeo4W64\apps\Qt5\bin
path %PATH%;C:\OSGeo4W64\apps\Python37\Scripts

set PYTHONPATH=%PYTHONPATH%;%OSGEO4W_ROOT%\apps\qgis\Python
set PYTHONHOME=%OSGEO4W_ROOT%\apps\Python37
cmd.exe
```

At this point, it is important to check that the paths exist. If not, make the changes to match your installation. Once saved, double-click on your `pyqgis.cmd` and then type the following commands:

python3
import qgis.core

These should both return with no errors. If not, review the preceding installation paths again.

Extending QGIS with Python

A working Python interpreter with QGIS Python libraries available to it can be seen in the following screenshot:

qgis.core

Setting up the pb_tool

Within the shell created previously, install `pb_tool` using the following command:

```
python3 -m pip install pb_tool;
```

Once installed, type `pb_tool` at the command line:

```
C:\WINDOWS\system32\cmd.exe
Successfully installed Click-7.0 Sphinx-1.8.2 alabaster-0.7.12 babel-2.6.0 colorama-0.4.0 docutils-0.14 imagesize-1.1.0
packaging-18.0 pb-tool-3.0.6 snowballstemmer-1.2.1 sphinxcontrib-websupport-1.1.0

C:\Users\andre\Desktop>pb_tool
Usage: pb_tool [OPTIONS] COMMAND [ARGS]...

  Simple Python tool to compile and deploy a QGIS plugin. For help on a
  command use --help after the command: pb_tool deploy --help.

  pb_tool requires a configuration file (default: pb_tool.cfg) that declares
  the files and resources used in your plugin. Plugin Builder 2.6.0 creates
  a config file when you generate a new plugin template.

  See http://g-sherman.github.io/plugin_build_tool for for an example config
  file. You can also use the create command to generate a best-guess config
  file for an existing project, then tweak as needed.

  Bugs and enhancement requests, see:
  https://github.com/g-sherman/plugin_build_tool

Options:
  --help  Show this message and exit.

Commands:
  clean       Remove compiled resource and ui files
  clean-docs  Remove the built HTML help files from the build directory
  compile     Compile the resource and ui files
  config      Create a config file based on source files in the current...
  create      Create a new plugin in the current directory using either the...
  dclean      Remove the deployed plugin from the .qgis2/python/plugins...
```

> **TIP**
> If you get an error, check that `C:\OSGeo4W3\apps\Python37\Scripts` is in your PATH.

Navigate to the path where you saved your new plugin and type the following:

pb_tool deploy

Extending QGIS with Python

Select y to proceed, as shown in the following screenshot:

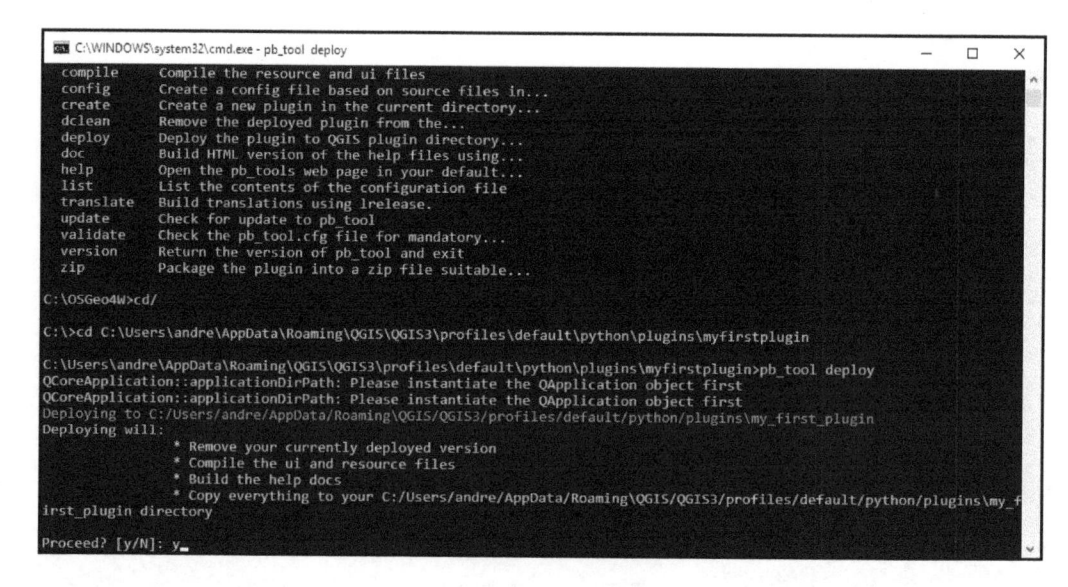

Following the deployment instructions

When the build is finished, your command will look like the following screenshot:

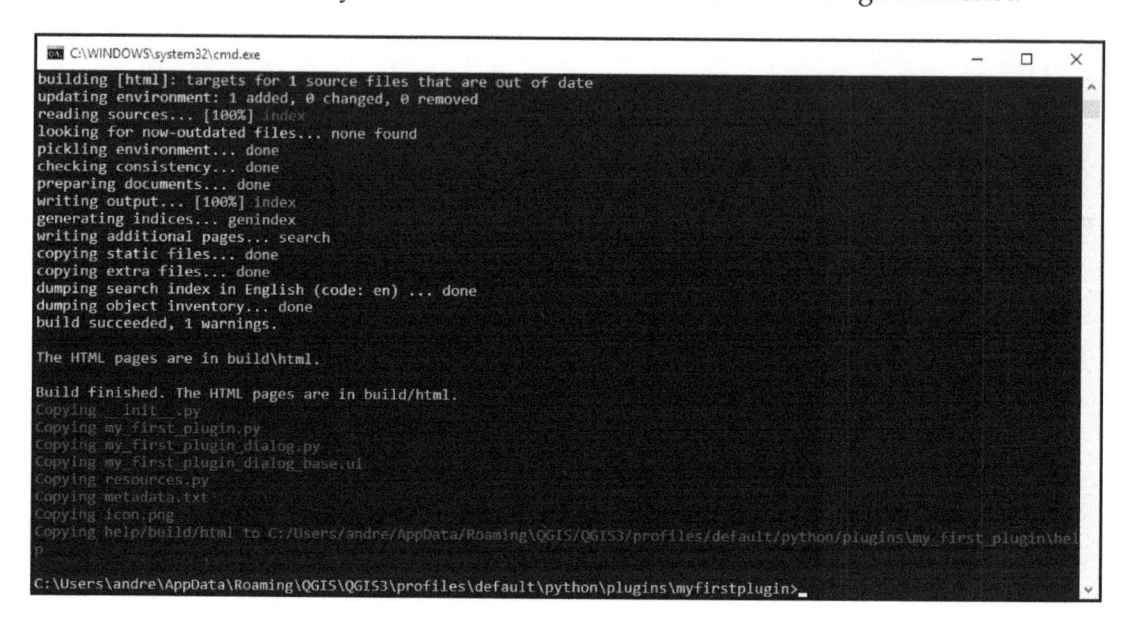

Plugin deployed via the command line

Our plugin is now available to QGIS. In the next section, we will create an icon for the toolbar. If you were to install it in the plugin manager, it should now appear like the following screenshot:

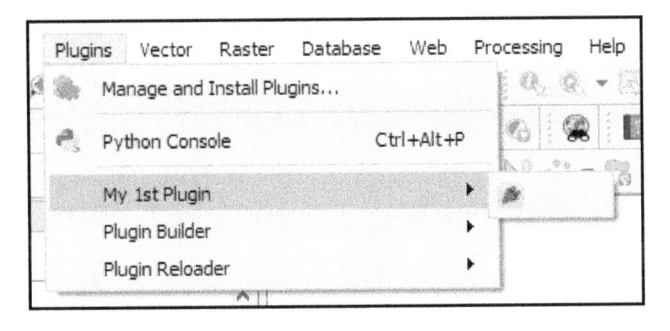

My 1st Plugin

Assigning a logo to the plugin

One thing we still have to do is prepare the icon for the plugin toolbar. This requires us to compile the `resources.qrc` file, which Plugin Builder created automatically in order to turn the icon into usable Python code. This is done on the command line. On Windows, again I recommend using the OSGeo4W shell. This is because it makes sure that the environment variables are set in such a way that the necessary tools can be found. Navigate to the plugin folder and run the following command:

```
pyrcc5 -o resources.py resources.qrc
```

> **TIP**: You can replace the default icon (`icon.png`) to add your own plugin icon. Afterward, you just have to recompile `resources_rc.qrc`, as shown previously.

Extending QGIS with Python

Restart QGIS and you should now see your plugin listed in the Plugin Manager. Now activate your plugin in the Plugin Manager and you should see this listed in the plugins menu. When you start your plugin, it will display a blank dialog that is just waiting for you to customize it:

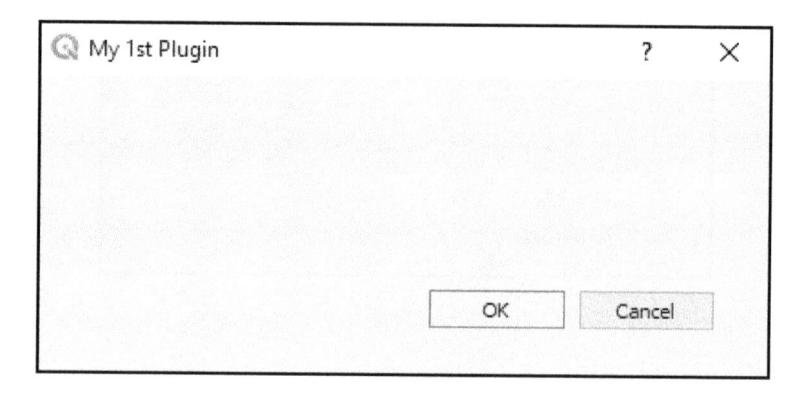

The dialog box for My 1st Plugin

Customizing the plugin GUI

To customize the blank default plugin dialog, use Qt Designer. You can find the dialog file in the `plugin` folder. In my case, it is called `my_first_plugin_dialog_base.ui` (derived from the module name I specified in Plugin Builder). When you open your `plugin's .ui` file in Qt Designer, you will see the blank dialog. Now you can start adding widgets by dragging and dropping them from the Widget Box on the left-hand side of the Qt Designer window. In the following screenshot, you can see that I added a label and a drop-down list widget (listed as Combo Box in the Widgetbox). You can change the label text to `Layer` by double-clicking on the default label text. Additionally, it is good practice to assign descriptive names to the widget objects.

For example, I renamed the combo box to **layerCombo**, as you can see here in the bottom-right corner:

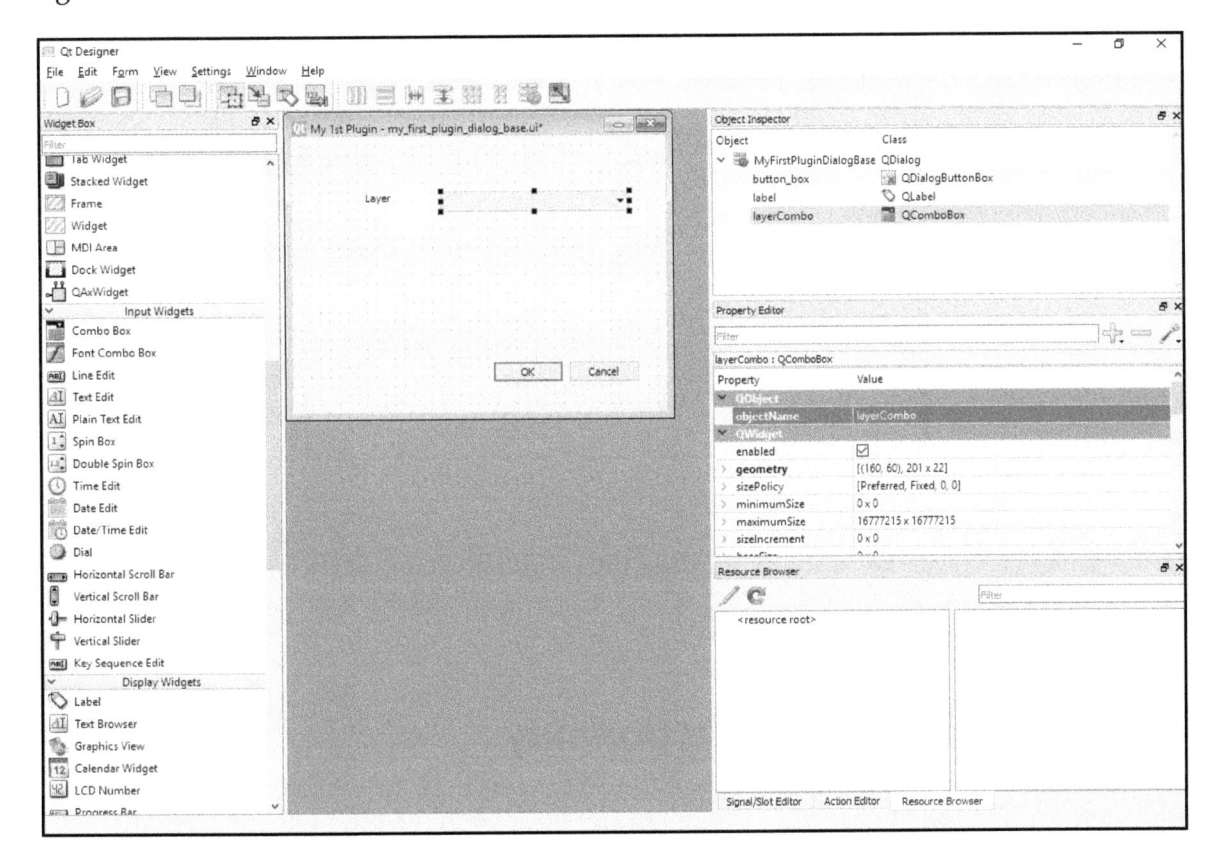

Qt Designer

Extending QGIS with Python

Once you are finished with the changes to the plugin dialog, you can save them. Then you can go back to QGIS. In QGIS, you can now configure Plugin Reloader by clicking on the **Choose a plugin to be reloaded** button in the Plugins toolbar and selecting your plugin. If you now click on the **Reload Plugin** button and the **press your plugin** button, your new plugin dialog will be displayed. It should now look like the following screenshot:

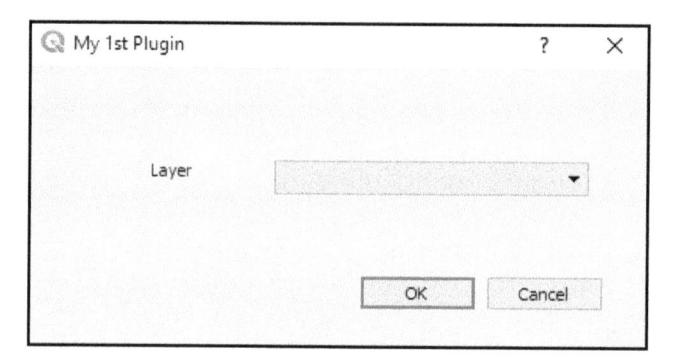

My 1st Plugin GUI updated

This is great! However, we want to populate the combo box with all the layers in the QGIS project. Make sure you have loaded a few vector layers into QGIS. Next, we will add this functionality to the plugin.

Implementing plugin functionality

The layer combo box is empty and we want to add layers to it. To achieve this, we need to add a few lines of code to `my_first_plugin.py` (located in the plugin folder). Firstly, make sure all the imports are correct:

```
from PyQt5.QtCore import QSettings, QTranslator, qVersion, QCoreApplication
from PyQt5.QtGui import QIcon
from PyQt5.QtWidgets import QAction
from qgis.core import *
# Initialize Qt resources from file resources.py
from .resources import *
# Import the code for the dialog
from .my_first_plugin_dialog import MyFirstPluginDialog
import os.path
```

Then change the `run()` method:

```
def run(self):
    """Run method that performs all the real work"""
    # show the dialog
    self.dlg.show()
    # clear the combo box
    self.dlg.layerCombo.clear()
    layers=QgsProject.instance().mapLayers().values()
    for layer in layers:
        if layer.type() == QgsMapLayer.VectorLayer:
            self.dlg.layerCombo.addItem( layer.name(), layer )
    result = self.dlg.exec_()
```

Once you are done with the changes to `my_first_plugin.py`, you can save the file and use the Reload Plugin button in QGIS to reload your plugin. If you start your plugin now, the combo box will be populated with a list of all the layers in the current QGIS project. This is demonstrated in the following screenshot:

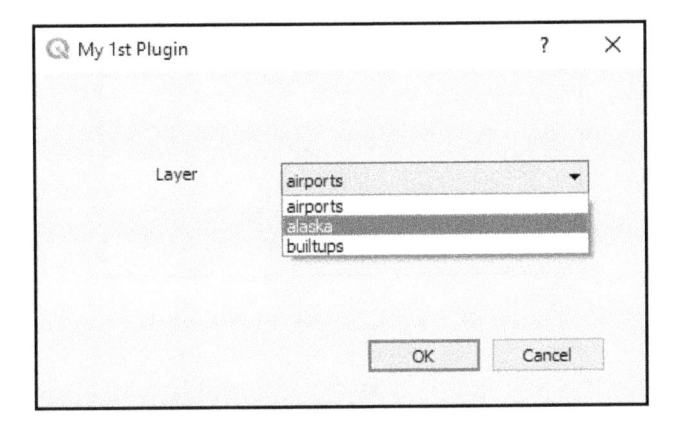

Layers in the map appearing in the drop-down list in My 1st Plugin

Plugins are fully customizable. QT Designer offers many GUI tools that you can use to build a more comprehensive plugin.

Extending QGIS with Python

Adding a message box when OK is clicked

At the top of the `my_first_plugin.py` script, add `QMessagebox` to the imports. This is shown in the following code:

```
from PyQt5.QtWidgets import QApplication, QAction, QWidget, QPushButton,
QMessageBox
```

Now add the following two lines of code to the bottom of the `run` method. Make sure they are within the `if` statement.

```
msgbox = QMessageBox(QMessageBox.Information, "How many layers?", "Number of features in layer: %s" % layer.featureCount(), QMessageBox.Ok)
msgbox.exec_()
```

Save and reload your plugin in QGIS. You will find that after clicking **OK**, the number of layers in the layer selected in the drop-down box will appear as an information box. This is shown in the following screenshot:

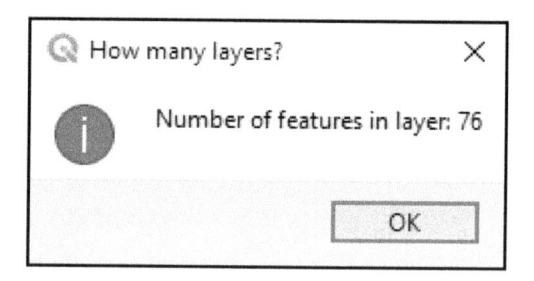

Messagebox showing the number of features in the selected layer

Clicking **OK** on this message box will now close the plugin.

3D view

In QGIS 3, we have the ability to view our data in 3D. To begin, add the `Landcover.img` raster and then add the `SRTM_05_01.tif` file that we used in Chapter 4, *Creating Great Maps*, and Chapter 5, *Spatial Analysis*, to the map. Now raster as well. Set `Landcover` as the top layer in the layer panel.

[246]

Chapter 6

This should look like the following screenshot, with the default styling:

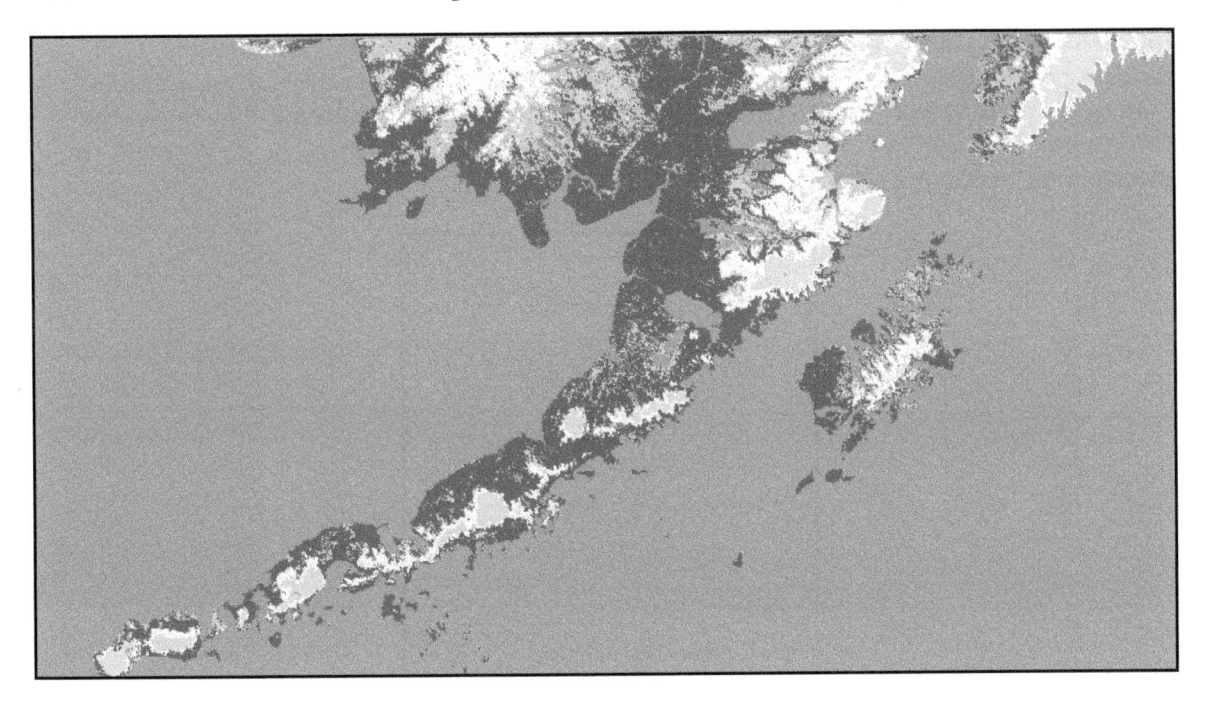

Landcover data in QGIS – default styling

The `landcover.img` raster has a cell size of 1 km x 1 km, so any 3D results will be coarse because the underlying elevation data has a cell size of 30 m x 30 m. To enable a 3D window, click on **View** | **New 3D Map View,** as shown in the following screenshot:

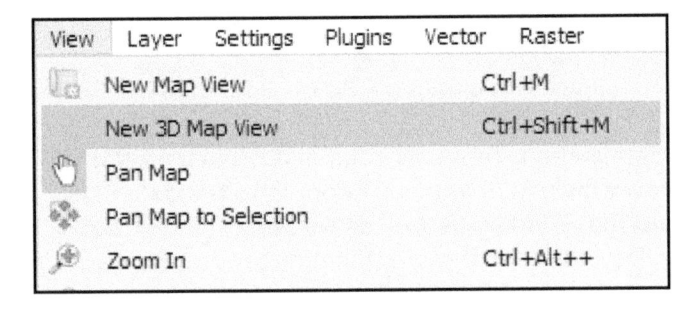

Setting up a 3D Map view

Extending QGIS with Python

You can dock this new view. I prefer to have it above the map window view, but set it up as best suits you and your screen. The 3D view has five buttons associated with it. They are **zoom to full** (the extent of data), **save as image, configure, animate,** and **identify**. First, click on configure, set the **Elevation** parameter to **srtm_05_01 layer** (the DEM), and then change the vertical scale to 10.0 (this is the exaggeration of the elevation). Finally, set the Tile resolution to 250 px (this will improve the rendering of the data). The parameters are shown in the following screenshot:

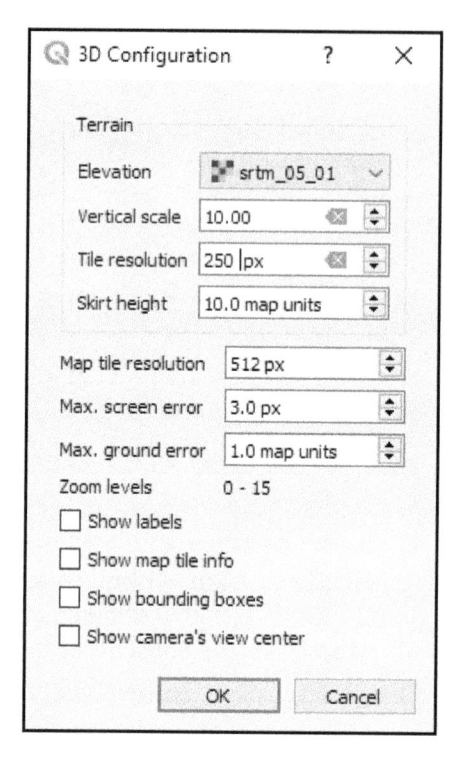

Setting the configuration of the 3D view

Click on **OK** and the data is then shown as a flat layer. Turn off the SRTM in the layer panel. Only the landcover layer will appear. Zoom in to the data using the mouse wheel. To rotate it, press and hold the *Shift* key as well as pressing the left mouse button. With practice, you will develop a familiarity with the navigational tools. 3D rendering can be a little slow, depending on the age and specification of your computer.

[248]

In the following screenshot, I am displaying the landcover draped over the DEM with a focus on the highest elevations in the data. It is useful to see the landcover and its relationship with the elevation. My 3D view and 2D view are shown in the following screenshot:

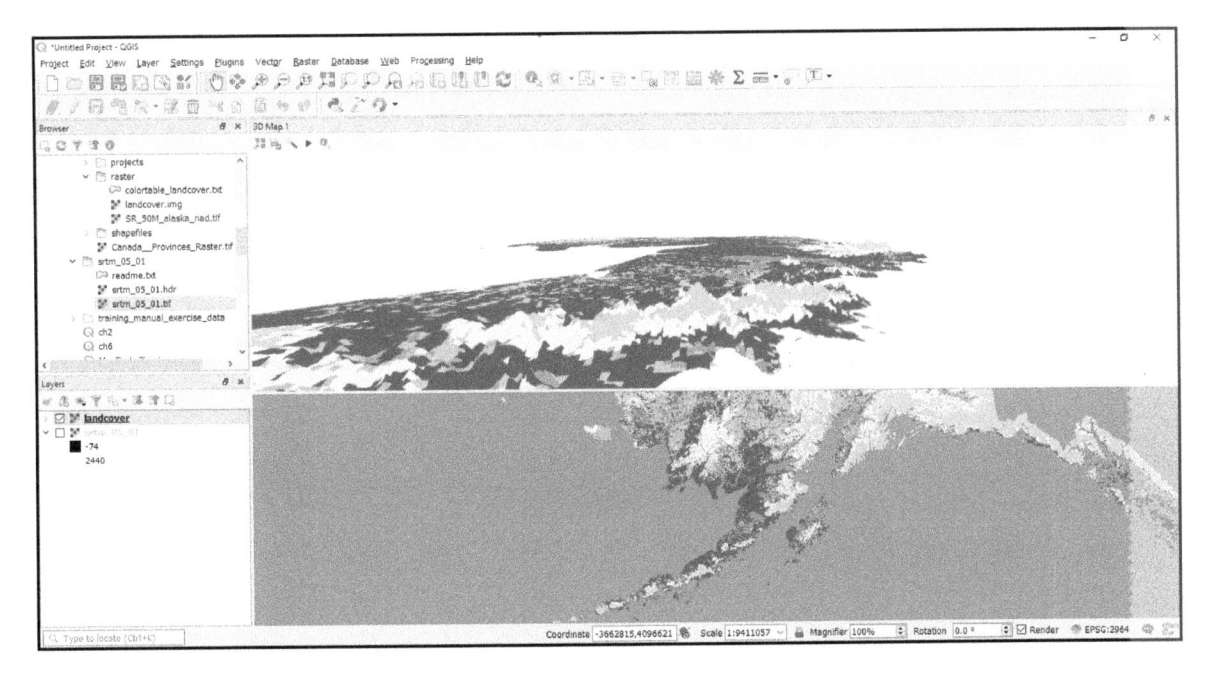

The landcover data appearing in 3D

You can open multiple map views and multiple 3D views, which will appear as tabs on your data. These new features give a richer viewing experience for your data than with previous versions of QGIS. In QGIS 3.4, the functionality to add 3D views to the print layout was added.

Extending QGIS with Python

Create a new layout as we did in `Chapter 4`, *Creating Great Maps*. This time, select **Add Item** | **Add 3D view** and draw the boundary on the canvas. In the **Item Properties** tab, choose **Copy Settings from a 3D View...** and select the 3D view we created previously. Your 3D map should now appear. This is shown in the following screenshot:

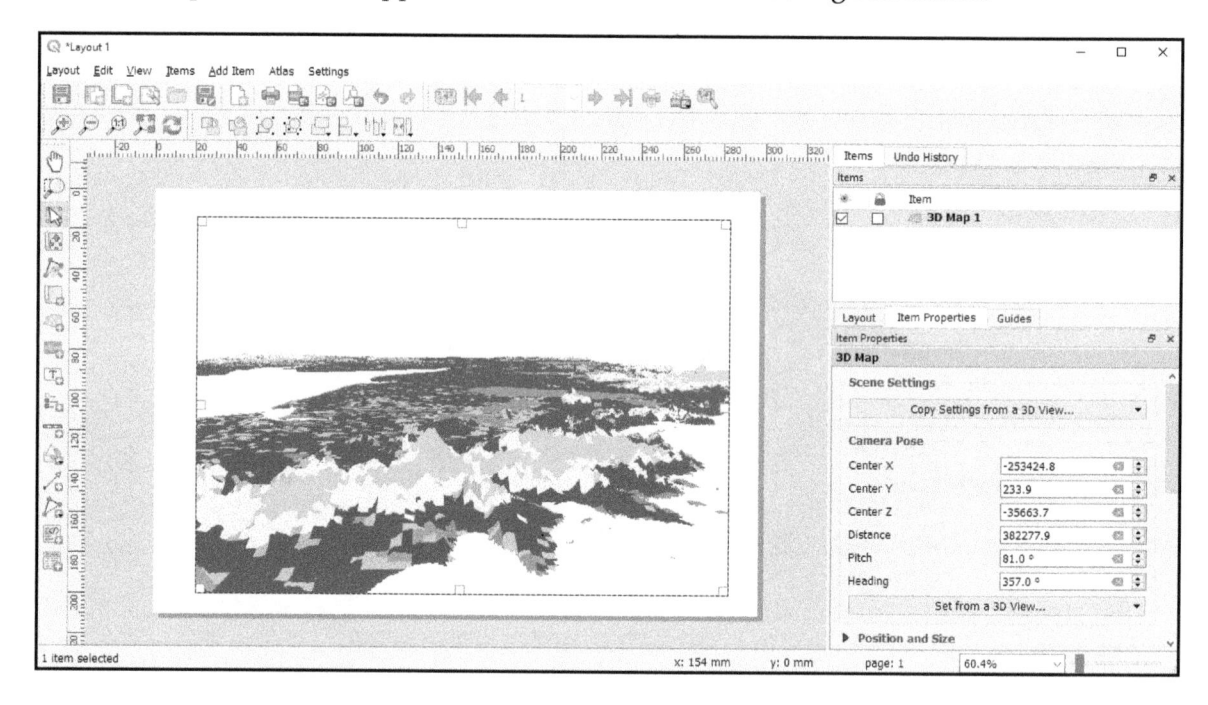

Creating 3D maps

QGIS 3.4 added the functionality to identify features in a 3D view and create animations within a 3D view. More controls and features are expected to be added in the future.

> The new 3D features in QGIS 3.4 were developed by Lutra Consulting and are detailed here: https://www.lutraconsulting.co.uk/blog/2018/10/17/qgis3d-new-features-qgis3-4/.

[250]

Summary

In this chapter, we covered the different ways to extend QGIS using actions and Python scripting. We started with different types of actions and then continued to the Python console, which offers a direct way to interact with the QGIS Python API. We also used the editor that is part of the Python console panel and provides a better way to work on longer scripts containing loops or even multiple class and function definitions. You can save, share, and load these scripts. Next, we applied our knowledge of PyQGIS to develop custom tools for the **Processing Toolbox**. These tools profit from Processing's automatic GUI generation capabilities, and they can be used in Graphical modeler to create geoprocessing models. We also developed and deployed a basic plugin based on a Plugin Builder template.

You should now have a feel for the capabilities of extending QGIS. You should also be familiar with model builder, console-based interaction, and building your own algorithms and plugins all with Python. With this background knowledge, you can now start your own PyQGIS development. There are several web and print resources that you can use to learn more about QGIS Python scripting. For the updated QGIS API documentation, check out http://qgis.org/api/. If you are interested in more PyQGIS recipes, take a look at the *PyQGIS Developer Cookbook* at http://docs.qgis.org/testing/en/docs/pyqgis_developer_cookbook and the QGIS programming books offered by Packt Publishing. It may also be useful to look at Gary Sherman's newly updated book, *The PyQGIS Programmer's Guide for QGIS 3*, Locate Press.

We finally looked at 3D in QGIS. This is a new and developing area, and you can expect to see more 3D interactions in future versions of QGIS.

QGIS is a constantly changing and improving software. In this book, we have tried to outline the main functions and features. If you are interested in all the new features in QGIS 3, have a look at the change log at the following link: https://www.qgis.org/en/site/forusers/visualchangelog30/index.html.

Other Books You May Enjoy

If you enjoyed this book, you may be interested in these other books by Packt:

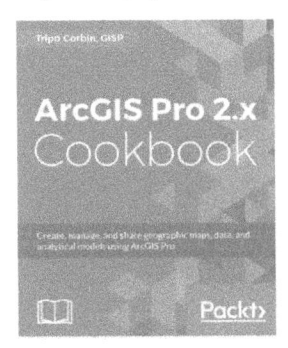

ArcGIS Pro 2.x Cookbook
Tripp Corbin, GISP

ISBN: 978-1-78829-903-9

- Edit data using standard tools and topology
- Convert and link data together using joins and relates
- Create and share data using Projections and Coordinate Systems
- Access and collect data in the field using ArcGIS Collector
- Perform proximity analysis and map clusters with hotspot analysis
- Use the 3D Analyst Extension and perform advanced 3D analysis
- Share maps and data using ArcGIS Online via web and mobile apps

Other Books You May Enjoy

Mapping with ArcGIS Pro
Amy Rock, Ryan Malhoski

ISBN: 978-1-78829-800-1

- Using ArcGIS Pro to create visually stunning maps and make confident cartographic decisions
- Leverage precise layout grids that will organize and guide the placement of map elements
- Make appropriate decisions about color and symbols
- Critically evaluate and choose the perfect projection for your data
- Create clear webmaps that focus the reader's attention using ArcGIS Online's Smart Mapping capabilities

Leave a review - let other readers know what you think

Please share your thoughts on this book with others by leaving a review on the site that you bought it from. If you purchased the book from Amazon, please leave us an honest review on this book's Amazon page. This is vital so that other potential readers can see and use your unbiased opinion to make purchasing decisions, we can understand what our customers think about our products, and our authors can see your feedback on the title that they have worked with Packt to create. It will only take a few minutes of your time, but is valuable to other potential customers, our authors, and Packt. Thank you!

Index

3
3D view 246, 248, 250

A
actions
 generic actions 207
 open actions 208
 operating system actions 208
 used, for adding functionality 207
 used, for opening files 211, 213
 used, for opening web browser 214
Analysis Ready Data (ARD) 90
application programming interface (API) 214
Atlas
 creating 144
automated geoprocessing
 with graphical modeler 199

B
batch processing
 multiple datasets 198
buffer script
 building 226, 228
 executing 229
 extending 230

D
data formats
 about 28
 GeoPackage 28
data joins 63, 67
data
 about 77
 attributes toolbar 33
 communicating with 116
 filtering 220
 GeoPackage, creating 77, 80
 inspecting 34
 interacting 32
 interactive styling 84
 loading 28
 measuring 35
 navigation 32
 obtaining, into QGIS 29, 31
 selecting 36, 39
 Spatial Databases 81
 styling 84
developer version (DEV) 6

F
functionality
 adding, actions used 207
 Python actions 207

G
Geographic Resources Analysis Support System (GRASS) 6
GeoPackage
 about 28
 creating 77, 80
 exporting, to format 81
geoprocessing scripts
 buffer script, building 226, 228
 creating, Python used 224
 writing 224

H
heatmap
 creating, from points 178

I

identify results 34

K

Kernel Density Estimation (KDE) 101

L

labeling
  about 118, 127
  line labels 124
  polygon labels 127
labels
  editing, interactively 119, 121
  used, for displaying information 121, 124
latest release (LR) 6
Layer styling
  about 86
  parameters 87
  Raster Toolbar 91
layers
  styling 218
line labels 124, 127
line styles
  creating 105, 108
list comprehension
  reference link 216
long term release (LTR) 6

M

map images
  exporting 222
map outputs 143
map
  attribute table, adding 141
  creating 129, 130
  data, loading 131, 132
  grids, adding 139
  layout items, adding 133, 134
  online, presenting 145
  options, creating 138
  saving, to share 143
  title, adding 135, 137
memory layer 221
model
  creating, for automation of hexagonal heatmaps 201, 204
  documenting 205
  sharing 205

O

overview map
  adding 140

P

pixels 27
Plugin Builder 232
plugin template
  creating, with Plugin Builder 233, 234, 236
  logo, assigning 241
  message box, adding 246
  pb_tool, setting up 238
  plugin functionality, implementing 244
  plugin GUI, customizing 242
  qgis.core, accessing from command line external to Python 237
plugin
  developing 232
point styles
  creating 98, 101
polygon labels 127
polygon styles
  creating 109, 113
  symbol layer types 110
processing toolbox 154
Python action
  configuring 208, 210
Python console
  about 214
  data, filtering 220
  layers, styling 218
  map images, exporting 222
  memory layer, creating 221
  raster data, exploring 217
  raster data, loading 217
  vector data, exploring 215, 217
  vector data, loading 215, 216
Python
  used, for creating geoprocessing scripts 224

[258]

Q

QGIS 3.4
  installing 5
QGIS2Web
  3D web map, exporting 147, 149
  about 147
QGIS
  installing, on Windows 6
  installing, OSGeo4W installer used 7
  releasing 7, 8

R

raster data
  about 73, 76
  analyzing 154
  clipping rasters 154
  converting, to vector data 166
  elevation/terrain data, analyzing 156, 159
  exploring 217
  integrating, with vector data 166
  loading 217
  raster calculator, using 161, 163
  terrain projections 160
  versus vector data 166
raster layer statistics
  accessing 171
raster layers
  data, styling 92, 95
  hillshade 86
  Layer styling 86, 89, 90
  multi-band color 86
  paletted 86
  single-band gray 86
  single-band pseudo-color 86
  styling 85
raster processing
  analysis 179
  area shares, calculating with region 192, 194, 196
  density, mapping with hexagonal grids 188
  features, identifying in proximity 184
  nearest neighbors, finding 180
  points, converting between lines and polygons 181

  sampling, at point locations 186
  workflows, building with processing tools 183
Raster Toolbar 92

S

shapefile
  creating 51
Shuttle Radar Topography Mission (SRTM) 156
simple marker tool
  about 101
  default symbols 103
  SVG 102
Spatial Databases 81
stretching 87
styles
  saving 95
SVG Mapbox symbol
  URL, for downloading 101
System for Automated Geoscientific Analyses (SAGA) 6

T

temporary scratch layers
  using 68
topological errors
  finding, with Topology checker 69
  fixing 69
  invalid geometry errors, fixing 72

V

vector 187
vector data
  about 40
  attribute data, editing 40, 43, 47
  attribute data, populating 62
  building 47
  converting, to raster data 169
  data joins 63, 67
  data, creating 51
  exploring 215
  geometries edit, correcting 57, 60
  integrating, with raster data 166
  loading 215
  projections 49
  snapping 56

temporary scratch layers, using 68
tools, editing 53, 56
topological errors, checking 69
topological errors, fixing 69
versus raster data 166
vector layer statistics
  accessing 171
vector layers
  2.5D 97
  categorized 97
  graduated 97
  heatmap 97
  inverted polygons 97
  line styles, creating 105, 108
  point cluster 97
  point displacement 97
  point styles, creating 98, 101
  polygon styles, creating 109, 113
  rule-based 97
  simple marker tool 101
  single symbol 97
  styling 96
vector processing
  analysis 179
  area shares, calculating with region 192, 194, 196
  features, identifying in proximity 184
  nearest neighbors, finding 180
  points, converting between lines and polygons 181
  workflows, building with processing tools 183

W

web map
  exporting 146

Z

zonal statistics
  computing 174

Lightning Source UK Ltd.
Milton Keynes UK
UKHW031836181120
373651UK00004B/203

9 781788 997423